HOOKED-CLASPS & EYES

A Classification & Catalogue of Sharp- or Blunt-Hooked Clasps
& Miscellaneous Objects with Hooks, Eyes, Loops, Rings or Toggles

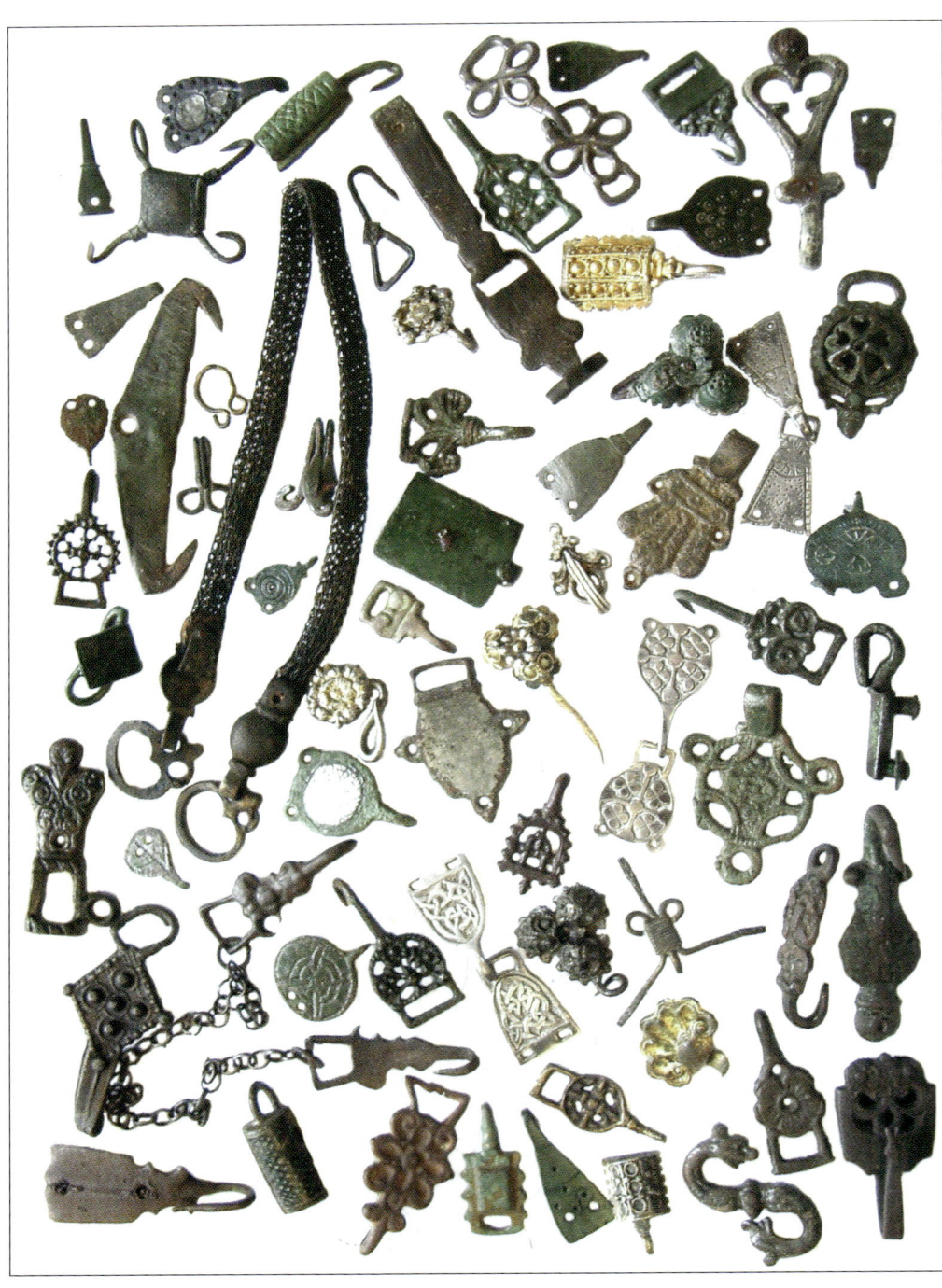

HOOKED-CLASPS & EYES

A Classification & Catalogue of Sharp- or Blunt-Hooked Clasps
& Miscellaneous Objects with Hooks, Eyes, Loops, Rings or Toggles

by

Brian Read

principal illustrators

Nick Griffiths & Patrick Read

Sponsored by

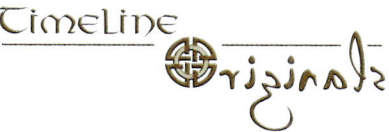

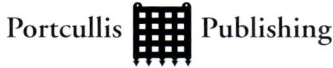

Portcullis Publishing

First published 2008 by
Portcullis Publishing, Meadow View, Wagg Drove, Huish Episcopi, Langport, Somerset, TA10 9ER

© Brian Read 2008

ISBN 978-0-9532450-5-5

Reproduction of any part of this publication, storage in a retrieval system, or transmission in any form or by any means, electronic, mechanical, photocopying, recording or otherwise, is prohibited without the prior permission of the publisher.

Book and cover design and typesetting by Philippa Foster, 5D Illustration.
Printed by Short Run Press Limited, Exeter, Devon.

By the same author:
History Beneath Our Feet. 1988. Merlin Books.
History Beneath Our Feet. 1995. Anglia Publishing.
Cockington Bygones, vol 1. 1999. Portcullis Publishing.
Cockington Bygones, vol 2. 2000. Portcullis Publishing.
Metal Artefacts of Antiquity, vol 1. 2001. Portcullis Publishing.
Cockington Bygones, vol 3. 2003. Portcullis Publishing.
Metal Buttons *c.*900 BC - *c.*AD 1700. 2005. Portcullis Publishing.

Brian Read was born in 1939 in Essex and raised in East and South-East London. With no formal qualifications, in 1954 he left Secondary Modern School and became a trainee millwright and then a trainee groundsman before joining the Merchant Navy in 1955 where he travelled widely. In 1961 he embarked on a fire service career, first with Devon County Fire Service, then the City of Plymouth Fire Brigade, and finally the newly formed Devon Fire Brigade. While on duty in 1983, in the rank of assistant divisional officer, he sustained an injury that, in 1986, resulted in his medical discharge.

Since leaving the fire service he has worked as a freelance writer. His first book *History Beneath Our Feet*, published in 1988, was a bestseller and after extensive revision underwent re-publication in 1995 and again proved successful. In 1999 he extended into self-publishing, using the imprint Portcullis Publishing, under which *Hooked-Clasps & Eyes* is the sixth title.

Since 1979, metal-detecting and its associated study of small metal artefacture has been his primary leisure interest.

Knowledge unshared is knowledge lost

Dedication

To Val, for her support and encouragement

Contents

	Page:
Illustrations other than catalogue items	IV
Notes on illustrations	VI
Drawing conventions for enamel	VI
Abbreviations	VI
Acknowledgements	VII
Foreword	X
Introduction	XI

1: ROMAN PERIOD CLASPS — 1
  Corbridge Types B-C, Category G vertical sharp-hooked and eye clasps and
    Category H horizontal tie-loops. — 1
  Class A necklace blunt-hooked and eye clasps. — 3
  Class B necklace blunt-hooked and eye clasps. — 4

2: EARLY MEDIEVAL CLASPS — 5
  Class A single sharp-hooked clasps. — 7
  Class B single sharp-hooked clasps. — 21
  Class C single sharp-hooked clasps. — 23
  Class D single sharp-hooked clasps. — 24
  Class E single sharp-hooked clasps. — 30
  Class F single sharp-hooked clasps. — 34
  Class G single sharp-hooked clasps. — 35
  Class H single sharp-hooked clasps. — 36
  Class I single sharp-hooked clasp. — 36
  Class J single sharp-hooked clasp. — 37
  Unclassified single sharp-hooked clasps. — 37
  Class K double sharp-hooked clasps. — 39
  Class L double sharp-hooked clasp. — 39
  Class M double sharp-hooked clasps. — 40

3: LATE MEDIEVAL CLASPS — 42
  Class A single sharp-hooked clasps. — 43
  Class B possible single blunt-hooked clasp. — 44

4: EARLY POST-MEDIEVAL CLASPS — 45
  Class A single sharp-hooked clasps. — 50
  Class B single sharp-hooked clasps. — 52
  Class C single sharp-hooked clasps. — 53
  Class D single sharp-hooked clasps. — 58
  Class E single sharp-hooked clasps. — 87
  Class F single sharp-hooked clasps. — 118
  Class G single sharp-hooked clasp. — 119
  Class H single sharp-hooked clasps. — 119
  Class I single sharp-hooked clasps. — 123
  Class J single sharp-hooked clasps. — 124
  Class K single sharp-hooked clasp. — 125
  Class L single sharp-hooked clasps. — 128
  Class M single sharp-hooked clasps. — 129
  Class N single sharp-hooked clasp. — 129
  Class O single sharp-hooked clasp. — 130

Class P single sharp-hooked clasp.	130
Class Q single sharp-hooked clasps.	131
Unclassified single sharp-hooked clasps.	132
Class R double sharp-hooked clasps.	133
Class S double sharp-hooked clasps.	134
Class T double sharp-hooked clasp.	135
Class U triple sharp-hooked clasp.	136
Class V quadruple sharp- and blunt-hooked clasps.	139

5: EARLY POST-MEDIEVAL WIRE CLASPS — 140

Class A wire single sharp-hooked clasps.	140
Class B wire single sharp-hooked clasp.	141
Class C wire single sharp-hooked clasps.	141
Class D wire double sharp-hooked clasps.	143
Class E wire double sharp-hooked clasps.	144
Class F wire triple sharp-hooked clasps.	145
Class G wire quadruple sharp-hooked clasps.	146
Class H wire single blunt-hooked clasp.	146
Class I wire chatelaine blunt-hooks.	146
Unclassified wire possible clasps.	148

6: LATE MEDIEVAL TO EARLY POST-MEDIEVAL WIRE BLUNT-HOOKED AND EYE CLASPS AND EARLY POST-MEDIEVAL WIRE RINGS — 150

Class A wire single blunt-hooked and eye clasps.	150
Class B wire single blunt-hooked and eye clasps.	158
Class C wire single blunt-hooked and eye clasps.	162
Class A wire rings.	162

7: EARLY POST-MEDIEVAL BLUNT-HOOKED AND EYE CLASPS — 164

Class A single blunt-hooked and eye clasps.	164
Class B single blunt-hooked and eye clasps.	183
Class C single blunt-hooked clasp.	185
Class D single blunt-hooked clasp.	186
Class E single blunt-hooked clasp.	186
Class F single blunt-hooked and eye clasps.	187
Class G single blunt-hooked clasps.	187

8: MISCELLANEOUS OBJECTS WITH HOOKS, EYES OR LOOPS — 189

Early post-medieval hat-hooks.	189
Early post-medieval single sharp-hooked collar-clasp.	196
Early and late medieval nummular brooches.	199
Late medieval and early post-medieval havettes.	202
Early and late post-medieval possible single blunt-hooked clasps.	205
Early post-medieval unclassified eyes.	207
Early post-medieval unclassified toggle-clasps.	208
Early medieval and early post-medieval unclassified hooks, eyes or loops.	212
Early post-medieval strap-hooks with integral loops.	232

Bibliography — 234

Illustrations Other Than Catalogue Items

Frontispiece
A cornucopia of hooked-clasps and miscellaneous hooks, eyes, loops and toggles.

Fig. 1.1. Legio Secunda Augusta infantryman wearing a Corbridge Type B *lorica segmuntata* cuirass.
Fig. 1.2. Corbridge Type B *lorica segmuntata* Category G vertical sharp-hooked and eye clasps and Category H horizontal tie-loops.
Fig. 1.3. Corbridge Type B lorica segmuntata Category G vertical sharp-hooked and eye clasps.
Fig. 2. Roman bead-necklace from Bishops Canning, Wiltshire.
Fig. 3. Roman bead-necklace from Bishops Canning, Wiltshire.
Fig. 4. The Three Magi, altar front from Espinol, late 13th century.
Fig. 5. The Bayeux Tapestry: the Norman Count Guy and a Norman guard both wearing spiral leg-wrappings or banded hose.
Fig. 6. A possible Anglo-Saxon warrior wearing spiral leg-wrappings.
Fig. 7. The Bayeux Tapestry: a mounted Norman knight wearing cross-banded leg-wrappings.
Fig. 8. Tiny rings from South-West Wiltshire.
Fig. 9. Reconstruction of possible use of a tiny ring and sharp-hooked clasp.
Fig. 10. A Thomas Class B, Type 1 Anglo-Saxon sharp-hook strapend.
Fig. 11. A late medieval possible drape or curtain ring.
Fig. 12.1. The Marriage of Cana, 1480-95, showing possible hooked-clasp.
Fig. 12.2. Detail of possible hooked-clasp in the Marriage of Cana.
Fig. 13. English Woman in Contemporary Dress *c.*1532-35 showing probable single sharp-hooked clasps.
Fig. 14. Peasant Dance, *c.*1567 showing possible single sharp-hooked trefoil clasp.
Fig. 15. Reconstruction of one possible attachment-method of an early post-medieval Class C, Type 3 sharp-hooked clasp.
Fig. 16.1. St Margaret of Antioch wearing a possible sharp-hooked clasp, in a *c.*1518-27 stained-glass window, the Chapel of the Vyne.
Fig. 16.2. Detail of St Margaret's possible sharp-hooked clasp.
Fig. 17. Catherine of Aragon wearing a pair of trefoil-jewels, in a 16th-century stained-glass window, the Chapel of the Vyne.
Fig. 18.1. Queen Elizabeth I wearing a circular throat-jewel, Axbridge Town Charter, 1599.
Fig. 18.2. Detail of Queen Elizabeth's throat-jewel.
Fig. 19.1. Sir Edward Hoby wearing a high hat with sharp-hooked clasp/s, 1577.
Fig. 19.2. Detail of Sir Edward Hoby's sharp-hooked hat-clasp/s.
Fig. 20. Reuse of an indeterminate form of early post-medieval wire clasp as a suspension-mount for an early 13th-century harness pendant.
Fig. 21. Incomplete Class A wire chatelaine blunt-hook, *c.*17th-century.
Fig. 22. The Ferraran court jester, Gonella, wearing Class A, Type 1 wire single blunt-hooked and eye clasps, *c.*1445.
Fig. 23. Early post-medieval Class A, Type 1 wire single blunt-hooked and eye clasps attached to men's breeches and doublets.
Fig. 24. Class A, Type 1 wire blunt-hooked and eye clasp on the back of a 1742-44 woman's robe.
Fig. 25. Class A, Type 1 wire blunt-hooked and eye clasps on the back of an 1821-25 woman's dress.
Fig. 26. Class A, Type 1 wire blunt-hooked and eye clasps on the back of a probable *c.*18th - *c.*19th-century woman's dress.
Fig. 27. Class A, Type 1e probable silver wire blunt-hooks on the back of an 1824-26 woman's dress.
Fig. 28. Class A, Type 1 silver wire bar-type eye on the back of an 1824-26 woman's dress.

Fig. 29. Reconstruction of a Class A, Type 1 wire eye and 17th-century button from the Dutch East India Company fluit *Lasdrage*.
Fig. 30. Class A, Type 1 wire blunt-hooked and eye clasp linked together.
Fig. 31. Class A, Type 1 wire blunt-hooks and Class A, Type 1b wire eyes from the Dutch East India Company jacht *Vergulde Draeck*.
Fig. 32.1. Class B blunt-hooked and eye clasps on a 1620-30 man's woollen felt-coat in the Museum of London.
Fig. 32.2. Class B blunt-hooked and eye clasps on the Museum of London woollen felt-coat.
Fig. 33. A possible Hines Type D early medieval Double Spiral-Headed dress- or hair-pin.
Fig. 34. Arthur, Prince of Wales, wearing a Milan bonnet with two possible hat-hooks, *c.*1520.
Fig. 35. Link from a Gothic gold livery-collar of SS.
Fig. 36. Gold livery-collar of SS worn by a *c.*1350 - *c.*1500 woman.
Fig. 37. Arms of the Clothworkers' Company of London, from the grant of 1530.
Fig. 38. Arms of the Shearmen of London, incorporated 1527/8 with the Fullers as the Company of Clothworkers.
Fig. 39. Havette on a 1677 version of the Clothworkers' Arms.
Fig. 40. Havette on a 19th-century unattributed version of the Clothworkers' Arms.
Fig. 41.1. A young woman wearing a girdle fastened with a metal-clasp and chain, 1523-24.
Fig. 41.2. Detail of the young woman's clasp and chain.
Fig. 42.1. Robert Dudley, Earl of Leicester, wearing an S-shaped clasp and other metal-fittings on his sword-belt and hanger, *c.*1575.
Fig. 42.2. Detail of the S-shaped clasp and other metal-fittings on the Earl of Leicester's sword-belt.
Fig. 43. Buff-leather sword-belt hanger and metal-fittings, *c.* mid-17th-century.

Notes on Illustrations

Each artefact is illustrated either by a line-drawing, one or more photographs, or both a line-drawing and a photograph or photographs. Most images are smaller than actual-size while for clarity some are enlarged - maximum dimensions for the surviving material are included within the text. Some seriously misshapen objects are drawn in their original form. Both professional and amateur sources provided the drawings and photographs, therefore, inevitably, the orientation and style varies: these orientation differences mean there is a mixture of hook-ends towards the top, together with towards the bottom and towards either side which on some, adversely affects figurative motifs. Every object has an individual catalogue-number. Respective Treasure case, Portable Antiquities Scheme Database, United Kingdom Detector Finds' Database, museum accession, and private record-numbers are mentioned within the text, as are copyright and courtesy acknowledgements. Photographs without a copyright acknowledgement are copyright of the author. The photograph of Sir Edward Hoby's portrait, and detail, are published courtesy of its anonymous owner. To no avail, the Somerset Record Office made every effort to obtain permission to reproduce the drawing of Queen Elizabeth I in the Axbridge Town Charter: any infringement is the sole responsibility of the author/publisher and not Somerset Record Office. Despite exhaustive enquiries, several other images are reproduced without approval and again any infringement is the sole responsibility of the author/publisher. Reproduction of illustrations is prohibited without express permission in writing from the respective copyright owner. Inevitably, much of the material submitted for study was repetitive of which the best respective examples are illustrated and described: the author is sorry for disappointing those contributors whose objects are absent.

Drawing conventions for enamel

| Black or Dark-Blue | Light-Blue | Green | White |

Abbreviations

acc. no.	accession number
D	diameter
De	depth
L	length
W	width

Acknowledgements

This book is the product of many years researching and recording small metal artefacture, including objects with hooks, eyes, loops, rings or toggles. As with my other works, its compilation is entirely due to the enthusiastic co-operation of many people and it is to them that any credit should be aimed, especially landowners throughout the country who willingly encourage metal-detecting on their respective properties. For allowing their finds to be recorded for inclusion herein, or making me aware of an interesting object or assisting in another way, my gratitude is extended to members of metal-detecting clubs, and independent metal-detectorists, namely: Blackpool and Fylde Metal-Detecting Club - John Rigby; Coventry Moles Metal-Detecting Club - Ian Turvey; Derby Artefact Recovery Group - Lisa Grace and Adam Staples; East Devon Metal-Detecting Club - Pete Barrell, Jim Cobley, Andy Down, Ron Gibson, Gordon Glover, Ian Griffin, Colin Hancock, Colin Hart, Mark Hanley, Ian MacFadzean, Paul Maeer, Sam Weller and Win Weller; Fenland Finders Metal-Detecting Club - Cheryl Hodgson; Hertfordshire and District Metal-Detecting Society - Chris Brook; Hinkley Search Society - John Caluori and Tessa Caluori; Hoyland and District Searchers - Joseph M Arbones; Hucclecote Metal-Detecting Club - Kath Hurcombe; Isle of White Metal-Detecting Club - Peter Hopkinson and Gavin Leng; Norton Metal-Detecting Club - Tim Binns, Dave Derby and Sue Johnston; Quakers Acres Metal-Detecting Club - Lance Todd; Rally UK Metal-Detecting Club - Joseph Rayner; Redditch Historical Detecting Society - Mark Pugh; Sevendale Historical Research Metal-Detecting Society - Dave Whalley; South Ribble Metal-Detecting Club - Matthew Rush; Society of Thames Mudlarks - Ken Bellringer, John Dunford, Firth Fairbank, Tony Pilson, Bill Yendall and Tony Yendall; Stockport Metal-Detecting Club - Kevin Jones; Stour Valley Search and Recovery Club - John Hinchcliffe, Andy Mitchell, Bob Tydeman, Ken Wheatley and Bernard Yarosz; Taynton Metal-Detecting Club - Dave Mayes and Mary Mayes; Torbay Metal-Detecting Club - David Martin, Dina Parnell, John Parnell and Ross Whitehead; Trowbridge Metal-Detecting Club - Duncan Carrier; Two Dales Metal-Detecting Club - Garry Jones; Vectis Searchers Metal-Detecting Club - Terry Barrett, Joan Robson and Tom Winch; Weston Historical Research and Detecting Association - Paul Gardner and Nick Martin; Weymouth and Portland Metal-Detecting Club - John Fugler, Dave Cobb, David Grenfell, Margaret Hamilton, Roy Mcleod, Paul Rainford, Jim Walmsley and Steve Wootton; Yeovil and District Bottle and Metal-Detecting Club - Chris Adams, Ken Bellringer, Paul Burton, Phil Burton, Roger Evans, Nigel Hallett, Tony James, Anne Laverty, Graham Libbey, Jean Lovett, Robert Lovett, Val MacRae, Alan Maidment, Bob March, Hugh Morgan, Mike Pittard, Lee Purdy, A Sawyer, Alan Swinnerton, Gordon Sinfield and Hugh Vincent; Independents - J Adams, Mr Armstrong, Mark Arrowsmith, Ian Atkinson, Mike Bailey, H Barbour, John Barbour, Terry Barrett, Peter Beazley, Derrick Bell, Mark Benwell, P Berry, A Bewick, Tim Binns, Neal Blatherwick, S Boniface, G Bowes, John Bromley, S Brown, Charles Bullock, Edward Burns, Nigel Butler, D Button, Stephen Button, Steven Carpenter, A Calver, Richard Calver, Chris Chandler, Mike Charles, Ian Chubbock, Mr Collins, Gary Crace, Gary Croucher, David Cummings, Marjorie Dandy, Ian Darke, A Davies, Gill Davies, Trevor Davies, A Dixon, R A Duquemin, Mark Duell, Phil Edwards, B Eeles, H Elliott, D Everingham, Ivor Faye, Russell Fergie, B Fitzjohn, R Freemantle, Mr Ferguson, D Fox, Mike Gaines, Paul Gardner, Helene Garnett, Andy Germaney, A Gibbens, Roland Gill, Ted Godfrey, Martin Green, Robert Green, Jim Halliday, Franky Hayes, Chris Hepple, H Hibbard, Malcolm Higginbotham, Paul Hipwell, Chris Hodgson, Colin Holmes, Neil Hopper, Graham Hunt, Gary Kelly, Tim Kennett, W Kitching, G Knight, Helen Labrooy, Richard Last, Tony Laverick, Paul Linford, J Linton, Ray Lewis, D Locke, K Logan, John Lyons, Fred Meadows, Ray Merrell, John Middleton, Danny Mills, John Mills, Jerry Morris, Nigel Nicholson, Chris Osbourne, Jim Patterson, Duncan Patey, J Pederson, Bill Pegg, Charlie Pelham,

S Pickles, L Pimbifft, Malcolm Price, Mark Pugh, John Radford, Clive Rasdall, R Ratford, Stan Raymond, Martin Reed, Alan Ridgeway, David Roberts, Paul Roberts, D Robinson, Wilf Robinson, Ken Ross, Steve Rourke, Tony Russell, Mike Ruczynski, R Sharp, J Sinclair, Barry Sherlock, Margaret Sherlock, John Slade, Brian Smith, Dennis Smith, Des Smith, D Soanes, Bryan Smyth, Steve Strong, R Sykes, A Thomas, Patrick Thorn, Lance Todd, J Trout, Roy Turland, M Turner, Ken Umpleby, John Williams, Anne Weller, Malcolm White, D Whitfield, Barry Wilson, Mary Winch, John Winter, Lynda Winter, Ian Winkles, Peter Woods and S Zaremba.

Both at home and overseas, many institutions, commercial enterprises and learned individuals from within the world of professional archaeology, the museums' service and private life assisted with research and provided wise council, for which I am deeply appreciative, namely: Amsterdams Historisch Museum - Vanessa Vroon-Najem; Amsterdam Bureau of Monuments and Archaeology, Department of Archaeology - Wiard Krook; Ashmolean Museum - Amanda Turner (Photographic Services); Bath Museum of Costume - Elly Summers and Elaine Uttley; Berkshire Record Office - Lisa Spurrier; The British Museum - Barry Ager (Department of Prehistory and Europe); Clwyd-Powys Archaeological Trust - Jeff Spencer; Colchester and Ipswich Museum Service - Joan Lyall; Courtolds Institute of Art - Jane Cunningham and Louisa Dare; The Clothworkers' Company - Jessica Collins; Dorset County Museum - Peter J Woodward; Dei Gratia - Dave Shelley; Sword In The Stone - Mike Pegg, Germanisches Nationalmuseum, Nuremburg - Jutta Zander-Seidel; Geoff Hobson (militarist and collector); Kunsthistorisches Museum, Vienna - Florian Kugler; Legio Secunda Augusta - Shaun McDermott and David Richardson; the Museum of London -Hilary Davidson (Fashion and Decorative Arts, Later Department), Geoff Egan (Specialist Services), Catherine Maloney and Roz Sherris (Administration) and Sean Waterman (Retail and Licensing); The National Trust - Karen Symonds (The Vyne), Nikita Hooper, Anna Harrison and Rosie Jordan (Photo Library), Dominic Hamilton and Althea MacKenzie (Snowshill Manor); National Portrait Gallery - Erica Ingham; National Museums of Scotland - Christina Brettle, Kristine Stankovski and Naomii Tarrant (retired); Nordiska Museet, Stockholm - Ingrid Roos and Annika Tegnér; Norfolk Finds' Identification and Recording Service, Norfolk Museums and Archaeology Service - Andrew Rogerson; Norfolk Visitor Services - Alison Newbery; Northampton Museums and Art Gallery - Rebecca Shawcross; Norwich Castle Museum - Tim Pestell; The Portable Antiquities Scheme - Caroline Barton, Fi Hitchcock, Dan Pett and Ian Richardson (Central Unit), Kevin Leahy (Finds' Advisor), Kurt Adams, Frank Basford, Dot Bruns, Laura Burnett, Charlotte Burrill, Amy Cooper, Erica Darch, Adam Daubney, Elizabeth Gill, David Graham, Katie Hinds, Simon Holmes, Mark Lodwick, Francis McIntosh, Faye Minter, Naomi Payne, Peter Reavill, Andrew Richardson, Wendy Scott, Lisa Staves, Ciorstaidh Hayward Trevarthen, Anna Tyacke, Nina Steele, Kate Sutton, Rosalind Tyrrell, Philippa Walton, Julian Watters, Rob Webley, David Williams and Danielle Wootton (Finds Liaison Officers); One Guy From Barlick - Stanley Challenger Graham; Royal Armouries Museum - Stuart Ivinson and Thom Richardson; Somerset County Museums Service - Steve Minnitt; Somerset Records Office - Jane de Gruchy and Paula Lewis; Somerset County Library Service - Laurina Deacon, Jane Langton and Carole Ovorton; Statens Historiska Museet, Stockholm - Annica Ewing, Siv Falk, Lotta Fernstål, Mari-Louise Franzén, Annika Larsson, Pia Melin and Elisabet Regner; Southampton University - David A Hinton; Suffolk County Council Archaeology Service - Jude Plouviez; TimeLine Originals - Brett Hammond; United Kingdom Detector Finds' Database - Rod Blunt and John Winter; Victoria and Albert Museum - Richard Edgecumbe and Susan North; York Archaeological Trust - Peter Addyman (retired); Western Australian Maritime Museum - Patrick Baker, Susan Cox and Myra Stanbury; West Berkshire Museum -Jennie Currie and Elin Williams; West Berkshire Historic Environment Record - Sarah Orr; Wiltshire Heritage Museum - Paul Robinson and Lisa Webb; The Winchester Research Unit of the Winchester Excavations Committee - Katherine Barclay.

The task of drawing most of the objects was shared between master antiquarian and illustrator Nick Griffiths (who, as always, generously shared his encyclopaedic knowledge) and my son Patrick, while other artwork is predominantly Nick's, although Patrick is responsible for some. Patrick also advised on dating and identification of objects, and collected several items for drawing and returned them to their respective owners. To them both, my warmest gratitude. A number of other individuals contributed archaeological illustrations, photographs or a painting, and my thanks are extended to Frank Basford for all Isle of White Council and the Isle of White Archaeological Unit drawings; Donna Wreathall for all Suffolk County Council Archaeological Service drawings; Anne Hodgson for drawings of numerous finds from North Yorkshire; Roy Turland for his drawings of finds from Northamptonshire; Neil Hopper, Ray Lewis and Jackie Smith for their drawings of finds from their respective regions; Helen Stanford for permission to publish the reconstructive portrait of a medieval woman displayed in Wiltshire Heritage Museum; David Williams for his drawing of the Farnham Pin (hat-hook); Ken Wheatley for drawings of his clasps and photographing finds from Dorset; and David Graham who kindly provided the photograph of the Farnham Pin. Special thanks go to Peter Woods for enthusiastically supplying photographs of not only his clasps but also Roy Turland's; Jim Patterson for bringing to my attention the 16th-century silver-gilt triple-hooked clasp from Lincolnshire, and much additional assistance; Jim Halliday for the benefit of his wisdom and generously providing illustrations of clasps recorded by him over many years; and Harry Bain, editor of *The Searcher*, who kindly liaised between her readers and myself concerning interesting clasps published in the magazine. I am indebted to master goldsmith Barry Sherlock for advising on the technical aspects of his ancient craft and the correct terminology for individual elements of jewellery. To the legendary Geoff Egan, one of our foremost archaeologists and small finds experts, my thanks for his valuable time discussing aspects of the subject matter, proofreading the final draft and penning the foreword. Nick Griffiths, another expert on small finds, also proofread the final draft and I am grateful for his constructive comment. To delightful and talented Philippa Foster of 5D Illustration, my appreciation for designing the cover and book and undertaking the typesetting. My gratitude to the ever helpful Mark Couch and his team at Short Run Press Limited for producing another high-quality book. Lastly, to my partner Val who accompanied me on research trips, took notes and photographs, made constructive comments, proofread the manuscript at various stages and, importantly, furnished me with hot drinks - my love and gratitude.

Brian Read (Somerset, 2008)

Foreword

In this latest work on metal finds, Brian Read turns his attention to what might on first sight appear to be a single category of object with a common basic function, though they are actually from several different periods, from Roman to post-medieval. The hooked objects that are considered in this work are in fact extremely diverse, comprising not only a large number of apparently general-purpose clasps for dress but some were specifically used to hold swords about the waist, and there are a few that were highly specialised textile-finishing tools. In contrast with the most ornate of the highly elaborate, composite hooks there is a common but enigmatic category of eyes comprising simply a one-part loop of twisted wire. Despite the large numbers now catalogued of the extremely varied (and often viciously sharp) clasps from the late 15th/early 16th centuries their precise function or functions (they certainly had more than one) have yet to be established.

Drawing on his wide and diverse contacts across and beyond Britain, a catalogue of 831 items has been compiled and put into logical groupings. The finds included come from museums and private collections, the detecting fraternity (including Jim Halliday's datasheets) and archaeological assemblages, making full use too of the Portable Antiquities Scheme database, Treasure records and the United Kingdom Detecting Finds' database. Splendidly clear drawings, mainly the work of Nick Griffiths and Patrick Read, are judiciously used, sometimes alongside photographs and sometimes on their own, enhancing the appreciation of all-important details.

Many items are at some level familiar or have parallels that are, but the extent of the diversity most notably of the late 15th/early 16th-century dress clasps in both precious and base metals will come as a surprise even to those who have followed the pertinent recent literature. While it is highly unlikely in dealing with such complicated material that any two researchers would arrive at the same classification scheme, the one used here should be applauded as a bold first attempt to tackle the full range now known.

Precise dating for many of the individual objects remains elusive (there are particular problems with one of the core periods here - the late 15th to early 17th centuries - the mainstream history of which is so well known). The surprisingly few but valuable indications so far located are carefully set out, and the strengths and weaknesses of the resulting view of implied developments are there to be considered. Details of contemporary paintings which seem to show some hooked clasps being worn are reproduced with clarity. Even so, there may be some doubt in each case (the artists were more interested in the clothes as worn than these small accessories which may have held them in place). These are the best indicators available, and they do suggest that despite the obvious peril the sharp hooks were indeed sometimes worn in positions where they might accidentally inflict damage on the person. This is an area where we can perhaps hope for significant fresh insights in future - it remains to be seen whether or not these will vindicate or overturn what is suggested in this present volume.

A broad category of often still puzzling objects has here been taken on and for the first time given an overall framework. This present work is a worthy ready reference of first resort to help clarify these intriguing items.

Geoff Egan (London, 2008)

Introduction

The advent of the metal-detector is responsible for a vast repertoire of small metal artefacts with one or more sharp- or blunt-hooks, either integral or separate, now being in the known record. Though few have been excavated from archaeological stratified contexts in Britain, members of The Society of Thames Mudlarks have recovered many from secure deposits of the River Thames foreshore or datable fly-tipping in or originating from London. Associated with several categories of such hooks is a separate eye or ring, of which various forms are apparent, but seemingly less ubiquitous. We have a good understanding of the function of some of these hooked objects, for example Roman infantry armour-clasps, Roman period necklace-clasps, early medieval wrist-clasps, early post-medieval wire blunt-hooked and eye clasps, late medieval and early post-medieval havettes, early post-medieval sword-belt fittings and late post-medieval clog-clasps, among others. Conversely, however, concerning so-called hooked-tags, hooked-fasteners, clothing-hooks, clothing-fasteners, cloak-fasteners, cloak-clasps, scarf-hooks, hat-hooks and nummular brooches, there is a dearth of knowledge of precisely where and how these were used. This latter nomenclature, for some, is inappropriate and misleading, and in this publication the author has elected to use (albeit sometimes elaborated) Geoff Egan's term 'clasp' to describe most objects with hooks; and Paul Robinson's expression 'blunt-hook' to differentiate from sharp-hooked pieces. Clasps are either single, double, triple or quadruple sharp- or blunt-hooked. Also included, but not classified, is a limited range of small metalwork provided with hooks, eyes, loops or toggles for which we have little or no knowledge of where and how they were used; notwithstanding, some probably had an association with sword-belts.

Evidence herein suggests that some, though perhaps by no means all, sharp-hooked clasps may have functioned in tandem with separate metal-eyes or rings: three early medieval and one early post-medieval single sharp-hooked clasps are complete with separate eyes but their genuineness is questionable. All four sets were allegedly found in Belgium and bought legitimately by the author. The opinion of a master goldsmith, who is highly experienced in ancient metalwork, is they are possibly authentic of their respective periods but equally perhaps very good copies cast from originals - their finishing indicates the edges and file marks are exceedingly sharp, they seem too highly-polished, and one pair appears repatinated. Notwithstanding, the sin of over-polishing excavated items is frequently seen, therefore in itself this is inconclusive, and if they were buried soon after manufacture, this would explain the lack of wear. If matching pairs of sharp-hooked and eye clasps did exist, as random metal-detecting finds is doubtful for the chances of finding them together is remote, therefore the implication is they are from intentional graves or accidental burials, where matching sets would be expected. The question must be asked, why imitate something that is unknown (that is the eyes), which implies they are either genuine or copies of? The obvious answer to establishing authenticity is scientific analysis but although the author tried, such a procedure proved unobtainable. If their discovery circumstances is above board, it is frustrating that this knowledge is not available to a wider audience for it would contribute immensely with our understanding of these sharp-hooked clasps. Despite these misgivings, they are included here to show what some eyes for sharp-hooked clasps may have looked like.

It is probable that most blunt-hooked clasps functioned with en suite eyes. Despite a lack of definitive proof that they adorned hats, Tudor period objects with distinctive S-shaped or recurving sharp-hooks on their reverse, and lacking attachment-loops, and spuriously named 'hat-hooks', are correctly clasps, however, here, as a more general term, hat-hooks is used. The same is said for part of another intriguing category of object, 'nummular-brooches', and a case is made for some actually being clasps and not brooches or badges, but in the interests of continuity, in the text the name remains as before.

Several contemporary portraits show possible sharp-hooked clasps or hat-hooks worn on dress, while similar iconography reveals various forms of blunt-hooked clasp. Although such images are helpful, because the objects are frequently partially obscured and only the front perspective is visible, positive conclusions are difficult or impossible (see below). There is no extant contemporary dress with sharp-hooked clasps or hat-hooks still attached, however, wire blunt-hooked and eye clasps are plentiful on dress surviving from the 16th - 20th centuries. These latter dress-accessories are evident on a 15th-century portrait (see below). Several probable gold blunt-hooked and eye clasps secure the front of a tunic worn by King Henry VIII depicted in a possible early 17th-century portrait after a portrait of *c.*1542 by an unknown artist after Hans Holbein the Younger; and the Ermine portrait of Queen Elizabeth I, 1585, shows her bodice and skirt secured by similarly rich blunt-hooked and eye clasps. Such opulence is beyond the scope of this present work which is confined mainly to utilitarian varieties.

The majority of the material catalogued here has a British provenance, however, some is from mainland Europe, namely Sweden, Belgium and the Netherlands, while a Dutch East India vessel wrecked of Western Australia provides an important assemblage. Although certain identical or very similar forms are known in Belgium, France, Germany and the Netherlands, the author's limited trawl revealed they appear unknown from the rest of the Continent; for example Nordiska Museet, Stockholm has an extensive collection of hooked-clasps, none of which appears to have a British parallel. Without wide-ranging further research it is impossible to draw any conclusions on this anomaly, but is it due to the prohibition or restriction on metal-detecting in large parts of the European mainland? From Britain the time span is broad for sharp- or blunt-hooked clasps of one sort or another, namely: Roman period (1st - 4th century AD), early medieval (*c.*5th - *c.*12th century), late medieval (*c.*14th - *c.*15th century), early post-medieval (*c.*16th - *c.*17th century) and late post-medieval (*c.*18th - *c.*21st century). The known record suggests that sharp-hooked clasps appear to have suffered a hiatus between the end of the 12th century and possibly the 1300s. Most dates assigned herein are tentative.

This famine of conclusive evidence means that for some categories of sharp- or blunt-hooked clasp, it is conjectural whether they definitely had a direct association with fastening dress components. No doubt some did; however, consideration should be given to other applications, for example fastening purses, bags, satchels or straps. Decoration, frequently to a high degree, is featured on the fronts of many sharp- or blunt-hooked clasps, presumably therefore they were attached in positions where they could be seen. In this publication, objects are classified according to perceived date, shape, whether one-piece or composite, and other constructional and design elements. Deciding the shape occasionally proved problematic, for example certain sub-circular or sub-triangular clasps arguably could be either. In the course of time, no doubt re-classification or sub-divisions will be deemed necessary, which is inevitable.

This catalogue of objects is not an accurate reflection of distribution, therefore it seemed pointless to produce distribution-maps that looked pretty but proved nothing. Suffice to say that early medieval sharp-hooked clasps were recorded from County Durham in the north-east to Somerset in the south-west, but there are none from Scotland, Wales or Northern Ireland. Early post-medieval sharp- or blunt-hooked clasps appear ubiquitous throughout most of England, however, Scotland and Northern Ireland produced nil returns and Wales only one example. These gaps may simply be due to insufficient interest, not only on the part of private individuals but also museums.

During this survey, literally many hundreds of sharp- or blunt-hooked clasps and eyes were studied, of which a goodly proportion is catalogued in this work, some of which are unparalleled in the known record; notwithstanding, it is not, and never could be, definitive, for new forms, or variants, of recorded examples are regularly coming to light. Wherever possible, each object underwent a thorough examination, regrettably without the benefit of scientific analysis, to extract constructional information; however, for those recorded on the Portable Antiquities Scheme Database, and some on the United Kingdom Detecting Finds' Database, first-hand re-examination proved impossible: in these instances the official report was heeded but, inevitably, may differ from what is written here. Any misinterpretation, misidentification or other error is solely the responsibility of the author. Due to this ignorance of the precise composition of metals used in the manufacture of objects within this present work, those of copper or its alloys, are described as *copper alloy*; and lead or its alloys, *lead/tin alloy* (albeit, some are perhaps pure tin). Like other small metalwork, although at first sight they often look the same, it is unusual to find two identical clasps, which suggests that different workshops operated, but all using common patterns.

With regard to the number of pieces an object comprises, a figure is stated in the respective description. Decorative or constructional rivets, split-pins, studs or roves are included in the total. Glass or bone beads; silver, glass, stone or shell appliqués; decorative wire, or individual elements in ground-supported or openwork filigree and granular ornamentation, and separate rivets that play no part in the construction and whose sole function is securing to a secondary object, are discounted.

1: ROMAN PERIOD CLASPS

Some Roman infantrymen wore a cuirass, known as *lorica segmuntata*, to protect the torso, of which certain components of the Corbridge Types B and C plates were linked together with substantial sheeting copper-alloy vertical sharp-hooked and eye clasps and horizontal tie-loops and leather thongs. The Corbridge Type A *lorica segmuntata* cuirass also has tie-loops but not vertical blunt-hooks and eyes. Eyes are either circular, therefore drilled, or semicircular. Tie-loops are similar to vertical hooks but have close-butted loops which repeated tensioning of thongs tended to partially spread apart, thereby making them similar to blunt-hooks. Even more confusing is that both vertical sharp-hooks and eyes and horizontal tie-loops are known in a variety of designs. Both sections of whatever form were attached by separate copper-alloy rivets. Here it is not the intention to dwell on these specialised objects, already categorised and catalogued by M C Bishop and M D Thomas in their informative *Lorica Segmentata* vols I and II, 2002 and 2003 respectively, which this author recommends highly to those who desire a greater understanding. Both vertical sharp-hooks and eyes and horizontal tie-loops are seemingly rare finds for metal-detectorists: notwithstanding, perhaps they are discovered but go unrecognised, hence their absence from this catalogue. Instead, reconstructive drawings demonstrate their appearance and function (Figs 1.2-3). Designation is according to Bishop and Thomas, that is Category G sharp-hooked and eye clasps and Category H tie-loops.

Though extremely rare from Britain, Roman high-status gold chain-necklaces and body-chains fitted with separate wire-clasps comprising a sharp- or blunt-hook and an eye, or hooks alone, are in museums. Less expensive copper-alloy or silver chain-necklaces, and bead-necklaces, prevailed alongside this opulent jewellery, both forms of which were secured with blunt-hooked and eye clasps. Each section of such clasps is one-piece and either cast or wrought from rods, the hooks of which are formed into a distinctive S-shape designated as Class A, Type 1 or shepherd's-crook designated as Class B, Type 1. It is impossible to say whether clasps found detached from their chain or string are from chain- or bead-necklaces. Nos 3-4 and figs 2-3 formed part of an early 5th-century hoard of Roman coins and jewellery found in Wiltshire, while nos 1-2 are best assigned as 4th - 5th century.

Roman Corbridge Types B-C, Category G vertical sharp-hooked and eye clasps and Category H horizontal tie-loops

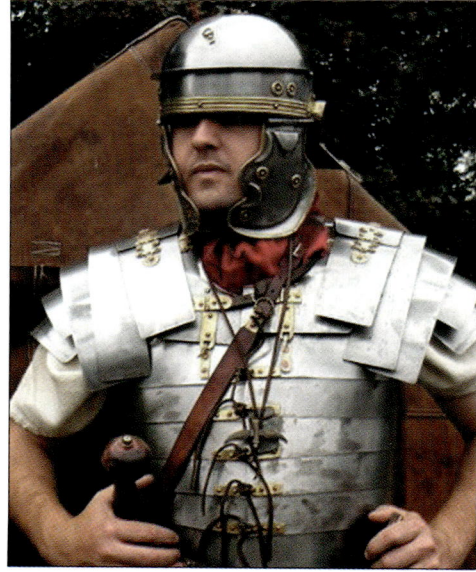

Fig. 1.1. Legio Secunda Augusta infantryman wearing a Corbridge Type B *lorica segmuntata* cuirass. Note copper-alloy Category G vertical sharp-hooked and eye clasps and Category H horizontal tie-loops riveted to the front. The back of the cuirass is also fitted with Category G vertical sharp-hooked and eye clasps. Photograph © Val MacRae.

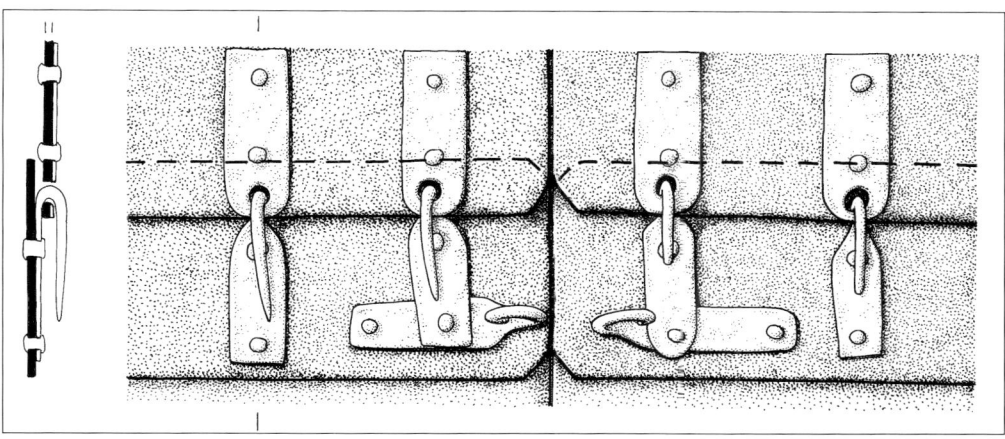

Fig. 1.2. Reconstructive drawing of sheeting copper-alloy Category G vertical sharp-hooked and eye clasps and Category H horizontal tie-loops riveted to the front of a Corbridge Type B *lorica segmuntata* cuirass. Hook-plates are elongated shield-shaped with two median drilled rivet-holes, hooks are forward-facing; actual size between 45-49 x 13-15.5mm. Eye-plates are also elongated shield-shaped with two median drilled rivet-holes and a drilled eye; actual size about 46 x 18mm. Drawing © Nick Griffiths.

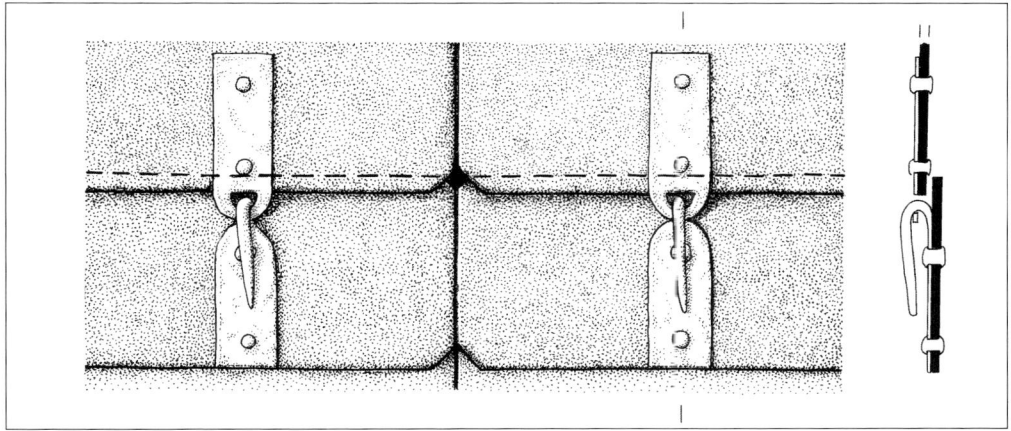

Fig. 1.3. Reconstructive drawing of sheeting copper-alloy Category G vertical sharp-hooked and eye clasps riveted to the back of a Corbridge Type B *lorica segmuntata* cuirass. Hook-plates are elongated shield-shaped with two median drilled rivet-holes, hooks are forward-facing; actual size 46.5 x 16.5mm. Eye-plates are also elongated shield-shaped with two median drilled rivet-holes and a semicircular eye; actual size about 45-46 x 15-17mm. Drawing © Nick Griffiths.

Roman period Class A necklace blunt-hooked and eye clasps

Type 1

1. Copper alloy; probably cast and wrought; each section is one-piece; moulded-relief. The sub-triangular shank of each part is rectangular-section, the attachment-ends of which are narrowed and drilled with an attachment-loop. The hooked-section has a slightly tapering circular-section S-shaped hook in the same plane as the shank. The eye-section has a flattened transverse circular eye. The front face of each shank has chevrons or crescents, while the lower edge of each has oblique lines; 38 x 11.5mm. *South Devon*. After Read 1995, no. 148. Drawing © Patrick Read.

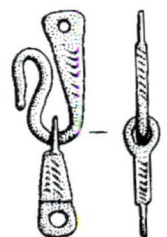

2. Silver; probably cast and wrought; one-piece; moulded-relief. Hooked-section: a circular-section shaft terminating with a rounded collared attachment-loop at one end and a slightly tapering circular-section shepherd's-crook blunt-hook at the other; all four faces at each end of the shaft are ribbed; L26mm. *Dorset*. Drawing © Nick Griffiths.

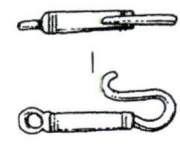

3. Silver; probably cast and wrought; each section is one-piece; punched and possibly moulded-relief. The shank of each part is tapering rectangular-section, both with a drilled attachment-loop at one end. The hooked-section has a circular-section S-shaped hook in plane with the shank, and a conical terminal. The eye-section has a flattened transverse circular eye. All four faces of each section have two longitudinal grooves and multiple random dashes; hooked-section 27 x 12mm, eye-section 24 x 4mm (Fig. 2). *Bishops Cannings, Wiltshire*. Wiltshire Heritage Museum acc. no. DZSWS:2004.252.7. Photograph reproduced courtesy of Wiltshire Heritage Museum.

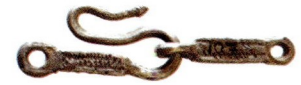

HOOKED-CLASPS & EYES

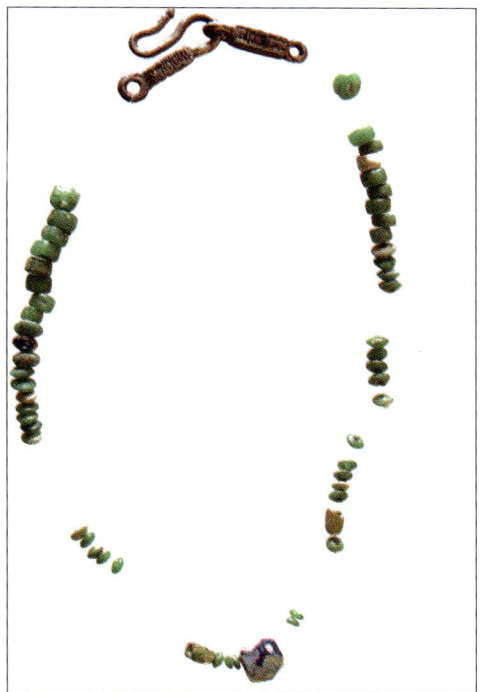

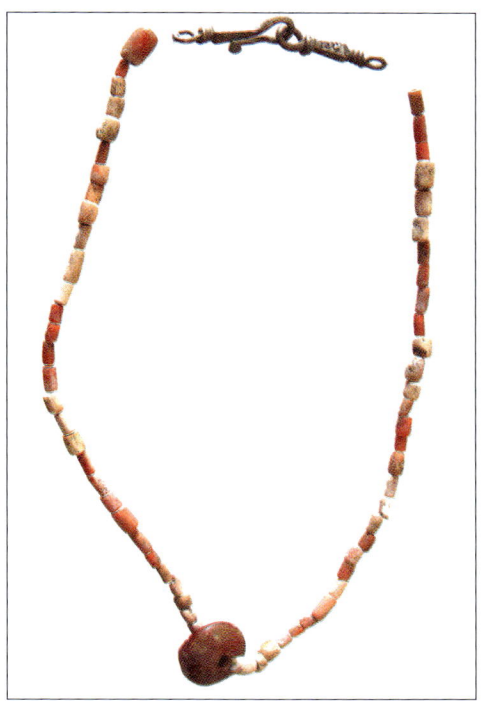

Fig. 2. A Roman bead-necklace with a Class A, Type 1 blunt-hooked and eye clasp. *Bishops Canning, Wiltshire.* Wiltshire Heritage Museum acc. no. DZSWS:2004.252.6 (restrung with monofiliment, invisible in photographs). Photograph reproduced courtesy of Wiltshire Heritage Museum.

Fig. 3. A Roman bead-necklace with a Class B, Type 1 blunt-hooked and eye clasp. *Bishops Canning, Wiltshire.* Wiltshire Heritage Museum acc. no. DZSWS:2004.252.7 (restrung with monofiliment, invisible in photographs). Photograph reproduced courtesy of Wiltshire Heritage Museum.

Roman period Class B necklace blunt-hooked and eye clasps

Type 1

4. Silver; wire; each section is one-piece; undecorated. The shank of each part is flattened tapering rectangular-section, both with a twisted wire attachment-loop at one end. The hooked-section has a part circular- and part square-section shepherd's-crook hook in plane with the shank, the hook terminal spirals outwards. The eye-section has a twisted wire eye; hooked-section 25 x 6mm, eye-section 24 x 5mm (Fig. 3). *Bishops Cannings, Wiltshire.* Wiltshire Heritage Museum acc. no. DZSWS:2004.252.6. Photograph reproduced courtesy of Wiltshire Heritage Museum.

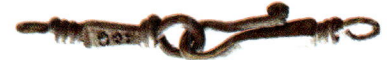

2: EARLY MEDIEVAL CLASPS

Most early medieval clasps are one-piece and flat, though composite or convex examples are recorded (see below). All forms are distinguishable by one or (rarely) two recurving sharp-hooks and attachment-holes pierced through the plate or knops. Griffiths *et al* 2007 states that 'The hooks are almost always integral to the plate...' which implies early medieval clasps with separate hooks are known; however, none were revealed during the course of this current survey. Either two or three attachment-holes is the norm, and more uncommonly, one or four. These are usually positioned in the plate at the end opposite the hook, though sometimes centrally and nearer the hook. Knops with attachment-holes always project from the end opposite the hook. A seemingly rarer form has ornamental knops, and attachment-holes within the plate. Attachment-holes are usually circular, therefore drilled, however, oval, rectangular and triangular are recorded here. Evidence for attaching by rivets is absent from the known record, therefore presumably stitching was favoured. Silver is not uncommon, however, copper-alloy is by far the prevalent metal and either may be sheeting or cast. Wrought-iron examples are recorded from Thetford, Norfolk (Rogerson and Dallas 1984, fig. 111, no. 40) and Winchester, Hampshire (Hinton 1990, nos 1406A, 1412 and 1414), and the probability is that many were made from this metal but have not survived: as random metal-detecting finds, iron is also unlikely due to the ferrous discriminating ability of modern detectors and as solid rust is non-magnetic, they will not provide a signal. Interestingly, Griffiths *et al* 2007 says '...lead alloys form a significant sub-group...', but again this author is unaware of any early medieval sharp-hooked clasps made of this metal.

Plain sharp-hooked clasps from this period are common; notwithstanding, the obverse of both sheeting or cast clasps typically display punch-work, engraving, compass inscribing, drilled-holes or pits; while some cast clasps are moulded-relief. Backs are usually plain, although nos 59 and 86 have annulets around the attachment-holes. Also current was the practice of inlaying copper-alloy clasps in this category with silver sheeting or wire. Niello decoration, particularly on silver clasps, is frequently seen and although uncommon openwork, enamel, mercury-gilding or white-metal coating also prevailed. Early medieval single sharp-hooked clasps with a drilled central-hole retaining a separate decorative-rivet are scarce, and clasps with an empty hole of sufficient diameter perhaps suggests a missing rivet. This survey revealed only one triangular single sharp-hooked clasp with such a rivet (No. 144).

Shapes of early medieval sharp-hooked clasps are predominantly triangular/sub-triangular or circular/sub-circular, however, sub-rectangular, lozenge/sub-lozenge, trefoil, heart, quatrefoil, trapezoid, asymmetrical and stylised figurative are catalogued here. A pronounced or shallow ridged collar, sometimes projecting either side, which may be zoomorphic or debased zoomorphic, at the juncture of the plate and hook, is a feature on some. Early medieval sharp-hooked clasps are designated as Classes A-J with respective classes sub-divided into types.

The earliest confirmed secure dating for triangular single sharp-hooked clasps is 7th century and this shape is thought to have predominated until the 9th when circular forms perhaps first appeared. Both these shapes, and others, as described here, seemed to have continued in use until about early post-Conquest 11th century or even into the early 12th. Archaeological evidence from Lincoln confirms that circular single sharp-hooked clasps were being made there in the 10th century (Leahy 2007). Those decorated with silver inlays and/or niello are thought to be 9th century onwards.

The flimsiness and small size of many early medieval sharp-hooked clasps, especially those of sheeting, implies their usage was restricted to functions lacking undue strain. We can but speculate whether they were solely for linking separate elements of personal dress, like leg-wrappings and trousers (see below); some feasibly performed multifarious tasks about the person, for example securing textile purses or bags (see below). Fig. 4 shows the Three Magi, of which Caspar and Melchior are wearing thigh-length hose (*chauses*) supported by a pair of suspenders, presumably somehow secured to a girdle hidden beneath their tunics, and, though by no means certain, they may have been attached to the hose by sharp-hooked clasps, as suggested by an obvious expansion at the end of each suspender where it joins the hose. As late as *c*.1260 hose had a point at the top, to which a cord was attached, that in turn was tied to the girdle (Kelly and Schwabe 1972). A trio of early medieval single sharp-hooked clasps catalogued here, two Class A, Type 1 and one Class C, Type 1 are complete with metal-eyes and they perhaps provide evidence not evident elsewhere of how they may have been used; but on which type of dress or other application remains unknown. Notwithstanding, as indicated in the main introduction, uncertainty surrounds the authenticity of these pieces, therefore caution is advised.

Some early medieval sharp-hooked clasps were undoubtedly utilitarian, uninspiring in their manufacture and decoration, perhaps intentionally so, as they were meant to be hidden from view. Conversely, there are many, and not only those totally or partially of silver, that exhibit craftsmanship of the highest order, their ornateness surely commanding to be seen by all.

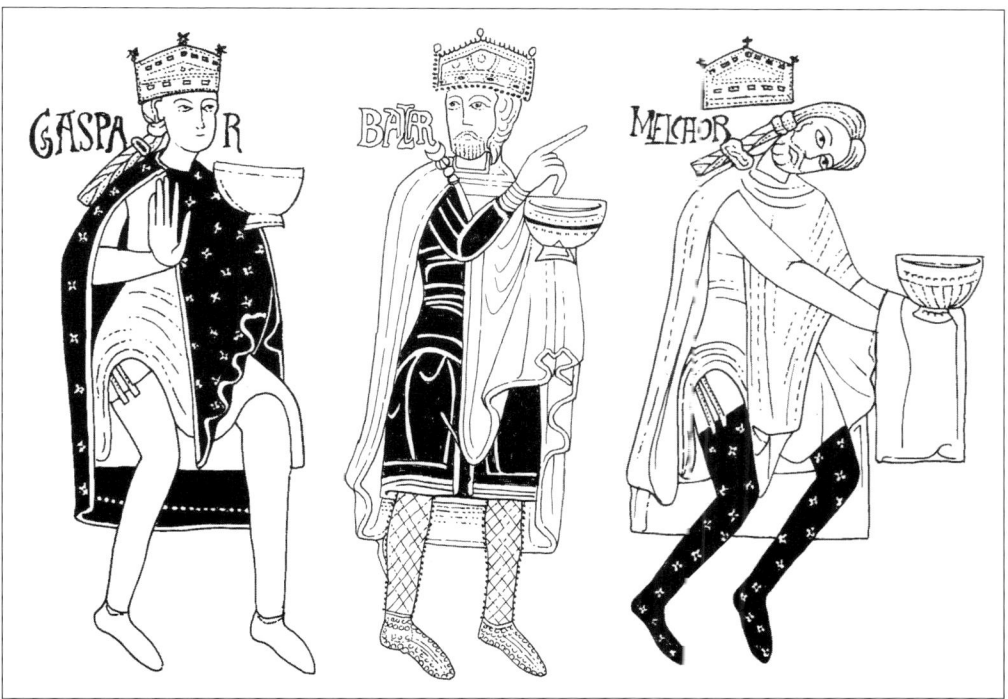

Fig. 4. Redrawing of the Three Magi, altar front from Espinol, late 13th century, Vich, Episcopel Museum. Note the expansion on the ends of the suspenders supporting Caspa's and Melchior's hose, and Balthasar's possible cross-band leg-wrappings.

HOOKED-CLASPS & EYES

Early medieval Class A single sharp-hooked clasps

Either cast or sheeting with engraved and/or punched, or openwork decoration. All are c.7th - c. early 12th century except no. 39 which is uncertain (see caveats in main introduction), and no. 84 could be 16th century, despite having attachment-holes instead of a loop.

Early medieval Class A, Type 1

Triangular/Sub-triangular

One attachment-hole

5. Copper alloy; sheeting; one-piece; drilled and compass-inscribed or engraved. A median band of four ring-and-dot motifs; 22 x 0.93mm. *Derbyshire*. Portable Antiquities Scheme E4488. Photographs © Derby City Council.

6. Copper alloy; sheeting; one-piece; punched. Dots forming a chevron surmounted by a triangle with a median band; a transverse rectangular attachment-hole; 33 x 13mm. *East Anglia*.

Two attachment-holes

7. Copper alloy; sheeting; one-piece; undecorated; 23.3 x 10.45mm. *South-West Wiltshire*. Drawing © Patrick Read.

8. Copper alloy; sheeting; one-piece; undecorated except for a transverse groove at the juncture of the plate and hook; 26 x 12.5mm. *Cambridgeshire*. United Kingdom Detecting Finds' Database 818. Photographs © Rod Blunt.

9. Silver; probably sheeting; one-piece; engraved. A linear border each side; a transverse groove at the juncture of the plate and hook; 27.7 x 14mm. *South Somerset*. Drawing © Patrick Read.

10. Copper alloy; sheeting; one-piece; engraved and punched. A median band of dots within a border of dots; two V-shaped notches either side at the juncture of the plate and hook. Incomplete, one corner and part of its attachment-hole broken off; 25.87 x 10mm. *South-East Dorset*. Drawing © Patrick Read.

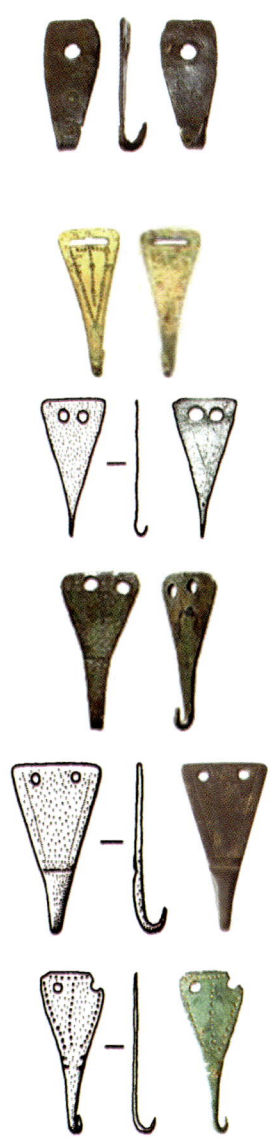

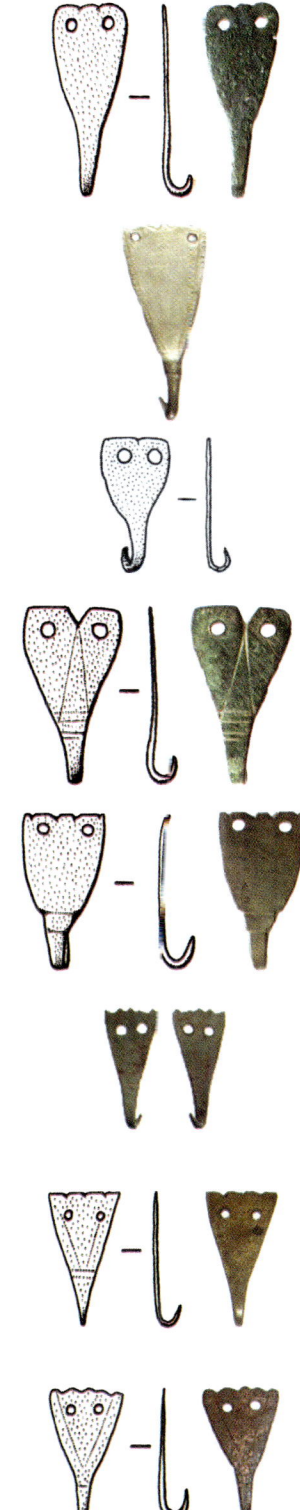

11. Copper alloy; sheeting; one-piece; undecorated. The attachment-end has an engrailed edge; 33.12 x 12.55mm. *South-East Dorset*. Drawing © Patrick Read.

12. Silver; possibly cast; one-piece; engraved. The attachment-end has an engrailed edge; a hatched linear border either side; a ridged and transverse grooved collar at the juncture of the plate and hook; 33 x 14mm. *Wiltshire*. Treasure case 2002 T252. Photograph © the Trustees of The British Museum.

13. Copper alloy; sheeting; undecorated. The attachment-end is shallow bifurcate; 23 x 11mm. *South-West Dorset*. Drawing © Patrick Read.

14. Copper alloy; sheeting; one-piece; engraved. Two lines radiate from the bifurcate attachment-end to the juncture of the plate and hook where they conjoin four transverse lines; 30 x 16mm. *Suffolk*. Drawing © Patrick Read.

15. Copper alloy; probably cast; one-piece; engraved. Two transverse grooves at the juncture of the plate and hook, otherwise plain; the attachment-end has an engrailed edge; 26.2 x 13.5mm. *South-West Wiltshire*. Drawing © Patrick Read.

16. Copper alloy; sheeting; one-piece; undecorated. The attachment-end has an engrailed edge; 18 x 0.79mm. *Buckinghamshire*. United Kingdom Detecting Finds' Database 4291. Photographs © Gordon Heritage.

17. Copper alloy; sheeting; one-piece; engraved. A linear border each side; three transverse lines at the juncture of the plate and hook; the attachment-end has an engrailed edge; 22.27 x 11.56mm. *Billingsgate fly-tip, London*. Drawing © Patrick Read.

18. Copper alloy; sheeting; one-piece; engraved. Comparable with no. 17 except one transverse line at the juncture of the plate and hook; 21.82 x 11.95mm. *Billingsgate fly-tip, London*. Drawing © Patrick Read.

19. Copper alloy; sheeting; one-piece; engraved. Two slightly oblique transverse lines at the junction of the plate and hook; the attachment-end has an engrailed edge; 27.5 x 14.2mm. *Billingsgate fly-tip, London*. Drawing © Patrick Read.

20. Copper alloy; sheeting; one-piece; engraved. A linear and cross-hatched border either side; the attachment-end has an engrailed edge; 28.24 x 15.36mm, *Suffolk*. Portable Antiquities Scheme SF-38A955. Drawing © Donna Wreathall.

21. Copper alloy; sheeting; one-piece; engraved, punched and compass-inscribed. A trefoil of ring-and-dot motifs within a linear border either side; two transverse lines at the junction of the plate and hook; the attachment-end has an engrailed edge; 25.85 x 14.7mm. *Billingsgate fly-tip, London*. Drawing © Patrick Read.

22. Copper alloy; sheeting; one-piece; engraved, drilled and compass-inscribed. A median band of three pierced ring-and-dot motifs within a linear border either side; traces of two transverse lines at the junction of the plate and hook; the attachment-end has an engrailed edge; 27.91 x 16.18mm. *Billingsgate fly-tip, London*. Drawing © Patrick Read.

23. Copper alloy; sheeting; one-piece; engraved, drilled and compass-inscribed. A trefoil formed from four ring-and-dot motifs, two slightly oblique transverse lines at the junction of the plate and hook; the attachment-end has an engrailed edge; 30 x 16mm. *Hampshire*. Drawing © Patrick Read.

24. Copper alloy; sheeting; one-piece; engraved, drilled and compass-inscribed. A Latin Cross formed from five ring-and-dot motifs, the upper dot pierces the plate; two slightly oblique transverse lines at the junction of the plate and hook; the attachment-end has an engrailed edge; 30.22 x 12.41mm. *South-West Wiltshire*. Drawing © Patrick Read.

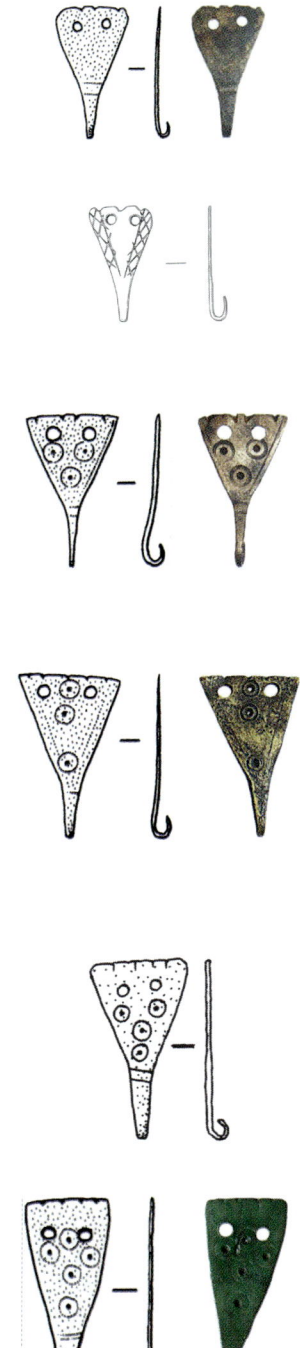

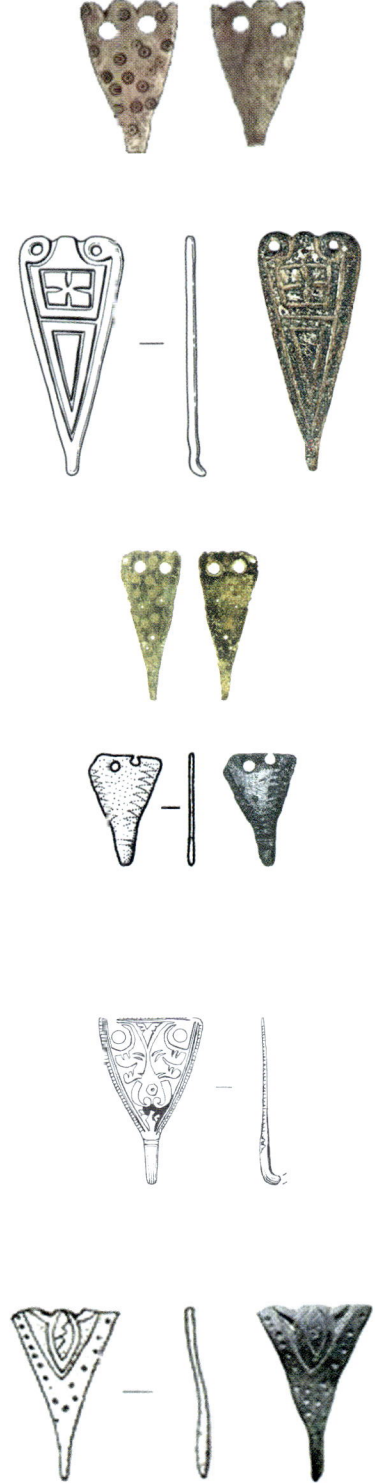

25. Copper alloy; sheeting; one-piece; punched or compass-inscribed. A field of random ring-and-dot motifs; the attachment-end has an engrailed edge. Incomplete, hook broken off; 24 x 14.9mm. *Buckinghamshire*. United Kingdom Detecting Finds' Database 3632. Photographs © Gordon Heritage.

26. Copper alloy; probably cast; one-piece; moulded-relief or engraved; gilded. The attachment-end has an engrailed edge; a trapezium-shaped panel divided in two sections, the upper one with a quatrefoil within a sub-rectangular panel, and the lower, a triangle. Hook-point distorted; 40 x 17mm. *Suffolk*. Portable Antiquities Scheme SF8362. Drawing © Donna Wreathall, photograph © Suffolk County Council Archaeological Service.

27. Copper alloy; sheeting; one-piece; punched. A field of random ring-and-dot motifs; much corroded; 16.31 x 5.66mm. *Somerset*. Taunton County Museum acc. no. OS. AA.2350 C518. Photographs © Somerset County Council.

28. Copper alloy; sheeting; one-piece; engraved. A zigzag border either side; two slightly oblique transverse lines at the junction of the plate and hook. Incomplete, hook and one corner broken off and the edge of one attachment-hole worn through; 18.89 x 11.59. *South-West Wiltshire*. Drawing © Patrick Read.

29. Silver; sheeting; one-piece; engraved. A panel of Winchester-style foliate inlaid with niello within a beaded border; two transverse lines at the junction of the plate and hook. Incomplete, hook-point broken off and broken in several pieces, drawn reconstructed; 27.5 x 16mm. *Surrey*. Portable Antiquities Scheme SUR-E4FAE7. Drawing © Surrey County Council.

30. Copper alloy; possibly cast; one-piece; possible moulded-relief or engraved and drilled. A triangular panel with a geometric-shape bordered by dots. Incomplete, part of the attachment-end broken off, outline of two attachment-holes; hook distorted or broken off; 28 x 17mm. *Oxfordshire*. Drawing and photograph © Rod Blunt.

HOOKED-CLASPS & EYES

31. Copper alloy; possibly cast; one-piece; engraved or moulded-relief. A sub-triangular panel of derived Trewhiddle-style decoration. Incomplete, the attachment-end of the plate and point of distorted hook broken off, outline of two attachment-holes; 33 x 17mm. *Worcestershire*. Photographs © Paul Roberts.

32. Copper alloy; sheeting; one-piece; drilled and compass-inscribed. A field of random ring-and-dot motifs. Incomplete, hook broken off; 22 x 19mm. *Norfolk*. United Kingdom Detecting Finds' Database 13791. Photographs © Robert Green.

33. Copper alloy; sheeting; one-piece; engraved. A median band and border of interlace; 17 x 12mm. *South Oxfordshire*. Photographs © Chris Hodgson.

34. Copper alloy; sheeting; one-piece; engraved. Geometric panels and a linear border; 21.93 x 13.3mm. *Derbyshire*. Drawing © Nick Griffiths.

35. Copper alloy; sheeting; one-piece; punched. Geometric panels outlined by voided addorsed triangles. Incomplete one corner broken off; 33 x 20mm. *Norfolk*. Portable Antiquities Scheme NMS-4B2380. Photographs © Norfolk Museums and Archaeology Service.

36. Copper alloy; sheeting; one-piece; punched. Geometric panels and a linear border; 19.17 x 9.2mm. *Derbyshire*. Drawing © Nick Griffiths.

37. Copper alloy; sheeting; one-piece; engraved and punched. A voided Plain Cross within a voided border, the two rectangular panels each have a curvilinear voided band; the edges of the attachment-end and sides have multiple notches; a transverse groove at the juncture of the plate and hook. Dimensions unrecorded. *East Yorkshire*. Jim Halliday.

38. Silver; possibly cast; one-piece; engraved. Extremely shallow acute angular interlace on a field of waffle-shapes; oval attachment-holes; 19.96 x 12.31mm. *Kent*. Portable Antiquities Scheme KENT-A5C3A1. Treasure case 2005 T331. Photographs © the Trustees of The British Museum.

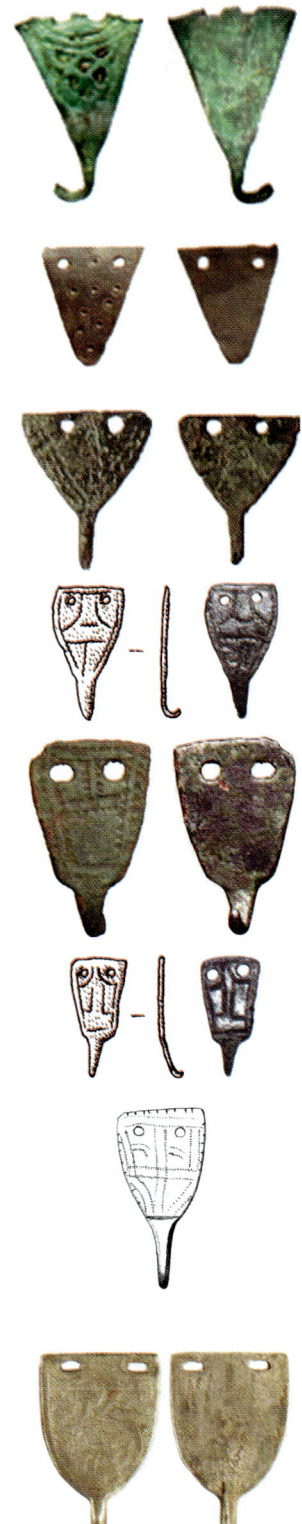

HOOKED-CLASPS & EYES

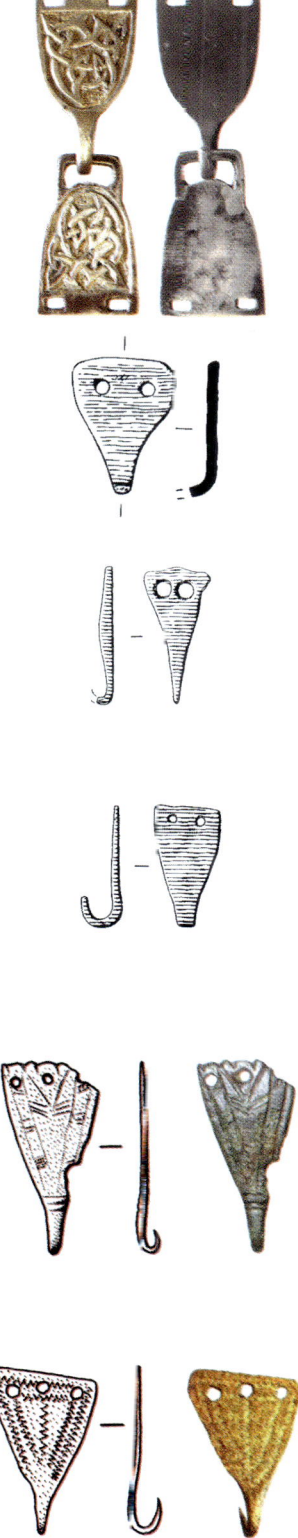

39. Silver; probably cast; each section is one-piece; moulded-relief. Each section has a panel of interlace the interstices of which are pitted, suggesting a key for niello or enamel; and rectangular attachment-holes; rectangular attachment-eye. Incomplete, hook-point broken off; hooked-section 28.87 x 14.76mm; eye-section 27.54 x 14.65. *Belgium*. Purchased in England.

40. Iron; wrought; one-piece; undecorated. Incomplete, hook broken off; 27 x 20mm. *Norfolk*. After Rogerson and Dallas 1984. Drawing © and reproduced courtesy of Andrew Rogerson, Finds' Identification and Recording Service, Norfolk Museums and Archaeology Service.

41. Iron; wrought; one-piece; undecorated except white-metal coated, possibly tin. 26 x 12mm. Incomplete, hook-point broken off. *Winchester, Hampshire*. After Hinton 1990, fig. 148, no. 1412. Drawing © and reproduced courtesy of The Winchester Research Unit of the Winchester Excavations Committee.

42. Iron; wrought; one-piece; undecorated. 23 x 12mm. *Winchester, Hampshire*. After Hinton 1990, fig. 148, no. 1414. Drawing © and reproduced courtesy of The Winchester Research Unit of the Winchester Excavations Committee.

Three attachment-holes

43. Copper alloy; sheeting; one-piece; engraved. A voided linear border either side, the attachment-end has two lines radiating from two triple bands of oblique lines; the attachment-end has an engrailed edge; three transverse grooves at the juncture of the plate and hook. Incomplete, one corner and most of its attachment-hole and a small section of one side broken off; 32 x 16mm. *South-East Dorset*. Drawing © Patrick Read.

44. Copper alloy; sheeting; one-piece; engraved. A median band of zigzags within a voided border of zigzags; 27.57 x 17.65mm. *Billingsgate fly-tip, London*. Drawing © Patrick Read.

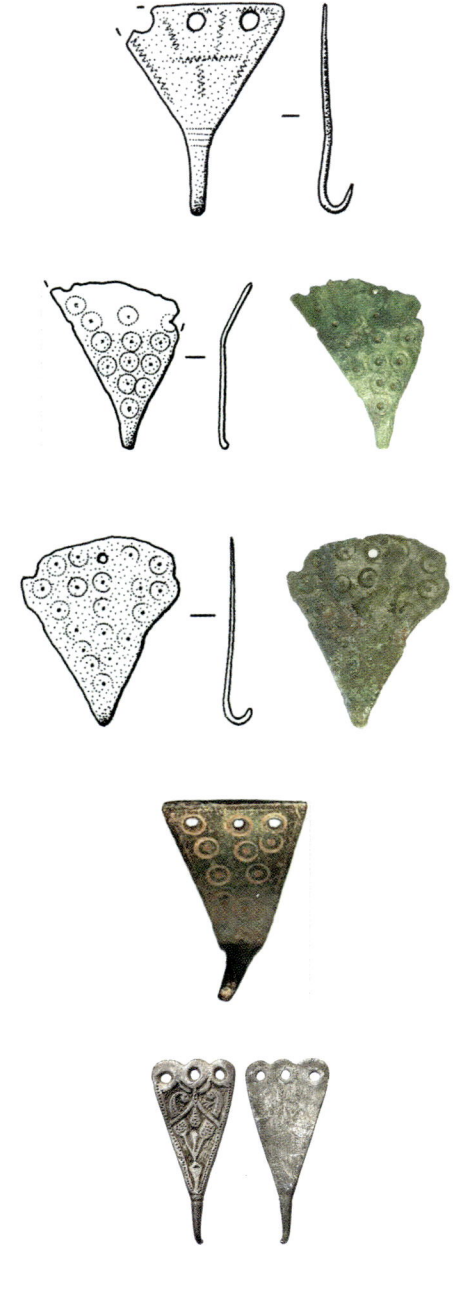

45. Copper alloy; sheeting; one-piece; engraved. Vertical, oblique and transverse bands of zigzags within a border of zigzags; four transverse lines at the juncture of the plate and hook. Incomplete, one corner and part of its attachment-hole broken off; 35 x 28mm. *South-East Lincolnshire*. Drawing © Patrick Read.

46. Copper alloy; sheeting; one-piece; drilled and compass-inscribed. A median band and border of ring-and-dot motifs. Incomplete, part of the attachment-end, sides and hook-point broken off, distorted; outline of one attachment-hole, probably three originally; 28 x 27mm. *South-East Dorset*. Drawing © Patrick Read.

47. Copper alloy; sheeting; one-piece; drilled or compass-inscribed. A field of ring-and-dot motifs; sporadic white-metal coating, probably tin. Incomplete, part of the attachment-end and each side broken off; probably three attachment-holes originally, one remaining; 31.17 x 25.31mm. *South-East Dorset*. Drawing © Patrick Read.

48. Copper alloy; sheeting; one-piece; engraved, drilled and compass-inscribed. An annulet around each attachment-hole; a field of ring-and-dot motifs within traces of a linear border; hook distorted; 33 x 19mm. *Suffolk*. Portable Antiquities Scheme SF3981. Photograph © Suffolk County Council Archaeological Service.

49. Silver; probably cast; one-piece; probably engraved and moulded-relief. Stippled stylised foliate within three panels the fields of which are scored; the attachment-end has an engrailed edge; a beaded border; two transverse lines at the juncture of the plate and hook. Incomplete, hook-point broken off and possible niello missing; 30 x 15.4mm. *South-East Dorset*. Treasure case 2004 T245. DORCM acc. no. 2006.28 in the collections at Dorset County Museum and published with the permission of The Dorset Natural History and Archaeological Society at the Dorset County Museum.

HOOKED-CLASPS & EYES

50. Silver; possibly sheeting; one-piece; engraved; probably nielloed. Geometric curvilinear and a linear border either side; the attachment-end has an engrailed edge; large attachment-holes. Curvilinear marks on the back possibly represent engraving mistakes; 15 x 14mm. *Isle of White*. Photographs © Mary Winch.

Early medieval Class A, Type 2

Circular/Sub-circular

One attachment-hole

51. Copper alloy; sheeting; one-piece; undecorated. The hook is exceptionally long; 32.31 x 21.02mm. *Staffordshire*. Drawing © Patrick Read.

52. Silver; sheeting; one-piece; engraved. A six-petalled flower; 16 x 10mm. *Kent*. United Kingdom Detecting Finds' Database 11434. Photographs © Patrick Thorn.

53. Copper alloy; possibly cast; one-piece; moulded-relief. A central large attachment-hole within three concentric circles; 20.5 x 13.4mm. *North Yorkshire*. Portable Antiquities Scheme SWYOR-A0E268. Photographs © West Yorkshire Archaeology Service.

Two attachment-holes

54. Copper alloy; sheeting; one-piece; undecorated. One large and one small attachment-hole (an unusual combination), distorted; 25.29 x 21.17mm. *South Somerset*. Taunton County Museum acc. no. 84.AA.22. C517. Photographs © Somerset County Council.

55. Copper alloy; sheeting; one-piece; undecorated. Two nicks in the edge above the attachment-holes; 16.38 x 14.85. *Billingsgate fly-tip, London*. Drawing © Patrick Read.

56. Copper alloy; sheeting; one-piece; punched. A border of dots; 19.81 x 11.26mm. *South Somerset*. Drawing © Patrick Read.

57. Copper alloy; sheeting; one-piece; engraved. A median line within a circle; 17.5 x 11.5mm. *South Somerset*. Drawing © Patrick Read.

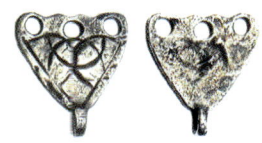
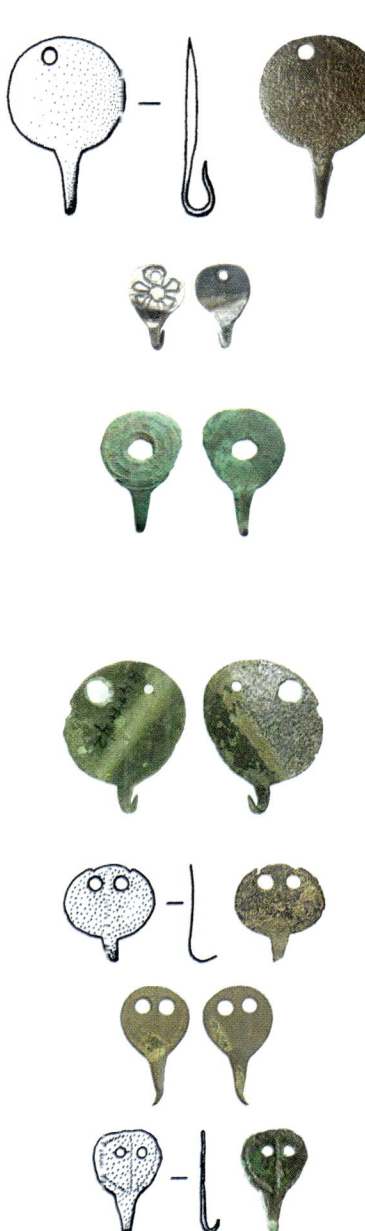

58. Copper alloy; sheeting; one-piece; engraved. Comparable with no. 57 except zigzags. Incomplete, hook-point broken off; 17.9 x 13mm. *South-West Wiltshire*. Drawing © Patrick Read.

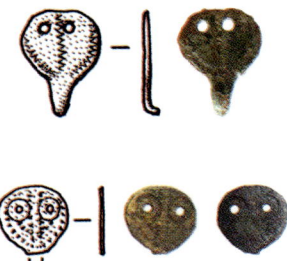

59. Copper alloy; sheeting; one-piece; punched and possibly compass-inscribed. An annulet around each attachment-hole and addorsed triangles forming two median bands and two concentric circles. The back has an annulet around each attachment-hole. Incomplete, hook broken off; 11.16 x 10.96 mm. *River Thames foreshore, London*. Drawing © Patrick Read.

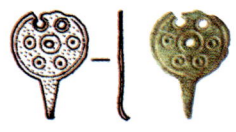

60. Copper alloy; sheeting; one-piece; engraved or possibly compass-inscribed, drilled and openwork. A small drilled-hole and each attachment-hole is within an annulet; four ring-and-dot motifs, all within a linear border. Incomplete, a small section of the edge near the attachment-holes is broken off and hook distorted; 18.5 x 12.5mm. *Suffolk*. Drawing © Patrick Read.

61. Copper alloy; sheeting; one-piece; engraved and openwork. A small drilled-hole within five concentric circles; 20.3 x 13mm. *South-East Lincolnshire*. Drawing © Patrick Read.

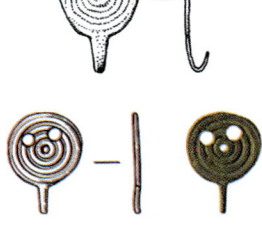

62. Copper alloy; possibly cast; one-piece; openwork and possible moulded-relief. Comparable with no. 61 except four concentric circles and a slightly larger central hole. Incomplete, hook-point broken off; 17 x 12.12mm. *Suffolk*. Portable Antiquities Scheme SF-4CB200. Drawing © Donna Wreathall, photograph © Suffolk County Council Archaeological Service.

63. Copper alloy; possibly cast; one-piece, possible moulded-relief and openwork. A small drilled-hole within four concentric circles, three linear and one formed from four ring-and-dot motifs; 18 x 13mm. *Norfolk*. United Kingdom Detecting Finds' Database 10373. Photographs © Robert Green.

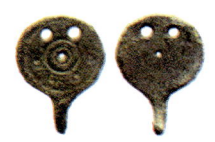

64. Copper alloy; possibly cast; one-piece; possible moulded-relief. Comparable with nos 62-63 except three concentric circles and a central pit; 15 x 11mm. *Kent*. United Kingdom Detecting Finds' Database 8986. Photographs © Patrick Thorn.

65. Silver; sheeting; one-piece, engraved. A discontinuous spiral with sporadic hatching in the field; much abraded; 12 x 8.5mm. *Norfolk*. Treasure case 2003 T233. Photograph © Trustees of The British Museum.

66. Copper alloy; sheeting; one-piece; engraved. A voided saltire and three concentric circles, the inner two dissected by the arms. Incomplete, hook-point broken off; 23.9 x 19.9mm. *South-West Wiltshire*. Drawing © Patrick Read.

67. Copper alloy; sheeting; one-piece; engraved. A voided saltire, an equal-armed cross and two concentric circles; 19.3 x 18.8mm. *South Somerset*. Taunton County Museum acc. no. 878/1990/30.

68. Copper alloy; sheeting; one-piece; engraved. A voided curved-arm saltire with a median line in one quadrant within a circle; 16.63 x 9.57mm. *Suffolk*. Portable Antiquities Scheme SF-580E38. Drawing © Donna Wreathall, photograph © Suffolk County Council Archaeological Service.

69. Copper alloy; sheeting; one-piece; engraved. An off-centre equal-armed cross formed from voided zigzags within a circle; 18.1 x 12.6mm. *North Lincolnshire*. Portable Antiquities Scheme NLM4303. Drawing © Portable Antiquities Scheme and North Lincolnshire Council.

70. Copper alloy; sheeting; one-piece; engraved. An off-centre equal-armed cross formed from zigzags; 19 x 14mm. *Lincolnshire*. United Kingdom Detecting Finds' Database 8755. Photographs © Graham Hunt.

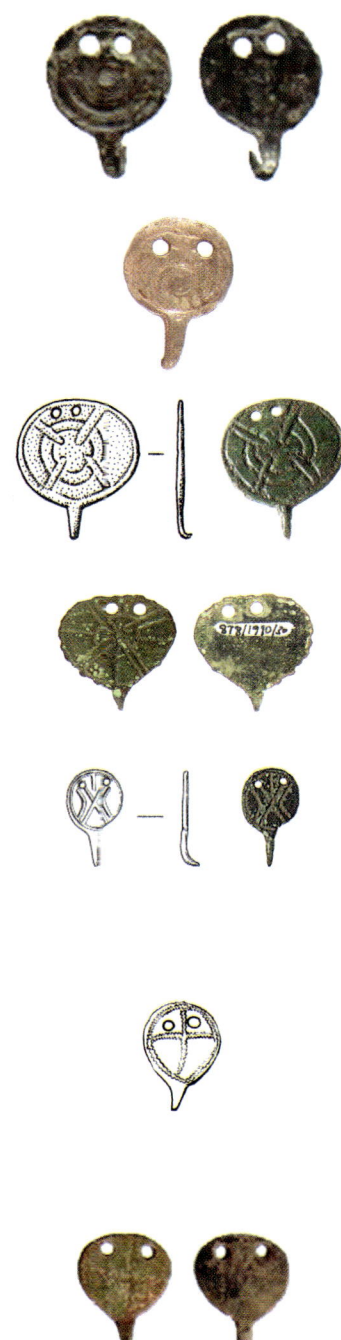

71. Copper alloy; sheeting; one-piece; engraved. A voided equal-armed cross, the two quadrants nearest the hook each contain a crescent, within a circle. Incomplete, the edge of one attachment-hole worn through; 18 x 11mm. *Suffolk*. Portable Antiquities Scheme SF-29AA63. Drawing © Donna Wreathall, photograph © Suffolk County Council Archaeological Service.

72. Copper alloy; sheeting; one-piece; engraved. An equal-armed cross; plate split near one attachment-hole, and corroded; 17.22 x 10.96mm. *Derbyshire*. Drawing © Nick Griffiths.

73. Copper alloy; sheeting; one-piece; engraved. An ornate cross paty within a circle; sporadic off-white residue in the engraving; a tiny angular knop on one side at the juncture of the plate and hook is probably a manufacturing defect. Incomplete, a small nick in the edge; 21.87 x 12.56mm. *Billingsgate fly-tip, London*. Drawing © Patrick Read.

74. Silver; possibly cast; one-piece; engraved or moulded-relief. A stylised cross paty, each arm dissecting two concentric circles; an engrailed edge; sporadic possible niello inlay. Incomplete, a small section of plate broken off; 21.52 x 13.01. *Suffolk*. Portable Antiquities Scheme SF-1EFD68. Drawing © Donna Wreathall, photographs © Suffolk County Council Archaeological Service;.

75. Silver; sheeting; one-piece; engraved. A cross paty, each arm has two transverse lines, within a circle; 23 x 14.9mm. *Kent*. Treasure case 2004 T327. Photographs © the Trustees of The British Museum.

76. Copper alloy; sheeting; one-piece; engraved. A circle with a median line and an arc in each segment; 16.63 x 9.57mm. *Suffolk*. Portable Antiquities Scheme SF-580E38. Drawing © Donna Wreathall, photograph © Suffolk County Council Archaeological Service.

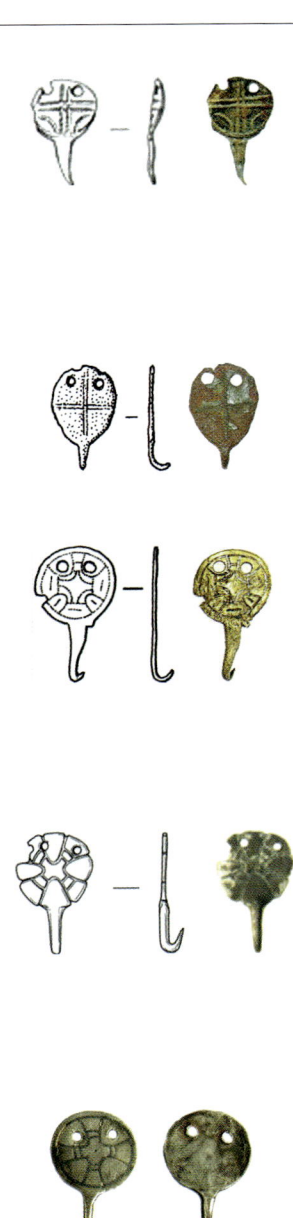

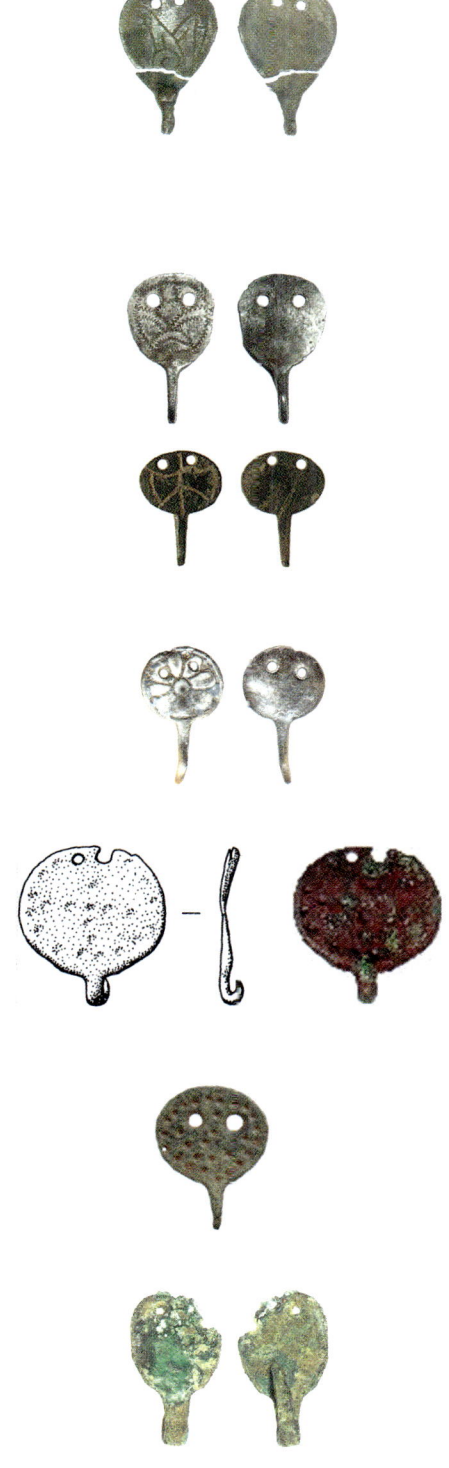

77. Silver; possibly cast; one-piece; engraved. Ringerike-style decoration; a ridged collar at the juncture of the plate and hook. Incomplete, plate fractured just above the juncture of the hook; hook-point broken off and probable niello inlay missing; 19.7 x 12.72mm. *Derbyshire*. Portable Antiquities Scheme DENO-93DBE4. Treasure case 2004 T351. Photographs © Derby City Council.

78. Silver; sheeting; one-piece; engraved. Geometric panels formed from zigzags, interpreted as a facing human-mask; 12.8 x 0.72mm. *North Essex*. Photographs © Joseph Rayner.

79. Copper alloy; sheeting; one-piece; engraved. A median line and curvilinear in each semi-circle; 19.5 x 13.6mm. *Suffolk*. Portable Antiquities Scheme SF-A8DDFS. Photographs © Suffolk County Council Archaeological Service.

80. Silver; possibly cast; one-piece; possible moulded-relief. An eight-petalled flower, each petal inlaid with degraded niello; 18.98 x 10.84mm. *Essex*. Portable Antiquities Scheme ESS-2C8575. Photographs © Colchester Museums.

81. Copper alloy; sheeting; one-piece; drilled. An equal-armed cross formed from pits within a circle; crudely-made. Incomplete, the edge of one attachment-hole worn through; 26.5 x 23.5mm. *South Somerset*. Drawing © Patrick Read, photograph © Somerset County Council.

82. Copper alloy; sheeting; one-piece; punched. A field of random dots, one of which has perforated the metal; 17 x 13mm. *Norfolk*. Portable Antiquities Scheme NMS-670893. Photograph © Norfolk Museums and Archaeology Service.

83. Copper alloy; cast; shallow convex; one-piece; undecorated. A solid-domed obverse, flat reverse. Incomplete, suffering from bronze disease and a section of the plate corroded away; 12.39 x 7.07mm. *Somerset*. Taunton County Museum acc. no. OS. AA.2344 C5 18.

84. Copper alloy; cast; convex; one-piece; moulded-relief; gilded obverse. A hollow-domed boss bearing a (?) human facing-mask; a laterally projecting edge; an attachment-hole each side of the mouth; 28.4 x 22mm. *Northamptonshire.* Portable Antiquities Scheme NARC-82E223. Photographs © Northamptonshire County Council.

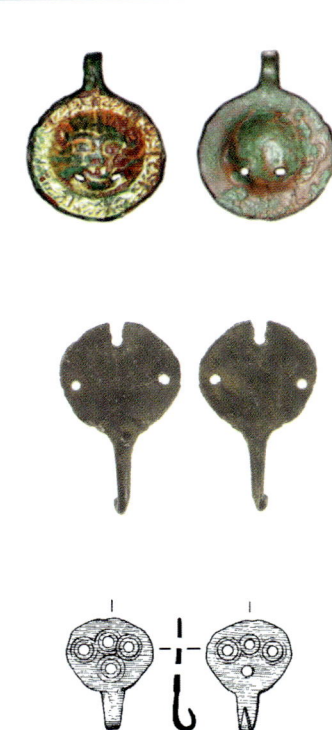

Three attachment-holes

85. Silver; possibly cast; one-piece; undecorated. A pellet at the juncture of the plate and hook; 3.08 x 1.22mm. Incomplete, edge of one attachment-hole broken off. *Bedfordshire.* Photographs © St Albans Museums.

Four attachment-holes

86. Copper alloy; sheeting; one-piece; compass-inscribed. The attachment-holes form an unequal-armed cross; on the front each attachment-hole is within an annulet, while on the back the upper three holes are similarly decorated; 22 x 17mm. *Norfolk.* After Rogerson and Dallas 1984. Drawing © and reproduced courtesy of Andrew Rogerson, Finds' Identification and Recording Service, Norfolk Museums and Archaeology Service.

87. Copper alloy; sheeting; one-piece; punched or drilled and compass-inscribed. Five ring-and-dot motifs forming an equal-armed cross; D15mm. Incomplete, hook broken off. *East Yorkshire.* United Kingdom Detecting Finds' Database 6163. Photographs © Richard Last.

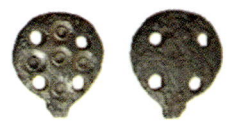

Early medieval Class A, Type 3

Sub-rectangular

One attachment-hole

88. Copper alloy; sheeting; one-piece; drilled. Three bands of pits, comprising eight in all, two of which have pierced the metal, possibly due to abrasion or excessive pressure on the drill-bit; 27.1 x 17.3mm. *Suffolk.* Portable Antiquities Scheme ESS-39FF15. Photographs © Suffolk County Council Archaeological Service.

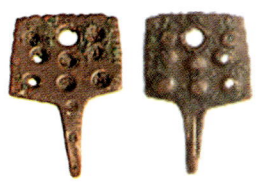

Early medieval Class A, Type 4

Stylised figurative

One attachment-hole

89. Copper alloy; sheeting; one-piece; engraved. Bands of zigzags forming a tribrach motif with a voided chevron near the hook-end and a sub-lozenge at the attachment-end, flanked by commas; resembles a stylised lily. Incomplete, hook-point broken off; 20.19 x 10.91mm. *Suffolk*. Portable Antiquities Scheme SF-D18A63. Drawing © Donna Wreathall, photographs © Suffolk County Council Archaeological Service.

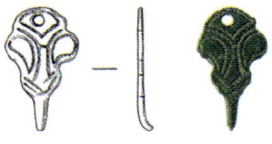

90. Silver; sheeting; one-piece; engraved. Comparable with no. 89 except two transverse grooves at the juncture of the plate and hook; 19 x 12.4mm. *North Yorkshire*. Treasure case 2004 T50. Photographs © the Trustees of The British Museum.

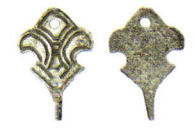

Early medieval Class A, Type 5

Trefoil-shaped

One attachment-hole

91. Copper alloy; cast; one-piece; moulded-relief. Interlace; the reverse is shallow concave. Incomplete, hook-point broken off; 19.4 x 14.2mm. *West Sussex*. Portable Antiquities Scheme SUSS-830C92. Photographs © Gary Crace.

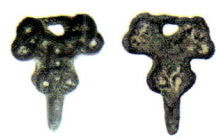

Early medieval Class A, Type 6

Heart-shaped

Two attachment-holes

92. Copper alloy; sheeting; one-piece; undecorated. Incomplete, hook broken off and the edge of one attachment-hole worn through; 13.07 x 13.16mm. *South-West Wiltshire*. Drawing © Patrick Read.

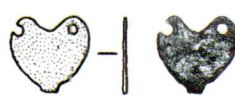

93. Copper alloy; sheeting; one-piece; punched. A field of random dots; the edges of the attachment-holes are ragged; 20 x 14mm. *Suffolk*. Portable Antiquities Scheme SF3692. Drawing © Donna Wreathall, photograph © Suffolk County Council Archaeological Service.

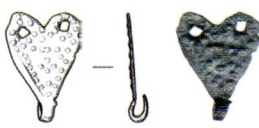

Early medieval Class B single sharp-hooked clasps

Comparable with Class A except having a projecting, frequently ridged, rounded or angular collar midway or at the juncture of the plate and hook: no. 94 has decorative knops. Either plain or engraved, compass inscribed and/or drilled. All except no. 95, which is perhaps early 16th century, are *c*.8th - *c*. early 12th century.

Early medieval Class B, Type 1

Triangular/Sub-triangular

One attachment-hole

94. Copper alloy, cast; one-piece; engraved and moulded-relief. A projecting shallow ridged angular collar midway; a rounded knop either side of the attachment-end; the attachment-end has a linear border; 22.68 x 8.1mm. *County Durham*. Drawing © Patrick Read.

95. Copper alloy; sheeting; one-piece; undecorated. A triangular attachment-hole; a stepped collar at the juncture of the plate and hook; 24 x 12mm. *Suffolk*.

Two attachment-holes

96. Copper alloy; possibly cast; one-piece; drilled and engraved. A border of pits either side; the projecting partially rounded and angular collar at the juncture of the plate and hook has two transverse bands of pits; the attachment-end is bordered with triangles while the edge has two small nicks; 23 x 15mm. *Lincolnshire*. Portable Antiquities Scheme LIN-506641. Photograph © and courtesy of the Portable Antiquities Scheme.

97. Copper alloy; sheeting; one-piece; engraved. Traces of a zigzag border either side; a projecting angular collar at the juncture of the plate and hook; 15.9 x 14mm. *South-West Wiltshire*. Drawing © Patrick Read.

Three attachment-holes

98. Copper alloy; sheeting; one-piece; undecorated. The attachment-end has an engrailed edge; a shallow ridged and slightly projecting rounded collar at the junction of the plate and hook. Incomplete, corner attachment-hole edges worn through; 27 x 15mm. *South-West Somerset*. Drawing © Patrick Read.

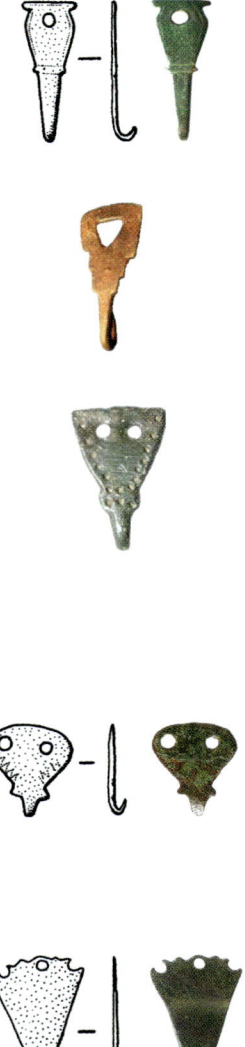

Early medieval Class B, Type 2

Circular/Sub-circular

Two attachment-holes

99. Copper alloy; sheeting; one-piece; compass-inscribed, punched and openwork. A small drilled-hole within three concentric circles bordered by dots, one of which has penetrated the metal; a projecting angular collar at the juncture of the plate and hook; 17.2 x 11.9mm. *Billingsgate fly-tip, London*. Drawing © Patrick Read.

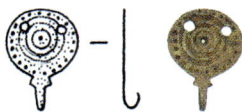

100. Copper alloy; sheeting; one-piece; compass-inscribed and drilled. A field of ring-and-dot motifs; a projecting angular collar at the juncture of the plate and hook. Incomplete, hook point broken off; 19.5 x 11.7mm. *Suffolk*. Drawing © Patrick Read.

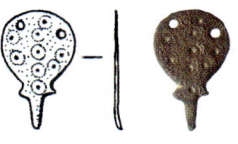

Early medieval Class B, Type 3

Heart-shaped

Two attachment-holes

101. Copper alloy; sheeting; one-piece; undecorated. A projecting rounded collar at the juncture of the plate and hook; 26.9 x 21.5mm. *North-West Norfolk*. Sedgeford Historical and Archaeological Research Project SH03 BYDNT JEWELL F1240 NSMR 1609.

102. Copper alloy; sheeting; one-piece; punched. A field of annulets; the bifurcate edge of the attachment-end has a central small slightly angular knop; a shallow projecting rounded collar at the juncture of the plate and hook; 35 x 19mm. *Cambridgeshire*. Portable Antiquities Scheme CAM-32AF23. Photographs © Cambridgeshire County Council.

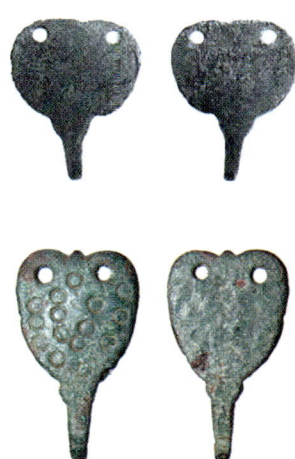

Early medieval Class C single sharp-hooked clasps

Comparable with Classes A and B except with a ridged zoomorphic collar at the juncture of the plate and hook; drilled attachment-holes in the main plate; decoration is engraved or engraved and drilled. Mid to late 11th century, except no. 105 which is uncertain (see caveats mentioned in the main introduction).

Early medieval Class C, Type 1

Triangular

Two attachment-holes

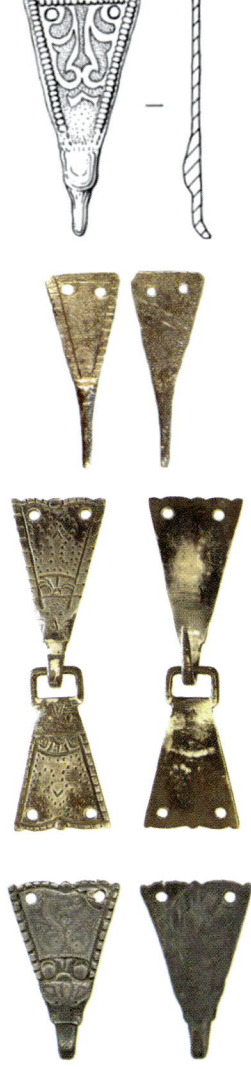

103. Silver; probably cast; one-piece; engraved. A panel of Winchester-style foliate inlaid with niello within a beaded border; a shallow projecting ridged debased zoomorphic collar at the juncture of the plate and hook. Incomplete, hook-point and two corners broken off; 41.86 x 23.68mm. *Dorset*. Portable Antiquities Scheme SOMDOR 1161. Drawing © Somerset County Council.

104. Silver; sheeting; one-piece; engraved. A hatched linear border; an annulet around each attachment-hole; a ridged zoomorphic collar at the juncture of the plate and hook; 34 x 12.35mm. *Cambridgeshire*. Treasure case 2004 T263. Photographs © the Trustees of The British Museum.

105. Silver; probably cast; each section is one-piece; engraved and drilled. The dimensions and decoration of the plates are sufficiently similar to assume they are a pair; each has curvilinear and linear bands of dots and a linear chevron within a linear and hatched border; the attachment-ends are engrailed; a ridged zoomorphic collar at the juncture of the plate and hook; a rectangular attachment-eye; hooked-section 24.99 x 14.39mm; eye-section 29.4 x 14.33mm. *Belgium*. Purchased in England.

106. Silver; probably cast; one-piece; engraved and drilled; sporadic niello. Comparable with no. 105 except two linear and dotted confronted beaked, winged snake-like animals; 29 x 17mm. *North Gloucestershire*. Portable Antiquities Scheme WAW-F2FAA5, Treasure case 2005 T181. Photographs © The Portable Antiquities Scheme.

Early medieval Class D single sharp-hooked clasps

Two or more distinct rounded knops drilled for attachment, positioned on the end of the plate opposite the hook, distinguish Class D from Classes A-C. Either cast or sheeting copper-alloy or silver, one-piece or composite construction, decoration may be relief, engraved, compass-inscribed, punched, drilled or inlays of silver or niello. All are c.9th - c. early12th century, except no. 108 where caveats apply (see main introduction).

A 10th-century male burial at Birka, Sweden (grave 905) contained two substantial copper-alloy Class D, Type 4 single sharp-hooked clasps, with moulded-relief and openwork decoration, one below each patella of the skeleton (see no. 122): remnants of woollen twill textile adhering to their reverses is interpreted as perhaps being from spiral or cross-band leg-wrappings (similar to modern puttees). Leg-wrappings were also made of linen. Interestingly, each hook-point remained linked to a small iron eye, each of which retained evidence of rusted linen tabby, possibly from the trousers (Hägg 1986). In the 10th and 11th centuries certain sharp-hooked-clasps were perhaps stitched, using their attachment-holes, on the ends of leg-wrappings and the eyes stitched on the trousers or stockings. Contemporary iconography, for example the Bayeux Tapestry, shows the legs of both Anglo-Saxons and Normans with horizontal bands (some in different colours) and a diagonal band at the top, often interpreted as spiral leg-wrappings though banded hose is a possibility (see fig. 5). A possible late Anglo-Saxon warrior wearing spiral leg-wrappings is shown in fig. 6. Cross-band leg-wrappings were apparently more uncommon and the Bayeux Tapestry shows very few examples, one being a mounted Norman knight attacking the Saxons (Fig. 7). It is thought that either form of leg-wrapping was worn over trousers or stockings or even covered bare legs. Other methods for securing leg-wrappings were cords with tassels or buckled garters - their free-ends possibly being simply tucked in. Frustratingly, Anglo-Saxon period sharp-hooked-clasps and metal-eyes are conspicuous by their absence in contemporary illustrations. Interestingly, a productive (a contentious description) Anglo-Saxon site in South-West Wiltshire has produced at least 12 single sharp-hooked clasps (various classes, most of which are catalogued here), and from this same confined area ten cast high-lead/tin copper-alloy rings have been recovered, all of which are tiny and range in external diameter from 6.71 - 9.14mm. These are described as possible late medieval pendent-loops (Portable Antiquities Scheme WILT-4E64F8); however, their alloy and distinctive lozenge-shaped sections are anomalous with pendent-loops in the known record. Each of these rings sits comfortably on the hook of any size of Anglo-Saxon single or double (see below) sharp-hooked clasp; and although not iron, are they therefore eyes from trousers? (Figs 8-9)

A second interment, at Cathedral Green, Winchester, revealed two Class D, Type 1 silver single sharp-hooked clasps in a c.871 indeterminate sex burial (grave 67), one being positioned on and the other beneath a knee-cap (Biddle and Hinton 1990). This perhaps adds weight to the leg-wrappings hypothesis.

A pair of early medieval Class D, Type 1 copper-alloy single sharp-hooked clasps formed part of The Forum Hoard of over 820 Anglo-Saxon coins (mainly Athelstan) excavated in 1883 near the House of the Vestal Virgins in Rome. These sharp-hooked clasps are extremely important, for not only did they help determine the hoard's disposition date, but for two other reasons: each is inscribed with part of the name of Marinus [+DOMNA MA] [+RINO PAPA] who was Pope from 942-46, which makes them the only Anglo-Saxon inscribed sharp-hooked clasps in the known record and they may have fastened a purse or bag in which the coins were carried (Blunt 1974).

Additional evidence for early medieval sharp-hooked clasps possibly being used with purses or bags comes from a hoard of Anglo-Saxon coins deposited c.963 and found at Tetney, Lincolnshire, which also contained a pair of silver single sharp-hooked clasps, class unknown (Hinton 1990).

Furthermore, Hinton tells us that 'tags' (sharp-hooked clasps) from two 7th-century graves '... are recorded as coming from below the head and beside the hip of their respective skeletons, and that the discovery of five tags in association at Shakenoak (Oxfordshire) may imply "some sort of multiple fastening", like a modern hook and eye.' All of this evidence suggests that sharp-hooked clasps of any class from this period probably had multifarious functions.

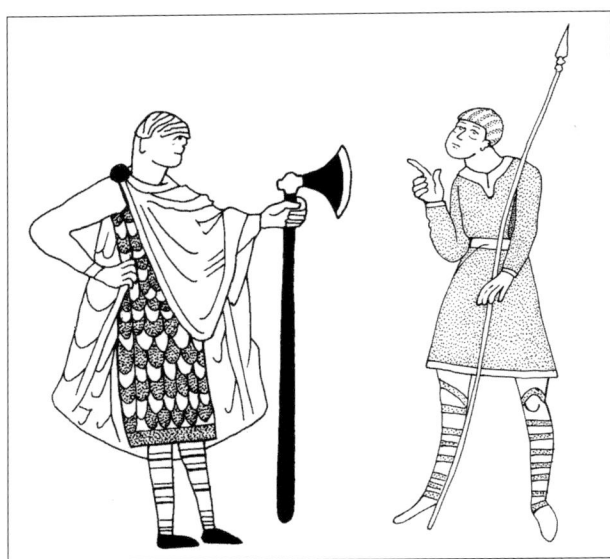

Fig. 5. Redrawn from the Bayeux Tapestry: the Norman Count Guy and a Norman guard both wearing either spiral leg-wrappings or banded hose. Note diagonal band above the guard's knees.

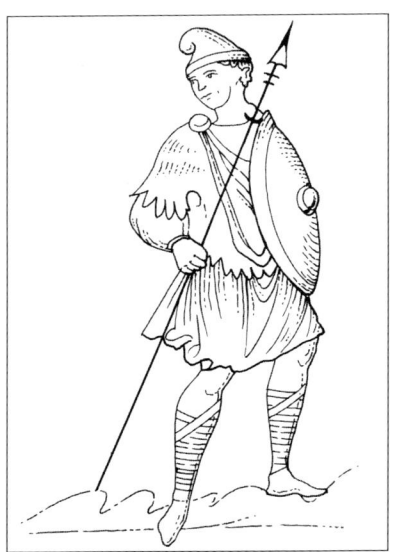

Fig. 6. From a 19th-century engraving, taken from a 11th-century Anglo-Saxon manuscript, a warrior wearing 'typical late Saxon robes', including spiral leg-wrappings (note diagonal bands below the knees); after Wise 1979. This illustration may be from a Carolingian manuscript, however, if it is an Anglo-Saxon manuscript, it is heavily influenced by continental illustrations (pers. comm. Nick Griffiths).

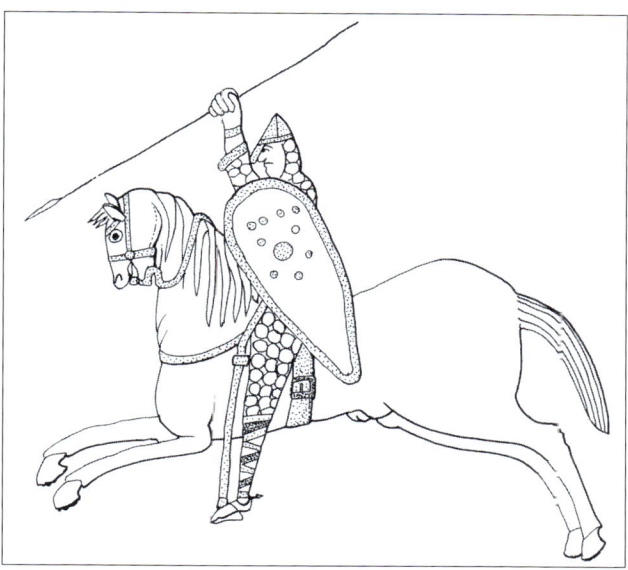

Fig. 7. Redrawn from the Bayeux Tapestry: a mounted Norman knight attacking the Saxons at Hastings. Note cross-banded leg-wrappings.

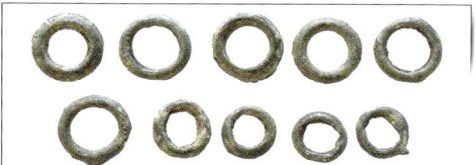

Fig. 8. Ten tiny high-tin/lead copper-alloy rings from South-West Wiltshire.

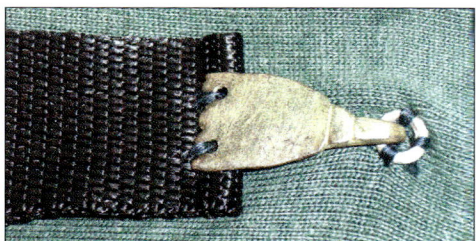

Fig. 9. Reconstruction showing possibly how early medieval sharp-hooked clasps and the tiny rings were stitched to trousers and leg-wrappings respectively and then attached together.

HOOKED-CLASPS & EYES

Early medieval Class D, Type 1

Circular/Sub-circular

Two attachment-knops

107. Silver; sheeting; one-piece; undecorated. Rounded attachment-knops; 19 x 13.7mm. *South Somerset*. Portable Antiquities Scheme SOM-D90C24. Photographs © Somerset County Council.

108. Silver; probably cast; each section is one-piece; moulded-relief. Hooked-section: a circular panel bearing a cross pommée variant, a quatrefoil in each quadrant; the interstices of each quadrant are stippled, suggesting a key for niello or enamel; rounded attachment-knops; 23.11 x 15.84mm. Incomplete, hook-point broken off. Eye-section: identical decoration, a rectangular attachment-eye; 30.4 x 16.11mm. *Belgium*. Purchased in England.

109. Silver; probably cast; one-piece; engraved; nielloed. A circular panel bearing a fabulous retrograde quadruped; 23 x 16mm. *Hampshire*. United Kingdom Detecting Finds' Database 12751. Photographs © Mark Duell.

110. Copper alloy; sheeting; one-piece; punched and engraved. A circular panel of random ring-and-dot motifs; rounded attachment-knops; 26 x 16mm. *South-West Wiltshire*. Drawing © Patrick Read.

111. Copper alloy; sheeting; one-piece; engraved. A circular panel of derived Trewhiddle-style decoration; two transverse grooves at the juncture of the plate and hook; rounded attachment-knops; 36 x 22.5mm. *Norfolk*. Portable Antiquities Scheme NMS-DF4534. Photographs © Norfolk Museums and Archaeology Service.

112. Copper alloy; cast; one-piece; engraved. A circular panel bearing a propeller-shape with triquetra knots in the interstices, a central small hollow-domed boss, all within a beaded border; three transverse grooves at the juncture of the plate and hook. Incomplete, probable rounded attachment-knops broken off; 26 x 21mm. *Norfolk*. Portable Antiquities Scheme NMS-345151. Photograph © Norfolk Museums and Archaeology Service.

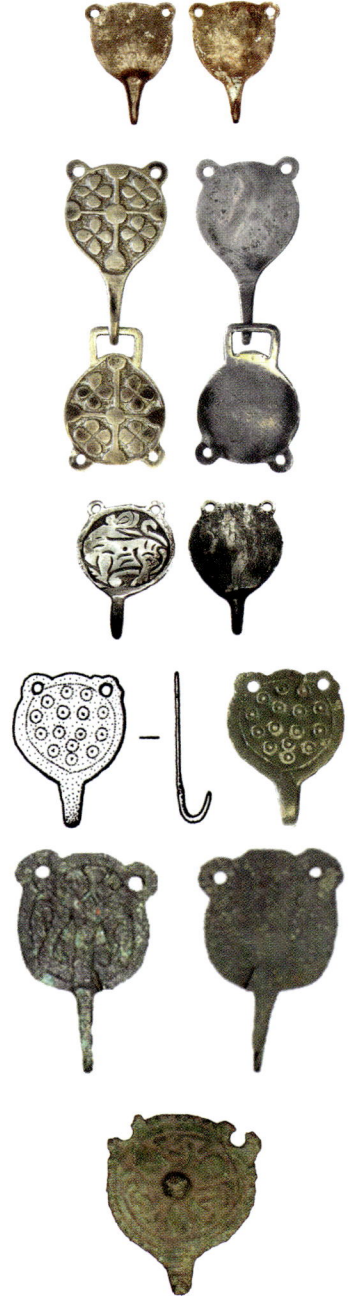

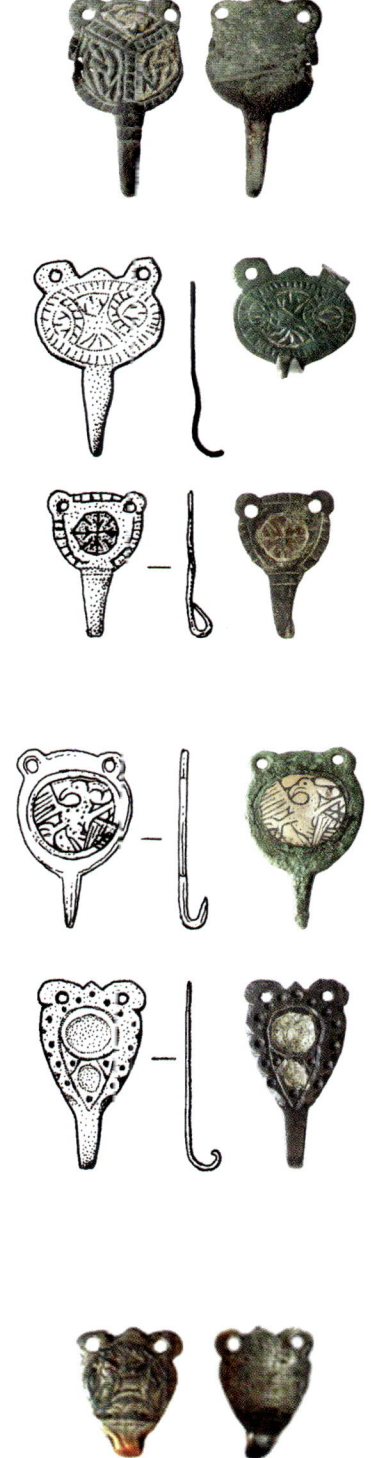

113. Copper alloy; sheeting; one-piece; engraved. A circular panel bearing a hatched tribrach motif, the interstices infilled with interlace, all within a hatched border; three transverse grooves at the juncture of the plate and hook; a small tear in the edge; 34 x 18.5mm. *Essex*. United Kingdom Detecting Finds' Database 12608. Photographs © John Mills.

114. Copper alloy; sheeting; one-piece; engraved. An oval panel in the Trewhiddle-style within a voided linear and hatched border; a small rounded knop between the slightly angular attachment-knops; the hook and one knop distorted; 34 x 21mm. *South-West Wiltshire*. Drawing © Patrick Read.

115. Copper alloy; possibly sheeting; one-piece; engraved; champlevé enamel. A sub-circular reddish (?) enamel panel with a black/blue (?) enamel four-petalled flower; a hatched border; rounded attachment-knops; two transverse lines at the juncture of the plate and hook; 24.16 x 15.62mm. *Fly-tip, East London*. Drawing © Nick Griffiths.

116. Copper-alloy and silver; possibly cast, and sheeting; two-piece; engraved. An inset roundel bearing an eagle with outspread wings (representing St John the Baptist), inlaid with niello; rounded attachment-knops; 30 x 19mm. *South-West Wiltshire*. Drawing © Nick Griffiths.

117. Copper alloy and silver; one-piece; sheeting and wire; drilled and engraved. Circular and smaller sub-circular panels outlined with silver wire and infilled with a whitish substance within an ovoid, two oblique lines project from the circle and over the sub-circle; a border of pits and further pits in the interstices; the side edges have V-shaped notches; rounded attachment-knops and a small angular knop between; 30.48 x 16.7mm. *County Durham*.

118. Silver; possibly cast; one-piece; engraved and nielloed. A circular panel in the Trewhiddle-style; a small angular knop between the rounded attachment-knops; 21.6 x 15.8mm. *East Yorkshire*. United Kingdom Detecting Finds' Database 11284. Photographs © Colin Popplewell.

119. Copper alloy; possibly cast; one-piece; engraved; sporadic white-metal coating on both sides (?) silver or tin. A sub-circular panel bearing addorsed curvilinear, the outer two interstices of which contain an oblique sub-rectangle; a small angular knop between the rounded attachment-knops; 26 x 19mm. *Norfolk*. United Kingdom Detecting Finds' Database 12421. Photographs © Robert Green.

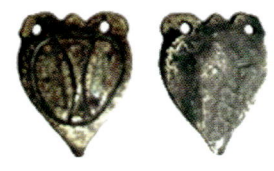

Early medieval Class D, Type 2

Quatrefoil

Two attachment-knops

120. Silver; sheeting; one-piece; engraved. Possibly a Winchester-style stippled lily-like motif; rounded attachment-knops; 17.17 x 10.83mm. *Kent*. Portable Antiquities Scheme KENT-0144D4. Treasure case 2005 T350. Photograph © Kent County Council.

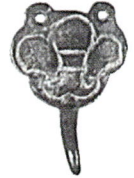

Early medieval Class D, Type 3

Lozenge-shaped

Two attachment-knops

121. Copper alloy; sheeting; one-piece; engraved. Three longitudinal bands of zigzags; rounded attachment-knops; 25 x 8.3mm. *Suffolk*. Portable Antiquities Scheme SF-084921. Drawing © Donna Wreathall, photograph © Suffolk County Council Archaeological Service.

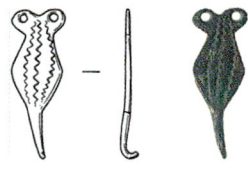

Early medieval Class D, Type 4

Sub-circular

Three attachment-knops

122. Copper alloy; cast; one-piece; moulded-relief and openwork. Curlicue ribs, a raised annulet around each openwork disc, and interlace. Resembles a zoomorphic facing-mask; 33.8 x 22.5mm. *Adelsö, Up, Birka, Sweden*. Photograph © Christer Åhlin/ Museum of National Antiquities, Stockholm, Sweden. Inventory no. 34000: Bj 905.

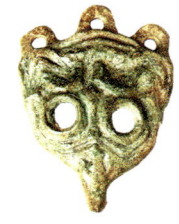

Asymmetrical

Three attachment-knops

123. Silver; sheeting, one-piece; engraved. Two bands of interlace with (?) foliate terminals, each band has linear borders; rounded attachment-knops; 18.7 x 1.02mm. *Gloucestershire*. Portable Antiquities Scheme GLO-721AD7. Photographs © Birmingham City Council.

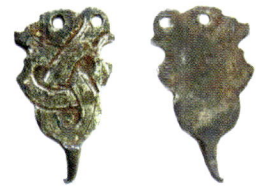

Early medieval Class E single sharp-hooked clasps

All are comparable with Class D except for a projecting angular or rounded collar, often slightly ridged, at the juncture of the plate and hook. One has a central drilled tiny hole. Either plain or engraved, punched and/or drilled or inlaid. Designated as Types 1 and 2; *c*.9th - *c*. early 12th century.

Early medieval Class E, Type 1

Circular/Sub-circular

Two attachment-knops

124. Copper alloy; sheeting; one-piece; undecorated. A shallow projecting rounded collar at the juncture of the plate and hook; rounded attachment-knops. Incomplete, one attachment-knop broken off; 20 x 15mm. *South-East Dorset*. Drawing © Patrick Read, photograph © Andy Mitchell.

125. Copper alloy; sheeting; one-piece; undecorated. A shallow angular collar at the juncture of the plate and hook; rounded attachment-knops; 24.1 x 20.7mm. *South Wiltshire*. Drawing © Patrick Read.

126. Copper alloy; sheeting; one-piece; undecorated. A slightly projecting and ridged collar at the juncture of the plate and hook; a small angular knop between the rounded attachment-knops; one attachment-knop and hook distorted; 25.5 x 13mm. *South Somerset*. Drawing © Patrick Read.

127. Copper alloy; sheeting; one-piece; undecorated apart for minimal engraving. A projecting rounded collar at the juncture of the plate and hook; rounded attachment-knops, each hole outlined by a crescent; 25 x 20mm. *Northamptonshire*. Peter Woods CH4. Drawing © Roy Turland, photograph © Peter Woods.

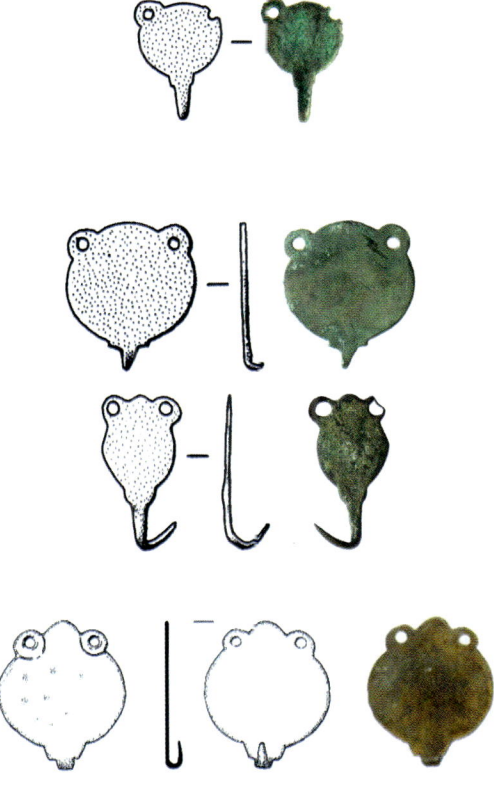

128. Silver; sheeting; one-piece; engraved. A voided curved-edged cross within a circle; rounded attachment-knops; a shallow angular collar at the juncture of the plate and hook. Incomplete, one attachment-knop and a small part of the plate broken off; 21 x 12mm. *South Oxfordshire*. Photographs © Chris Hodgson.

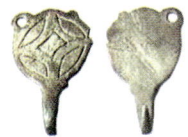

129. Copper alloy; sheeting; one-piece; engraved. An ovoid panel bearing a voided trident with an internal voided hatched trident; the side interstices are in the Trewhiddle-style and the other two are dissected by a pair of transverse lines; a linear and hatched border; a shallow projecting rounded collar at the juncture of the plate and hook; rounded attachment-knops. Incomplete, hook and one attachment-knop broken off; 26.35 x 20.8mm. *Suffolk*. Portable Antiquities Scheme SF-6F6046. Drawing © Donna Wreathall, photographs © Suffolk County Council Archaeological Service.

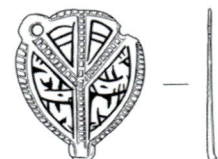 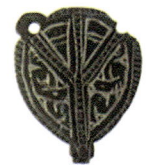

130. Copper alloy; sheeting; one-piece; engraved. A circular panel bearing a tribrach motif with ovoids in the interstices, a shallow projecting angular collar at the juncture of the plate and hook; rounded attachment-knops; 23 x 21mm. *Leicestershire*. Portable Antiquities Scheme LEIC-82D676. Photographs © Leicestershire County Council.

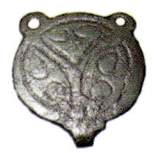 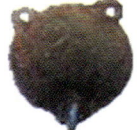

131. Copper alloy; sheeting; one-piece; engraved. A sub-circular panel of Trewhiddle-style interlace within a circle and hatched border; voided curvilinear on the projecting partially rounded and angular collar at the juncture of the plate and hook; rounded attachment-knops. Incomplete, hook-point and one attachment-knop broken off; 24.5 x 16.47mm. *Berkshire*. Portable Antiquities Scheme BERK-EE3806. Photographs © West Berkshire Council.

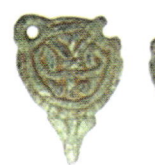 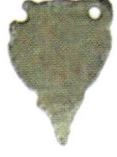

132. Copper alloy; sheeting; one-piece; compass-inscribed and openwork. A small drilled-hole within four concentric circles; a projecting angular collar at the juncture of the plate and hook; angular attachment-knops; one of which is distorted; 18 x 10mm. *South-West Wiltshire*. Drawing © Patrick Read.

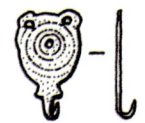

133. Copper alloy; cast; one-piece; moulded-relief; sporadic white-metal coating, probably tin. A circular panel bearing an eight-petalled flower, a shallow projecting rounded collar with one transverse and two vertical lines at the juncture of the plate and hook; rounded attachment-knops. Incomplete, the edge of one knop with attachment-hole worn through; 26.56 x 15.7mm. *Essex*. Portable Antiquities Scheme ESS-B2ABB3. Photographs © Colchester Museums.

 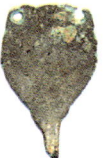

134. Silver; possibly cast; one-piece; probably moulded-relief and drilled. A circular panel bearing a stylised eight-petalled flower comprising four large triangular petals with lily motifs and four small triangles with a sub-lozenge; the sepals, ridges between the petals, around the attachment holes and border are filled with contiguous tiny triangles; a projecting angular collar with two drilled pits at the juncture of the plate and hook. Incomplete, one attachment knop broken off; 27 x 20mm. *Hampshire*. Photographs © Mike Gains.

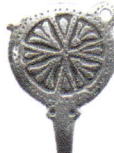 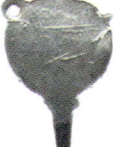

135. Copper-alloy and silver; possibly cast; one-piece; drilled. A circular panel of a blackish substance inlaid with three addorsed spirals of wire; the panel and each attachment-hole is bordered by pits; a single pit is positioned between the shallow projecting rounded collar at the juncture of the plate and hook; rounded attachment-knops. Incomplete, hook broken off; 23 x 15mm. *Cambridgeshire*. Portable Antiquities Scheme CAM-A1B9B1. Photographs © Cambridgeshire County Council.

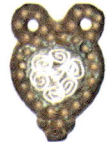 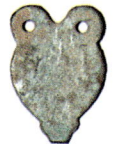

136. Copper-alloy and silver; cast and wire; one-piece; moulded-relief. A circular panel of a blackish substance inlaid with three silver wire addorsed spirals and crescents; bordered by ring-and-dot motifs creating an engrailed edge; rounded attachment-knops; a debased fleur-de-lis collar at the juncture of the plate and hook. Incomplete, hook broken off; 19.8 x 16.1mm. *Suffolk*. Portable Antiquities Scheme SF-DC3B75. Drawing © Donna Wreathall, photograph © Suffolk County Council Archaeological Service.

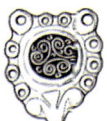 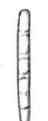 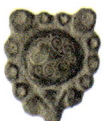

HOOKED-CLASPS & EYES

137. Copper-alloy and silver; cast and wire; one-piece; moulded-relief. Comparable with nos 136, 138, except with a bird-like collar. Incomplete, hook-point broken off; 19.8 x 16.1mm. *Suffolk*. Portable Antiquities Scheme SF-DC3B75. Drawing © Donna Wreathall, photograph © Suffolk County Council Archaeological Service.

138. Copper-alloy and silver; cast and wire; one-piece; moulded-relief. Comparable with nos 136-137, except with a smaller panel and a Y-shaped collar with two transverse grooves. Incomplete, hook-point broken off; 30 x 16mm. *Suffolk*. Portable Antiquities Scheme SF9916. Drawing © Donna Wreathall, photograph © Suffolk County Council Archaeological Service.

Early medieval Class E, Type 2

Sub-lozenge shaped

Two attachment-knops

139. Copper alloy; sheeting; one-piece; punched. Three median ring-and-dot motifs; a projecting angular collar at the juncture of the plate and hook; inordinately large rounded/angular attachment-knops; 17 x 11.8mm. *Norfolk*. Portable Antiquities Scheme no. unavailable. Photograph © Norfolk Museums and Archaeology Service.

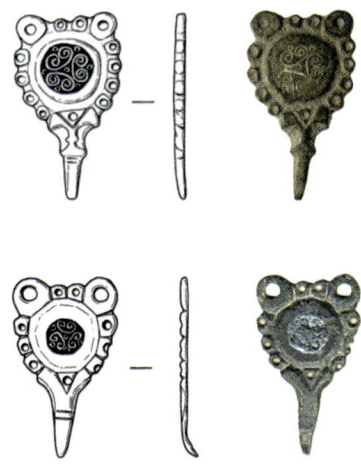

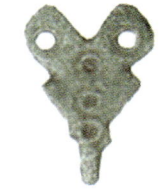

Early medieval Class F single sharp-hooked clasps

Two or three rounded knops pierced with attachment-holes and a slightly projecting and ridged zoomorphic collar at the juncture of the plate and hook differentiate Class F cast single sharp-hooked clasps from Class E. One is inlaid with silver wire and the other has openwork decoration; both are possibly mid to late 11th century.

Early medieval Class F, Type 1

Circular/Sub-circular

Two attachment-knops

140. Copper-alloy and silver; cast and wire; one-piece; moulded-relief. Two longitudinal sub-rectangular panels filled with a blackish substance inlaid with silver wire S-spirals; a slightly projecting and ridged zoomorphic collar at the juncture of the plate and hook; a small angular knop between the presumably rounded attachment-knops. Incomplete, both attachment-knops broken off, one wire S-spiral missing; much abraded; 31 x 15.5mm. *South-East Dorset*. Drawing © Patrick Read.

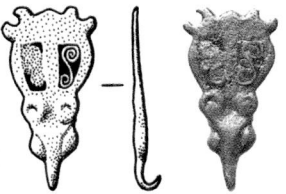

Three attachment-knops

141. Silver; cast; one-piece; moulded-relief and openwork. An animal in the Urness-style; a projecting shallow-ridged and zoomorphic collar at the juncture of the plate and hook; rounded and angular attachment-knops; 40 x 14.3mm. *Hampshire*. Drawing and photograph © Peter Beazley.

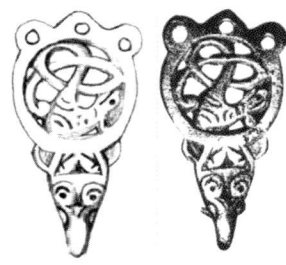

Early medieval Class G single sharp-hooked clasps

Designated as Class G, Types 1 and 2, these single sharp-hooked clasps are differentiated from all others by having attachment-holes in the main plate at the end opposite the hook, and two ornamental knops. Decoration is drilled, compass-inscribed and openwork. Both are *c.*9th - *c.* early 12th century.

Early medieval Class G, Type 1

Sub-triangular

Two ornamental angular knops, two attachment-holes in the main plate

142. Copper alloy; sheeting; one-piece; compass-inscribed, and openwork. The obverse has a chevron of small drilled-holes, each hole within an annulet; both attachment-holes are also within an annulet. On the back the attachment-holes are within annulets. Incomplete, hook broken off; 20 x 14mm. *North Yorkshire.* United Kingdom Detecting Finds' Database 6289. Photographs © Neil Blatherwick.

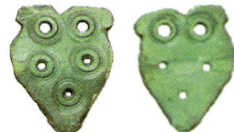

Early medieval Class G, Type 2

Circular

Two rounded ornamental knops, one or two attachment-holes in the main plate

143. Copper alloy; sheeting; compass-inscribed and drilled. A central large ring-and-dot motif bordered by smaller ring-and-dot motifs; the rounded knops each have a ring-and-dot motif; 17.36 x 14.5mm. *Norfolk.* SH04 BYD NT 1264. Photographs © Norfolk Museums and Archaeology Service.

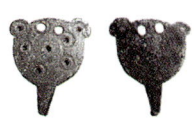

Early medieval Class H single sharp-hooked clasp

A central drilled-hole filled with a separate decorative rivet differentiates this category of single sharp-hooked clasp from all preceding early medieval single sharp-hooked clasps. Designated as Class H, Type 1. Other decoration is engraved; *c.*7th - *c.* early 12th century.

Early medieval Class H, Type 1

Triangular

Two attachment-holes

144. Silver; probably sheeting; two-piece; engraved. A triangular panel bearing a hatched tribrach motif with interlace snake-like animals in the interstices, all within a hatched border; a chevron and a sub-lozenge at the juncture of the plate and hook; a central rivet-hole. A separate domed-head rivet is secured in the rivet-hole; 35.7 x 27.5mm. *Provenance unknown*. Photographs © TimeLine Originals.

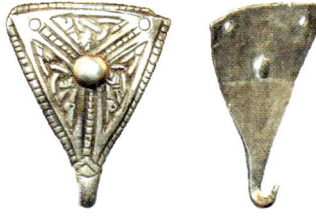

Early medieval Class I single sharp-hooked clasp

Being cast, circular with attachment-knops and drilled for a separate decorative rivet differentiates Class I, Type 1 from the immediately preceding early medieval Class H, Type 1 single sharp-hooked clasp; *c.*9th - *c.* early 12th century.

145. Copper alloy and silver; cast and probably wire; two-piece; moulded-relief. An eight-petalled flower within a circle and hatched border; a ribbed collar at the juncture of the plate and hook; rounded attachment knops. A separate silver domed-head rivet is secured in a central rivet-hole; 17.5 x 14.5mm. *Lincolnshire*. Photographs © Andy Germaney.

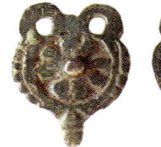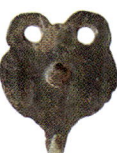

Early medieval Class J single sharp-hooked clasp

A projecting collar at the juncture of the plate and hook differentiates Class J, Type 1 from the preceding Class I, Type 1. Other decoration is engraved; c.7th - c. early 12th century.

Early medieval Class J, Type 1

Circular

Two attachment-knops

146. Silver; sheeting; two-piece; engraved. A circular panel bearing a triple-stranded cross, the centre strand beaded, a beaded border; a rounded collar at the juncture of the plate and hook; rounded attachment-knops and a central rivet-hole. A separate domed-head rivet is secured in the rivet-hole; 25 x 15mm. *Gloucestershire*. United Kingdom Detecting Finds' Database 9483. Photographs © Dave Mayes.

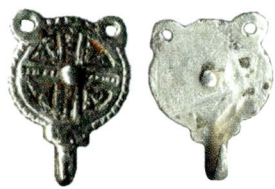

Early medieval unclassified single sharp-hooked clasps

Incompleteness precludes ascribing a precise classification and typology for these single sharp-hooked clasps: no. 147 is possibly Class A or B, no. 148 perhaps Class I, and no. 149 possibly Class C or F. Although outside of the present remit, fig. 9 shows a Thomas Class B, Type 1 Anglo-Saxon strapend: whether these not uncommon artefacts functioned similarly as sharp-hooked clasps is unknown.

Early medieval unclassified

Circular

147. Silver; possibly cast; one-piece; moulded-relief or engraved and niello. A probable circular panel bearing foliate and floriate on a niello field. Incomplete, hook-point and a section of plate with attachment-holes broken off; 21 x 20mm. *Wiltshire*. Wiltshire Heritage Museum acc. no. DB 1708. Drawing © Nick Griffiths.

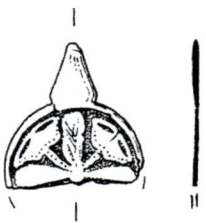

HOCKED-CLASPS & EYES

148. Silver; sheeting; two-piece; engraved and nielloed. A circular panel bearing a cross paty, the arms of which are speckled; the interstices resemble stylised leaves; a rounded attachment-knop; a central rivet-hole. A separate domed-head silver-gilt rivet is secured in the rivet-hole. Incomplete, one attachment-knop and hook broken off; D17mm. *Norfolk*. Treasure case M&ME 436. Photographs © the Trustees of The British Museum.

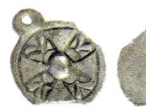
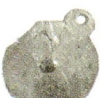

Indeterminate shape

149. Silver; cast; one-piece; engraved and moulded-relief. A ridged zoomorphic collar and three slightly oblique transverse grooves at the juncture of the plate and hook. Incomplete, plate broken off; 24 x 9mm. *Kent*. Portable Antiquities Scheme KENT-8FD147. Treasure case 2003 T107. Photograph © Kent County Council.

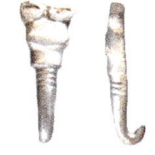

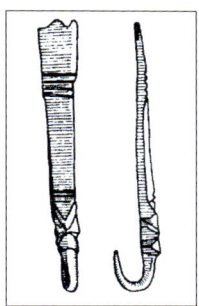

Fig. 10. A Thomas Class B, Type 1 Anglo-Saxon cast high-lead copper-alloy sharp-hooked strapend, L45mm; late 8th or 9th century but may have continued into the 11th. *Southampton*. After Hinton *et al* 1995, fig. 4, no. 169/2622. Drawing © and reproduced courtesy of Southampton Museums.

Early medieval Class K double sharp-hooked clasps

Two recurving sharp hooks, placed side by side at the narrow end, differentiate Class K one-piece sharp-hooked clasps from single sharp-hooked clasps of this period. Attachment-holes are within the plate and decoration engraved. Each is *c.* 9th century.

Early medieval Class K, Type 1

Trapezoid

Indeterminate number of attachment-holes

150. Silver; sheeting; one-piece; engraved. Trewhiddle-style foliate within two panels, one dentate and the other triangular, outlined by a beaded border. Incomplete, a section of the attachment-end and attachment-holes broken off; 30 x 14mm. *Barking Abbey, Essex,* site no. BA.1.85 1025. After Webster, L and Reversehouse, J, 1991, no. 67 (b). Drawing © Nick Griffiths.

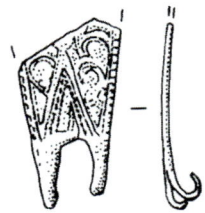

Three attachment-holes

151. Silver; probably cast; one-piece; engraved and moulded-relief and possible niello. A panel of Trewhiddle-style foliate and floriate on a (?) niello field outlined by a dotted and beaded border; the attachment-end is engrailed; each hook has a ridged zoomorphic collar at the juncture of the plate; 34.75 x 19.25. *South Dorset.* Drawing © Nick Griffiths.

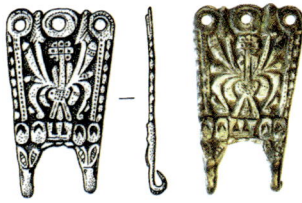

Early medieval Class L double sharp-hooked Clasp

Rounded knops with attachment-holes differentiate this Class L double sharp-hooked clasp from Class K. Decoration is engraved; *c.* mid-9th century.

Early medieval Class K, Type 1

Circular

Two attachment-knops

152. Silver; probably cast; one-piece; engraved and moulded-relief and niello. A circular panel of Trewhiddle-style foliate on a niello field; the splayed recurving hooks, each of which appears to be circular-section, resemble horns; rounded attachment-knops; 35 x 20.1mm. *Berkshire.* Drawing © Nick Griffiths, photographs © reserved West Berkshire Museum A705.

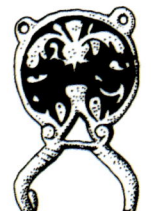 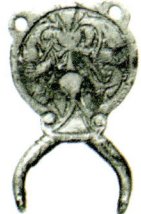

Early medieval Class M double sharp-hooked clasps

Designated as Class M, Type 1, these cast copper-alloy clasps comprise a moulded-relief in-the-round or flat bar with a circular-section tapering recurving sharp hook at either end, lying in the same plane as the bar. A distinguishing feature is a central hole in the bar, drilled from side to side, presumably used for suspending from a chain, cord or thong. An example assigned as '... subsequent to ... 507' was recovered from a Frankish cemetery at Herpes, France (Smith 1923, fig. 196); while one from Norwich came from a 11th- - 12th-century context; however, it is perhaps earlier, even pre-Conquest or Middle Saxon (Margeson 1993, fig. 9, no. 79). Frustratingly, no mention is made of where in the grave the one from Herpes was positioned, therefore provides no clue as to its possible function.

The double-hook arrangement seems suitable for fastening a cloak at the throat (though seemingly somewhat hazardous), for a sharp-hook could have easily pierced the fabric either side, though such an action done repeatedly would surely be prejudicial to the integrity of the fabric; alternatively, metal-eyes secured to the two parts would have mitigated such damage: however, this function is questionable (see below). They are frequently called 'shroud hooks' used in burials, a hypothesis implied by the above mentioned two burials, though as to why shrouded bodies required such substantial and decorative clasps defies imagination. Another possibility is they are havettes used in woollen cloth-making; however, the piercing and angle of the hooks are anomalous with most confirmed havettes (see below). Notwithstanding, no. 153 is marked with a saltire as found on several recorded havettes and the Arms of the Clothworkers' Company of London.

Early medieval Class M, Type 1

Oval-section bar

153. Copper alloy; cast; one-piece; moulded-relief. An in-the-round bar with seven varying width ribs and a saltire positioned over the suspension hole; 45 x 14.5. *South-West Wiltshire*. Drawing © Nick Griffiths.

154. Copper alloy; cast; one-piece; moulded-relief. Comparable with no. 153 except the ribs differ and without a saltire; L45.5mm. *Norfolk*. After Margeson 1993, fig. 9, no. 79. Drawing © and reproduced courtesy of Norfolk Museums and Archaeology Service.

Rectangular-section bar

155. Copper alloy; cast; one-piece; moulded-relief. A wide flat bar with a grooved spiral around the sides and edges; one side has a median shallow channel that interrupts the spiral run; 44 x 17mm. *Suffolk*. Portable Antiquities Scheme SF-E1B756. Drawing © Donna Wreathall, photograph © Suffolk County Council Archaeological Service.

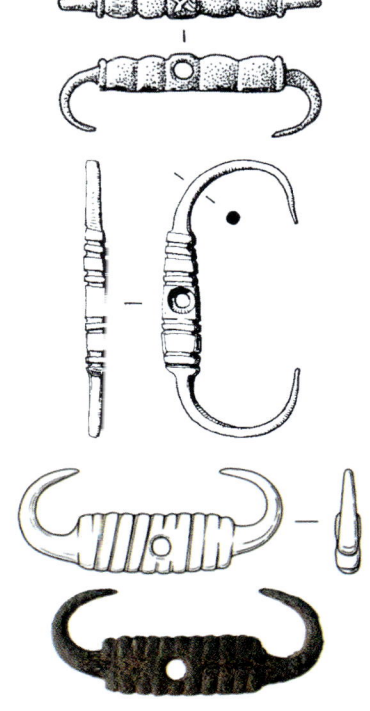

156. Copper alloy; cast; one-piece; moulded-relief. A wide flat bar tapered at each end; the four faces of the centre are plain, while all four sides of both ends have a series of transverse ribs. Incomplete, corroded and both hooks broken off; 38 x 7mm. *Suffolk*. Portable Antiquities Scheme SF11037. Drawing © Donna Wreathall, photograph © Suffolk County Council Archaeological Service.

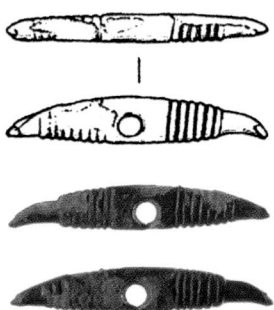

3: LATE MEDIEVAL CLASPS

The *Household Book of Queen Isabella of England 1311-12* (wife of Edward II) BM MS. Cotton Nero C VIII, fols. 121-152 Further Necessities, lists expenses occurred by John De Falaise of the Queen's Tailor's Office, 'Four dozen hooks for the use of the queen, 8s.' Mention is made of various items of clothing, including '15 robes, 3 cloaks, 6 bodices ... and one new curtain for the chapel of the queen, for rings for the same curtains, 12d'. Queen Isabella's 48 hooks cost 2d each, and if the curtain-rings are considered at the same unit price, 2d, their quantity was six. A simple ring would have been far cheaper to produce than a more complicated hook; therefore the unit cost may have been as low as a farthing, which equates to 48. However, we can infer from the above entries that the hooks and rings are separate entities and not the late medieval (*c.*1270-*c.*1350) plain rings with integral hooks possibly used with drapes and curtains (Fig. 8) (Egan 1998, fig. 43, nos 135-37 and 2005, fig 59, no. 311). Interestingly, some century and a half later, in 1464, an official restriction was imposed on the import of curtain-rings (C Blair and J Blair 1991). It is reasonable to accept that Queen Isabella's 'four dozen hooks' were for use with dress and not a curtain. Whatever, apparently it is the earliest documented evidence for the use of hooks with textiles. Other than the form described below, Class A, Type 1, it is uncertain whether hooked-clasps of any kind were a feature of late medieval dress or accessories thereof.

Invaluable information about hooks, eyes or rings and clasps worn with both women's and men's dress is found in several informative scholarly works, for example C W and P Cunnington 1963, 1966, 1970 and 1973. These latter volumes are profusely illustrated with line-drawings but, frustratingly, depictions of actual hooks, eyes or rings, or clasps used in a particular application are inadequate or nonexistent, and no explanation is provided of how substantial, strong or large they were. Nonetheless, they tell us the following:

Men's dress
*c.*1350-1400 - short boots fastened on their outer sides with *hooks*.
*c.*1400 - cote-hardies [coats] probably fastened down their fronts with *hooks* and *eyes*.
*c.*1400-50 - houppelandes [gowns] fastened down their fronts with buttons or *hooks* and *eyes*.
*c.*1400-50 - shoes fastened with buckles, buttons, lacing or *hooks* through eye holes without metal reinforcing.
1400-1500 - short buskins [calf-length boots] fastened with buckles, lacing or *hooks* and *eyes*.

Curiously, the known record has no evidence for hooks as fasteners on late medieval men's boots or shoes (or indeed women's footwear), and uncertainty surrounds the source of the Cunnington's information.

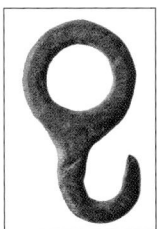

Fig. 11. A *c.*1270 - *c.*1350 possible drape- or curtain-ring; 30.5 x 16.6mm. *Hampshire*. Portable Antiquities Scheme Hamp-62EF31. Photograph © Winchester Museum Service.

Late medieval Class A single sharp-hooked clasps

Just two possible late medieval Class A single sharp-hooked clasps are in the known record, each of which is designated as Type 1. Both are crafted from one piece of copper-alloy triangular sheeting into a splayed unsoldered butt-seamed hollow cone: close to the broader open end of each is a drilled small hole, presumably used for securing to a leather thong or textile cord. Either riveting or stitching would have been suitable but which method was favoured is unknown. The narrow end forms a recurving sharp-hook expedient for piercing textile or linking to a metal or worked-eye.

Apart from being wider, and with splayed butt-seams and a hook, they can be paralleled with *c.*1350 - *c.*1400 lace-chapes riveted to leather thongs or textile cords and used for lacing personal dress (Egan 1991). The 7th-century word *aiglet* - modern *aglet* (see below) - (Walton Rogers 2007), describes a metal lace-tag that, except for the hook, is similar to those catalogued here. There is no obvious reason for lace-chapes or -tags to have hooks, therefore these two sharp-hooked clasps may have linked separate elements of personal dress, or associated articles, perhaps in tandem with metal- or worked-eyes. Of course, though it would be coincidental, both could indeed be lace-chapes with accidentally distorted points; however, the hooks appear to be intentionally formed.

A post-hole of the East Hall of the Saxon and medieval palaces at Cheddar, Somerset revealed no. 158: the post-hole fill was assigned as *c.*1250 - *c.*1300, therefore this clasp could be either residual or intrusive, which means it could be anti or post these dates. Interestingly, the provenance of no. 157 is also a confirmed early to late Anglo-Saxon site; however, here it is tentatively assigned the same date.

Late medieval Class A, Type 1

Cone-shaped

157. Copper alloy; sheeting; one-piece; undecorated. A splayed unsoldered butt seam; one attachment-hole; a circular-section tapering hook; 20.05 x 5mm. *South-West Wiltshire*. Drawing © Patrick Read.

158. Copper alloy; sheeting; one-piece; undecorated. Comparable with no. 157; 18 x 8.7mm. *Cheddar, Somerset*. Taunton County Museum acc. no. OS. AA. 2/299. Photographs © Somerset County Council.

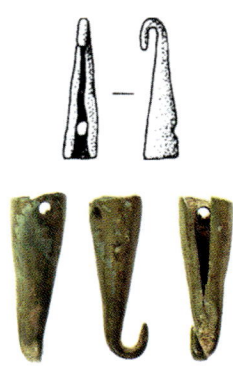

Late medieval Class B possible single blunt-hooked clasp

Whether this curiosity is a functional blunt-hooked clasp worn with a matching or worked-eye is uncertain. Wiard Krook, Department of Archaeology, Bureau of Monuments and Archaeology, Amsterdam, commented that its Gothic style implied a late medieval or possibly early post-medieval attribution and suggested the hook is unintentional and originally had a straight shank: if this hypothesis is correct, what was its function? The relatively soft lead/tin from which it is made, appears similar with the alloys used with late medieval pilgrims' badges, and its excellent condition is indicative of coming from a waterlogged context. It is apparently unparalleled in the Netherlands or Britain.

Lozenge-shaped

159. Lead/tin; cast; one-piece; moulded-relief. A cross formed from five pellets within annulets on a cross-hatched field; a beaded border, and a rounded knop on each apex, a further pellet and a median line on the hook-shank; a rounded loop; 53.63 x 26.05mm. *Amsterdam*. Drawing © Patrick Read.

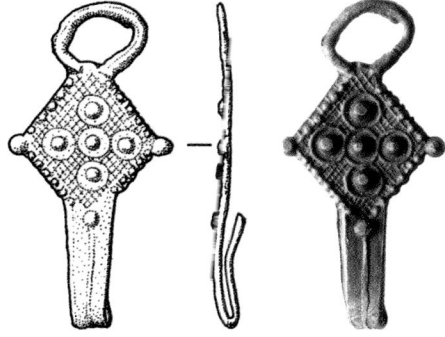

4: EARLY POST-MEDIEVAL CLASPS

A *Tudor Book of Rates* for the year 1582 (Willan 1962) has an entry which reads, 'Curten rings the pound viiid', that is, curtain rings are subjected to an import duty of 8d to the pound. In the same book a further two entries for import duty are noteworthy, 'Hook ends the groce iiiis' (a gross of hook ends attracts an import duty of four shillings), and 'Hookes the groce viijs' (a gross of hooks attracts an import duty of eight shillings). These curtain-rings may have been the same as the now ubiquitous copper-alloy sub-hexagonal section type of ring, invariably exhibiting filing striations, some of which are now thought of as possible late medieval or early post-medieval drape- or curtain-rings (Egan 1998, fig. 43, no. 104); notwithstanding, their varying sizes suggests multifarious uses extending into the early post-medieval period (Read 1995, nos 390-393). Presumably, hooks were different from hook ends, but this remains unknown. Archaeological proof of how curtains and drapes were suspended is lacking, though contemporary depictions do survive (Egan 1998).

Eight entries of dog-hooks, either gold, enamelled gold, gold and turquoise, gold-plate and silver-gilt are found in *The Inventory of King Henry VIII*. Whether these hooks were purely decorative or for attaching leashes to collars is unknown, though precious-metals, enamels and gems seem unsuitable for the latter purpose. In the same record, one listed under 'Aglettes and Buttons of Golde', along with sundry buttons, aglettes and clasps, are 'twoo hookes ...'. The only other mention of a hook in the inventory is 'a small hoke Silver and gilte ...'. These three hooks were possibly worn on dress, but as to whereabouts and their appearance we can only wonder. Why hooks are listed in the inventory along with aglettes and buttons is an enigma, and it begs the question, were buttons, aglettes and hooks considered as the same thing, their names being interchangeable? The same confusion arises with the term 'tache', which sometimes is interpreted as a hook.

That hooks and eyes were worn by Elizabeth I is confirmed by two entries in a *Day Book* which records items of clothing and jewels lost or given away by the queen between 1561 and 1585 (Arnold 1980): "[350] 'Lost the 13 of August at nonesuch from the ((gown)) Jacquet of black taffeta one eye of gold wiar worke parcell of uppon the same Jacquet of hookes and eyes lviij pere 1582.' [351] 'Lost the 19 of September at Otelands 1582 j ey[e] of gold from a Jacqet of black vellat, parcel of uppon the same Jacquet ((L)) {0}69 pere j od[d] hooke.'" Tantalisingly, these entries provide no insight into what the hooks and eyes looked like and where they were worn on the respective jackets.

The aforementioned Cunnington volumes continue:

Men's dress
1500-30 - doublets [jackets] fastened down their fronts with a lace, buttons or *hooks*.
1545-1600 - doublets fastened down their fronts from waist to the top of the collar with *hooks* and *eyes*.
1545-1600 - jerkins [jackets] fastened down their fronts from the waist to the top of the collar with *hooks* and *eyes*, buttons, lacing or points [metal chapes].
1590s-1630 - Style 1 doublets fastened down their fronts with buttons and more rarely, *hooks* and *eyes*.
1630 or c.1645 - Style 2 doublets fastened down their fronts with buttons or *hooks* and *eyes*.
From c.1630 breeches secured to doublets with *substantial hooks* stitched to the breeches waist-band - with *hooks* facing outwards - secured to *strong metal rings* suspended from or stitched to the underside of the doublet lower edge and hidden by the doublet skirt [Fig. 23]; the number of *hooks* and *rings* varied and some long, narrow breeches were suspended by only a couple of *hooks* and *rings* positioned at the back.
1660s-70s - petticoat breeches similarly attached to doublets using *hooks* and *eyes*.
c.1600-30 - fronts and or sides of jerkins or jackets [worn over doublets] fastened with lacing, points, buttons or *hooks* and *eyes*.

1630-45, revived 1660-70 - long-legged breeches or Spanish hose attached as before to Style 2 doublets with large *hooks* and *eyes*.

1700-50 - cloaks fastened under the chin by a *clasp*.

1750-1800 - coats with sham buttonholes down the front, instead of buttons a few *hooks* and *eyes* were used for closure.

Women's dress

1495-1530s - Style 1 kirtles [dress/gown] fastened down their fronts with buttons, laces and probably, *hooks* and *eyes*.

1500-45 - gowns fastened down their fronts with possible *hooks* and *eyes* or pins.

1525-60 - Style 2 kirtles fastened down their left sides from waist to armpit, or alternatively down their fronts, with pins or *hooks*.

1545-80s - cassocks [probably similar to coats] fastened with *hooks*.

1545-90s - Style 1 bodices fastened down their left sides, probably with *hooks*.

1545-90s - Style 1B high-necked bodices fastened down their fronts with buttons or probably *hooks* and *eyes*.

1545-1600 - doublets or padded bodices fastened with *hooks* and *eyes* or buttons.

c.1600-25 - fronts of jackets or waistcoats [doublets] fastened by *hooks* and *eyes*, buttons or ribbon bows.

1625-50 - back-fastening bodices fastened with laces or *hooks* or a series of jewelled *clasps*, and bodices without basques were frequently fastened down their fronts with *hooks*, buttons or lacing.

1700-50 - jacket bodices fastened down the front by lacing or copper *hooks* and *eyes*.

1700-50 - corsets adorned with silver stay *hooks* set with stones, for suspending watches.

1708-c.1750 - wrapping-gowns may be secured at the bosom or waist by a brooch, ribbon tie or jewelled *clasp*.

1730s-40s - front edge-to-edge closure of bodices were secured by jewelled *clasps*, pins or *hooks* and *eyes*.

1730-1800 - laced tippets [cape] closed by *clasps* or pins.

1770-85 - bodice waistcoat of the short polonese [open robe] *hooked*, buttoned or laced down the front, or on the back laced and *hooked*.

1780s - bodices of open robes fastened down the front with either ribbons, laces, buttons or *hooks*.

1780s - caracos [thigh-length jackets] fastened down the front with tapes and *hooks* and *eyes*.

1750-1800 - jackets [separate bodices] fastened down the front by lacing or by *hooks* and *eyes*.

1770-1800 - on closed bodices, laced or *hooked* down the front.

1770s-1800 - bodices of The English Gown closed down the front with lacing, pins or *hooks* and *eyes*.

Late 1700s - optional accessories worn with round gowns [thigh-length bodices] 'gold straps and *clasps*'.

Study of fastening methods on surviving contemporary dress in museum collections indicates that the majority of the Cunningtons clasps, hooks and eyes are probably the early and late post-medieval utilitarian base-metal or, more rarely, silver, wire blunt-hooked and eye clasps as catalogued herein (see below). Janet Arnold's outstanding *Patterns of Fashion* volumes are probably the finest scholarly works which explain clearly, both textually and illustratively, when, where and how these distinctive objects were used on men's and women's dress.

Surviving 16th- - 17th-century breeches and doublets reveals no evidence whatsoever of any category of sharp-hooked clasp being used to secure one to the other, another fact confirmed by Arnold.

It is well attested that many early post-medieval sharp-hooked clasps have decorated obverses, some highly so, therefore it seems a pointless exercise to have hidden them from view. While three contemporary portraits demonstrate a couple of ways of where and how a form of hooked-clasp secured components of women's dress, there is no surviving iconographic proven evidence for their use as fasteners on men's. However, a 1577 portrait of Sir Edward Hoby (Fig. 19.1-2) possibly demonstrates a sharp-hooked clasp (or clasps) worn for decoration. It is reasonable to accept that certain classes of more ornate sharp-hooked clasp may have been dual function, firstly as true fasteners and secondly purely for decoration.

Concerning ground-supported and openwork filigree wirework and granules, the former a decoration and the latter both constructional and decorative, but each highly intricate, found on not only clasps but other smallwares such as buttons and dress- and hair-pins; it is convenient here to dispel its romantic origin hypothesised by the author (Read 2005). Further research revealed it is not traditionally Swedish, specifically the province of Skåne, and brought to England during the reign of Elizabeth I. At that time Skåne actually belonged to Denmark. Sharp-hooked clasps of the forms prolific in England, with either of these styles of filigree and granular decoration, appear to be absent from Sweden or indeed elsewhere on the Continental mainland, therefore English manufacture is probable. This latter hypothesis is supported by a Swedish law of 1485 which states that all objects of gold or silver should be stamped with a maker's mark; furthermore from 1596 some Swedish cities stamped all gold or silver items made within city limits with their city symbol, a practice that later spread nationwide. Since 1689 all such gold or silver objects have a stamped letter code, indicating the year of manufacture. Several sharp-hooked clasps and an eye catalogued below carry a maker's mark, none of which is Swedish, therefore they are presumably English.

A painting *The Marriage of Cana* by the Master of the Altarpiece of St Bartholemew at Cologne, 1480-95, in the Musées Royaux des Beaux-Arts, Brussels (Fig. 12.1-2) shows the back of a woman with what seems to be a hooked-clasp attached to the pointed end of her kirtle. If it is a hooked-clasp, and as a separate eye is not visible, it suggests the hook directly pierced the outer garment. The hook-shank appears quite wide, therefore the clasp could be either sheeting with an integral or separate soldered hook or cast one-piece or composite. Whatever, it appears to be a form absent from the present assemblage. The date of the painting means that this type of clasp was perhaps in use as early as the late medieval period.

A *c.*1532-35 watercolour drawing *English Woman in Contemporary Dress* by Hans Holbein the Younger (Fig. 13) appears to show an evidently sharp-hooked clasp secured (presumably by stitching) either end of a short, textile or leather strap: one hook is attached to a girdle and the other pierces and raises the hem of her dress, thereby preventing soiling. It is unclear which class of sharp-hooked clasp they are; whatever, they appear to be used independently of separate metal-eyes or rings (see comments below). Apart from on textile or leather straps, loops may have been stitched or knotted directly to a garment, and they were certainly alternatively attached to a short chain (see below). Confirmation that sharp-hooked clasps were stitched to textile straps or garments is attested by nos 187, 254, both of which retain a remnant of textile in its loop.

Pieter Breugel the Elder's painting *Peasant Dance*, *c.*1567, in the Kunsthistoriches Museum, Vienna, depicts what seems to be a sharp-hooked clasp, possibly shaped as a trefoil of domed-bosses, attached to the pointed end of a woman's kirtle, while the hook pierces the dress fabric. To which class this clasp belongs is impossible to say (Fig. 14).

Allowing for the reservations stated in the main introduction, apart from early medieval Class A, Type 1; Class C, Type 1; Class D, Type 1; and early post-medieval Class E, Type 5 sharp-hooked clasps, there is no positive evidence for other clasps with sharp hooks being used in conjunction with separate metal-eyes. As mentioned earlier, the repeated insertion of a sharp hook would soon destroy the integrity of the textile, therefore it would have been sensible to use a metal- or thread worked-eye. The number of sharp-hooked clasps found by metal-detectorists now runs into many, many hundreds, of which the majority are in private collections, but other than the few in this catalogue (which may be unrelated to clasps), corresponding eyes are absent. Why? Perhaps because certain classes of sharp-hooked object thought of as clasps (particularly early post-medieval Class D) were not used for securing dress at all, but, as discussed earlier, arguably are simply ornaments hooked and stitched to dress.

Interestingly, none of the early medieval or early post-medieval single or double sharp-hooked clasps examined during this survey showed any sign whatsoever of wear on the inside bend of the hook - an anomaly also pointed out in Gaimster *et al* 2000 - which seems to imply that sharp hooks directly pierced the textile and not metal-eyes. Such a hypothesis is possibly supported by apparent wear frequently visible on the inside edges of eyes of early post-medieval Class A blunt-hooked clasps (see below), although their corresponding hooked sections appear unabraded.

Due consideration of the aforementioned evidence means that at this time it must remain conjectural whether sharp-hooked clasps were intended to be used in tandem with metal- or worked-eyes.

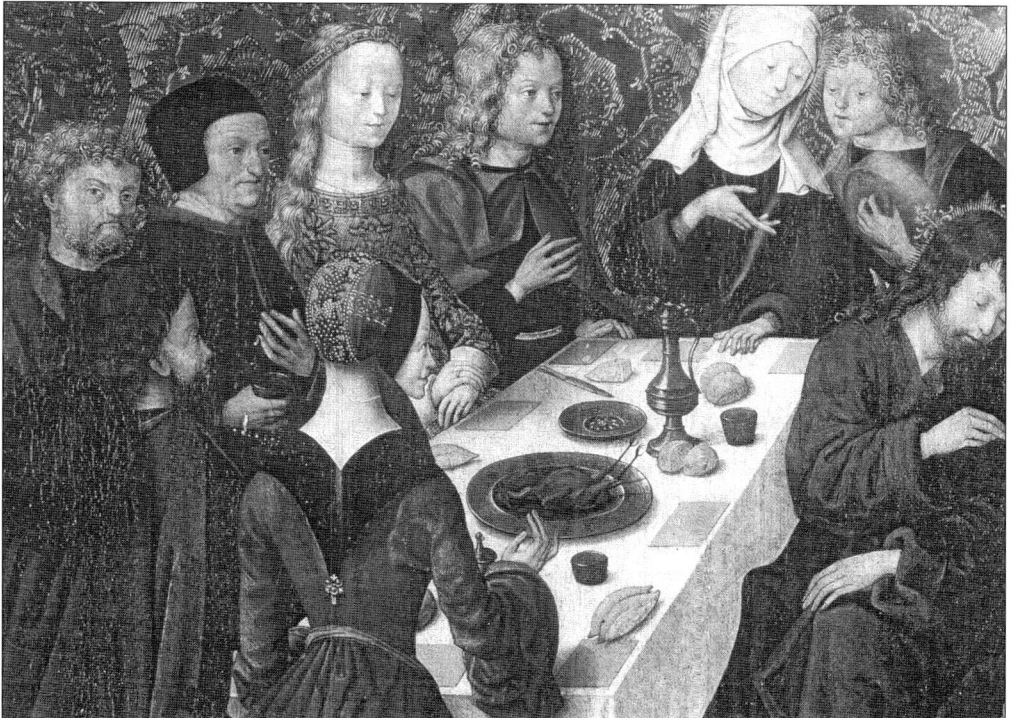

Fig. 12.1. *The Marriage of Cana* by the Master of the Altarpiece of St Bartholemew at Cologne, 1480-95, in the Musées Royaux des Beaux-Arts, Brussels. Note possible sharp-hooked clasp worn on the back of the woman in the foreground.

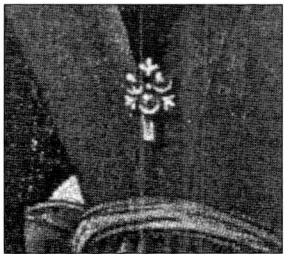

Fig. 12.2. Detail of the possible sharp-hooked clasp.

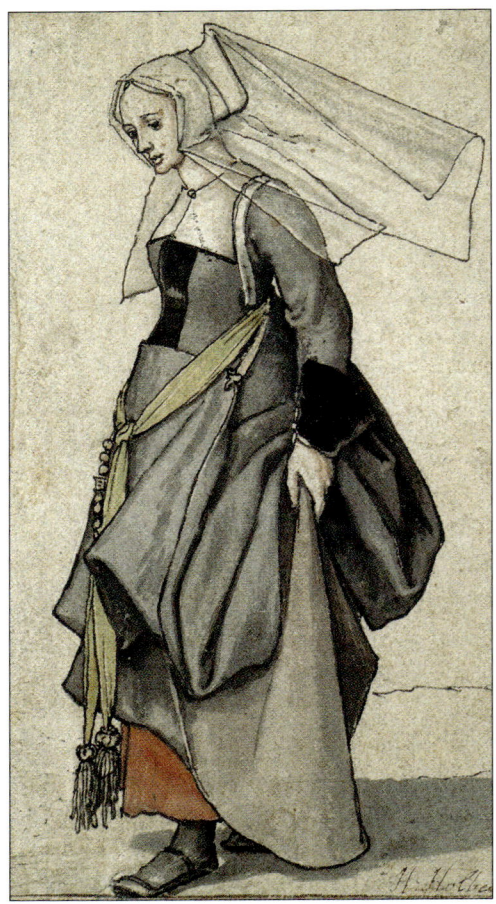

Fig. 13. A *c*.1532-35 watercolour drawing, *English Woman in Contemporary Dress*, by Hans Holbein the Younger. Note the indeterminate probable sharp-hooked clasps, one either end of a strap between the hem of her dress and girdle. Reproduced courtesy of the Ashmolean Museum, Oxford WA1863.423PI/ 298.

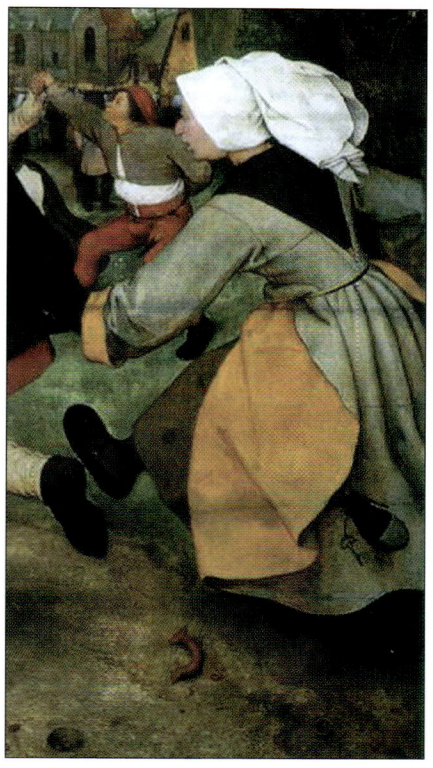

Fig. 14. Detail of *Peasant Dance* c.1567, Pieter Breugel the Elder in the Kunsthistoriches Museum, Vienna. Note (?) trefoil clasp attached to the pointed end of the kirtle while the hook pierces the dress fabric.

Early post-medieval Class A single sharp-hooked clasps

Perhaps an uncommon category, Class A single sharp-hooked clasps are comparable with certain sword-belt hooks though their small size suggests otherwise. Construction is composite and copper alloy, either part cast and part sheeting or sheeting: hooks are recurving and sharp-pointed circular- or flattened-section (or combined) tapering wire, or sheeting. Decoration is engraved or moulded-relief. The twin-plates design, with a space between, indicates that a textile or leather strap was secured between them. All are stylistically assigned c. late 15th early 16th century.

Early post-medieval Class A, Type 1

Rectangular/Sub-rectangular

160. Copper alloy; sheeting and wire; four-piece; engraved and punched. The plate is folded longitudinally from one piece of metal with on the obverse a transverse voided band near each end, the central panel has a field of random crescents; the attachment-end has an engrailed edge; two median rivet-holes. A separate flattened wire hook inserted between the plates is secured by separate copper-alloy rivets; 20.5 x 11.3mm. *Hertfordshire*. Portable Antiquities Scheme BH-CA7794. Photographs © St Albans Museum.

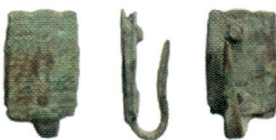

161. Copper alloy; cast, sheeting and wire; four-piece; moulded-relief. The cast front-plate bears a black-letter (?) N (?) U within a rectangular hatched panel; the attachment-edge has V-shaped notches over a transverse line, while the hook-edge has two semi-circular notches. Two median rivet-holes pierce the front- and sheeting back-plates and are secured together, with a space between, by two separate copper-alloy rivets, the one nearest the hook is copper-alloy and the other, iron. The flattened end of a circular-section wire hook is secured between the two plates by the copper-alloy rivet; 24 x 14mm. *River Thames foreshore, London.* Drawing © Nick Griffiths.

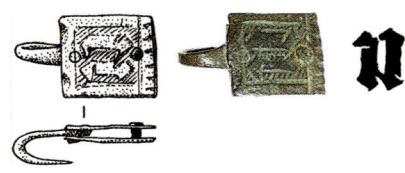

162. Copper alloy; cast and sheeting; two-piece; moulded-relief. A cast plate bearing a black-letter (?) N within a rectangular hatched panel; two median rivet-holes each retains a separate copper-alloy rivet one of which secures a separate sheeting hook. Probably incomplete, back-plate is missing; 23.7 x 10.57mm. *River Thames foreshore, London.* Drawing © Nick Griffiths.

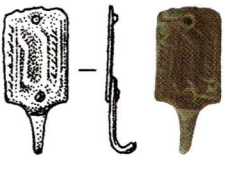

163. Copper alloy, sheeting; four- or six-piece; engraved. The obverse-plate has a transverse line either end; the attachment-edge is engrailed. The back-plate is bent forwards at the hook-end thereby forming a basal-plate; the hook is inserted through an aperture in the basal plate and secured between the front- and back-plate by a separate copper-alloy rivet; a further two rivet-holes, each retaining a separate copper-alloy rivet, pierce the front- and back-plate near the attachment-end; 23 x 12mm. *River Thames foreshore, London.* Portable Antiquities Scheme LON-669433. Photographs © Museum of London.

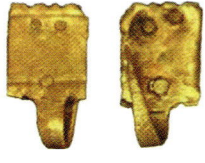

Early post-medieval Class B single sharp-hooked clasps

Again, so far as the known record reveals, the two Class B single sharp-hooked clasps catalogued here are unusual. Of composite box construction, one is copper-alloy sheeting and the other silver-gilt sheeting and cast, and each has a circular-section tapering wire recurving sharp hook. Components are soldered together. Attachment to a textile or leather strap was achieved by riveting. No. 164, which is engraved, is possibly late 15th century, while the moulded-relief and openwork decoration on no. 165 is stylistically *c.* late 16th.

Early post-medieval Class B, Type 1

Rectangular

164. Copper alloy; sheeting and wire; three-piece; hollow rectangular-section; engraved. The front-plate has cross-hatching and one rivet-hole. The back-plate has one rivet-hole and turned-over tapering sides and similarly turned-over base; iron staining around the back-plate rivet-hole suggests an iron rivet secured the clasp to a strap. A separate wire hook is soldered between the two plates; 23.75 x 10.58. *River Thames foreshore, London*. Drawing © Nick Griffiths.

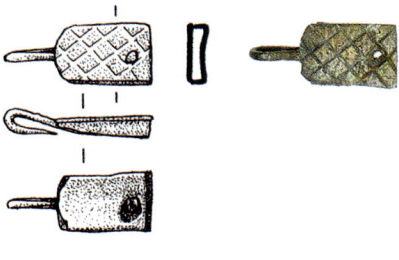

Early post-medieval Class B, Type 2

165. Silver-gilt; cast, sheeting and wire; three-piece; hollow rectangular-section; moulded-relief and openwork. The cast front-plate comprises intertwined vine tendrils, the attachment-end edge is shallow bifurcate with a rounded knop at each corner; the tendrils protrude over the edges of three sides and form a point at the juncture of the plate and hook. The sheeting back-plate, which has two rivet-holes, has turned-over sides and base. A separate wire hook pierces the base and is soldered to the inside of the back-plate. Incomplete, the hook-point and small sections of the tendrils are broken off; 27.96 x 18.44 x 5.17mm. *East Wiltshire*. Drawing © Nick Griffiths.

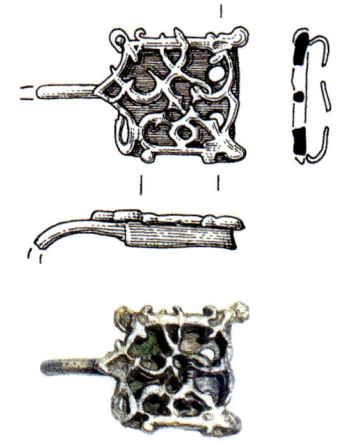

Early post-medieval Class C single sharp-hooked clasps

Distinguished by either a rectangular, square, circular, semi-circular or triangular aperture in their reverse-plate, thereby forming transverse loops, Class C single sharp-hooked clasps are composite hollow-box construction, and designated as Type 1 sub-rectangular-section; Type 2 sub-rectangular section; Type 3 semi-circular section; Type 4 semi-circular or trapezoid-section; Type 5 rectangular- or semi-circular section; and Type 6 cylindrical. Plates are rectangular/sub-rectangular and either cast one-piece, composite sheeting or part cast and part sheeting. Copper-alloy is the predominant metal, followed by silver and then lead/tin. Hooks are recurving, sharp-pointed and tapering circular- or flattened-section wire. Components are soldered or embedded together. Decoration is frequently elaborate and may be engraved, moulded-relief, ground-supported filigree and granules, imitative ground-supported filigree and granules, gilding or niello. Filigree and imitative filigree is invariably gilded. A collar, either plain or elaborate, at the juncture of the plate and hook, is a feature on some.

Presumably, a textile strap or cord or leather thong was inserted in the open-end and returned through the aperture in the reverse and then secured on itself by riveting, seizing, stitching or knotting (Fig. 15). Two composite sheeting and wire single sharp-hooked clasps from London are similar to nos 178-180, except the London examples have an internal 'spring' which folds towards the open-end (Egan 2005, nos 159 and 160); none are noted here. Types 2-3 clasps may have been in use during the late medieval period; while Types 1, nos 4-6 are *c*.16th century.

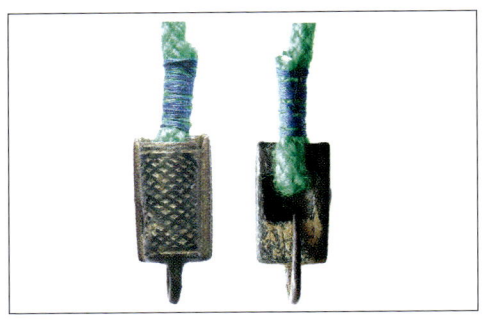

Fig. 15. An early post-medieval Class C, Type 3 sharp-hooked clasp: reconstruction of one possible method of attaching, by seizing, to a cord.

Early post-medieval Class C, Type 1

Rectangular

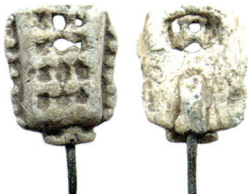

166. Lead/tin and copper-alloy; cast and wire; two-piece; moulded-relief; rectangular-section. A hatched front, the long sides of which have laterally projecting beaded edges, and a debased swag forming a ridged collar where the hook shank is inserted. The back has a sub-rectangular aperture near the attachment-end and at the other end is a sub-rectangular thickened section into which is embedded a separate copper-alloy wire hook. Incomplete, hook-point broken off; several holes in the front are possibly casting flaws; 31.7 x 18.36mm. *South Yorkshire*. Portable Antiquities Scheme SWYOR-D9ED91. Photographs © West Yorkshire Archaeology Service.

HOOKED-CLASPS & EYES

Early post-medieval Class C, Type 2

167. Copper alloy; sheeting and wire; three-piece; engraved; sub-rectangular-section. The front-plate has a four-petalled flower within a rectangular panel with three transverse bands at the attachment-end, one cabled and two transversely hatched, while the opposite end of the panel has a transverse cabled band; the apex near the hook has a triangular panel of foliate. The back-plate has a transverse rectangular aperture and turned-over sides. A separate wire hook is soldered between the two plates; 36.6 x 15.59mm. *River Thames foreshore, London.* Drawing © Patrick Read.

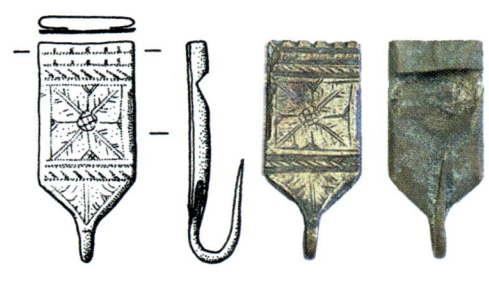

Early post-medieval Class C, Type 3

Rectangular

168. Copper alloy; cast, sheeting and wire; three-piece; convex; engraved; niello; semi-circular section. The front-plate has a rectangular panel of cross-hatching with two transverse bands near the attachment-end and one at the hook-end, all inlaid with niello. The sheeting back-plate, which is wider than the obverse-plate, thereby forming laterally projecting long edges, has a square aperture. A separate wire hook is inserted through the base and then soldered between the two plates; 30 x 13.5 x 8mm. *South Somerset.* Drawing © Patrick Read.

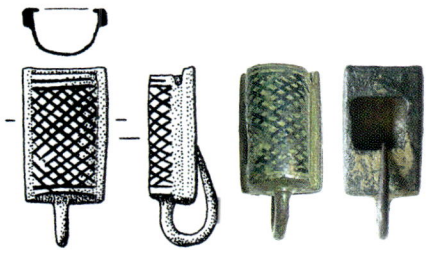

169. Copper alloy; cast, sheeting and wire; three-piece; convex; engraved; niello; semi-circular section. Comparable with nos 168, 170-171 except the cross-hatched panel is slightly smaller, and a transverse rectangular aperture is near the attachment-end, which slopes towards the front. Incomplete, the strip of metal forming the edge of the attachment-end and the aperture is broken off; 32.62 x 15.4 x 7.4mm. *Northamptonshire.* Peter Woods CHR1000. Drawing © Roy Turland, photographs © Peter Woods.

170. Copper alloy; cast, sheeting and wire; three-piece; convex; engraved; niello; semi-circular section. Comparable with nos 168-169, 171 except the lozenges formed by the cross-hatching are much larger; 30.5 x 14mm. *South Devon.* Drawing and photograph © Patrick Read.

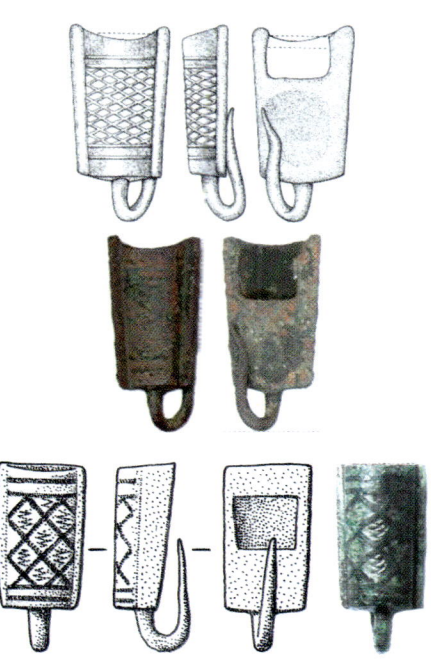

HOOKED-CLASPS & EYES

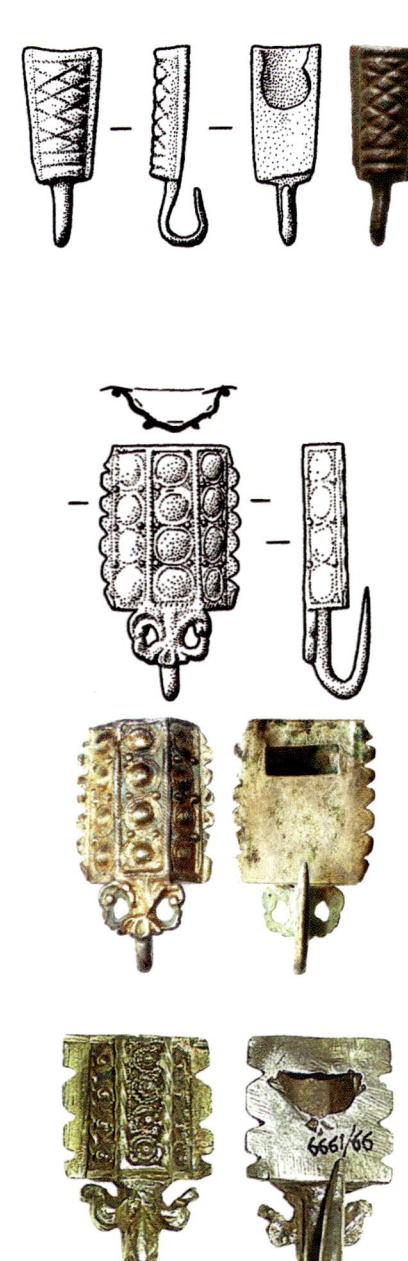

171. Copper alloy; cast, sheeting and wire; three-piece; convex; engraved; niello; semi-circular section. Comparable with nos 168-170 except the lozenges formed by the cross-hatching are larger than on nos 168-169 but smaller than no. 170, and the aperture is circular and near the attachment-end. Incomplete, the strip of metal forming the edge of the attachment-end and the aperture is broken off; 32.06 x 11.55 x 5.5mm. *Staffordshire*. Drawing © Patrick Read.

Early post-medieval Class C, Type 4

Rectangular

172. Silver-gilt; cast, sheeting and wire; four-piece; convex; moulded-relief; semi-circular section. A cast front-plate divided into three longitudinal panels, each with four domed bosses and imitative ground-supported twisted wire filigree and granules; a collar, formed from addorsed debased fleurs-de-lis, integral with the front-plate, provides support for the hook. The sheeting back-plate has laterally-projecting engrailed long edges, and a transverse rectangular aperture. A separate wire hook pierces the basal-plate and is then soldered to the back of the collar and the front-plate; 42.98 x 22.66 x 7.86mm. *South Devon*. Drawing © Patrick Read.

173. Silver-gilt; cast, sheeting, wire and ground-supported twisted wire filigree and granules; four-piece; convex; trapezoid-section. A sheeting front-plate with three longitudinal rectangular panels each edged with wire, the central panel contains four granules, each within two concentric annulets of thinner-gauge wire, while the outside panels contain four granules, each within a wire annulet. The back-plate, which has a semi-circular aperture, and basal-plates are formed from a single piece of sheeting bent at 90°. A separate wire hook is soldered to the reverse of a separate cast fleur-de-lis collar and the basal-plate; 24.3 x 12.1 x 8.6mm. *West Somerset*. Taunton County Museum acc. no. 99/1999. Photographs © Somerset County Council.

HOOKED-CLASPS & EYES

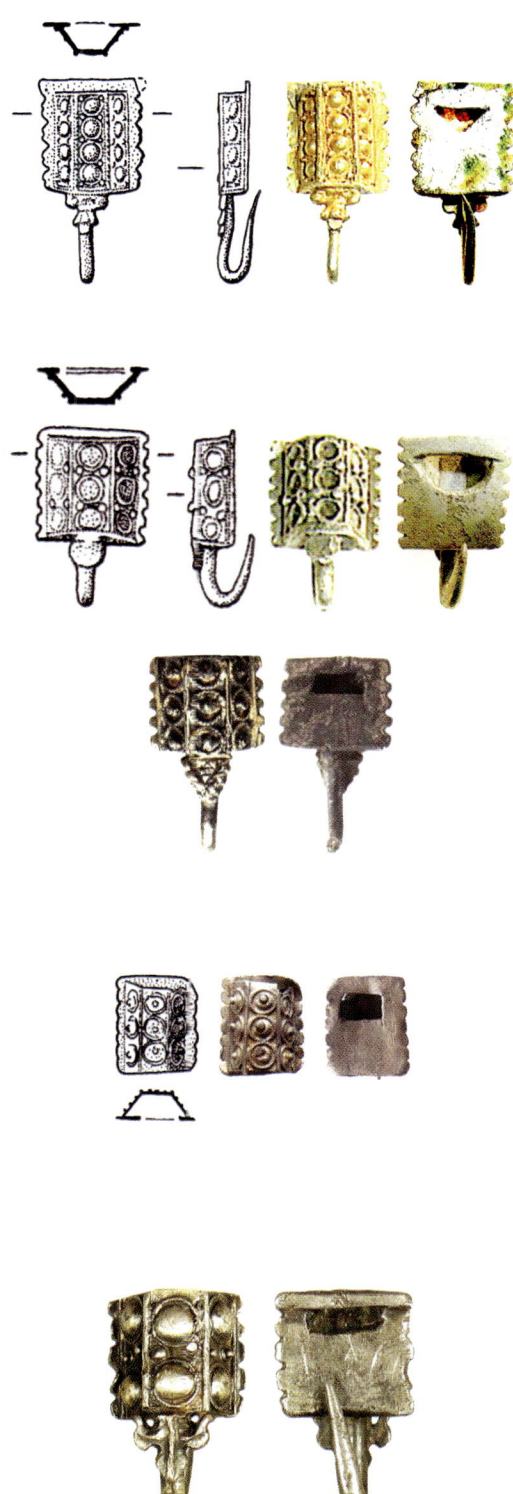

174. Silver-gilt; cast, sheeting, wire and ground-supported twisted wire filigree and granules; four-piece; convex. Comparable with nos 172-173, 175-177 except all of the annulets are single, each of which encloses a small domed boss lined either side by tiny granules, and a separate soldered addorsed debased fleurs-de-lis collar, and a triangular aperture in the back-plate. Incomplete, several annulets and granules missing; 36 x 18 x 6mm. *South Somerset*. Drawing © Patrick Read.

175. Silver-gilt; sheeting, wire and ground-supported twisted wire filigree and granules; four-piece; convex. Comparable with nos 172-174, 176-177 except three rectangular panels each containing three domed bosses within annulets, a separate soldered rounded collar, and a semi-circular aperture in the back-plate; 21.5 x 12.5 x 4mm. *South Somerset*. Drawing © Patrick Read.

176. Silver-gilt; sheeting, wire; ground-supported twisted wire filigree and granules and engraved; convex; three-piece. Comparable with nos 172-175, 177-178 except a triangular collar with a triangle and engrailed edges integral with the front-plate, a granule within each wire annulet, and lacking the granules in the interstices; 20 x 12mm. *North Yorkshire*. United Kingdom Detecting Finds' Database 13662. Photographs © Kevin Jones.

177. Silver-gilt; sheeting and ground-supported twisted wire filigree and granules; convex; probably four-piece. Comparable with nos 172-176, 178 except each boss is surmounted by a tiny granule, and a transverse rectangular aperture in the back-plate. Incomplete, a small section of the front- and basal-plates are broken off, and one granule and separate soldered wire hook missing; 16.81 x 13.59 x 5mm. *East Devon*. Drawing © Patrick Read.

178. Silver-gilt; sheeting, wire and ground-supported twisted wire filigree and granules; convex; probably four-piece. Comparable with nos 172-177 except two domed bosses in each panel, a fleur-de-lis collar and a transverse narrow rectangular aperture in the back-plate; 22.36 x 13.05. *Kent*. Treasure case 2003 T332. Photographs © the Trustees of The British Museum.

HOOKED-CLASPS & EYES

Early post-medieval Class C, Type 5

Rectangular

179. Copper alloy; sheeting and wire; convex; seven-piece; engraved; rectangular-section. The front-plate is divided into four longitudinal rectangular panels by separate soldered ribs; each panel has zigzags of which the angles of one side are hatched. The back-plate has laterally projecting engrailed long edges and a square aperture. A rectangular-section strengthening wire, obliquely grooved, is soldered along each side in the angle of the back- and front-plate. For support, a separate sheeting plate, bent at 90º, has its angular end soldered to the basal-plate while the other end forms a trefoil pierced collar for riveting to the hook's flattened shank; additionally, the hook would have been soldered to the back-plate which retains sporadic solder. Incomplete, separate wire hook missing and front-plate slightly distorted; 30.05 x 14.4 x 7mm. *River Thames foreshore, London.* Drawing © Nick Griffiths.

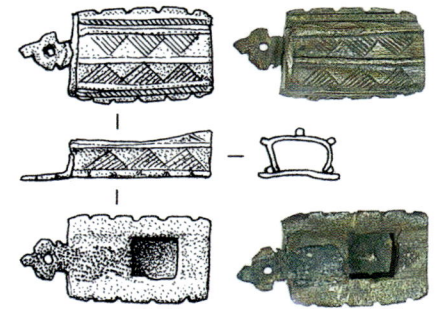

180. Copper alloy; sheeting and wire; six-piece; engraved. Comparable with no. 179 except semicircular-section; the wire hook is soldered to the back of the trefoil collar and the back-plate. Incomplete, hook-point broken off and front-plate slightly distorted; 33 x 14 x 5.2mm. *River Thames foreshore, London.* Drawing © Nick Griffiths.

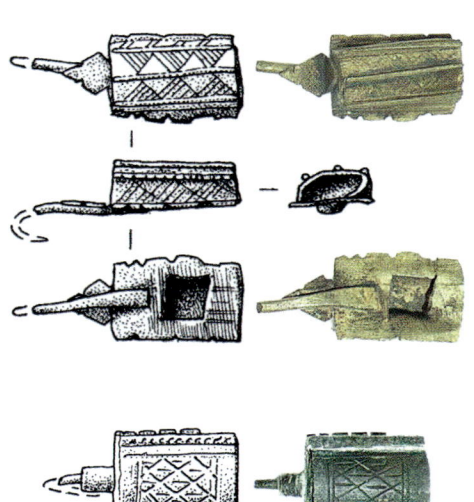

181. Copper alloy; sheeting and wire; eight-piece; convex; engraved; semi-circular-section. The front-plate has a cross-hatched rectangular panel within two longitudinal lines: each lozenge has a median line. The back-plate has laterally projecting engrailed long edges and a transverse rectangular aperture; a strengthening circular-section wire, with V-shaped grooves, is soldered along each side in the angle of the front- and back-plate; the hook-end is sealed by a separate soldered sheeting plate; a separate sheeting small plate inside the back-plate, between the aperture and attachment-end, presumably provides additional strength (this plate is not a spring, as in Egan 2005, no. 159). Incomplete, a small section of one edge of the back-plate broken off; a remnant of separate wire hook passes through a cylindrical collar and pierces the basal-plate where it is soldered to the inside of the back-plate; additionally, the end of the hook returns through a hole in the back-plate where it is secured with a separate rivet; 28.6 x 17 x 6.5mm. *River Thames foreshore, London*. Drawing © Nick Griffiths.

Early post-medieval Class C, Type 6

182. Silver-gilt; cast and wire; possibly two-piece; moulded-relief. A cylinder, open at one end and sealed at the other, with four longitudinal rectangular panels, three of which have a band of three circular knops, the panels are divided by bands of cabling; the fourth panel has a rectangular aperture near the open-end which is rimmed with a wide band while the closed-end has a similar band. A probable separate wire hook perhaps pierces the closed-end and then soldered; 35 x 13mm. The inside edge of the aperture near the attachment-end is abraded. Described as resembling a miniature lantern (Gaimster *et al* 2002, fig. 12, no. 12). *Kent*. Treasure case MME 78. Photographs © the Trustees of The British Museum.

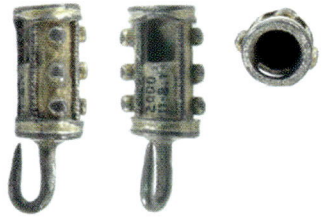

Early post-medieval Class D single sharp-hooked clasps

Of composite construction, Class D single sharp-hooked clasps are distinguished by a transverse laterally projecting attachment-loop on the back. Loops are either angular sheeting or circular-section wire and may be integral or separate soldered; however, on no. 231, on which a sizeable section of the front-plate is missing, each end of the wire loop pierces the back-plate and is then soldered. Examination of numerous Class D sharp-hooked clasps revealed that most attachment-loops are soldered to the back-plate though some do penetrate the plate before soldering. Obviously, on clasps with a front-plate, the two ends of the loop are concealed; however, on those clasps lacking loops, one can see whether or not the loops pierce the plate. Attachment-loops are normally lateral, though on no. 199 it is combined lateral and in the same plane as the plate. Characteristically, some have a decorative collar at the juncture of the plate and hook.

In this present work, with the exception of no. 249, which is riveted, all clasps in this category have either a separate embedded, soldered, or both embedded and soldered circular-section tapering wire or angular sheeting recurving sharp hook. Designated as Type 1 rectangular, Type 2 circular, Type 3 lozenge-shaped, Type 4 triangular, Type 5 heart-shaped/ovoid, Type 6 trefoil, Type 7 quatrefoil, Type 8 cinquefoil, Type 9 pentagonal, Type 10 sexfoil and Type 11 figurative. Plates are either flat or convex, base-metal or silver-gilt. Some are entirely cast while others are part cast and part sheeting. Components, additional to hooks and loops, are soldered together unless otherwise stated. Decoration is either moulded-relief, die-stamped, repoussé, openwork filigree, ground-supported filigree, imitative ground-supported filigree, openwork, gilding or (rarely) set with gems.

Two silver-gilt single sharp-hooked clasps catalogued here, from Devon and Norfolk respectively, are noteworthy, for the transverse bar of their respective loop is punched with the maker's mark IF.

This same mark is punched on a single sharp-hooked clasp found in Lincolnshire, Gaimster *et al* 2002, in which it is stated that makers' marks with initials appeared *c*.1580, and '... coincidentally, one of the earlier known initialled London makers' marks is 'IF', which is also found on apostle- and seal-top spoons from 1551. At this date 'I' was used for both 'I' and 'J'. Unfortunately, 'JF' are common initials but it is interesting to note that on 7 September 1554, a John Fox was fined for rings and pins worse than standard.' Whether this same John Fox made the Norfolk and Devon sharp-hooked clasps is unknown. Three others in this publication have makers' marks, namely: a possible foliate spray within a parade shield; possibly two chevrons, and a cross patonce.

Evidence for these clasps being attached to straps or directly on garments comes from nos 188, 255, each of which retains a fragment of textile in the loop, rare survivals. As suggested earlier, it is this class of single sharp-hooked clasp, particularly the elaborate silver-gilt examples, which lend themselves as pure dress-ornaments: the hook may have pierced the fabric and then a couple of stitches around the loop for additional security. All are *c*.16th century, and all are flat unless otherwise stated.

Early post-medieval Class D, Type 1

Rectangular

183. Lead/tin and probably copper alloy; cast and wire; two-piece; moulded-relief. A rectangular panel, the outline of which is recessed; two equidistant rounded knops on the sides and similar knops on the attachment-edge and each apex; a ridged collar at the juncture of the plate and hook. An integral loop. Incomplete, one side and one corner knop broken off and the embedded probable copper-alloy wire hook is missing, two holes in the plate are probably casting flaws; 23 x 16.5mm. *River Thames foreshore, London*. Drawing © Nick Griffiths.

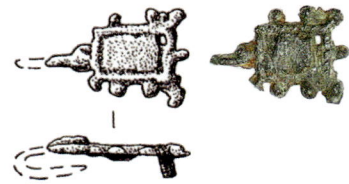

184. Lead/tin and copper alloy; cast and wire; convex; two-piece; moulded-relief; trapezoid-section. The three faces of the plate have ring-and-dot motifs; the laterally projecting engrailed long edges also have ring-and-dot motifs; a ridged collar at the juncture of the plate and hook. Incomplete, one long edge is slightly abraded, and a remnant of embedded separate copper-alloy wire hook. This clasp differs from others in this category, for the integral D-section loop projects only slightly; 31 x 18.5 x 5mm. *South Somerset*. Drawing © Patrick Read.

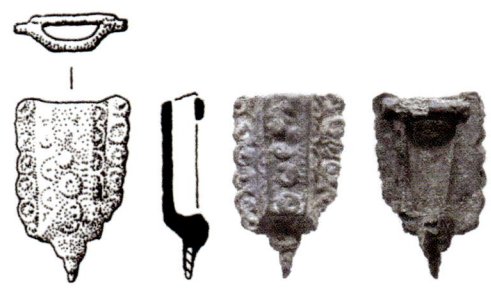

HOOKED-CLASPS & EYES

185. Silver-gilt; cast, sheeting, wire and ground-supported twisted wire filigree and granules; three-piece; moulded-relief. A rectangular panel with two large annulets, each surrounding a trefoil of small annulets with a central granule; in the field of the rectangle, each side of the annulets are smaller annulets, all with a central granule; the long edges have equidistant alternate globular and smaller rectangular knops while the attachment-edge and each apex has a globular knop; a debased fleur-de-lis collar at the juncture of the plate and hook. A separate soldered sheeting loop and wire hook. Incomplete, several small annulets and granules missing; 26 x 14mm. *Suffolk*. Portable Antiquities Scheme SF-9C8492. Photographs © Suffolk County Council Archaeological Service.

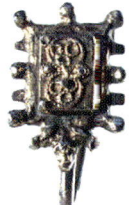 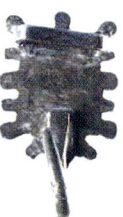

186. Silver-gilt; cast, sheeting, wire and ground-supported twisted wire filigree and a granule; three-piece; moulded-relief. Comparable with nos 185, 187-191 except a six-petalled flower with a central granule imitating a cabochon gem and a granule in each corner of the rectangular panel, and lacking the small rectangular knops. Incomplete, one corner knop broken off; 27.3 x 16.3mm. *Suffolk*. Portable Antiquities Scheme SF-3983. Photographs © Suffolk County Council Archaeological Service.

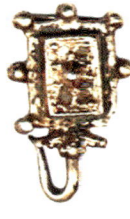 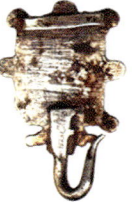

187. Silver-gilt; cast, sheeting, wire and ground-supported straight wire filigree and a granule; five-piece; moulded-relief. Comparable with nos 185-186, 188-191 except a recessed rectangular panel in which sits a rectangular sheeting appliqué applied with a central six-petalled flower and a central granule, and a small annulet in each corner, all within a wire border; this plate is secured to the main-plate by a separate domed-head (imitating a cabochon gem) split-pin that pierces both plates before splaying; 25 x 15mm. *Suffolk*. Portable Antiquities Scheme SF-C87E64. Photographs © Suffolk County Council Archaeological Service.

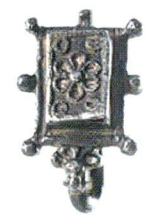 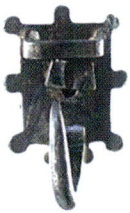

188. Silver; cast, sheeting and wire; three-piece; moulded-relief. The letter A (Amor) within a rectangular panel, otherwise comparable with nos 185-187, 189-191. The loop retains a fragment of textile; 20 x 0.9mm. *Somerset*. Photograph © Somerset County Council.

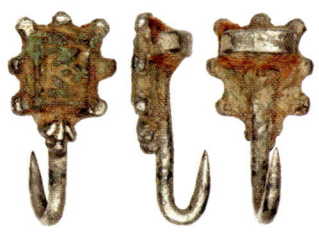

HOOKED CLASPS & EYES

189. Silver-gilt; cast, probably sheeting and wire; three-piece; moulded-relief. Comparable with nos 185-188, 190-191 except a trefoil of recessed pits surmounted by a recessed heart. Incomplete, a separate soldered probable sheeting loop missing; 17.4 x 0.69mm. *Hampshire*. Portable Antiquities Scheme HAMP-5C0711, Treasure case 2007 T05. Drawing and photographs © Winchester Museum Service.

190. Silver-gilt; cast, probably sheeting and wire; three-piece; moulded-relief. Comparable with nos 185-189, 191 except a shorter hook-shank. Incomplete, a separate soldered probable sheeting loop missing; 15 x 0.98mm. *Hampshire*. Treasure case 2004 T308. Photographs © the Trustees of The British Museum.

191. Silver-gilt; cast, probably sheeting, and wire; three-piece; moulded-relief. Comparable with nos 185-190 except a heart, and the collar resembles a bunch of grapes. Incomplete, separate soldered probable sheeting loop missing; 18.5 x 10mm. *Isle of White*. Treasure case 2006 T500. Drawing and photograph © Isle of White Council.

192. Copper alloy; sheeting and wire; three-piece; shallow convex; repoussé. A cinquefoil within a rectangular panel bordered by rectangular segments some of which contain a pellet; the apex-end of the plate has a panel with two addorsed fronds, each terminating in a pellet. A separate soldered sheeting loop and wire hook. The concave back is filled with white-metal, probably lead, and coated with a now black substance, possibly bitumen which is asphaltum, 'a brown carbonaceous pigment diluted and ground up with drying oil or varnish'; 25.7 x 12.93mm. *River Thames foreshore, London*. Drawing © Nick Griffiths.

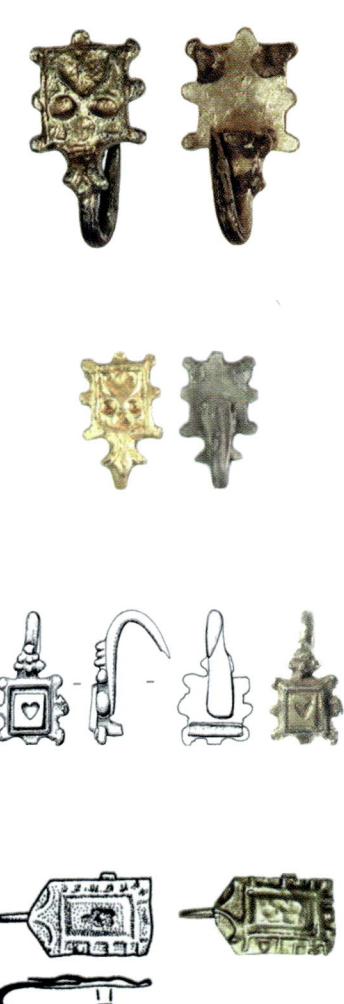

HOOKED-CLASPS & EYES

Early post-medieval Class D, Type 2

Circular/Sub-circular

193. Lead/tin and copper alloy; cast and wire; two-piece; moulded-relief. A curved-edge lozenge with a central pellet within three concentric circles, two beaded and the outer cabled, between the two inner circles are four equidistant pellets; an engrailed edge, and a trefoil collar at the juncture of the plate and hook. A separate embedded wire hook; 45 × 27.3mm. *River Thames foreshore, London.*

194. Lead/tin and copper alloy; cast and wire; two-piece; moulded-relief. A roundel bearing a stylised rose within a cabled border creating an engrailed edge; a shallow ridged collar at the juncture of the plate and hook. Incomplete, integral loop and separate embedded wire hook broken off; 18 × 14mm. *River Thames foreshore, London.* Drawing © Nick Griffiths.

195. Lead/tin and probably copper alloy; cast and wire; two-piece; moulded-relief. Comparable with no. 194 except a cinquefoil encircled by oblique lines and a voided linear border and an engrailed edge; a debased fleur-de-lis collar at the juncture of the plate and hook. Incomplete, separate embedded probable copper-alloy wire hook missing, plate and loop distorted, a small hole in the plate is possibly a casting flaw; 21 × 19.5mm. *South Somerset.* Drawing © Patrick Read.

196. Lead/tin and copper alloy; cast and wire; two-piece; moulded-relief. Probably circular. A roundel bearing a central pellet bordered by alternate annulets and pellets surmounted by a large pellet with a small pellet either side. Incomplete; edge and decoration corroded away, loop broken off, hook distorted; 36.04 × 14.48mm. *Warwickshire.* Photographs © Mark Pugh.

197. Silver-gilt; cast and wire; three-piece; moulded-relief and openwork. A six-petalled rose encircled by openwork and bordered by a wreath and equidistant small flowers. A separate soldered wire loop and wire hook. Incomplete, hook-point broken off; 21.59 × 15.39mm. *Hampshire.* Drawing © Patrick Read.

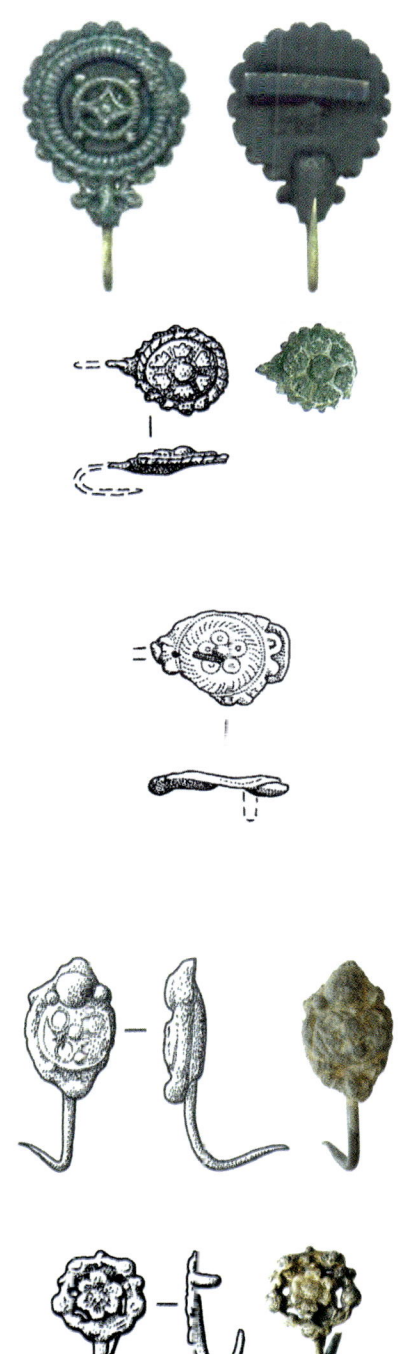

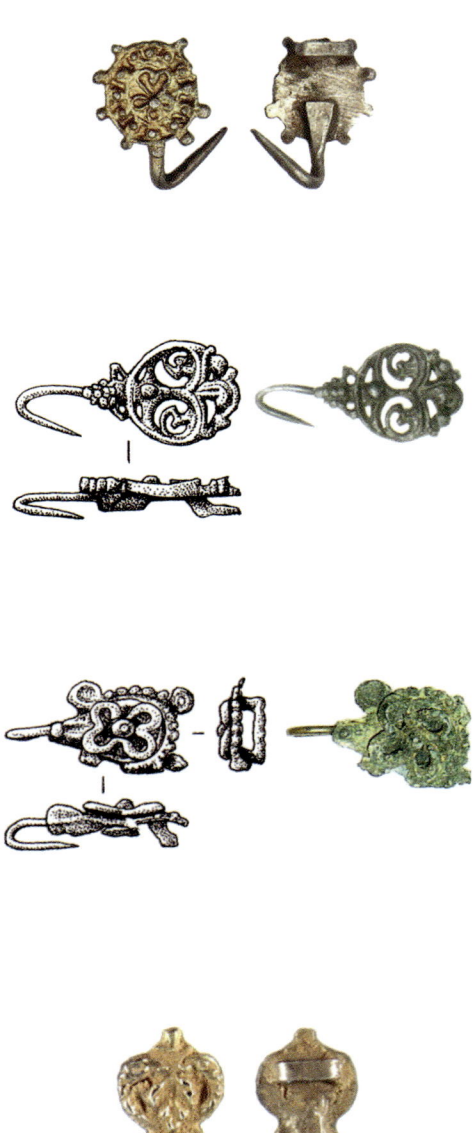

198. Silver-gilt; cast and wire; three-piece; moulded-relief. A five-petalled flower bordered by alternate pellets and bars; a raised edge and peripheral globular knops, one of which forms a raised collar at the juncture of the plate and hook. A separate soldered wire loop and wire hook. Incomplete, two knops broken off and hook distorted; plate 15 x 12mm. *North Wiltshire.* Photographs © Dennis Smith.

199. Copper alloy; cast and wire; two-piece, moulded-relief and openwork. A heart and stylised foliate; a projecting and ridged collar, possibly representing a bunch of grapes, at the juncture of the plate and hook. A separate both embedded and probably soldered wire hook; the integral loop projects laterally and then turns in the same plane as the plate, an unusual characteristic; 37 x 18mm. *River Thames foreshore, London.* Museum of London 1681/5 23.8.02. Drawing © Nick Griffiths.

200. Lead/tin and copper alloy; cast and wire; three-piece; moulded-relief. Four rounded recessed knops and a beaded border creating an engrailed edge; a ridged collar at the juncture of the plate and hook. A separate revolving openwork quatrefoil-headed rivet is secured through a central hole in the main-plate. An integral loop and separate embedded wire hook. Incomplete, part of the edge broken off; 30 x 16.67mm. *River Thames foreshore, London.* Drawing © Nick Griffiths.

201. Silver-gilt; cast, sheeting and wire; three-piece; moulded-relief. A leaf motif with confronted foliate scrolls; a rounded knop on the attachment-end and a projecting foliate collar at the juncture of the plate and hook. A separate soldered sheeting loop. Incomplete, hook missing; 17.8 x 9.6mm. *Hertfordshire.* Treasure case 2004 T315. Photographs © the Trustees of The British Museum.

HOOKED-CLASPS & EYES

202. Lead/tin and copper alloy; cast and wire; three-piece, convex obverse and partial convex back; moulded-relief. A solid-dome with imitative ground-supported twisted wire filigree and granules - a quatrefoil formed from annulets, each annulet encircling seven pellets simulating a six-petalled flower, the whole on a field of pellets; a beaded border creating an engrailed edge. An integral loop and separate embedded copper-alloy wire hook. Incomplete, loop and part of the edge broken off; 25 x 19.5mm. *North Wiltshire.* Drawing © Nick Griffiths.

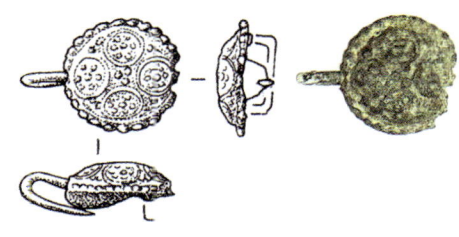

203. Copper alloy; sheeting; (?) wire and ground-supported twisted wire filigree and granules; four-piece; die-stamped; convex; sporadic white-metal coating, (?) tin. A hollow-domed front-plate with six collets, in the base of each is an off-centre pierced hole; applied with a wire annulet around each collet, a further wire annulet between each collet and a wire border below; two granules between each collet. The back-plate has an engrailed edge. Incomplete, separate (?) riveted attachment-loop, one granule and posts to set gems in the collets are missing, and hook-point broken off; 19 x 9mm. *Norfolk.* Portable Antiquities Scheme NMS-F22106. Photograph © Norfolk Museums and Archaeology Service.

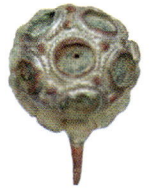

204. Copper alloy; sheeting; wire and straight, twisted and beaded wire openwork filigree; five-piece; die-stamped; convex. A hollow-domed nine-petalled rose with an S within each petal (see enlargement), and a central granule imitating a cabochon gem, overlaying a separate hollow-dome. The sheeting back-plate has an engrailed edge. A separate soldered wire loop and wire hook. Incomplete, hook-point broken off; 28.5 x 18mm. *River Thames foreshore, London.* Drawing © Nick Griffiths.

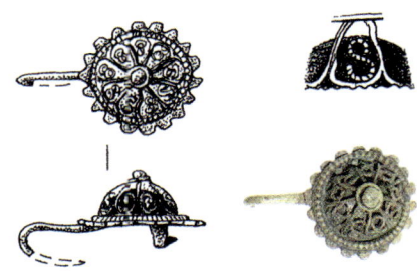

Early post-medieval Class D, Type 3

Lozenge-shaped

205. Silver-gilt; sheeting, wire and ground-supported twisted wire filigree and granules; three-piece; die-stamped; convex. A hollow-domed back-plate applied with a central imitative cabochon gem, an annulet, smaller annulets and granules and a lozenge, all bordered by small annulets and granules. The back-plate has engrailed edges. A separate soldered wire loop and wire hook; 32.09 x 23.37mm. *River Thames foreshore, London.* After Egan 2005, fig 27a. Drawing © Patrick Read.

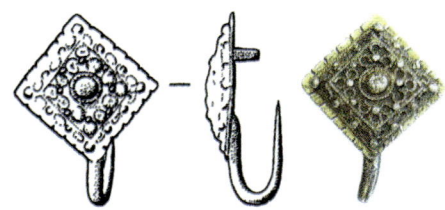

206. Silver-gilt; sheeting, wire and ground-supported twisted wire filigree and granules; five- or six-piece. A raised lozenge bordered by annulets, small granules and wire edging. A separate rove shaped as a four-petalled flower with sepals, each petal striated and ragged edged, is pierced by a separate domed-head split-pin and splayed on the back. A separate soldered sheeting loop and wire hook; 39.5 x 29.7mm. *South-West Yorkshire.* Portable Antiquities Scheme SWYOR-699EE7, Treasure case 2006 T423. Photographs © West Yorkshire Archaeology Service.

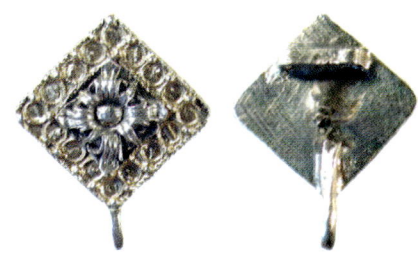

207. Silver-gilt; sheeting, wire and ground-supported twisted wire filigree and granules; convex; die-stamped; possibly nine-piece. A quatrefoil of hollow-domed bosses, each boss within an annulet, a central drilled-hole within a large annulet, two small annulets, each containing a granule, in each interstice. The back-plate has engrailed edges and trefoil knops on the apexes. A separate soldered sheeting loop and wire hook. Incomplete, most of each boss is broken off, several granules missing, a decorative rove and rivet or split-pin missing; hook fractured and soldered at least once; 36 x 27mm. *Wrexham, Wales.* Portable Antiquities Scheme CPAT-922557. Photograph © Clwyd-Powys Archaeological Trust.

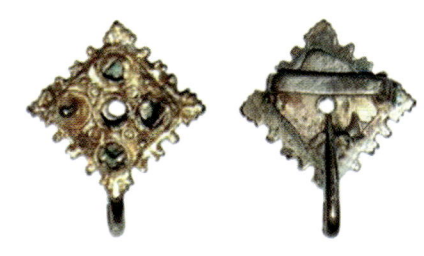

208. Silver-gilt; cast; three-piece; moulded-relief. A four-petalled flower within a border of pellets. A separate soldered wire loop and wire hook; 24 x 15mm. *Lincolnshire.* Treasure case 2004 T479. Photographs © the Trustees of The British Museum.

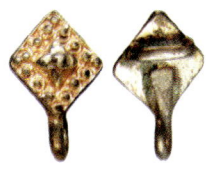

209. Silver-gilt; cast or sheeting and wire; three- or four-piece. The description in the *2003 Treasure Report* precludes saying whether the plate is cast or sheeting; if cast, the decoration is probably imitative ground-supported twisted wire filigree and granules; if sheeting, probably ground-supported twisted wire filigree and granules. A four-petalled flower, which is perhaps separate soldered, surrounded by 16 granules within wire annulets, all within a wire border. A separate soldered wire loop and wire hook; dimensions unrecorded. *Warwickshire*. Treasure case 2003 T356. Photographs © the Trustees of The British Museum.

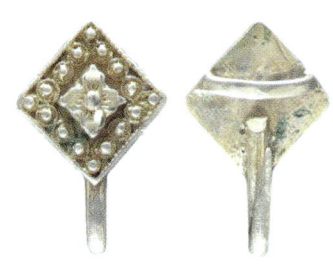

210. Silver-gilt; probably sheeting and wire and ground-supported twisted wire filigree and granules; three-piece. Nine large and three small granules within a wire border; each side is pierced by several small holes and has an engrailed edge. A separate soldered sheeting loop. Incomplete, separate soldered hook and one small granule missing; dimensions unrecorded. *North Yorkshire*. Treasure case 2002 T106. Photographs © the Trustees of The British Museum.

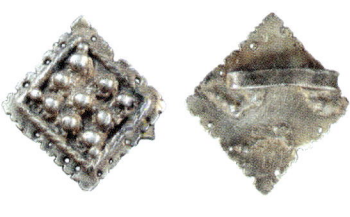

211. Silver-gilt; convex; cast, sheeting, wire and ground-supported twisted wire filigree and granules and moulded-relief. A shallow hollow-domed sheeting obverse-plate applied with five wire annulets, each encircling a granule within a small wire annulet, smaller wire annulets and granules in the interstices, all enclosed by a wire border. A cast reverse-plate with a large trefoil knop on each apex and in the centre of each side, interspaced with smaller rounded knops, a central drilled blow-hole. Incomplete, one large granule missing and one impressed into the hollow-dome, separate soldered loop missing and hook broken; dimensions unrecorded. *Cheshire*. Treasure case 2002 T303. Photographs © the Trustees of The British Museum.

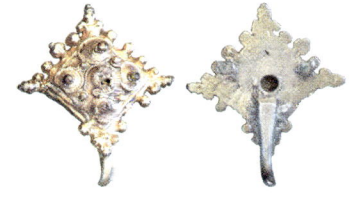

212. Silver-gilt; cast, sheeting and wire; four-piece; moulded-relief. A raised edge with a large rounded, slightly concave, knop on each apex and a small rounded knop in the centre of each side. A central drilled-hole retains a separate domed-head split-pin with four trefoil knops and is then splayed. A seperate soldered sheeting loop and wire hook. Incomplete, hook-point broken off; 25 x 20mm. *Norfolk.* Treasure case 2002 T280. Photographs © and courtesy The Portable Antiquities Scheme.

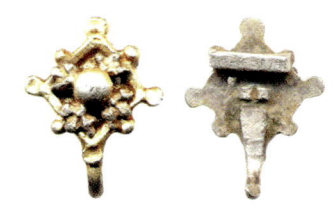

213. Silver-gilt; cast and possibly wire; five-piece; shallow concave; moulded-relief. A raised linear border and rounded knops on the edges and apexes; the reverse is punched with an illegible maker's mark resembling a foliate spray within a parade shield (see enlargement). A large multi-petalled flower rove and the main-plate are drilled centrally and pierced by a domed-head split-pin and then splayed. Incomplete, one side of the split-pin broken off and the separate soldered hook and loop are missing. *Hampshire.* Portable Antiquities Scheme HAMP-D69E85, Treasure case 2006 T450. Photographs © Winchester Museum Service.

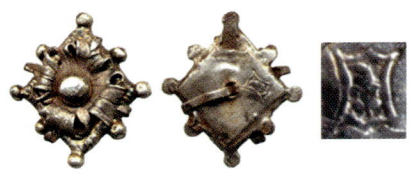

214. Silver-gilt; cast and wire; four-piece; moulded-relief. Fleur-de-lis knops on the edges and apexes. A separate quatrefoil hatched domed-head rivet with fleur-de-lis arms pierces the plate and is secured on the reverse. A separate soldered (?) wire (?) sheeting loop and wire hook. Incomplete, hook-point broken off; 30 x 20mm. *Lincolnshire.* Portable Antiquities Scheme 3BD8B2, Treasure case M&ME 370. Photograph © and courtesy of the Portable Antiquities Scheme.

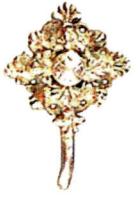

215. Silver-gilt; cast and wire; three-piece; shallow convex; moulded-relief. A thistle flanked by palmate leaves within two concentric stepped lozenges; a laterally projecting border with equidistant globular knops on the edges and apexes. A separate soldered wire loop and wire hook. Incomplete, hook-point broken off and loop distorted; 24 x 21.5mm. *Isle of White.* Portable Antiquities Scheme IOW-B5DFF7. Treasure case 2005 T202. Photographs © Isle of White Council.

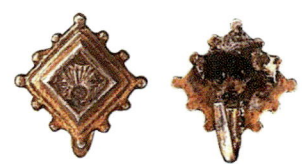

216. Copper alloy; sheeting and wire; convex; six-piece; die-stamped. The plate has engrailed edges, two transverse drilled-holes and a central rivet-hole. Two hollow-domed roves, each with four angular arms and four with bosses, surmounted one above the other, the outer one smaller. A separate domed-head rivet pierces the roves and the plate before securing. A separate soldered sheeting or flattened wire hook. A separate wire loop with oblique grooves is secured between the plate and the roves, presumably soldered. The two holes in the plate suggest they originally held the loop, therefore the present position of the loop perhaps represents a repair; the holes are an example of one method of attaching loops to the reverse-plate; 31.4 x 23.7mm. *North Yorkshire*. Portable Antiquities Scheme NLM-CA4D13. Photographs © Portable Antiquities Scheme and North Lincolnshire Council.

217. Copper alloy; sheeting and wire; three-piece; engraved. Undecorated apart from a linear border and engrailed edges. A separate soldered sheeting loop and wire hook. Incomplete, hook-point broken off; 29.5 x 19mm. *North Yorkshire*. Drawing © Nick Griffiths.

218. Copper alloy; sheeting and wire; three-piece; convex; die-stamped; undecorated. A hollow-domed boss and laterally projecting sides. A separate soldered flattened wire hook and sheeting annular loop; 30 x 16.6mm. *North Yorkshire*. United Kingdom Detecting Finds' Database 4626. Photographs © Nick Carter.

219. Lead/tin and copper alloy; cast and wire; two-piece; moulded-relief. A central solid lozenge within three concentric lozenges, two of which are linear and one pelleted. An integral loop. Incomplete, a remnant of separate embedded copper-alloy wire hook; 26.14 x 24.74mm. *Essex*. Portable Antiquities Scheme ESS-4519C4. Photographs © Colchester Museums.

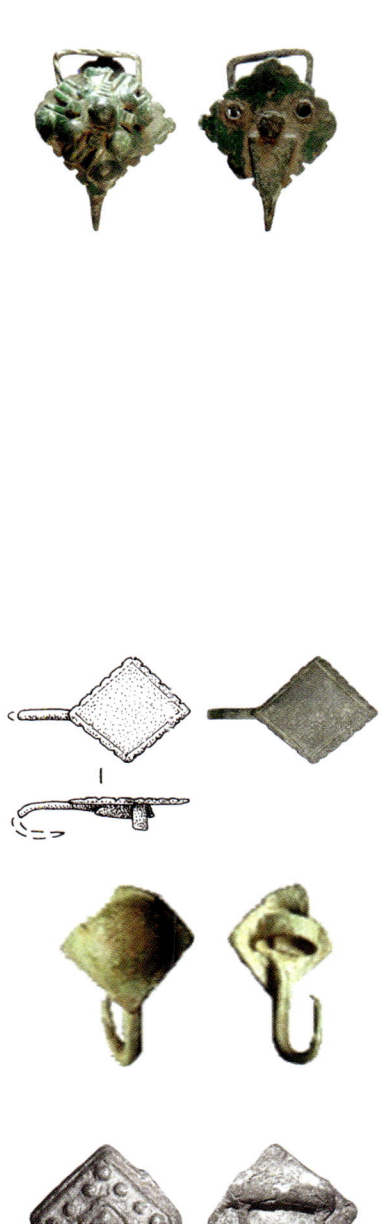

220. Lead/tin and copper alloy; cast and wire; two-piece; moulded-relief. Inscribed in Lombardic with the sacred monogram IHS - Jesus Saviour of Men (used as a protection against sudden death) within a circle; a beaded border creating engrailed edges and rounded knops on the side apexes; a trefoil collar at the juncture of the plate and hook. An integral loop and separate embedded copper-alloy wire hook. Incomplete, one apex broken off; 34.5 x 27.5. *River Thames foreshore, London.* Drawing © Nick Griffiths.

221. Lead/tin and probably copper alloy; cast and wire; two-piece; moulded-relief and possibly engraved. A circular panel bearing a black-letter (?) S (partially obscured by a hole) on a hatched field - possibly meaning 'Salvator', an invocation to Christ, the Saviour; all four edges have multiple nicks. An integral loop. Incomplete, separate embedded probable copper-alloy wire hook missing; 19.96 x 19.06mm. *River Thames foreshore, London.* Drawing © Patrick Read.

222. Lead/tin and copper alloy; cast and wire; three-piece; shallow concave; moulded-relief. A raised linear border and trefoil knops on three apexes. A separate quatrefoil-headed rivet is secured through a central hole. An integral loop and separate embedded copper-alloy wire hook. Incomplete, a probable trefoil collar at the juncture of the plate and hook broken off; 28.77 x 23.73mm. *River Thames foreshore, London.* Drawing © Patrick Read.

223. Lead/tin and copper alloy; cast and wire; three-piece; moulded-relief. Comparable with no. 222 except smaller trefoil knops and collar. Incomplete, a remnant of separate embedded copper-alloy wire hook; a ragged hole in the centre of the plate suggests a missing separate decorative feature; loop distorted; 29 x 23mm. *River Thames foreshore, London.* Drawing © Nick Griffiths.

224. Lead/tin and copper alloy; cast and wire; three-piece; moulded-relief. Comparable with nos 222-223 except a beaded border and a separate sexfoil-headed rivet; a separate embedded copper-alloy wire hook; 29.72 x 25.42mm. *River Thames foreshore, London.* Drawing © Patrick Read.

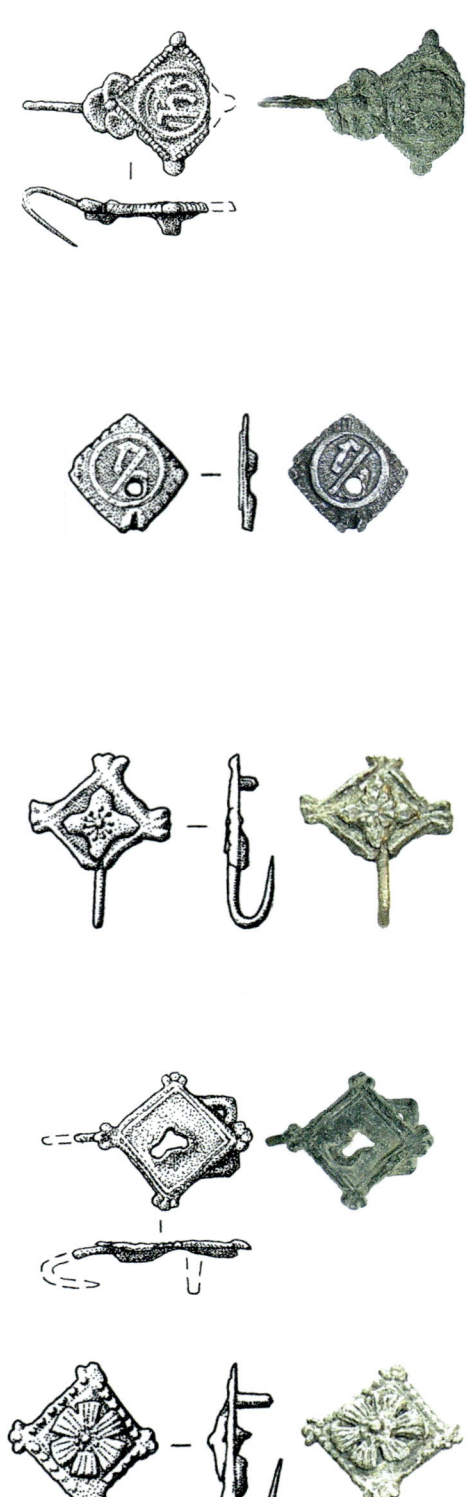

HOOKED-CLASPS & EYES

Early post-medieval Class D, Type 4

Triangular

225. Silver-gilt; cast; three-piece; engraved. A trefoil motif within a voided triangle; stylised foliate sides with engrailed edges. Incomplete; separate soldered hook broken and loop missing; 27 x 16.4mm. *North Yorkshire*. Treasure case 2003 T292. Photographs © the Trustees of The British Museum.

226. Silver-gilt; cast and wire; five-piece; moulded-relief. A triangle within laterally projecting sides; equidistant small rounded knops on the edges and acorn knops on the apexes; a (?) acorn collar at the junction of the plate and hook. A separate domed-head rivet pierces a separate triangular rove on the obverse before securing - the rove has debased fleur-de-knops on each apex and a rounded knop on each edge, the rivet-hole is within a sub-circular ridge. A separate soldered wire hook. Incomplete, one knop broken off the main plate, loop missing; 20 x 14mm. *Wiltshire*. Portable Antiquities Scheme WILT-2FF254. Photographs © Salisbury and South Wiltshire Museum.

227. Silver; cast and wire; possibly four- or five-piece. Comparable with no. 226. Probably incomplete, separate rivet appears to be missing; dimensions unknown. *Provenance unknown*. Photograph © TimeLine Originals.

228. Lead/tin and probably copper alloy; cast and wire; two-piece; moulded-relief. A central pellet within a cable-edged triangle, rounded knops on the apexes and a smaller pellet near the internal apex at the juncture of the plate and hook; engrailed edges and an integral loop. Incomplete, a separate embedded probable copper-alloy wire hook missing; 21.5 x 19.9mm. *South-East Dorset*. Drawing © Nick Griffiths.

229. Lead/tin and copper alloy; cast and wire; two-piece; moulded-relief. A panel of foliate and flowers within a linear border. An integral loop and separate embedded copper-alloy wire hook. Incomplete, loop fractured and distorted; 31 x 24.65mm. *River Thames foreshore, London*. Drawing © Nick Griffiths.

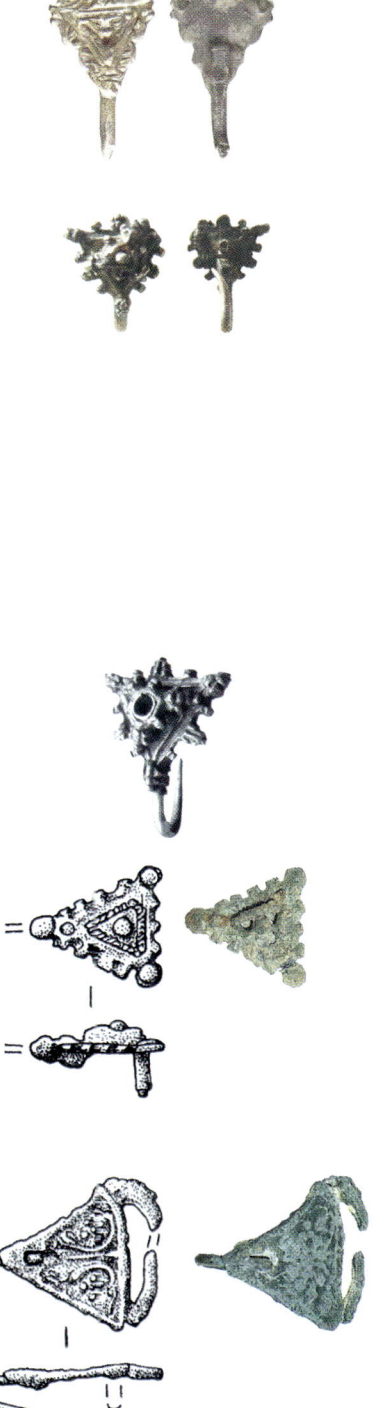

Early post-medieval Class D, Type 5

Heart-shaped/Ovoid

230. Copper alloy; cast and wire; three-piece; moulded-relief. A flower and foliate and engrailed edges. A separate soldered wire loop and wire hook. Plate and loop distorted; 36 x 20mm. *East Yorkshire*. Jim Halliday/030. Drawing © Anne Hodgson.

231. Copper alloy; sheeting, wire and ground-supported twisted wire filigree; four-piece; convex; die-stamped. A hollow-domed front-plate originally with several large wire annulets. The back-plate has engrailed edges. Incomplete, a large section of the front-plate and filigree, edge of the back-plate, separate soldered wire hook, and most of loop are broken off. The loop was secured by soldering into two holes in the back-plate, with just a stub remaining in one hole; 23 x 18mm. *South Somerset*. Drawing © Patrick Read.

232. Lead/tin and copper alloy; cast and wire; two-piece; convex; moulded-relief. A hollow-dome with imitative ground-supported twisted wire filigree and granules - a trefoil of annulets each annulet encircling a quatrefoil of small annulets and a central granule, a central large granule and smaller annulets and granules in the interstices; a laterally projecting engrailed edge. An integral loop and separate embedded copper-alloy wire hook; 39 x 24.79mm. *River Thames foreshore, London*. Drawing © Patrick Read.

233. Lead/tin and probably copper alloy; cast and wire; two-piece; convex; moulded-relief. A hollow-dome with imitative ground-supported twisted wire filigree and granules - small annulets each encircling a granule, and several smaller granules in the interstices, possibly imitating a berry. An integral loop. Incomplete, an embedded probable copper-alloy wire hook missing; 24.8 x 18.79mm. *River Thames foreshore, London*. Drawing © Patrick Read.

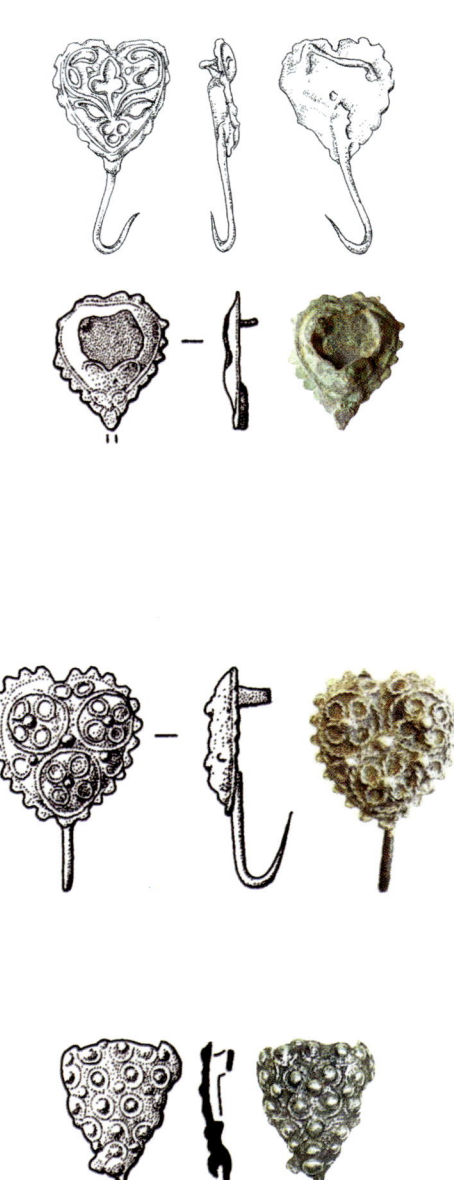

234. Silver-gilt; sheeting, wire and ground-supported twisted wire filigree and granules; four-piece; convex; die-stamped. A hollow-domed front-plate applied with a quatrefoil of large annulets each encircling a trefoil of small annulets and a granule, small annulets and granules in the interstices. The back-plate has engrailed edges. A separate soldered sheeting loop. Incomplete, separate soldered wire hook missing; 17 x 13.6mm. *South Somerset*. Drawing © Patrick Read.

235. Silver-gilt; sheeting, wire and ground-supported twisted wire filigree and granules; four-piece; convex; die-stamped. Comparable with nos 234, 236-242 except the large annulets each enclose a quatrefoil of small annulets and a granule. A separate soldered sheeting loop and wire hook; 25 x 16mm. *South-West Somerset*. Taunton County Museum acc. no. 151/2000. Treasure case M&ME 134. Photographs © Somerset County Council.

236. Silver-gilt; sheeting, wire and ground-supported twisted wire filigree and granules; four-piece; convex; die-stamped. Comparable with nos 234-235, 237-242 except a trefoil of large annulets each encircling a small annulet and a granule, small granules in the interstices. A separate soldered sheeting loop. Incomplete, separate soldered wire hook missing; 14.37 x 10.95mm. *South Somerset*. Taunton County Museum acc. no. 4505 109/2006. Treasure case 2005 T172. Photographs © Somerset County Council.

237. Silver-gilt; sheeting, wire and ground-supported twisted wire filigree and granules; four-piece; convex; die-stamped. Comparable with nos 234-236, 238-242 except each large annulet of the trefoil encircles a trefoil of small annulets and a small granule; small annulets and granules in the interstices. Incomplete, separate soldered wire loop, hook and several small granules missing; 15.4 x 11.3mm. *Mid-Somerset*. Drawing © Patrick Read.

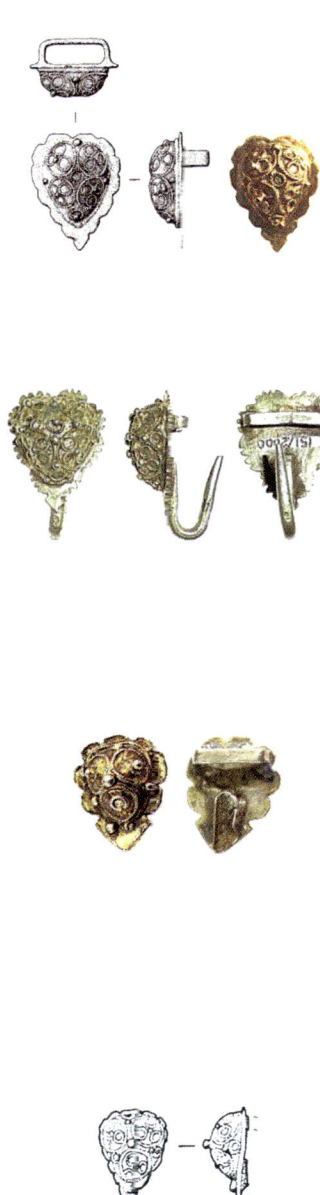

238. Silver-gilt; sheeting, wire and ground-supported twisted wire filigree and granules; four-piece; convex; die-stamped. Comparable with nos 234-237, 239-242 except a quatrefoil of large annulets each encircling a nippled-granule, smaller annulets, each encircling a nippled-granule in the interstices. A separate soldered sheeting loop and wire hook; 25.08 x 13.26mm. *East Devon*. Drawing © Nick Griffiths.

239. Silver-gilt; sheeting, wire and ground-supported twisted wire filigree and granules; four-piece; convex; die-stamped; engraved. Comparable with nos 234-238, 240-242 except each large annulet encircles a quatrefoil of small annulets and a central pellet; smaller annulets and granules in the interstices; each segment of the partially distorted engrailed edge has three oblique striations; 29.86 x 18.31mm. *South Somerset*. Taunton County Museum acc. no. 112/2006. Treasure case 2005 T525. Photographs © Somerset County Council.

240. Silver-gilt; sheeting, wire and ground-supported twisted wire filigree and granules; four-piece; convex; die-stamped. Comparable with nos 234-239, 241-242 except the small granules are absent from each trefoil of small annulets, as are the small annulets in the interstices. Incomplete, several annulets and separate soldered loop missing; slightly flattened; 27 x 17mm. *East Devon*. Drawing © Patrick Read.

241. Silver-gilt; sheeting, wire and ground-supported twisted wire filigree and granules; four-piece; convex; die-stamped. Comparable with nos 234-240, 242 except seven large annulets each encircling a small granule, small granules in the interstices. Incomplete, separate soldered loop missing; 29 x 21mm. *East Devon*. Drawing © Patrick Read.

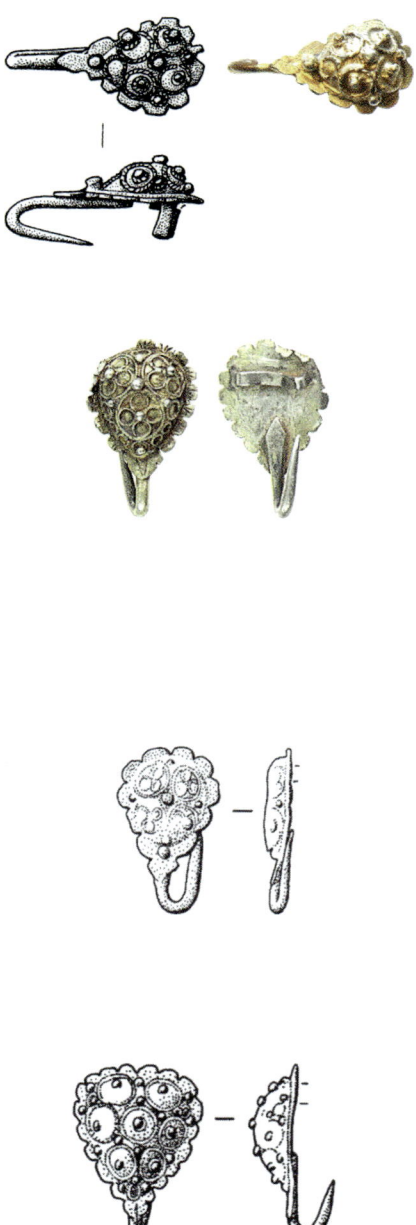

HOOKED-CLASPS & EYES

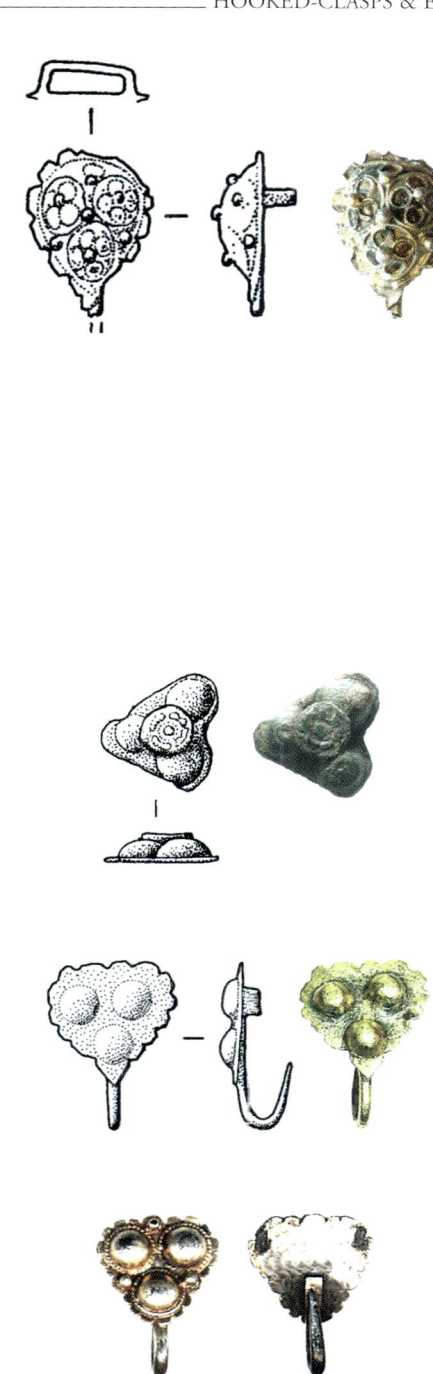

242. Silver-gilt; sheeting, wire and ground-supported twisted wire filigree and granules; four- or five-piece; convex; die-stamped. Comparable with nos 234-241 except a trefoil of large annulets each encircling a quatrefoil of small annulets and a central granule, small granules and annulets in the interstices. Incomplete, a separate angular-section tapering hollow folded piece of sheeting is soldered to the reverse-plate into which is inserted a tiny piece of wire: whether this wire is a remnant of the original hook is uncertain, if so, it would appear to be too flimsy; possibly it represents a repair. The folded hollow sheeting raises the question - rather than being solid wire, are other hooks on this category of clasp similarly made? This hypothesis will only be solved by examining each example by X-Ray; 27 x 17mm. *South Devon*. Drawing © Patrick Read.

243. Copper-alloy and lead/tin; sheeting and wire; five-piece; convex; die-stamped. A trefoil of hollow-domed bosses; a laterally projecting border. A separate rivet pierces a circular rove, imitating a rose, and the plate before securing; the reverse is filled with lead/tin. Incomplete, a small section of edge broken off and separate soldered loop and wire hook missing; 19.5 x 18.5mm. *Wiltshire*. Drawing © Nick Griffiths.

244. Copper alloy; sheeting and wire; three-piece; flat and convex; die-stamped. A trefoil of hollow-domed bosses and an engrailed edge. A separate soldered sheeting loop and wire hook. The back is coated with a now black substance, possibly bitumen, which fills the bosses; 27.77 x 20.92mm. *River Thames foreshore, London*. Drawing © Patrick Read.

245. Silver-gilt; sheeting, wire and ground-supported twisted wire filigree and granules; six-piece; convex; die-stamped. Comparable with no. 244 except the hollow-domed bosses are separate soldered and each boss is within an annulet, a granule within a small annulet is located in the interstices on the edge of the plate. Incomplete, separate soldered loop missing; 27 x 19.3mm. *Suffolk*. Portable Antiquities Scheme SF8565. Treasure case 2002 T125. Photographs © Suffolk County Council Archaeological Service.

Early post-medieval Class D, Type 6

Trefoil

246. Copper alloy; sheeting and wire; three-piece; shallow convex; die-stamped. A trefoil of hollow-domed bosses and a central smaller hollow-domed boss. A separate soldered sheeting loop and wire hook. The back is filled with a now black substance, possibly bitumen; 19.81 x 14.53mm. *River Thames foreshore, London*. Drawing © Patrick Read.

247. Copper alloy and lead/tin; sheeting and wire; three-piece; shallow convex; die-stamped. Comparable with no. 246 except the back is filled with lead/tin. Separate possibly soldered and embedded hook and distorted loop; 20.94 x 13.49mm. *River Thames foreshore, London*. Drawing © Nick Griffiths.

248. Copper alloy; sheeting and wire; three-piece; convex; die-stamped. A trefoil of hollow-domed bosses separated by bars radiating from a central pellet; a laterally projecting border. A separate soldered loop and wire hook. A now black substance, possibly bitumen, coats both the front and back which on the latter fills the bosses; 29.27 x 16.4mm. *River Thames foreshore, London*. Drawing © Patrick Read.

249. Copper alloy; cast and sheeting; three-piece; convex; moulded-relief. A trefoil of hollow-domed bosses, each boss has several ring-and-dot motifs and a central indentation; a laterally projecting border; each arm of a central trefoil is grooved and is pierced with a rivet-hole in which a separate rivet secures a separate sheeting hook to the back; one side of the attachment-end of the hook has an integral lateral projection bent to form the loop and then soldered to the opposite side; 31 x 17mm. *Lincolnshire*. After *Treasure Hunting* June 2001, pp33. Photographs © Rod Blunt.

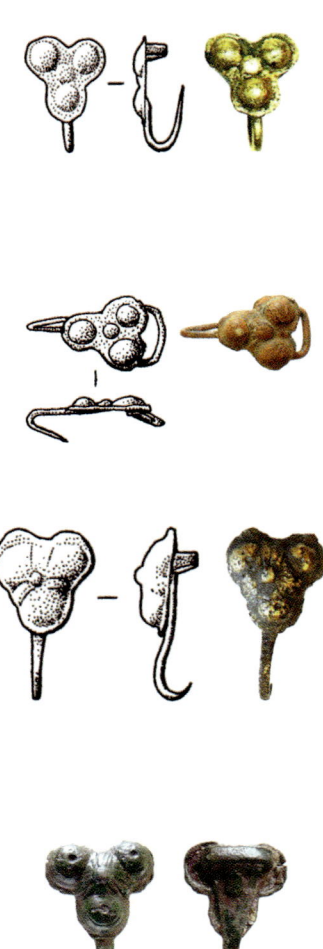

HOOKED-CLASPS & EYES

250. Copper-alloy and lead/tin; sheeting, wire and ground-supported twisted wire filigree; seven-piece; convex; die-stamped. The front-plate comprises a trefoil of hollow-domed bosses soldered to the back-plate, forming a laterally projecting border. A separate copper-alloy domed-head rivet pierces a circular rove with a beaded border and then a trefoil rove with a median wire on each arm, and then both plates before securing. A separate soldered wire loop and hook; the back is filled with lead/tin; 25 x 19.5. *River Thames foreshore, London.* Drawing © Nick Griffiths.

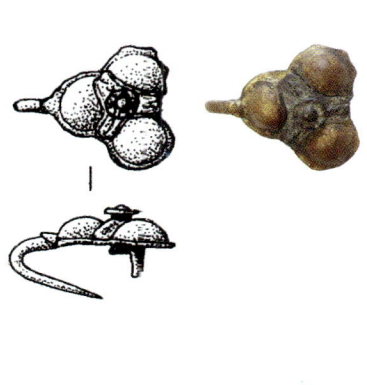

251. Lead/tin and copper alloy; cast and wire; two-piece, shallow convex; moulded-relief. A trefoil of hollow-domed bosses separated by bars radiating from a central smaller domed boss; rounded knops in the angles and a laterally projecting border. A distorted integral loop and separate embedded copper-alloy wire hook; 21.95 x 15.23mm. *River Thames foreshore, London.* Drawing © Patrick Read.

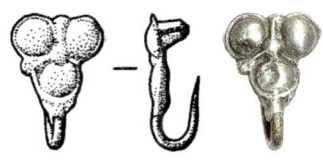

252. Lead/tin and iron; cast and wire; two-piece, convex; moulded-relief. A trefoil of hollow-domed bosses, a central small domed boss and four even smaller domed bosses; a laterally projecting beaded border. Incomplete, loop distorted and part broken off, separate embedded iron wire hook missing; 26 x 21mm. *North Yorkshire.* Jim Halliday. Drawing © John Middleton.

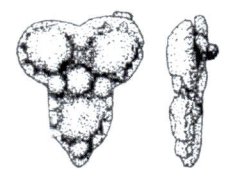

253. Silver; cast and wire; three-piece; moulded-relief. A large domed-boss in each lobe, a small pellet in the centre and between each lobe, all within a raised border. A separate soldered wire hook. Incomplete, separate soldered loop missing; 16.6 x 11.5mm. *Hampshire.* Treasure case 2004 T298. Photographs © the Portable Antiquities Scheme.

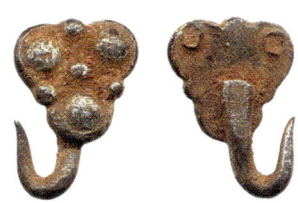

HOOKED-CLASPS & EYES

254. Silver-gilt; cast or sheeting and wire; convex; four-piece; moulded-relief or die-stamped. The front-plate comprises a trefoil of large hollow-domed-bosses, each boss within a twisted wire annulet, a pellet in the centre and between each lobe, all within twisted wire annulets. The back-plate has an engrailed edge. Incomplete, separate soldered loop and hook missing; dimensions unrecorded. The *Treasure Report 2004* provides an inadequate description: if the obverse-plate is cast, the decoration will probably be imitative ground-supported filigree; if sheeting, ground-supported filigree. *Suffolk*. Treasure case 2004 T285. Photographs © the Trustees of The British Museum.

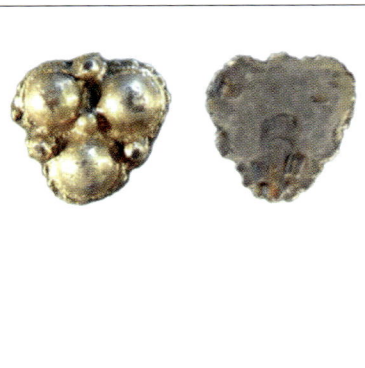

255. Copper alloy; sheeting and wire; five-piece; convex; die-stamped. A trefoil of hollow-domed bosses soldered to a plate with engrailed edges. A separate sheeting hook is fastened by a separate globular-head rivet that pierces a sheeting trefoil rove and then the plate. A separate soldered sheeting loop retaining a fragment of textile, either from a strap or garment. The back is coated with a now black substance, possibly bitumen, that fills the bosses; 22.75 x 13mm. *River Thames foreshore, London*. Drawing © Nick Griffiths.

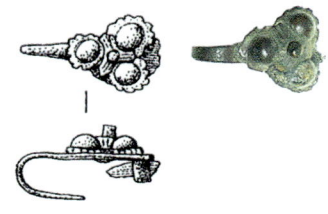

256. Silver-gilt, sheeting, wire and ground-supported twisted wire filigree and granules; seven-piece; convex; die-stamped. A trefoil of hollow-domed bosses soldered to a plate with a wire border, each boss is encircled by an annulet, a trefoil of large granules imitate cabochon gems. A partially flattened wire hook is both soldered and riveted to the back by a separate domed-head rivet, imitating a cabochon gem. Incomplete, separate soldered loop missing; 16.12 x 12mm. *Isle of White*. Photographs © Isle of White Council.

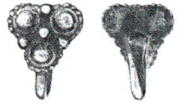

257. Copper alloy; sheeting and wire; six-piece; convex; die-stamped and engraved. A trefoil of hollow-domed bosses, each with a ring-and-dot motif. The back-plate has an engrailed edge. A partially flattened wire hook is both soldered and riveted to the back-plate by a separate globular-head rivet that pierces a trefoil rove with voided striations and engrailed edges, and then both plates. A separate soldered sheeting loop; 31.18 x 22.99mm. *River Thames foreshore, London*. Drawing © Patrick Read.

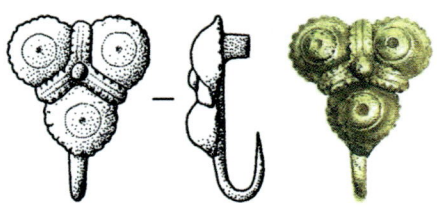

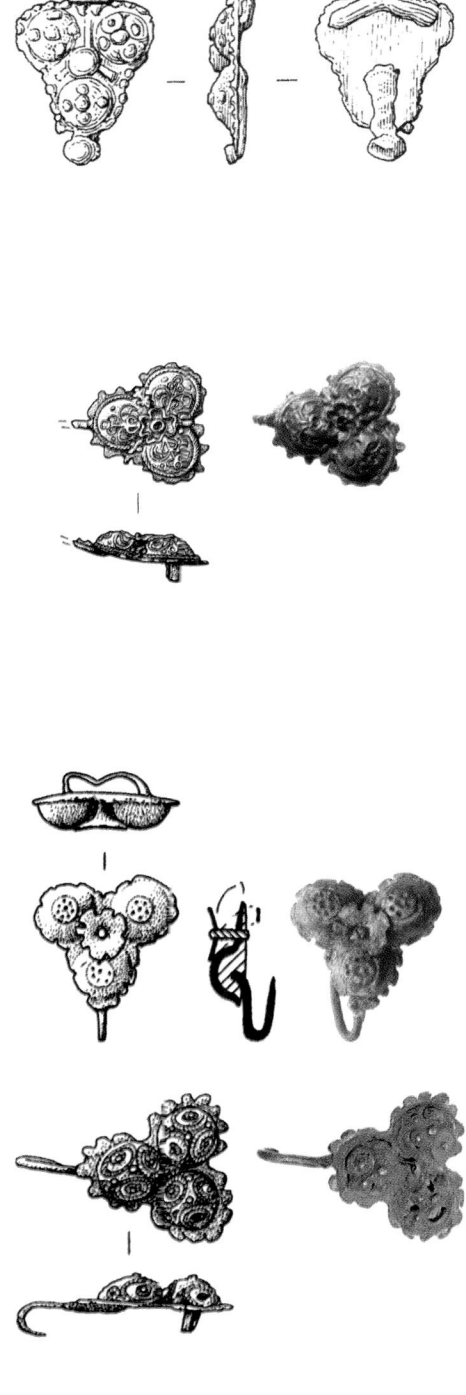

258. Lead/tin and probably copper alloy; cast and wire; two-piece; convex; moulded-relief. A trefoil of solid-domed bosses and imitative ground-supported twisted wire filigree and granules - each boss has five granules and the bosses are separated by bands radiating from a central smaller boss; a laterally projecting beaded border creates an engrailed edge. The integral loop is distorted. Incomplete, separate embedded probable copper-alloy wire hook missing; 29 x 22.5mm. *Lincolnshire*. Drawing © Nick Griffiths.

259. Copper alloy; sheeting and wire; five-piece; convex; die-stamped. The front-plate comprises a trefoil of hollow-domed bosses, each with a three-petalled flower and foliate and small pellets within an imitative ground-supported twisted wire annulet, in each angle a fleur-de-lis; a central six-petalled flower is pierced. The back-plate has an engrailed edge. A separate soldered sheeting loop and wire hook. Incomplete, hook broken off and a central possible separate appliqué is missing; 23.37 x 20.04mm. *South Wiltshire*. Drawing © Nick Griffiths.

260. Copper alloy; sheeting and wire; six-piece; convex; die-stamped, engraved and punched. The front-plate comprises a trefoil of hollow-domed bosses, each boss with a central annulet infilled with dots. The back-plate has an engrailed edge. A separate rivet pierces a sheeting seven-petalled rove and then the two plates. A separate soldered sheeting loop and wire hook; 26.9 x 23.5. *South-West Wiltshire*. Drawing © Patrick Read.

261. Copper alloy; sheeting, wire and ground-supported twisted wire filigree and granules; five-piece; convex; die-stamped. A trefoil of hollow-domed bosses, each applied with a trefoil of large annulets, each annulet encircling a small annulet and granule. The back-plate has an engrailed edge. A separate soldered wire loop and wire hook. Incomplete, a central separate decorative appliqué missing and several small holes in one boss; 34 x 24mm. *River Thames foreshore, London*. Drawing © Nick Griffiths.

HOOKED-CLASPS & EYES

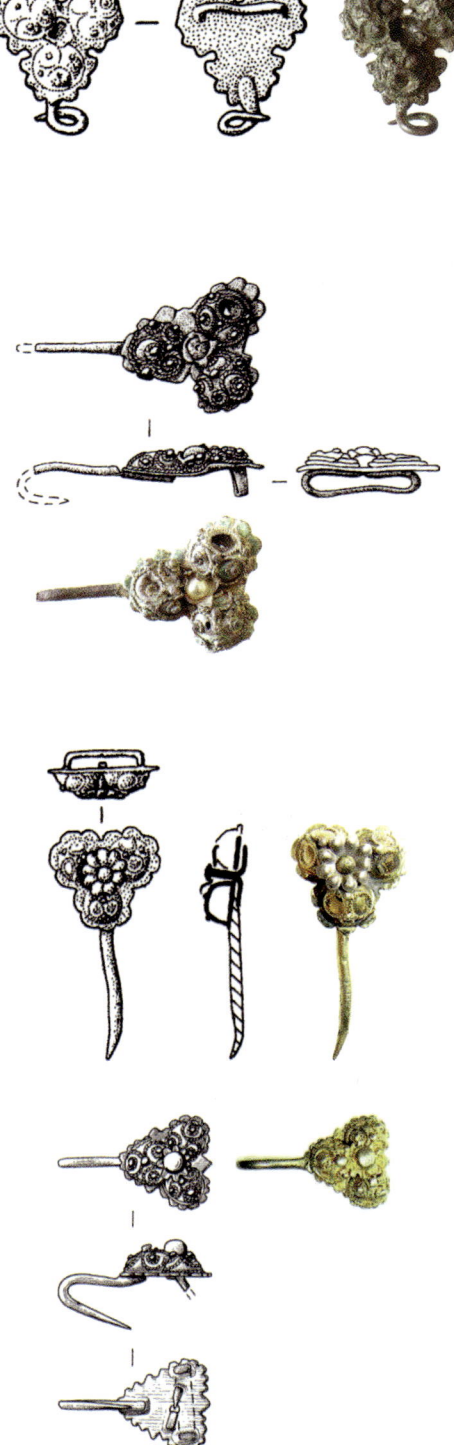

262. Copper alloy; sheeting, wire and ground-supported twisted wire filigree and granules; four-piece; convex; die-stamped. Comparable with nos 261, 263-272 except each trefoil has a small granule in each petal, and a central six-petalled appliqué. A separate soldered wire loop and wire hook; 25.4 x 21.5mm. *South-West Wiltshire*. Drawing © Patrick Read.

263. Copper alloy; sheeting, wire and ground-supported twisted wire filigree and granules; six-piece; convex; die-stamped. Comparable with nos 261-262, 264-272 except each boss comprises several small annulets, all with central small granules, encircled by larger annulets; a central white glass bead imitates a pearl. The separate soldered loop differs from the norm, for it is annular sheeting, about half of which, including the butt-seam, is soldered to the back-plate. Incomplete, point of separate soldered wire hook broken off, annulets broken in places and edge of the plate distorted; 37 x 23mm. *Wiltshire*. Wiltshire Heritage Museum, acc. no. 1986.76. Drawing © Nick Griffiths.

264. Silver-gilt; sheeting, wire and ground-supported twisted wire filigree and granules; eight-piece; convex; die-stamped. Comparable with nos 261-263, 265-272 except each boss has two small annulets spaced by two granules. A separate domed-head split-pin pierces a nine-petalled rove and then the plate before splaying. A separate soldered wire loop and distorted wire hook, now straight; 38.5 x 18mm. *South Somerset*. Drawing © Patrick Read.

265. Silver-gilt; sheeting, wire and ground-supported twisted wire filigree and granules; five-piece; convex; die-stamped. Comparable with nos 261-264, 266-272 except each boss has a trefoil of large annulets, each annulet encircles a small annulet and a granule. A separate soldered wire hook. A separate globular-head split-pin - imitating a cabochon gem - pierces a nine-petalled rove and both plates before splaying. Incomplete, separate soldered wire loop broken off; 25 x 16mm. *South-East Dorset*. Drawing © Nick Griffiths.

266. Silver-gilt; sheeting, wire and ground-supported twisted wire filigree and granules; six-piece; convex; die-stamped and engraved. Comparable with nos 261-265, 267-272 except the rove has multiple parallel striations. A separate globular-head split-pin - imitating a cabochon gem - pierces a sub-circular rove and both plates before splaying. The flattened end of a separate soldered wire hook is stamped with a cross patonce maker's mark (see enlargement). Incomplete, separate soldered loop missing, one splayed arm of the split-pin broken off and hook distorted; 22 x 16mm. *Norfolk*. Portable Antiquities Scheme NMS-E1FD52. Photograph © Norfolk Museums and Archaeology Service.

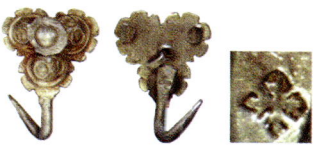

267. Silver-gilt; sheeting, wire and ground-supported twisted wire filigree and granules; six-piece; convex; die-stamped and engraved. Comparable with nos 261-266, 268-272 except the rove has multiple radiating, transverse and oblique striations. A separate domed-head split-pin - imitating a cabochon gem - pierces a sub-circular rove and both plates before splaying. Incomplete, separate soldered wire loop missing and one splayed arm of the split-pin broken off; 27 x 24mm. *East Yorkshire*. Photographs © Stan Raymond.

268. Silver-gilt; sheeting, wire and ground-supported twisted wire filigree and granules; six-piece; convex; die-stamped and engraved. Comparable with nos 261-267, 269-272 except the rove has three concentric beaded circles. A separate soldered flattened wire loop and wire hook. A separate domed-head split-pin - imitating a cabochon gem - pierces the sub-circular rove and both plates before splaying; 20 x 16mm. *East Yorkshire*. Photographs © Stan Raymond.

269. Silver-gilt; sheeting, wire and ground-supported twisted wire filigree and granules; six-piece; convex; die-stamped. Comparable with nos 261-268, 270-272 except a five-petalled rove A separate soldered wire hook. Incomplete, separate soldered loop missing; 26.7 x 18.3mm. *South-West Wiltshire*. Portable Antiquities Scheme SOMDOR-9B24F7. Treasure case 2006 T501. Photographs © Somerset County Council.

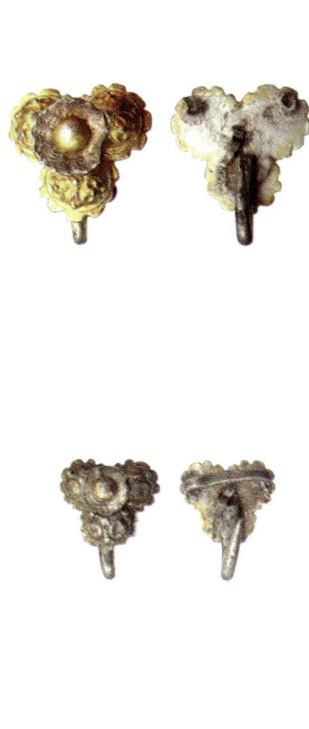

HOOKED-CLASPS & EYES

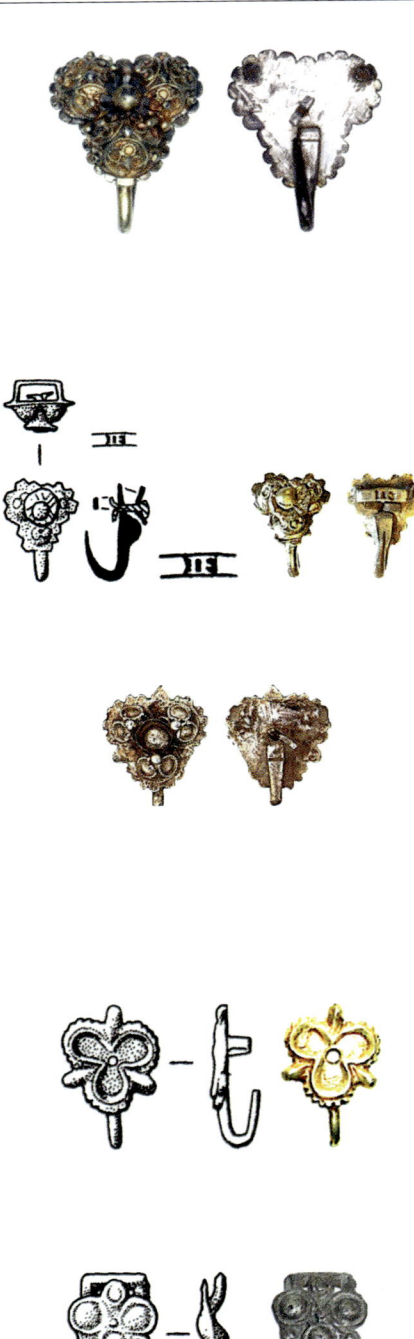

270. Silver-gilt; sheeting, wire and ground-supported twisted wire filigree and granules; six-piece; convex; die-stamped. Comparable with nos 261-269, 271-272 except each boss has a large annulet encircling a quatrefoil of smaller annulets, each of which encircles a smaller granule; and a twelve-petalled rove. A separate soldered wire hook. Incomplete, separate soldered wire loop missing; 30.3 x 25.06mm. *South-West Dorset.*

271. Silver-gilt; sheeting, wire and ground-supported twisted wire filigree and granules; five-piece; convex; die-stamped and engraved. Comparable with nos 261-270, 272 except each boss has two small annulets, and a circular rove with a voided saltire. A separate soldered wire hook. The back of the separate soldered flattened wire loop is punched with the maker's mark IF (see enlargement); 17.6 x 12mm. *East Devon.* Drawing © Patrick Read.

272. Silver-gilt; sheeting, wire and ground-supported twisted wire filigree and granules; five-piece; convex; die-stamped and engraved. Comparable with nos 261-271 except a pointed knop in the cusp of each side, resembling a three-petalled flower with sepals, and the circular rove has a peripheral circle. Incomplete, the separate soldered wire hook is broken and wire loop missing. Dimensions unknown. *Provenance unknown.*

273. Silver-gilt; cast and wire; probably four-piece; moulded-relief. A stylised three-petalled flower with sepals, engrailed edges. A separate soldered wire loop and wire hook. Incomplete, hook-point broken off; and a central drilled-hole presumably held a now missing decorative feature; 24 x 15.9mm. *North Dorset.* Drawing © Patrick Read.

274. Lead/tin and copper alloy; cast and wire; two-piece; shallow convex; moulded-relief. A stylised three-petalled flower with sepals. A distorted integral loop and separate embedded copper-alloy wire hook; 25.5 x 14.8. *River Thames foreshore, London.* Drawing © Patrick Read.

Early post-medieval Class D, Type 7

Quatrefoil

275. Silver-gilt; sheeting, wire and ground-supported straight and twisted wire filigree and granules; three-piece. Two central large concentric annulets, the inner straight wire and the outer twisted, the edges of which break four similarly formed large annulets; all five large annulets enclose a trefoil of small twisted wire annulets; the cusp each side is infilled with metal; one of the trefoils of small annulets retains a central granule; resembles a four-petalled rosette with sepals. Incomplete, separate soldered loop and wire hook missing; a central granule is missing from four trefoils of small annulets and a mark on each sepal suggests lost granules; D19.02mm. *North Dorset*. Acc. No. DORCM 2000.92.2 in the collections at Dorset County Museum and published with the permission of The Dorset Natural History and Archaeological Society at the Dorset County Museum. Photographs © Val MacRae

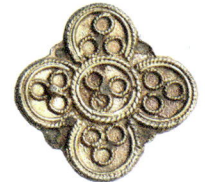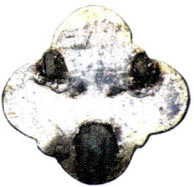

276. Silver-gilt; cast and wire; probably five-piece; convex; moulded-relief. A stylised four-petalled rose with sepals. Incomplete, a central drilled-hole is presumably for a now missing decorative feature; 24 x 18mm. *Suffolk*. Portable Antiquities Scheme SF-EE91A8. Photographs © Suffolk County Council Archaeological Service.

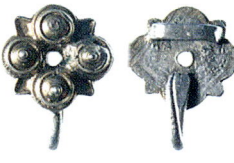

277. Silver-gilt; sheeting, wire and ground-supported twisted wire filigree and granules; probably six- or five-piece; convex; die-stamped. A quatrefoil of hollow-domed bosses, each boss applied with a peripheral annulet containing a trefoil of large annulets, each annulet encircling a small annulet and granule, soldered to a plate with an engrailed edge. A separate soldered wire hook. Incomplete, separate soldered loop missing, and a central drilled-hole is presumably for a now missing decorative feature; 20 x 18mm. *Essex*. United Kingdom Detecting Finds' Database 8924. Photographs © Duncan Patey.

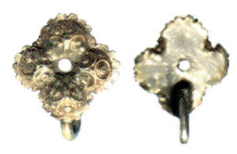

HOOKED-CLASPS & EYES

278. Silver-gilt; sheeting, wire and ground-supported twisted wire filigree and granules; seven-piece; convex; die-stamped. Comparable with no. 277 except each boss has a granule at the centre of each trefoil of large annulets and another near the base and each large annulet encircles a trefoil of small annulets with a central granule. A separate domed-head split-pin pierces two sexfoil roves, one larger than the other, through a central drilled-hole before splaying. The base of the separate soldered wire hook is punched with a maker's mark that appears to be two chevrons (see enlargement); 23 x 22mm. *Berkshire*. Photographs © John Caluori.

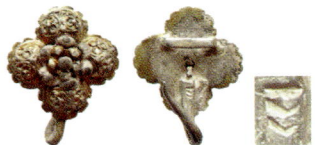

279. Silver-gilt; sheeting, wire and ground-supported twisted wire filigree and granules; six-piece; convex; die-stamped. Comparable with nos 277-278 except each boss lacks the small annulets. A separate shallow domed-head split-pin pierces a cinquefoil rove and central drilled-holes in both plates before splaying. A separate soldered flattened wire loop and hook. Incomplete, hook-point broken off; 20 x 15mm. *Cambridgeshire*. United Kingdom Detecting Finds' Database 14672. Photographs © J Pederson.

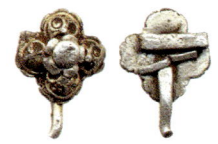

280. Silver-gilt; cast and wire; four-piece; moulded-relief and openwork. Four conjoined fleurs-de-lis radiating from a central hole inlaid with a large granule that imitates a cabochon gem. Incomplete, marks on the reverse indicate a missing separate soldered loop and hook; 20 x 18mm. *South Somerset*. Drawing © Patrick Read.

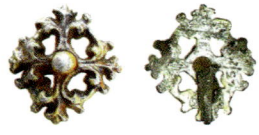

Early post-medieval Class D, Type 8

Cinquefoil

281. Silver-gilt; cast and wire or sheeting; convex; probably five-piece; moulded-relief. A stylised five-petalled rose with sepals. Incomplete, separate soldered loop and wire hook missing; a central drilled-hole is presumably for a now missing decorative feature; D19.1mm. *South Devon*. PAS DEV-E3E103, Treasure case 2005 T23. Photograph © Exeter City Council.

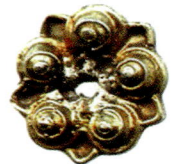 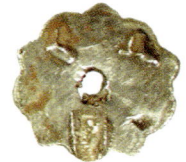

HOOKED-CLASPS & EYES

282. Silver-gilt; sheeting, wire and ground-supported twisted wire filigree and granules; six-piece; convex; die-stamped. The front-plate comprises a cinquefoil of hollow-domed bosses, each boss applied with large annulets, each encircling a trefoil of small annulets and a central granule. The back-plate has an engrailed edge. A separate domed-head split-pin pierces a domed sexfoil rove and both plates before splaying. A seperate soldered wire loop and wire hook; *c*.2.04 x 16.16mm. *Essex*.

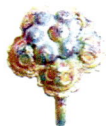

Early post-medieval Class D, Type 9

Pentagonal

283. Silver-gilt; cast, sheeting, wire and ground-supported twisted wire filigree and granules; four-piece; convex; moulded-relief. The front-plate comprises six hollow-domed bosses, one central and five peripheral; each boss is applied with six wire annulets, one central and five peripheral, the central annulet with a granule; five smaller granules surround each boss. The back-plate has a wreathed border with a tiny flower on each knop interspaced by a pellet. Incomplete, several bosses damaged, some filigree broken off and several granules missing, hook-point broken off and loop missing; 33 x 26mm. *Shropshire*. Treasure case 2003 T329. Photographs © the Trustees of The British Museum.

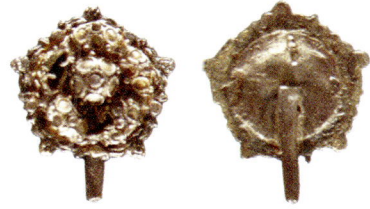

Early post-medieval Class D, Type 10

Sexfoil

284. Silver-gilt; sheeting, wire and ground-supported twisted wire filigree and granules; three-piece; convex; die-stamped. The front-plate comprises a hollow-dome applied with a sexfoil of alternate large wire annulets and rectangles, each annulet has a central granule and S-spirals, while the rectangles enclose three small annulets; a small domed boss on each apex. The back-plate has an engrailed edge. A separate soldered wire loop and wire hook. Incomplete, one apex broken off and a small hole in the front-plate; 40 x 25mm. *Cheshire*. After Gaimster *et al* 2002, fig. 6, no. 6. Treasure case M&ME 2001, 11-6.

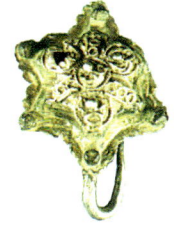

285. Silver-gilt; sheeting, wire and ground-supported twisted wire filigree; seven- or ten-piece. The plate has four separate soldered collets, the outer three within annulets, each set with a facetted garnet (see enlargement); a turquoise cabochon glass stone is set in the central collet; between the outer collets formerly were pearls affixed on separate posts within annulets, one pearl survives; engrailed edges. A separate soldered wire loop and wire hook. Incomplete, two pearls missing and their annulets are either missing or broken, hook-point broken off; 26 x 16.8mm. *River Thames foreshore, London*. Museum of London enquiry 4341/05, private collection. Drawing © Nick Griffiths, photograph © Tony Yendall.

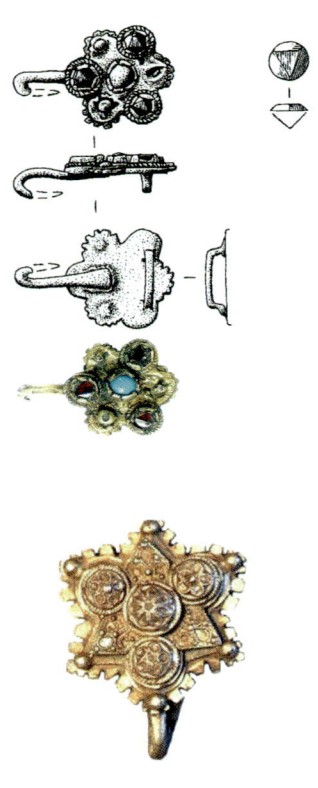

286. Silver-gilt; sheeting, possibly cast, wire and ground-supported twisted wire filigree and granules; possibly four-piece; convex. A possibly cast sexfoil front-plate with a trefoil of hollow-domed bosses bordered by wire, all of which are applied with five small wire annulets around a granule, within a large wire annulet, the field of each apex is applied with wire foliate and a flower and six tiny granules, a central rivet-hole. A probable sheeting back-plate has a raised linear outline, which mirrors the front-plate, and an engrailed edge with a large granule on each apex, a central rivet-hole. A separate split-pin, the head of which is a domed multi-petalled flower within a wire annulet, secures the two plates together. A separate soldered wire loop and wire hook; 39 x 29mm. *Norfolk*. Treasure case 2003 T23. Photographs © the Trustees of The British Museum.

Early post-medieval Class D, Type 11

Figurative

287. Silver-gilt; cast and wire; three-piece; openwork and moulded-relief. A portcullis; two chain-loops on the attachment-end; the opposite edge is engrailed. A separate soldered wire hook and flattened wire loop; 31.4 x 18.1mm. *Suffolk*. Portable Antiquities Scheme SF-33C358. Drawing © Donna Wreathall, photograph © Suffolk County Council Archaeological Service.

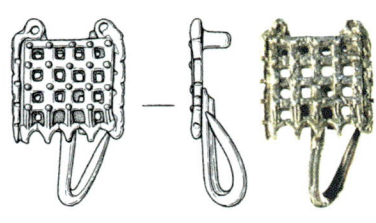

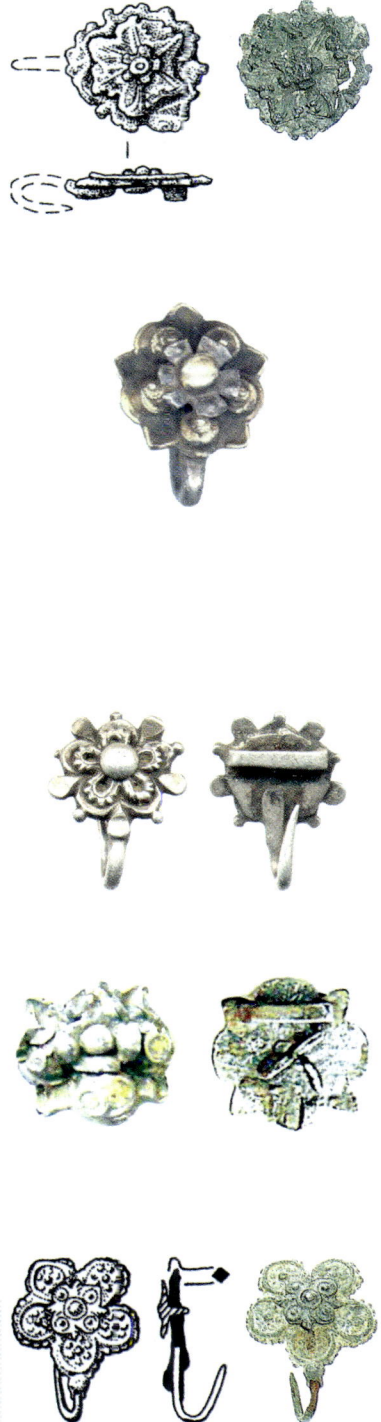

288. Lead/tin and probably copper alloy; cast and wire; four-piece; moulded-relief. A stylised double six-petalled rose - a ragged-edge plate overlaid with a six-petalled rose, both pierced centrally and secured together with a separate cinquefoil-headed rivet. An integral loop. Incomplete, a separate embedded probable copper-alloy wire hook is missing; D22.9mm. *River Thames foreshore, London.* Museum of London 2019/1. Drawing © Nick Griffiths.

289. Silver-gilt; cast, sheeting, wire and ground-supported twisted wire filigree and granules; five-piece; moulded-relief. A five-petalled rose with sepals and a raised border, each petal has a domed boss with a central small granule within an annulet. A separate domed-head split-pin pierces a separate sheeting sex-foil rove and the main-plate before splaying. A separate soldered sheeting loop and wire hook. The transverse section of the loop is punched with the maker's mark IF; 19 x 15mm. *Norfolk.* Portable Antiquities Scheme NMS-A28D98. Photograph © Norfolk Museums and Archaeology Service.

290. Silver; cast and wire; five-piece; moulded-relief. A five-petalled rose, each petal with a small rounded knop, and large rounded sepals, a central drilled rivet-hole. A separate five-petalled rove, each petal with an engrailed edge at the rounded end, is secured in the rivet-hole by a separate domed-head rivet; 27 x 20mm. *Norfolk.* Treasure case 2002 T39. Photographs © Portable Antiquities Scheme.

291. Silver-gilt; cast, sheeting and wire; five-piece; shallow convex; moulded-relief. A double four-petalled rose, each petal domed and with two annulets, and angular incuse sepals with raised edges. A separate domed-head split-pin pierces a quatrefoil rove and the plate before splaying. A separate soldered sheeting loop. Incomplete, separate soldered wire hook missing; 1.94 x 1.94mm. *North Yorkshire.*

292. Lead/tin and copper alloy; cast and wire; three-piece; moulded-relief. A five-petalled rose, an annulet on each petal encircles a sex-foil formed from tiny pellets; a beaded border; a ridged collar at the juncture of the plate and hook. A central hole retains a separate quatre-foil-headed rivet, resembles a four-petalled flower with angular sepals. An integral loop and separate embedded copper-alloy wire hook; 27.5 x 21mm. *River Thames foreshore, London.* Drawing © Patrick Read.

Early post-medieval Class E single sharp-hooked clasps

Undoubtedly the most ubiquitous category of all early post-medieval single sharp-hooked clasps is designated as Class E, Types 1-9, the distinguishing feature of which is an integral attachment-loop in the same plane as the plate. Attachment-loops are angular, with either a rectangular or sub-rectangular aperture. Hooks are recurving, the shanks of which are either rounded, angular a combination of both. A decorative collar is a feature found at the juncture of the plate and hook on many. Silver is uncommon and copper-alloy is by far the prevalent metal. Whatever the metal, and although sheeting examples are recorded here, casting is the norm, frequently partially or wholly unfettled, often with a sprue on the outside edge of the loop, perhaps indicative of mass production lacking adequate finishing. All are one-piece. Designated as Type 1 rectangular/sub-rectangular, Type 2 shield, Type 3 circular, Type 4 lozenge/sub-lozenge, Type 5 trefoil, Type 6 quatrefoil, Type 7 heart-shaped, Type 8 figurative and Type 9 asymmetrical. Decoration is either moulded-relief, openwork, drilled and, rarely, punched or engraved. Variations of a human-mask, predominantly classical-style, are common, some of which are frequently described as representing Christ or St John the Baptist, contentious descriptions.

Rare survivals testify that theses clasps, and other comparable classes (see below), were stitched through their attachment-loops, one either end of a short textile or perhaps leather strap, or knotted or stitched directly to a garment, or linked either end of a short length of chain.

With the exception of those attached to a chain, and no. 439, which has a separate eye, to which the caveat mentioned in the main introduction applies, all early post-medieval Class E single sharp-hooked clasps catalogued here are individual finds. A further two of Class E, Type 3 each retains an S-link from a chain. A pair of early post-medieval Class E, Type 1 single sharp-hooked clasps, both similar to nos 294-296, linked by a short chain, were found at Wharram Percy, North Yorkshire (Goodall 1979, fig. 56, no. 25).

Each of the linked pair of Class E, Type 1 single sharp-hooked clasps (No. 293) is crudely cut from sheeting and has simple engraved decoration that stylistically is perhaps late medieval. Two possibilities arise therefore - their attribution is possibly late medieval, which if correct broadens the usage period, or they perhaps represent later reuse of medieval metalwork. The archaeological record - particularly Norwich 1971-8 - suggests their use continued into at least the first quarter of the 17th century; however, all Class E clasps recovered by Thames Mudlarks are from secure *c*.1500 - 1550 deposits. Notwithstanding, no. 340 bears a human-mask wearing an 18th-century tie-wig, thereby seemingly extending even further their usage period.

Early post-medieval Class E, Type 1

Rectangular/Sub-rectangular

293. Copper alloy; sheeting; each clasp is one-piece; engraved. The obverse of both has several notches from which run oblique short lines, a longer line passes from one side at the juncture of the plate and hook and across to just below the loop; each attachment-loop is simply a 5mm long rectangular aperture. One hook is incomplete, being broken off at the bend. One clasp is 15 x 11mm, and the other 14 x 12mm. The chain comprises nine sheeting S-shaped links and the overall length of chain and hooks is 150mm. *North Yorkshire*. Portable Antiquities Scheme SF6654. Drawing © Donna Wreathall, photographs © Suffolk County Council Archaeological Service.

HOOKED-CLASPS & EYES

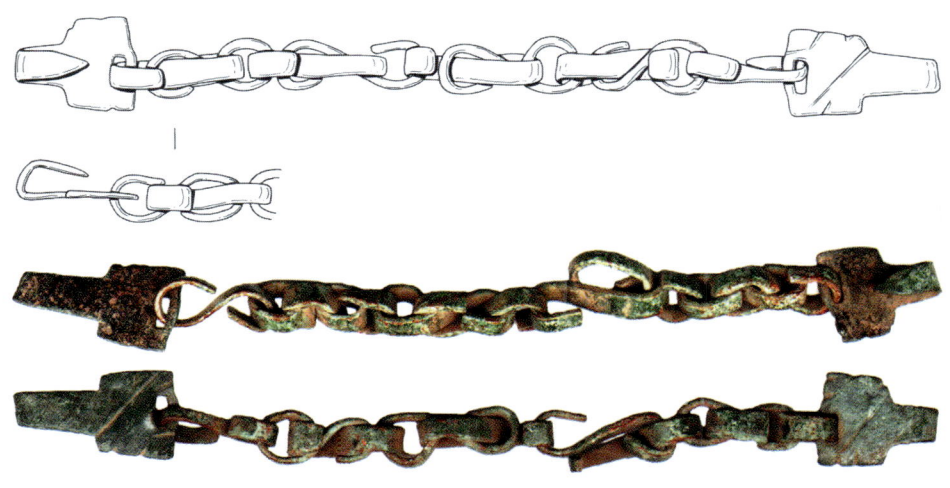

294. Copper alloy; cast; one-piece; moulded-relief. A longitudinal rectangular panel; each side edge is engrailed; a ridged ribbed collar at the juncture of the plate and hook; 30 x 14mm. *South Somerset.* Drawing © Patrick Read.

295. Copper alloy; cast; one-piece: moulded-relief. Comparable with no. 294 except less engrailing. Incomplete, hook-point broken off; 31 x 15mm. *South Somerset.* Drawing © Patrick Read.

296. Copper alloy; cast; one-piece; moulded-relief. Comparable with nos 294-295 except with two longitudinal concentric rectangular panels with a cabled border either side, and a ridged double ribbed collar; 31.68 x 16.25mm. *River Thames foreshore, London.* Drawing © Nick Griffiths.

297. Copper alloy; cast; one-piece; moulded-relief. Comparable with nos 294-296 except a six-petalled flower and a border of debased trefoils either side, and a ridged ribbed collar with two oblique bars; 27 x 13mm. *Yorkshire.* United Kingdom Detecting Finds' Database. Photographs © Ian Chubbock.

298. Copper alloy; cast; one-piece; moulded-relief. A transverse broad groove with a beaded ridge on the loop side and a plain ridge on the hook side; a swag and a ridged ribbed collar at the juncture of the plate and hook; 28.16 x 14.08mm. *River Thames foreshore, London.* Drawing © Nick Griffiths.

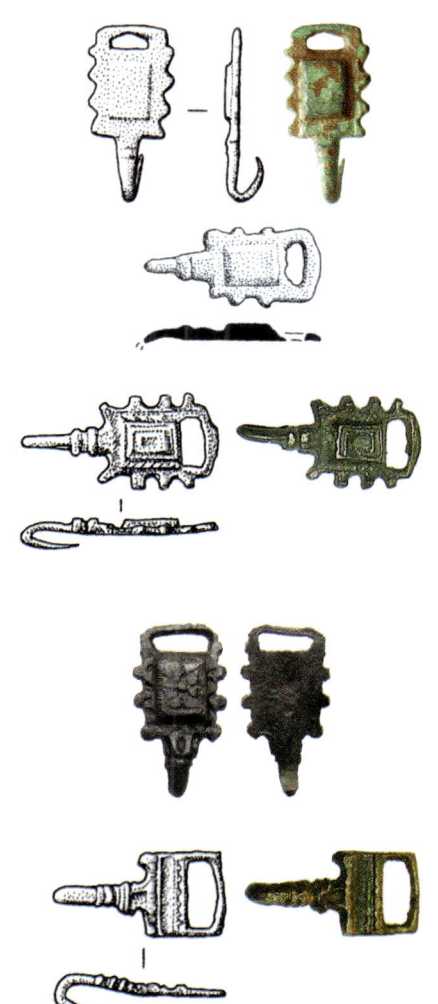

HOOKED-CLASPS & EYES

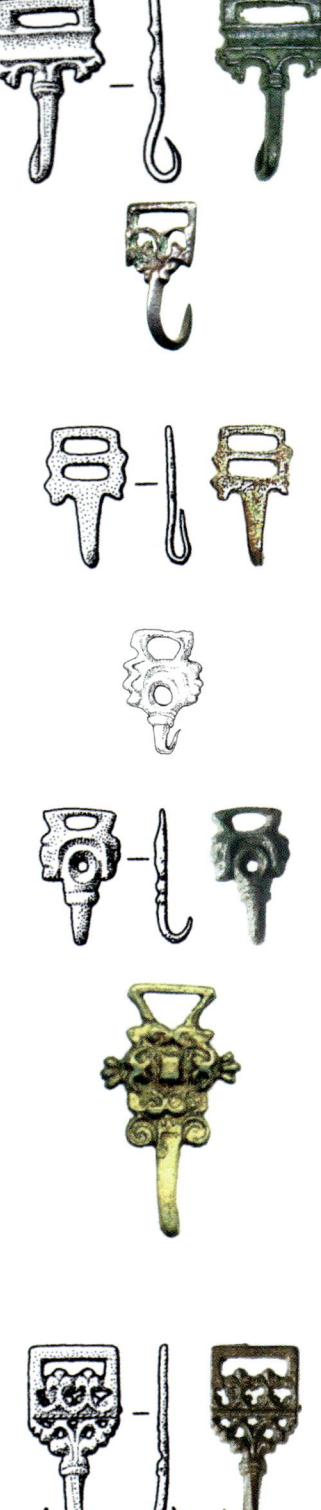

299. Copper alloy; cast; one-piece; moulded-relief. Comparable with no. 298 except both ridges are plain and fewer ribs on the collar; 30.58 x 18.34mm. *River Thames foreshore, London*. Drawing © Patrick Read.

300. Silver-gilt; cast; one-piece; moulded-relief and openwork. Two tendrils curve from the centre of a swag at the juncture of the plate and hook and conjoin with the sides of the loop; 24.9 x 14.23mm. *Buckinghamshire*. Portable Antiquities Scheme BUC-6B02F6. Photograph © Buckinghamshire County Council.

301. Copper alloy; probably cast; one-piece; undecorated apart from an openwork oval near the hook which is possibly a second attachment-loop; three slightly angular knops either side; 24 x 14mm. *River Thames foreshore, London*. Drawing © Patrick Read.

302. Copper alloy; cast; one-piece; moulded-relief and openwork. Several ridged arcs on the loop side of a central hole; engrailed side edges; a projecting ridged collar at the juncture of plate and hook; 21 x 13mm. *North Yorkshire*. Jim Halliday/063. Drawing © Anne Hodgson.

303. Copper alloy; cast; one-piece; moulded-relief and openwork. Comparable with no. 302 except the sides have V-shaped nicks and the openwork is smaller; 24.32 x 13.58mm. *North-East Kent*. Drawing © Patrick Read.

304. Copper alloy; cast; one-piece; moulded-relief. A central longitudinal rectangle flanked on all four sides by addorsed spirals; a trefoil knop either side; a projecting angular collar at the juncture of the plate and loop; a projecting collar with spirals at the juncture of the plate and hook; 40 x 22mm. *River Thames foreshore, London*.

Early post-medieval Class E, Type 2

Shield-shaped

305. Copper alloy; cast; one-piece; moulded-relief and openwork. A transverse cabled band surmounted by two fleurs-de-lis; the opposite side has a swag and a ridged ribbed collar at the juncture of the plate and hook. The openwork is partially unfettled; 35 x 15mm. *South-East Lincolnshire*. Drawing © Patrick Read.

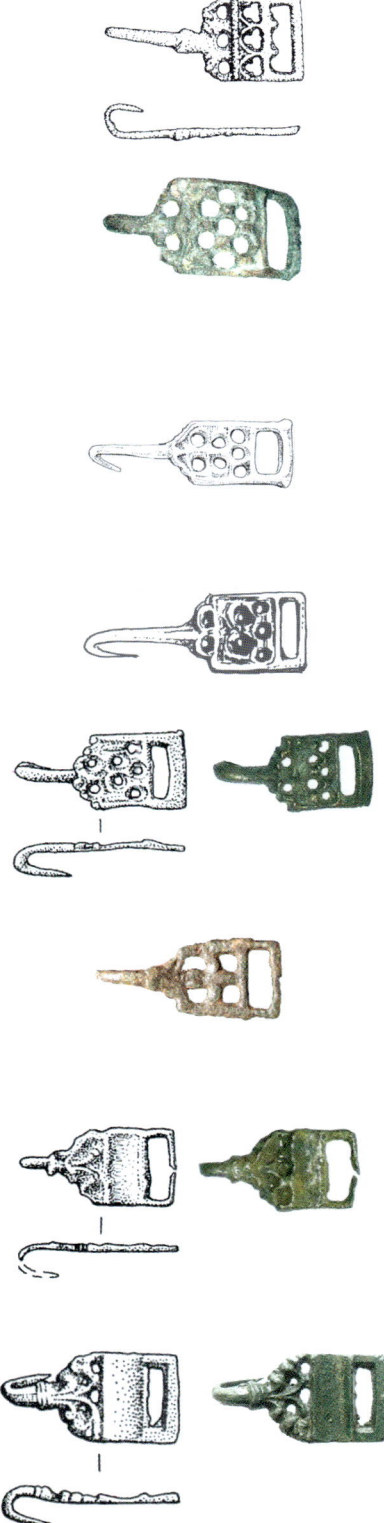

306. Copper alloy; cast; one-piece; moulded-relief and openwork. Comparable with no. 305 except the swag is shallower and has less openwork; 32 x 14mm. *North Yorkshire*. Jim Halliday.

307. Copper alloy; cast; one-piece; moulded-relief and openwork. Resembles a six-petalled flower; a raised rim around each hole, a shallow swag at the juncture of the plate and hook; slightly distorted; 33 x 15mm. *Norfolk*. Portable Antiquities Scheme NMS-900C42. Photograph © Norfolk Museums and Archaeology Service.

308. Copper alloy; cast; one-piece; moulded-relief and openwork. Possible foliate; a small rounded knop on each external apex of the loop; 33 x 11mm. *North Yorkshire*. Jim Halliday. Drawing © Anne Hodgson.

309. Copper alloy; cast; one-piece; moulded-relief and openwork. Possible foliate; a pierced collar at the juncture of the plate and hook; 36 x 15mm. *North Yorkshire*. Jim Halliday/025. Drawing © Anne Hodgson.

310. Copper alloy; cast; one-piece; moulded-relief and openwork. Comparable with no. 309; 28 x 13mm. *River Thames foreshore, London*. Drawing © Nick Griffiths.

311. Copper alloy; cast; one-piece; moulded-relief, punched and openwork. A fleur-de-lis; annulets around the sides of the plate; a swag and a ridged double-pellet collar at the juncture of the plate and hook; 33 x 14mm. *Cornwall*. Portable Antiquities Scheme CORN-7416E5. Photograph © Cornwall County Council.

312. Copper alloy; cast; one-piece; moulded-relief. Comparable with no. 313 except a transverse broad groove with a swag and a ridged collar at the juncture of the plate and hook. Incomplete, hook-point broken off and loop fractured; 26 x 14mm. *River Thames foreshore, London*. Drawing © Nick Griffiths.

313. Copper alloy; cast; one-piece; moulded-relief and openwork; sporadic gilding. Comparable with no. 312 except a ribbed collar; the attachment-aperture and openwork is slightly unfettled; 29 x 15mm. *South-West Wiltshire*. Drawing © Patrick Read.

314. Copper alloy; cast; one-piece; moulded-relief. A transverse broad groove and a swag of pellets and a ridged collar at the juncture of the plate and hook. Incomplete, hook-point broken off; 30 x 19mm. *South-West Lincolnshire*. Portable Antiquities Scheme LIN-CFC354. Photograph © and courtesy of the Portable Antiquities Scheme.

315. Copper alloy; cast; one-piece; moulded-relief and openwork. A small flower and foliate; a ridged double-pellet collar at the juncture of the plate and hook. Incomplete, hook broken off; 20 x 16mm. *East Yorkshire*. Jim Halliday/034. Drawing © Anne Hodgson.

316. Copper alloy; cast; one-piece; moulded-relief and openwork. Possibly a human facing-mask, a ridged collar at the juncture of the plate and hook; the loop is inset from the sides; 26 x 10mm. *South-East Lincolnshire*. Drawing © Patrick Read.

317. Copper alloy; cast; one-piece; moulded-relief and openwork. Three debased fleurs-de-lis within a shield surmounted by a crown; engrailed edges; the loop is slightly inset from the sides. Incomplete, hook broken off and openwork partially unfettled; 27 x 16.6. *South Somerset*. Drawing © Patrick Read.

318. Copper alloy; cast; one-piece; moulded-relief and openwork. Comparable with no. 317 except the loop is smaller and inset farther from the sides, a debased swag and a ridged collar at the juncture of the plate and hook. Incomplete, hook-point broken off; 35 x 15mm. *River Thames foreshore, London*. Drawing © Patrick Read.

Early post-medieval Class E, Type 3

Circular/Sub-circular

319. Copper alloy; cast; one-piece; shallow convex; moulded-relief. A solid-domed boss inscribed with the black-letter sacred monogram IHS within a cabled border; 31.5 x 13.5mm. *South-East Dorset*. Drawing © Patrick Read.

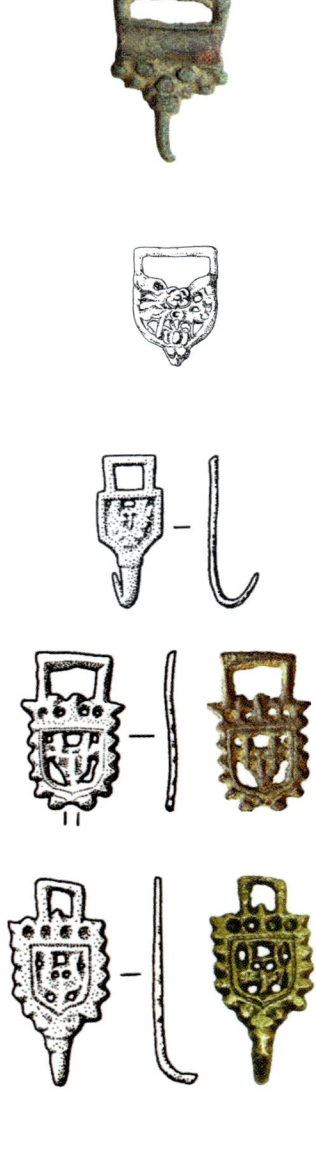

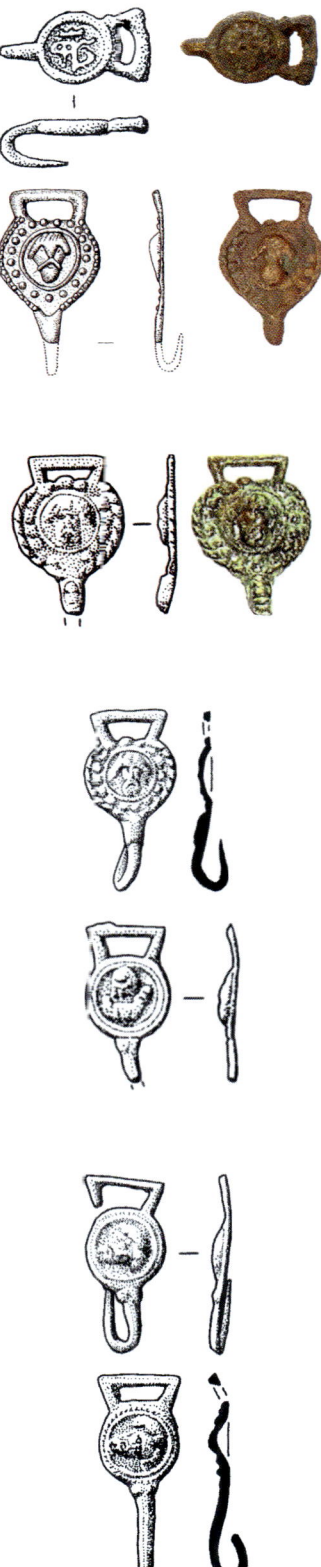

320. Copper alloy; cast; one-piece; moulded-relief. Inscribed with a stylised black-letter sacred monogram IHS surmounted by a coronet within a circle; 25.1 x 13.98mm. *Fly-tip, East London.* Drawing © Nick Griffiths.

321. Copper alloy; cast; one-piece; shallow convex; moulded-relief. A solid-domed boss bearing a classical-style human facing-mask within two concentric circles, the inner linear and the outer pellets, and a beaded border. Incomplete, hook broken off; 26 x 17mm. *Northamptonshire.* Peter Woods CH23. Drawing © Roy Turland, photograph © Peter Woods.

322. Copper alloy; cast; one-piece; shallow convex; moulded-relief. A solid-domed boss bearing a classical-style human facing-mask within two concentric circles, the inner linear and the outer pellets, and a cabled border; a ridged collar depicting what is perhaps a tiny human facing-mask at the juncture of the plate and hook. Incomplete, hook broken off; 29 x 19mm. *River Thames foreshore, London.* Drawing © Patrick Read.

323. Copper alloy; cast; one-piece; convex; moulded-relief. Comparable with no. 322 except with a hollow-domed boss and a plain ridged collar; 38 x 16mm. *South-East Lincolnshire.* Drawing © Patrick Read.

324. Copper alloy; cast; one-piece; convex; moulded-relief. A solid-domed boss bearing a classical-style human facing-mask within a beaded border; a ridged collar at the juncture of the plate and hook; a casting sprue on the outside edge of the loop. Incomplete, hook-point broken off; 26.5 x 14mm. *South-East Lincolnshire.* Drawing © Patrick Read.

325. Copper alloy; cast; one-piece; convex; moulded-relief. A hollow-domed boss bearing a classical-style human facing-mask within a beaded border; a ridged double-pellet collar at the junction of the plate and hook. Loop fractured; 31 x 13mm. *South Somerset.* Drawing © Patrick Read.

326. Copper alloy; cast; one-piece; convex; moulded-relief. Comparable with no. 325 except the beaded border is more pronounced and the hook has a longer shank; 37 x 15mm. *Suffolk.* Drawing © Patrick Read.

HOOKED-CLASPS & EYES

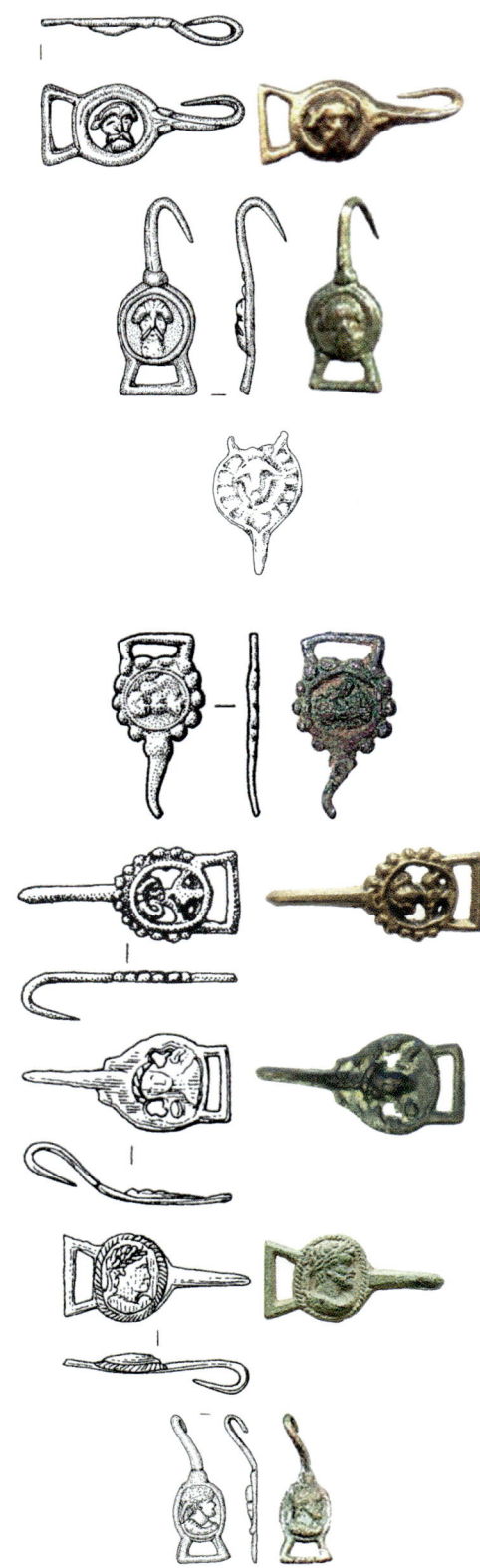

327. Copper alloy; cast; one-piece; convex; moulded-relief. Comparable with no. 326 except a linear border; 33 x 13mm. *Northamptonshire.* Peter Woods CH2. Drawing © Roy Turland, photograph © Peter Woods.

328. Copper alloy; cast; one-piece; convex; moulded-relief. A solid-domed boss bearing a classical-style human facing-mask within a linear border; a ridged collar at the juncture of the plate and hook; 33 x 12mm. *Northamptonshire.* Peter Woods CH2R. Drawing © Roy Turland, photograph © Peter Woods.

329. Copper alloy; cast; one-piece; moulded-relief. A possible human facing-mask bordered by sub-rectangular concave segments. Incomplete, hook-point and loop broken off; 24 x 11mm. *East Yorkshire.* Jim Halliday/041. Drawing © Anne Hodgson.

330. Copper alloy; cast; one-piece; moulded-relief. A classical-style human facing-mask within a linear circle and a beaded and engrailed edge; a ridged collar at the junction of the plate and hook. Incomplete, hook distorted and point broken off; 31.5 x 15.5mm. *East Devon.* Drawing © Patrick Read.

331. Copper alloy; cast; one-piece; moulded-relief and openwork. A human facing-bust within a linear circle and a beaded and engrailed edge; 34.4 x 16.02mm. *River Thames foreshore, London.* Drawing © Nick Griffiths.

332. Copper alloy; cast; one-piece; moulded-relief and openwork. A human facing-bust wearing a 16th century hat; a projecting angular collar at the juncture of the plate and hook; 35.5 x 17mm. *South-East Dorset.* Drawing © Nick Griffiths.

333. Copper alloy; cast; one-piece; convex; moulded-relief. A solid-domed boss bearing a classical-style human profile-mask right, within a cabled border; 34 x 16mm. *South-East Dorset.* Drawing © Nick Griffiths.

334. Copper alloy; cast; one-piece; convex; moulded-relief. A classical-style human profile-mask right; a ridged collar at the juncture of the plate and hook; 25 x 8.5mm. *Northamptonshire.* Peter Woods CH1. Drawing © Roy Turland, photograph © Peter Woods.

HOOKED CLASPS & EYES

335. Copper alloy; cast; one-piece; moulded-relief. A classical-style human profile-mask left, within a linear border; a projecting ridged collar at the juncture of the plate and hook; a casting sprue on the outside edge of the loop; 38 x 16mm. *South-East Dorset*. Drawing © Nick Griffiths.

336. Copper alloy; cast; one-piece; moulded-relief. A classical-style profile human-mask left; a ridged double-pellet collar at the juncture of the plate and hook. Incomplete, hook broken off; 24 x 14mm. *North Yorkshire*. Jim Halliday/017. Drawing © Anne Hodgson.

337. Copper alloy; cast; one-piece; moulded-relief. Triple-branched foliate emerging from a median stem, either side of which is a human profile-bust facing inwards. Incomplete, hook-point broken off and hook distorted, much corroded; 34 x 18mm. *Norfolk*. Portable Antiquities Scheme NMS-F68850. Photograph © Norfolk Museums and Archaeological Service.

338. Copper alloy; cast; one-piece; moulded-relief. Two confronted profile helmeted human masks, each within a transversely grooved frame resembling a vine and foliate which extends into a projecting collar at the juncture of the plate and hook. Several casting flaws in the plate; 37.5 x 19mm. *Norfolk*. Photographs © Steven Carter.

339. Copper alloy; cast; one-piece; moulded-relief and openwork. A bearded human profile-mask left, wearing a 16th century hat, within a cabled border. Incomplete, hook distorted and point broken off, corroded; 30.5 x 21.2mm. *Sussex*. Portable Antiquities Scheme SUSS-2E8753. Photographs © Portable Antiquities Scheme.

340. Copper alloy; cast; one-piece; moulded-relief and openwork. A human profile-mask right, wearing an 18th-century tie-wig, within a cabled border; a stylised swag and a ridged collar at the juncture of the plate and hook; 37.4 x 21.1mm. *Hertfordshire*. Portable Antiquities Scheme BH-4058D2. Photograph © St Albans Museum.

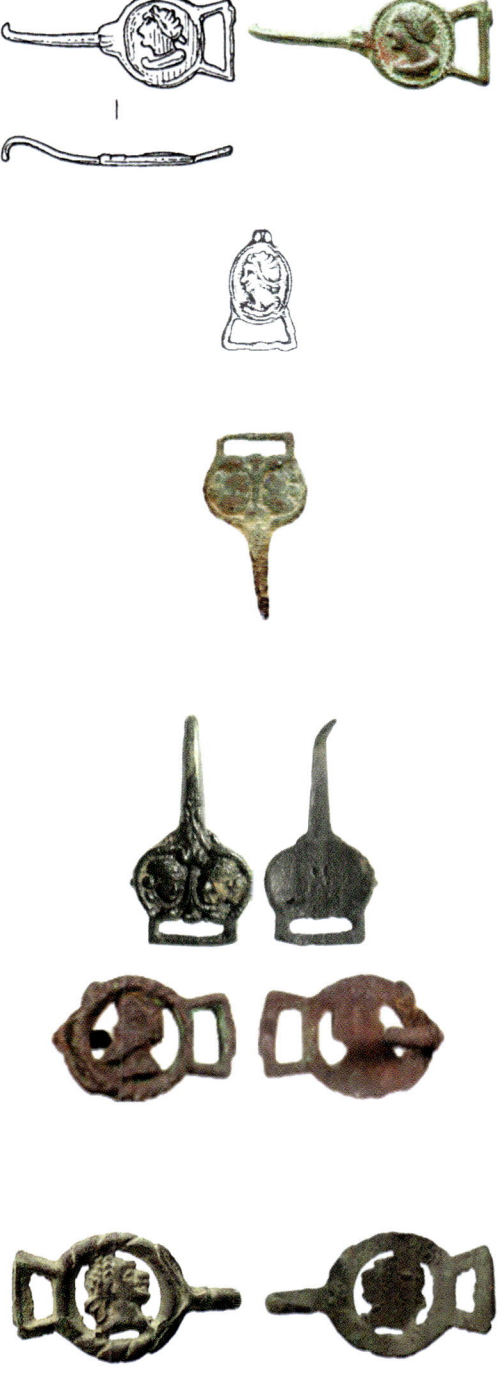

HOOKED-CLASPS & EYES

341. Copper alloy; cast; one-piece; moulded-relief and openwork. A small lozenge on a septum bar; adjoining the lozenge is a possible small flower, a petal of which forms a rounded knop inside the loop; a rounded knop, one of which is pierced, either side at the juncture of the plate and loop; a swag with a small flower at the juncture of the plate and hook; 35.1 x 14.1mm. *Hertfordshire*. Portable Antiquities Scheme BH-5DCC23. Photographs © St Albans Museum.

342. Copper alloy; cast; one-piece; moulded-relief. A four-petalled double rose. Incomplete, hook-point broken off; 37 x 16mm. *North Yorkshire*. Jim Halliday/021. Drawing © Anne Hodgson.

343. Copper alloy; cast; one-piece; moulded-relief and openwork. A four-petalled rose with sepals; an abraded ridged collar at the juncture of the plate and hook. Incomplete, hook-point broken off, openwork is possibly casting flaws; 30 x 12mm. *Staffordshire*. Drawing © Patrick Read.

344. Copper alloy; cast; one-piece; moulded-relief. A five-petalled rose within a cusped circle; 25 x 10mm. *Northamptonshire*. Peter Woods CH26. Drawing © Roy Turland, photograph © Peter Woods.

345. Copper alloy; cast; one-piece; convex; moulded-relief. A hollow-domed boss bearing a five-petalled double rose; hook distorted; 34 x 14mm. *South-East Dorset*. Drawing © Patrick Read, photograph © Ken Wheatley.

346. Copper alloy; cast; one-piece; convex; moulded-relief. Comparable with no. 345 except within a cabled border; 34 x 14. *River Thames foreshore, London*. Drawing © Patrick Read.

347. Copper alloy; cast; one-piece; convex; moulded-relief. A five-petalled rose within a circle of pellets and a linear border. Incomplete, loop and hook-point broken off; 35 x 17. *Northamptonshire*. Peter Woods CH13. Drawing © Roy Turland, photograph © Peter Woods.

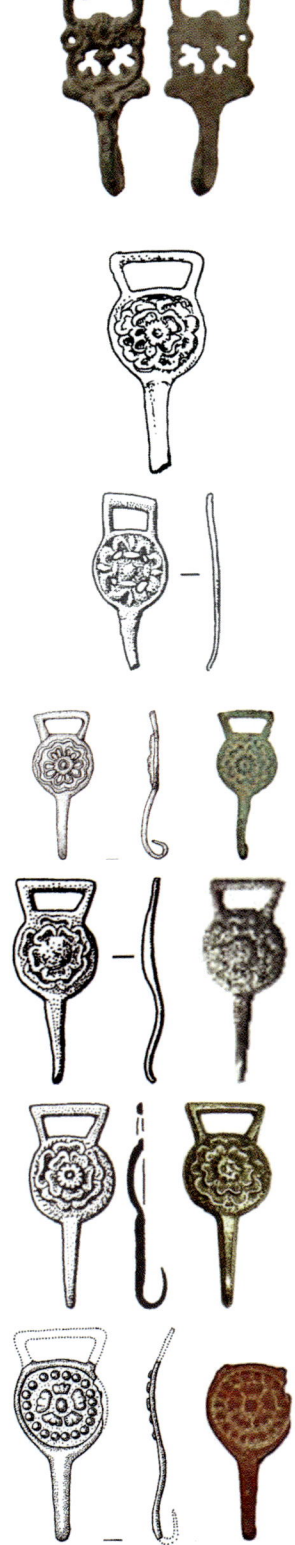

HOOKED-CLASPS & EYES

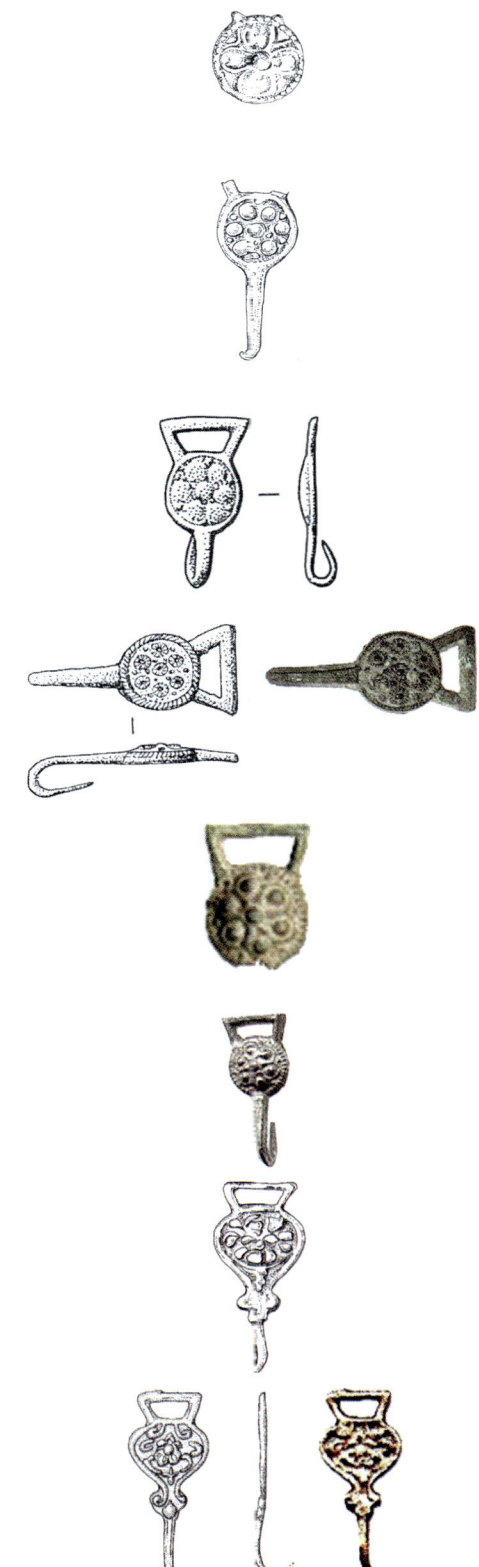

348. Copper alloy; cast; one-piece; moulded-relief. A four-petalled flower within a beaded border. Incomplete, loop and hook broken off; D15mm. *East Yorkshire*. Jim Halliday/ 037. Drawing © Anne Hodgson.

349. Copper alloy; cast; one-piece; moulded-relief. Resembles a six-petalled flower; a central pellet and a circle of six pellets, and tiny pellets in the interstices, within a linear border. Incomplete, loop broken off and hook distorted; 30 x 13mm. *North Yorkshire*. Jim Halliday. Drawing © Anne Hodgson.

350. Copper alloy; cast; one-piece; convex; moulded-relief. Resembles a six-petalled flower; a hollow-domed boss bearing a central small flower and a circle of small flowers, tiny pellets in the interstices, within a linear border; decoration abraded; 29 x 13mm. *South-East Lincolnshire*. Drawing © Patrick Read.

351. Copper alloy; cast; one-piece; moulded-relief. Comparable with no. 350 except within a cabled border; 34 x 15mm. *River Thames foreshore, London*. Drawing © Nick Griffiths.

352. Copper alloy; cast; one-piece; convex; moulded-relief. A solid-domed boss bearing a six-petalled flower, each petal enclosing a pellet, within a beaded border. Incomplete, hook broken off; 18 x 14mm. *Cambridgeshire*. United Kingdom Detecting Finds' Database 4321. Photographs © Cheryl Hodgson.

353. Copper alloy; cast; one-piece; convex; moulded-relief. Comparable with no. 352 except the central pellet is surrounded by six tiny pellets; 33.1 x 14.3mm. *North Yorkshire*.

354. Copper alloy; cast; one-piece; moulded-relief. A multi-petalled flower within a linear border; a trefoil collar at the juncture of the plate and hook; hook distorted; 31.5 x 15mm. *North Yorkshire*. Jim Halliday. Drawing © Anne Hodgson.

355. Copper alloy; cast; one-piece; moulded-relief. Comparable with no. 354 except the flower is different. Incomplete, hook-point broken off; 25 x 10mm. *Northamptonshire*. Peter Woods CH1R. Drawing © Roy Turland, photograph © Peter Woods.

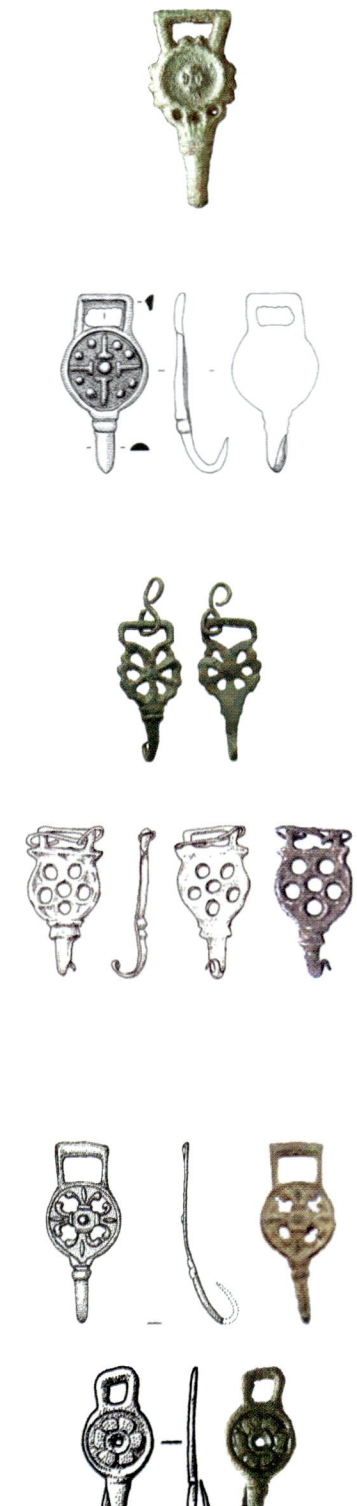

356. Copper alloy; cast; one-piece; moulded-relief. A quatrefoil within a recessed plate with a beaded border and an engrailed edge; a swag with three small pits one of which has pierced the metal; a ridged ribbed collar at the juncture of the plate and hook. Incomplete, hook-point broken off; 33 x 13mm. *Norfolk*. Portable Antiquities Scheme NMS-E71C50. Photograph © Norfolk Museums and Archaeology Service.

357. Copper alloy; cast; one-piece; moulded-relief. A pellet and four radiating T-shaped arms forming an equal-armed cross, two pellets in each quadrant, all within a linear border; the edges of the plate and loop are incised; a ribbed collar at the juncture of the plate and hook; the inside of the loop is unfettled; 30 x 14.3mm. *Isle of White*. Portable Antiquities Scheme IOW-2006-88-14. Drawing © Isle of White Council.

358. Copper alloy; cast; one-piece; moulded-relief and openwork. Resembles a six-petalled flower; a ridged ribbed collar at the juncture of the plate and hook. A circular-section wire S-link from a separate chain is attached to the loop; 31.9 x 14.9mm. *South Yorkshire*. Portable Antiquities Scheme SWYOR-C1A0. Photographs © West Yorkshire Archaeology Service.

359. Copper alloy; cast; one-piece; moulded-relief and openwork. Resembles a six-petalled flower; a central disc surrounded by five discs; a projecting ridged and ribbed collar at the juncture of the plate and loop; hook-point distorted. A circular-section wire S-link from a separate chain is attached to both sides of the loop; 30 x 15.5mm. Jim Halliday/PM1. *North Yorkshire*. Drawing © Anne Hodgson, photograph © Jim Halliday.

360. Copper alloy; cast; one-piece; moulded-relief and openwork. A cross flory with a central pellet; a projecting ridged and ribbed collar at the juncture of the plate and hook. Incomplete, hook-point broken off; 25 x 10mm. *Northamptonshire*. Peter Woods CH5. Drawing © Roy Turland, photograph © Peter Woods.

361. Copper alloy; cast; one-piece; moulded-relief and openwork. A six-petalled flower within a circle; a ridged collar at the juncture of the plate and hook; a central drilled-hole perhaps formerly held a decorative feature; 29.99 x 17.3mm. *South Gloucestershire*. Drawing © Patrick Read.

HOOKED-CLASPS & EYES

362. Copper alloy; cast; one-piece; moulded-relief. A cabled border; a swag at the juncture of the plate and hook. Incomplete, hook broken off; a central torn hole perhaps formerly held a separate decorative feature; 25 x 16mm. *North Yorkshire*. Jim Halliday/015. Drawing © Anne Hodgson.

363. Copper alloy; cast; one-piece; moulded-relief and openwork. A six-petalled rose within two linear concentric circles bordered by a beaded and engrailed edge; a projecting ridged and ribbed collar at the juncture of the plate and hook. Incomplete, hook-point broken off and loop fractured; 41 x 18mm. *River Thames foreshore, London*. Drawing © Patrick Read.

364. Copper alloy; cast; one-piece; moulded-relief and openwork. Comparable with no. 363 except one linear circle and a projecting ridged double-pellet collar; 30 x 15mm. *North Yorkshire*. Jim Halliday/046. Drawing © Anne Hodgson.

365. Copper alloy; cast; one-piece; moulded-relief and openwork. Comparable with nos 363-364 except a plain ridged collar. Incomplete, hook-point broken off; 34.46 x 16.93mm. *North-West Kent*. Drawing © Patrick Read.

366. Copper alloy; cast; one-piece; moulded-relief and openwork. Comparable with nos 363-365 except a six-pointed star; 35.63 x 15.37mm. *Kent*. Drawing © Patrick Read.

367. Copper alloy; cast; one-piece; convex; moulded-relief. Resembles a multi-petalled rose, a hollow-domed boss bearing a quatrefoil of pellets and a central pellet, the outer one within an annulet; a multi-petalled border with an engrailed edge; 31.91 x 14.89mm. *South-East Dorset*. Drawing © Patrick Read.

368. Copper alloy; cast; one-piece; moulded-relief and openwork. A six-petalled flower within a linear circle and a beaded and engrailed edge; a small rounded knop either side; a stylised swag and a projecting narrow ridged collar at the juncture of the plate and hook; 32.25 x 20.56mm. *South Somerset*. Drawing © Nick Griffiths.

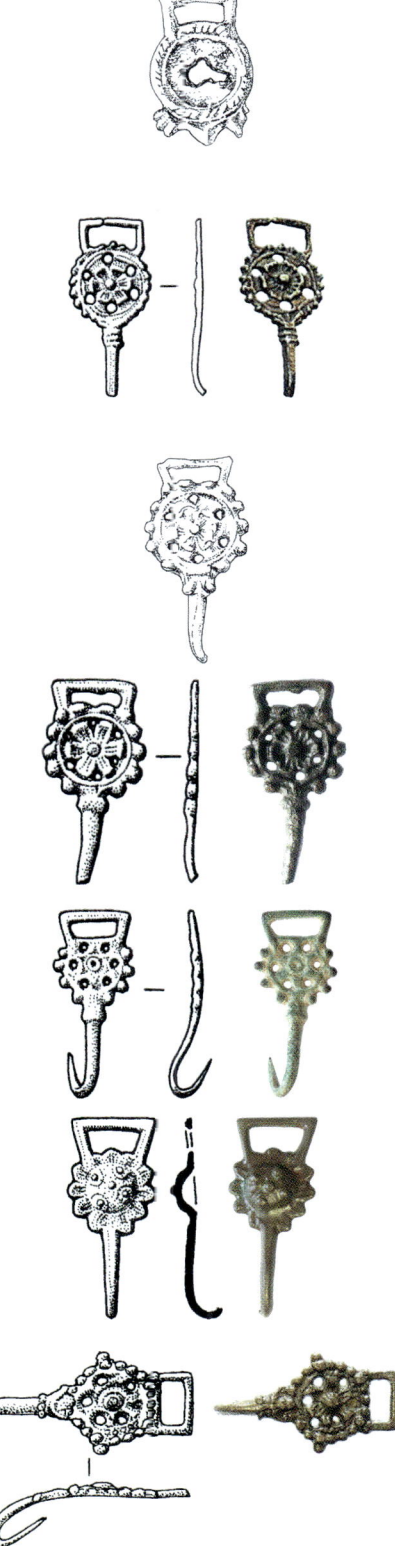

HOOKED-CLASPS & EYES

369. Copper alloy; cast; one-piece; moulded-relief and openwork. A multi-petalled flower within a beaded and engrailed edge; 26 x 17mm. *Northamptonshire*. Peter Woods CH3R. Drawing © Roy Turland, photograph © Peter Woods.

370. Copper alloy; cast; one-piece; moulded-relief and openwork. An equal-armed cross with a central pellet within a linear circle; a beaded and engrailed edge; partially unfettled; 32 x 16mm. *River Thames foreshore, London*. Drawing © Patrick Read.

371. Copper alloy; cast; one-piece; moulded-relief and openwork. Comparable with no. 370 except less openwork and the attachment-loop is different; hook distorted; 37 x 18mm. *Norfolk*. Portable Antiquities Scheme NMS-9BAC01. Photograph © Norfolk Museums and Archaeological Service.

372. Copper alloy; cast; one-piece; openwork, otherwise undecorated. An engrailed edge; 37 x 17mm. *East Devon*. Drawing © Patrick Read.

373. Copper alloy; cast; one-piece; moulded-relief and openwork. A six-petalled flower within a wreath and an engrailed edge; a swag and a ridged collar at the juncture of the plate and hook; hook distorted; 37.83 x 17mm. *South Somerset*. Drawing © Patrick Read.

374. Copper alloy; cast; one-piece; moulded-relief and openwork. A spray of small flowers and foliate on two stalks; a ridged collar at the juncture of the plate and hook; 30 x 16mm. *Kent*. United Kingdom Detecting Finds' Database 9863. Photographs © Patrick Thorn.

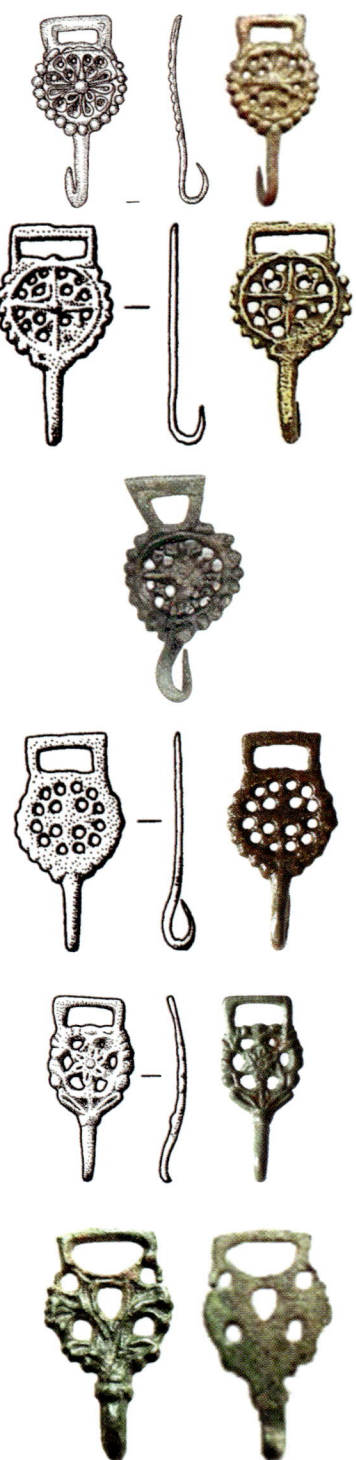

375. Copper alloy; cast; one-piece; moulded-relief and openwork. A spray of three small flowers whose stalks radiate from a pellet near the loop, within a beaded and slightly engrailed edge; a projecting ridged double-pellet collar at the juncture of the plate and hook; 38 x 16.5mm. *Buckinghamshire*. Drawing © Patrick Read.

376. Copper alloy; cast; one-piece; moulded-relief and openwork. A heart with a raised edge bordered by a beaded and engrailed edge; a projecting ridged collar at the juncture of the plate and hook; 32 x 17mm. *East Sussex*. United Kingdom Detecting Finds' Database 9603. Photographs © Dave Mayes.

377. Copper alloy; cast; one-piece; moulded-relief and openwork. A human facing-mask within a seven-pointed curved-edged star the points of which form peripheral equidistant small rounded knops; a projecting ridged and ribbed collar at the juncture of the plate and hook; 34 x 16.1mm. *Herefordshire*. Portable Antiquities Scheme HESH-0FD797. Photographs © Birmingham City Council.

378. Copper alloy; cast; one-piece; moulded-relief and openwork. Comparable with no. 377, 379-390 except a six-petalled flower; hook distorted; 25 x 13mm. *Northamptonshire*. Peter Woods CH8. Drawing © Roy Turland, photograph © Peter Woods.

379. Copper alloy; cast; one-piece; moulded-relief and openwork. Comparable with nos 377-378, 380-390 except a five-petalled rose. Incomplete, hook broken off and openwork is partially unfettled; 23.5 x 19mm. *Northamptonshire*. Peter Woods CH24. Drawing © Roy Turland, photograph © Peter Woods.

380. Copper alloy; cast; one-piece; moulded-relief and openwork. Comparable with nos 377-379, 381-390 except a fleur-de-lis within a linear circle; 37.66 x 18.24mm. Incomplete, hook-point broken off. *Staffordshire*. Drawing © Patrick Read.

381. Copper alloy; cast; one-piece; moulded-relief and openwork. Comparable with nos 377-380, 382-390 except a curved-edged triangle and without an openwork border; 39 x 19.5mm. *North Yorkshire*. Jim Halliday/76. Drawing © Anne Hodgson.

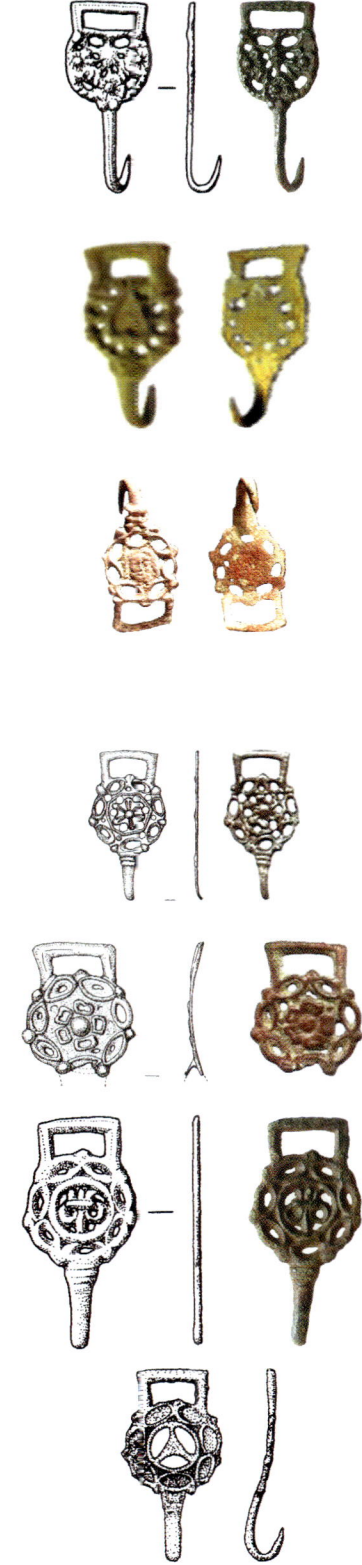

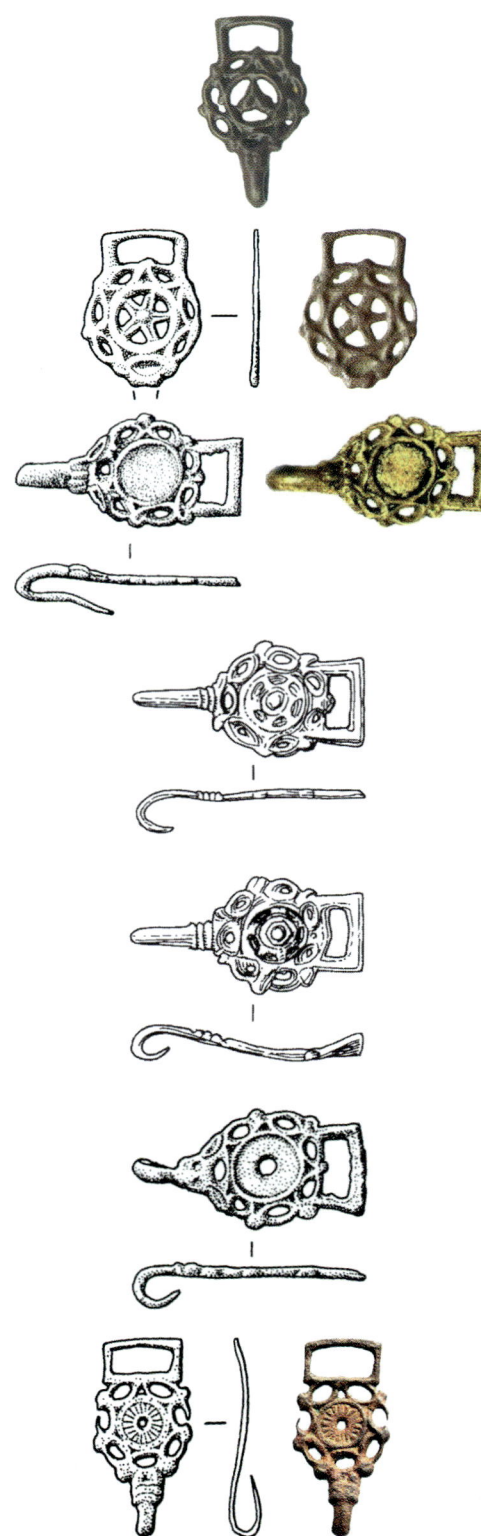

382. Copper alloy; cast; one-piece; moulded-relief and openwork. Comparable with no. 377-381, 383-390 except a heart and peripheral openwork; partially unfettled openwork; 32 x 19mm. *East Yorkshire*. Photographs © Stan Raymond.

383. Copper alloy; cast; one-piece; moulded-relief and openwork. Comparable with nos 377-382, 384-390 except a five-pointed star; 25.67 x 18.88mm. Incomplete, hook broken off. *Staffordshire*. Drawing © Patrick Read.

384. Copper alloy; cast; one-piece; moulded-relief and openwork. Comparable with nos 377-383, 385-390 except with a plain centre and a projecting ridged fluted collar; 38 x 20mm. *River Thames foreshore, London*. Drawing © Nick Griffiths.

385. Copper alloy; cast; one-piece; moulded-relief and openwork. Comparable with nos 377-384, 386-390 except a six-petalled rose and a ridged ribbed collar; 38 x 20mm. *South-East Dorset*. Drawing © Nick Griffiths.

386. Copper alloy; cast; one-piece; moulded-relief and openwork. Comparable with nos 377-385, 387-390 except a central small drilled-hole may have held a seperate decorative feature; 38 x 20mm. *South-East Dorset*. Drawing © Nick Griffiths.

387. Copper alloy; cast; one-piece; moulded-relief and openwork. Comparable with nos 377-386, 388-390 except the circle is undecorated and has a larger hole, and a swag and projecting ridged collar at the juncture of the plate and hook; 38 x 20mm. *River Thames foreshore, London*. Drawing © Nick Griffiths.

388. Copper alloy; cast; one-piece; moulded-relief and openwork. Comparable with nos 377-387, 389-390 except a multi-spoked wheel and a projecting ridged and ribbed collar. Incomplete, edge broken in places; 33 x 16mm. *East Devon*. Drawing © Patrick Read.

HOOKED-CLASPS & EYES

389. Copper alloy; cast; one-piece; moulded-relief and openwork. Comparable with nos 377-388, 390 except a flat-topped boss and a large swag; 45 x 21mm. *River Thames foreshore, London.* Drawing © Nick Griffiths.

390. Copper alloy; cast; one-piece; moulded-relief and openwork. Comparable with nos 377-389 except a central raised quatrefoil, 46 x 21mm. *Hampshire.* Portable Antiquities Scheme HAMP-51FB76. Drawing and photograph © Winchester Museum Service.

391. Copper alloy; cast; one-piece; moulded-relief. Resembles a seven-petalled rose with sepals; a raised linear circle bordered by seven pits; a projecting ridged and ribbed collar at the juncture of the plate and hook; 30 x 18.5mm. *South-East Dorset.* Drawing © Patrick Read.

392. Copper alloy; cast; one-piece; moulded-relief. Comparable with nos 391, 393-397 except a five-petalled rose and a projecting plain ridged collar; 41.58 x 19.28mm. *Staffordshire.* Drawing © Patrick Read.

393. Copper alloy; cast; one-piece; moulded-relief and openwork. Comparable with nos 391-392, 394-397 except a quatrefoil and two openwork holes; several peripheral pits are possibly unfettled; 32 x 17mm. *East Yorkshire.* Photographs © Stan Raymond.

394. Copper alloy cast; one-piece; moulded-relief and openwork. Comparable with nos 391-393, 395-397 except more openwork, a double-ridged collar and a shorter hook. Incomplete, loop broken off and several casting flaws in the quatrefoil; 24 x 15mm. *Isle of White.* Photographs © Mary Winch.

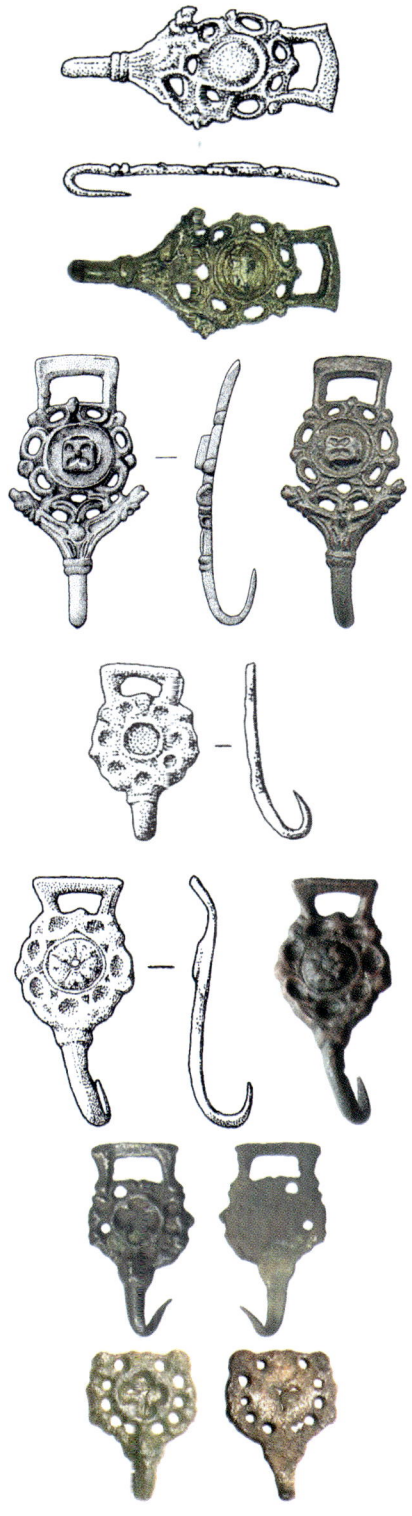

HOOKED-CLASPS & EYES

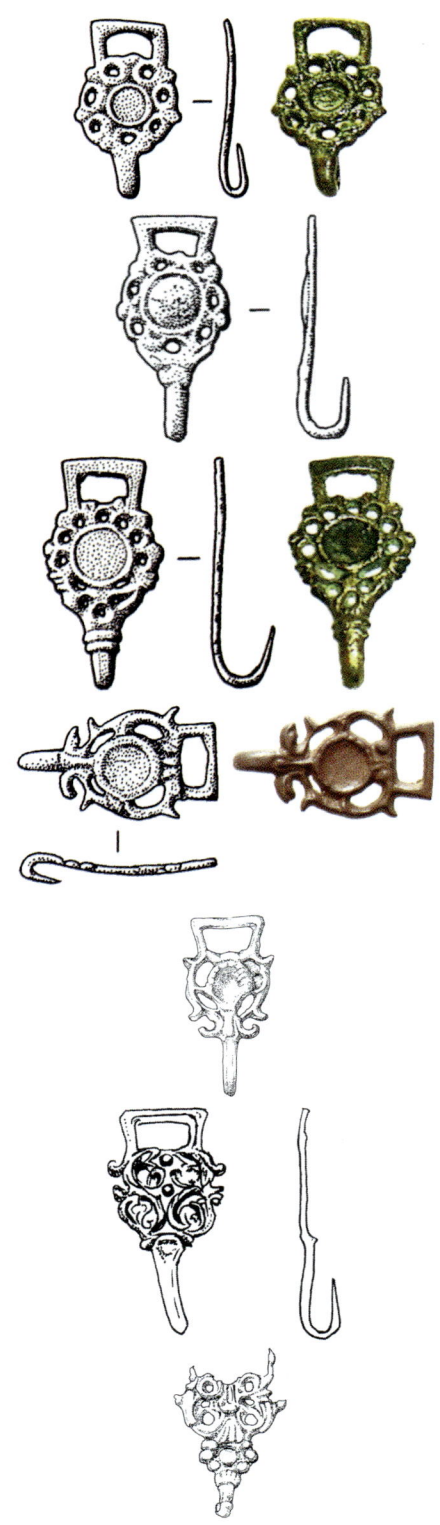

395. Copper alloy cast; one-piece; moulded-relief and openwork. Comparable with nos 391-394, 396-397 except without a collar and the holes are open; 30 x 18.5mm. *South-East Dorset*. Drawing © Patrick Read.

396. Copper alloy; cast; one-piece; moulded-relief and openwork. Comparable with nos 391-395, 397 except a shallow-domed boss within the circle, a swag and a ridged collar; 38 x 19mm. *South-East Lincolnshire*. Drawing © Patrick Read.

397. Copper alloy; cast; one-piece; moulded-relief and openwork. Comparable with nos 391-396 except a projecting ridged and ribbed collar; 39 x 20mm. *River Thames foreshore, London*. Drawing © Patrick Read.

398. Copper alloy; cast; one-piece; moulded-relief and openwork. A raised linear circle which perhaps originally had a beaded edge; two elongated angular knops either side and a swag at the juncture of the plate and hook; a pellet either side of two longitudinal voided ridges near the loop. 31.21 x 17.9mm. *South Somerset*. Drawing © Nick Griffiths.

399. Copper alloy; cast; one-piece; moulded-relief and openwork. Comparable with no. 398 except a beaded border to the upper half of the circle; 30 x 14mm. *North Yorkshire*. Jim Halliday/51. Drawing © Anne Hodgson.

400. Copper alloy; cast; one-piece; moulded-relief and openwork. Foliate, two pellets and spirals, the ends of which form two rounded knops either side; a projecting ridged collar at the juncture of the plate and hook; 38 x 20mm. *North Yorkshire*. Jim Halliday/019. Drawing © Anne Hodgson.

401. Copper alloy; cast; one-piece; moulded-relief and openwork. An indeterminate design, possibly scrolls and foliate; a small pointed knop either side; a six-petalled flower and a ridged fluted collar at the juncture of the plate and hook. Incomplete, loop broken off; 28 x 18mm. *North Yorkshire*. Jim Halliday/58. Drawing © Garry Kelly.

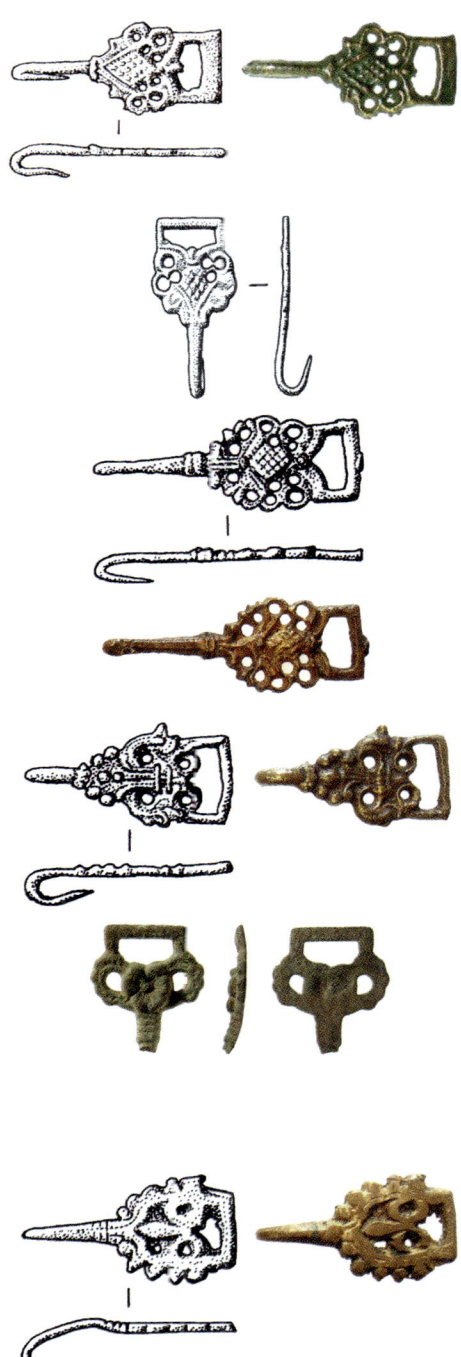

402. Copper alloy; cast; one-piece; moulded-relief and openwork. A chequered lozenge (frequently interpreted as a pineapple or thistle but is more likely a pinecone) within an engrailed edge; a ridged collar at the juncture of the plate and hook; 35 x 16mm. *River Thames foreshore, London.* Drawing © Nick Griffiths.

403. Copper alloy; cast; one-piece; moulded-relief and openwork. Comparable with no. 402 except less openwork and a projecting shallow collar; 35 x 16mm. *South-East Lincolnshire.* Drawing © Patrick Read.

404. Copper alloy; cast; one-piece; moulded-relief and openwork. Comparable with nos 402-403 except more openwork and a pellet and chevron surmounted by a hatched lozenge, and a small swag and a projecting ridged and ribbed collar; a casting sprue on the outside edge of the loop; 43.06 x 16.51mm. *River Thames foreshore, London.* Drawing © Nick Griffiths.

405. Copper alloy; cast; one-piece; moulded-relief and openwork. A swag; a multi-pellet collar at the juncture of the plate and hook; 32.3 x 17.8mm. *River Thames foreshore, London.* Drawing © Nick Griffiths.

406. Copper alloy; cast; one-piece; moulded-relief and openwork. A five-petalled rose; linear and oblique lines around each side; an engrailed edge; a ribbed collar at the juncture of the plate and hook. Incomplete, hook broken off; 20.2 x 17.3mm. *Isle of Wight.* Portable Antiquities Scheme IOW-ADA7B6. Photographs © Isle of White Council.

407. Copper alloy; cast; one-piece; moulded-relief and openwork. A fleur-de-lis within a sporadic linear border and an engrailed edge; a ribbed collar at the juncture of the plate and hook; openwork partially unfettled; 33.04 x 18.42mm. *River Thames foreshore, London.* Drawing © Nick Griffiths.

408. Copper alloy; cast; one-piece; moulded-relief and openwork. A pair of forearms emerging from what is interpreted as perhaps being clouds, the sleeve of each arm is ribbed and the hands grip handles which form a chevron connected to a ridged ribbed collar at the juncture of the plate and hook. The handles and shaft are reminiscent of a plough. Incomplete, hook-point broken off; 37 x 19mm. *Norfolk*. Portable Antiquities Scheme NMS-DE6A48. Photograph © Norfolk Museums and Archaeology Service.

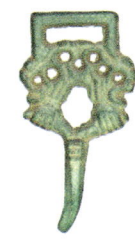

409. Copper alloy; cast; one-piece; openwork. A heart with a transverse bar either side; a slightly projecting angular collar at the juncture of the plate and the loop; a ridged ribbed collar at the juncture of the plate and hook; 27.8 x 14mm. *North Lincolnshire*. Portable Antiquities Scheme NLM-6A4072. Photographs © Portable Antiquities Scheme and North Lincolnshire Council.

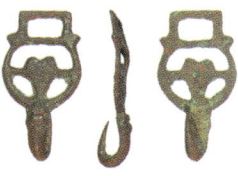

410. Copper alloy; cast; one-piece; moulded-relief and openwork. A stylised heart; a projecting angular collar at the juncture of the plate and loop; a projecting ridged and ribbed collar at the juncture of the plate and hook; side fractured near the collar; 17 x 14mm. *River Thames foreshore, London*. Drawing © Nick Griffiths.

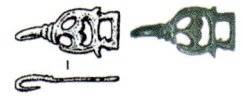

411. Copper alloy; cast; one-piece; moulded-relief and openwork. Comparable with no. 410 except a T-shaped centre design. Incomplete, section of loop broken off and hook distorted; 26.5 x 11mm. *North Yorkshire*. Drawing © Anne Hodgson.

412. Copper alloy; cast; one-piece; moulded-relief and openwork. An unequal-armed cross with a central pellet; a pellet either side at the juncture of the plate and loop; the quadrants nearest the hook each have a pit which probably represents unfettling; a ridged collar at the juncture of the plate and hook; 25 x 14mm. *Northamptonshire*. Peter Woods CH11. Drawing © Roy Turland, photograph © Peter Woods.

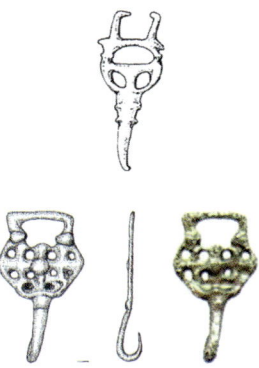

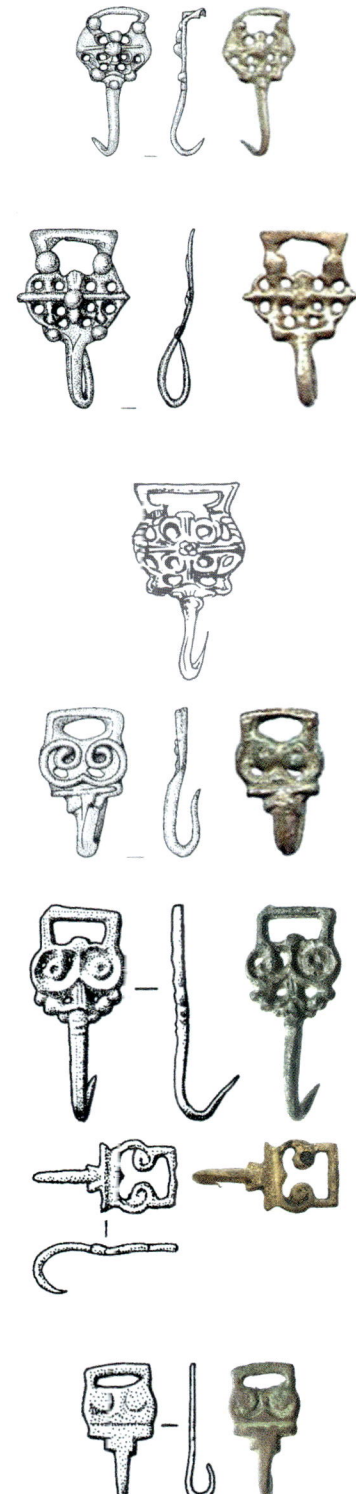

413. Copper alloy; cast; one-piece; moulded-relief and openwork. Comparable with no. 412 except less openwork and a pellet each side at the juncture of the plate and hook, a ridged single-pellet collar; loop distorted; 25 x 12mm. *Northamptonshire*. Peter Woods CH7R. Drawing © Roy Turland, photograph © Peter Woods.

414. Copper alloy; cast; one-piece; moulded-relief and openwork. Comparable with nos 412-413, 415 except the transverse arms of the cross protrude beyond the edges thereby forming small rounded knops, and without a ridged collar; 30 x 18mm. *Northamptonshire*. Peter Woods CH12. Drawing © Roy Turland, photograph © Peter Woods.

415. Copper alloy; cast; one-piece; moulded-relief and openwork. Comparable with nos 412-414 except with a central small quatrefoil, and each quadrant nearest the loop has a cabled edge; 34 x 19mm. *North Yorkshire*. Jim Halliday/029. Drawing © Anne Hodgson.

416. Copper alloy; cast; one-piece; moulded-relief and openwork. Conjoined confronted spirals; a transverse ridge and a projecting ridged collar at the juncture of the plate and hook; perhaps unfettled; 25 x 15mm. *Northamptonshire*. Peter Woods CH4R. Drawing © Roy Turland, photograph © Peter Woods.

417. Copper alloy; cast; one-piece; moulded-relief and openwork. Comparable with nos 416, 418-419 except a swag and a ribbed collar; perhaps unfettled; 35.81 x 15.98mm. *Oxfordshire*. Drawing © Patrick Read.

418. Copper alloy; cast; one-piece; moulded-relief and openwork. Comparable with nos 416-417, 419 except a larger area of openwork; an angular knop either side and a projecting angular collar at the juncture of the plate and hook; 23.59 x 12.35mm. *River Thames foreshore, London*. Drawing © Nick Griffiths.

419. Copper alloy; cast; one-piece; moulded-relief. Comparable with nos 416-418 except without openwork between the spirals; perhaps unfettled; 23 x 12mm. *South-East Lincolnshire*. Drawing © Patrick Read.

HOOKED-CLASPS & EYES

Early post-medieval Class E, Type 4

Lozenge/Sub-lozenge shaped

420. Copper alloy; cast; one-piece; moulded-relief. A transverse ridge surmounted by a recessed cross pommée and two pits; a trefoil of pellets either side; a projecting ridged collar at the juncture of the plate and hook; 28 x 15mm. *North Dorset.* Drawing © Patrick Read.

421. Copper alloy; cast; one-piece; moulded-relief. Comparable with no. 420 except a transverse beaded ridge surmounted by a recessed roundel; hook distorted and much abraded; 39 x 15mm. *South-East Lincolnshire.* Drawing © Patrick Read.

422. Copper alloy; cast; one-piece; moulded-relief. Comparable with nos 420-421 except a transverse ridge surmounted by a recessed heart flanked either side by three pits and a rounded knop; a slightly projecting and shallow ridged collar at the juncture of the plate and hook; 28 x 15mm. *South-East Dorset.* Drawing © Patrick Read.

423. Copper alloy; cast; one-piece; moulded-relief and openwork. A fleur-de-lis bordered by beaded and engrailed edges; partially unfettled; 32 x 17mm. *River Thames foreshore, London.* Drawing © Nick Griffiths.

424. Copper alloy; cast; one-piece; moulded-relief and openwork. Comparable with no. 423, 425 except the fleur-de-lis is within a raised linear lozenge, and a ridged double-pellet collar at the juncture of the plate and hook; partially unfettled; 30 x 21.5mm. *Norfolk.* United Kingdom Detecting Finds' Database 6336. Photographs © Malcolm Higginbotham.

425. Copper alloy, cast; one-piece; moulded-relief and openwork. Comparable with nos 423-424 except more openwork, a ridged single pellet collar and a longer hook-shank; a casting sprue on the outside edge of the loop; 38.5 x 18mm. *Lincolnshire.* Photograph © Rod Blunt.

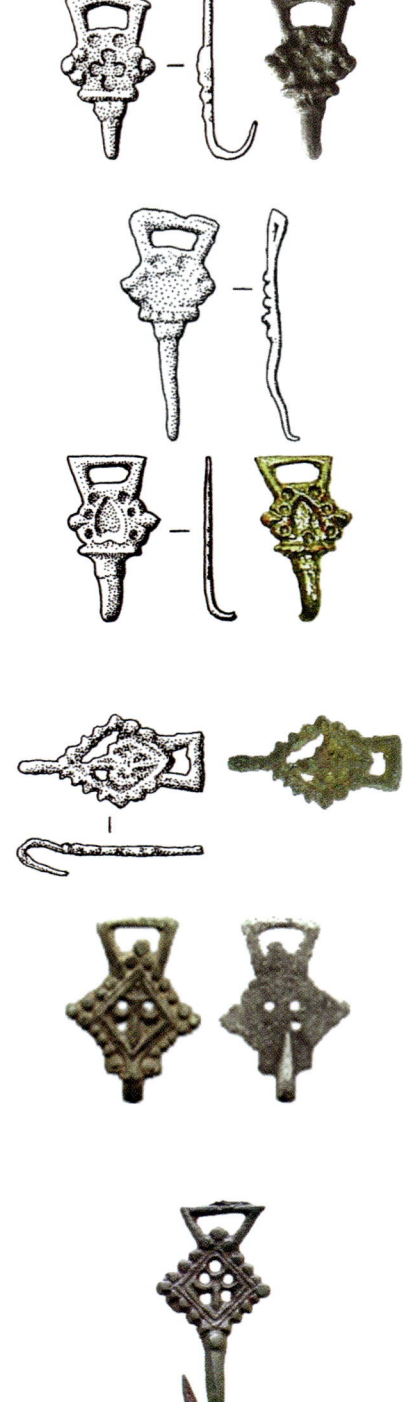

HOOKED-CLASPS & EYES

426. Copper alloy; cast; one-piece; moulded-relief and openwork. Comparable with nos 423-425 except a stylised fleur-de-lis and without a collar; distorted; 32 x 20mm. *East Yorkshire.* Jim Halliday/068. Drawing © Anne Hodgson.

427. Copper alloy; cast; one-piece; moulded-relief. A five-petalled rose; a trefoil knop either side; elongated beaded and engrailed edges; 35 x 21mm. *East Yorkshire.* Jim Halliday. Drawing © (?) Anne Hodgson.

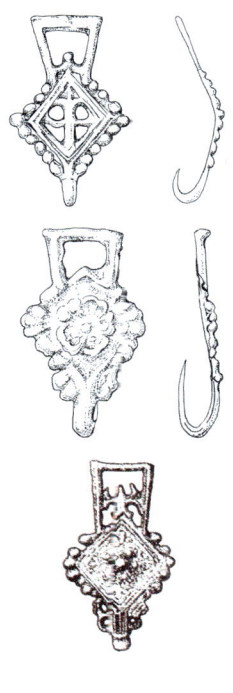

428. Copper alloy; cast; one-piece; moulded-relief and openwork. Six pellets resembling a small flower within a voided linear lozenge, beaded and engrailed edges; a fleur-de-lis in each internal angle; possibly a small bird with outstretched wings within the loop; two eyes on one side at the juncture of the plate and hook while the opposite side has a similar eye and another unpierced; a ridged collar at juncture of the plate and hook. Incomplete, hook and sections of the edges are broken off; probably slightly unfettled; 32 x 21mm. *North Yorkshire.* Jim Halliday. Drawing © John Middleton.

429. Copper alloy, cast; one-piece; moulded-relief. Comparable with no. 428 except without the fleur-de-lis in the angles; 45 x 22.8mm. *North Yorkshire.* United Kingdom Detecting Finds' Database 2708. Photographs © Paul Linford.

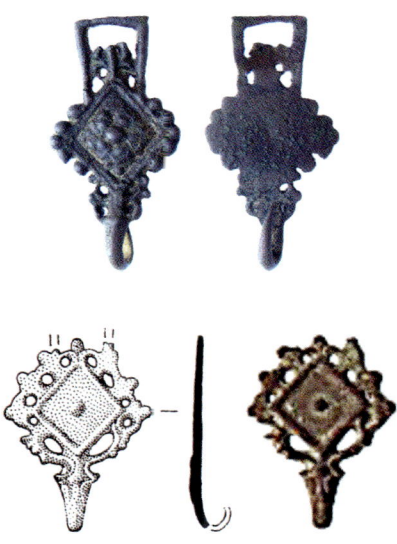

430. Copper alloy; cast; one-piece; moulded-relief and openwork. A central pellet within a raised linear lozenge; debased fleur-de-lis knops on the two edges nearest the loop; a swag and a projecting angular ridged collar at the juncture of the plate and hook. Incomplete, loop and hook-point broken off; 30.39 x 22.5mm. *Hampshire.* Portable Antiquities Scheme HAMP-A82766. Drawing and photograph © Winchester Museum Service.

HOOKED-CLASPS & EYES

431. Copper alloy; cast; one-piece; moulded-relief and openwork. Comparable with no. 430 except without a pellet in the lozenge, and with a projecting ridged collar; loop fractured; partially unfettled; 39.02 x 24mm. *South-West Lincolnshire*. Drawing © Nick Griffiths.

432. Copper alloy; cast; one-piece; moulded-relief. A quatrefoil within a lozenge with raised edges; a beaded border creating engrailed edges; a slightly projecting and shallow ridged collar at the juncture of the plate and hook. Much corroded and hook distorted; 34 x 16.1mm. *Dorset*. Portable Antiquities Scheme SOMDOR-25B110. Drawing © Patrick Read.

433. Copper alloy; cast; one-piece; moulded-relief. A five-petalled rose within a lozenge with raised edges; multiple rounded knops create engrailed edges which continue partially down the hook-shank; a ridged collar at the juncture of the plate and hook. Incomplete, loop broken off; 35 x 21mm. *Wiltshire*. Portable Antiquities Scheme WILT-4270C5. Photographs © Salisbury and South Wiltshire Museum.

Early post-medieval Class E, Type 5

Trefoil

434. Copper alloy; cast; one-piece; moulded-relief and openwork. Comparable with no. 435 except a trefoil of five-spoked wheels, a small rounded knop either side; a stylised small swag and a ridged collar at the juncture of the plate and hook. Incomplete, hook distorted and point broken off; 43 x 20mm. *South-East Dorset*. Drawing © Patrick Read.

435. Copper alloy; cast; one-piece; moulded-relief and openwork. Comparable with no. 434 except the openwork is circular, and a projecting collar comprised of two pellets; 37.47 x 20.31mm. *Buckinghamshire*. Portable Antiquities Scheme BUC-1D689.

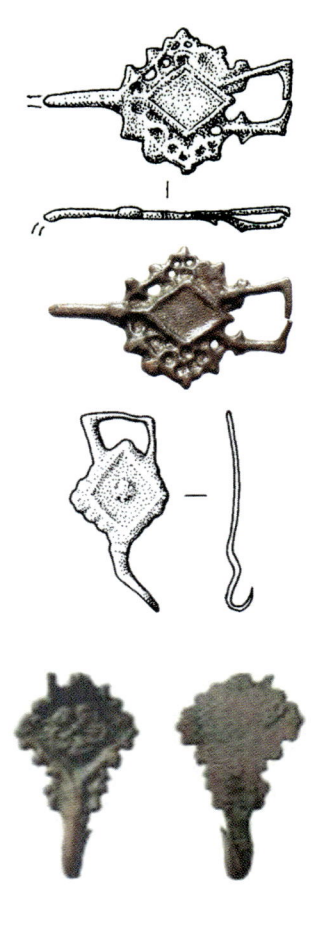

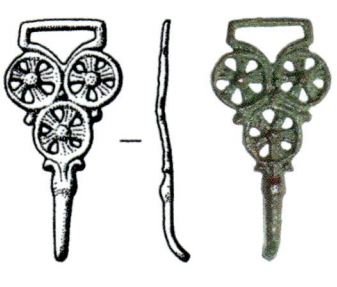

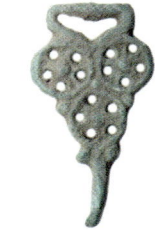

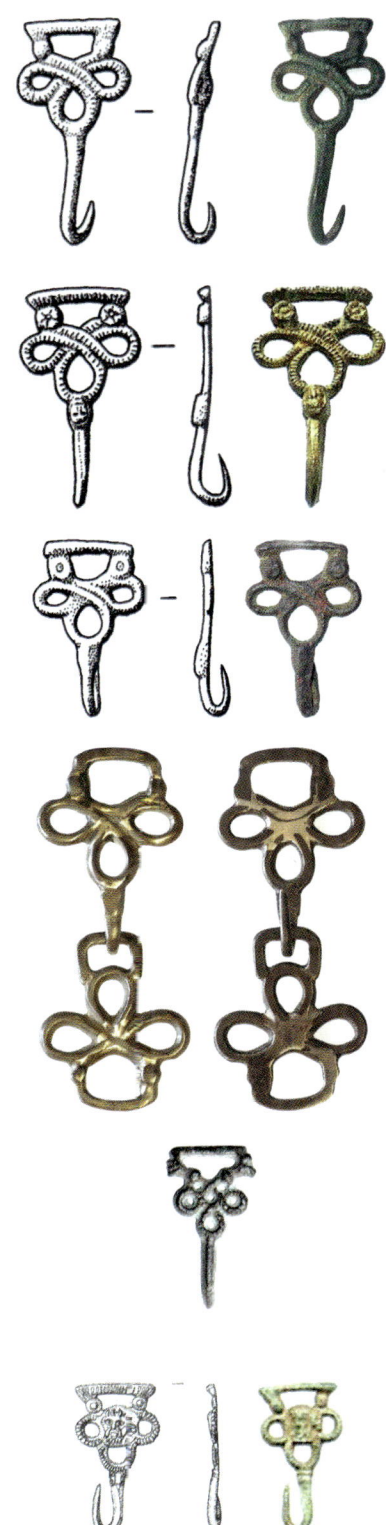

436. Copper alloy; cast; one-piece; moulded-relief and openwork. Comparable with nos 437-440 except a hatched Hungerford knot; each running-end of the cord terminates with a pellet; 38 x 18mm. *Hertfordshire*. Drawing © Patrick Read.

437. Copper alloy; cast; one-piece; moulded-relief and openwork. Comparable with nos 436, 438-440 except a small five-petalled rose at each running-end and a ridged collar bearing a tiny human facing-mask at the juncture of the plate and hook; 37 x 20mm. *River Thames foreshore, London*. Drawing © Patrick Read.

438. Copper alloy; cast; one-piece; moulded-relief and openwork. Comparable with nos 436-437, 439-440 except unhatched and a plain ridged collar at the juncture of the plate and hook; 30 x 18mm. *South Somerset*. Drawing © Patrick Read.

439. Silver-gilt; cast; each section is one-piece; moulded-relief and openwork. Comparable with nos 436-438, 440 except unhatched and plain pellets. Hooked-section 30.06 x 20.59, eye-section 26.17 x 21.55. *Belgium*. Purchased in England.

440. Copper alloy; cast; one-piece; moulded-relief and openwork. Comparable with nos 436-439 except the knot is bent more loosely and each running-end terminates with a tassel; 27 x 15mm. *Surrey*. Portable Antiquities Scheme SUR-FD1CF5. Photograph © Surrey County Council.

441. Copper alloy; cast; one-piece; moulded-relief and openwork. Comparable with no. 442 except a human facing-mask and a trefoil of rounded loops and a ridged ribbed collar; 25 x 13mm. *Northamptonshire*. Peter Woods CH3. Drawing © Roy Turland, photograph © Peter Woods.

442. Copper alloy; cast; one-piece; moulded-relief and openwork. Comparable with no. 441 except a multi-petalled flower and without a collar; 30 x 17mm. *North Yorkshire.* Jim Halliday. Drawing © Anne Hodgson.

443. Copper alloy; cast; one-piece; convex; moulded-relief. A trefoil of hollow-domed bosses, each boss with imitative ground-supported twisted wire filigree - a trefoil of annulets, each with a central small annulet, within a large annulet; a large central pellet; a ridged collar at the juncture of the plate and hook; 30 x 15.5mm. *Rutland.* After *Treasure Hunting* May 2001, pp 48. Photograph © Rod Blunt.

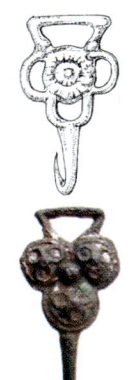

444. Copper alloy; cast; one-piece; convex; moulded-relief. A trefoil of hollow-domed bosses, each boss with a central pellet within a circle of five pellets on a hatched field; a ridged and hatched collar at the juncture of the plate and hook; 30 x 17mm. *East Yorkshire.* Photographs © Stan Raymond.

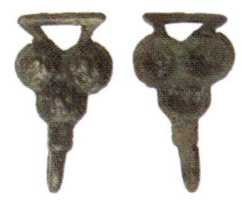

Early post-medieval Class E, Type 6

Quatrefoil

445. Copper alloy; cast; one-piece; moulded-relief. A human facing-mask with addorsed spirals on all four sides. Incomplete, hook broken off; 23 x 16mm. *East Yorkshire.* Jim Halliday/036. Drawing © Anne Hodgson.

446. Copper alloy; cast; one-piece; moulded-relief and openwork. Comparable with no. 447 except two conjoined figures-of-eight; a trefoil of small pellets; a slightly projecting ridged and ribbed collar at the juncture of the plate and hook; 33 x 13mm. *South-East Dorset.* Drawing © Nick Griffiths.

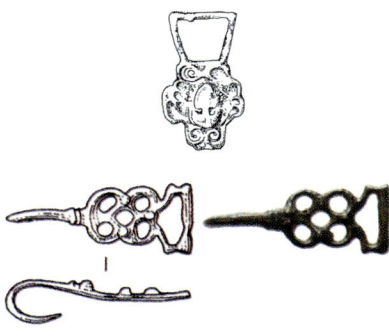

447. Copper alloy; cast; one-piece; moulded-relief and openwork; gilded overall. Comparable with no. 446 except the frame is hatched and a trefoil of pellets and two further pellets near the ridged ribbed collar; 36.76 x 13.44mm. *River Thames foreshore, London.* Drawing © Nick Griffiths.

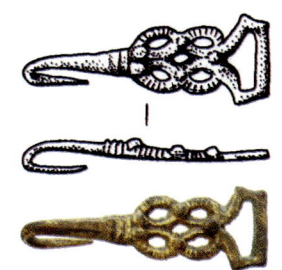

448. Copper alloy; cast; one-piece; moulded-relief and openwork. A saltire with two central transverse ribs; a projecting slightly angular ridged collar at the juncture of the plate and hook. Incomplete, hook-point broken off; 30.06 x 9.14mm. *Essex*. Portable Antiquities Scheme ESS-816456. Photographs © Colchester Museums.

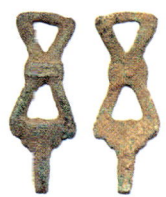

Early post-medieval Class E, Type 7

Heart-shaped

449. Copper alloy; cast; one-piece; moulded-relief and openwork. A cross-hatched heart surmounted by two chevrons, a swag extends either side almost to the openwork discs; a small rounded knop projects into the loop. Incomplete, hook broken off; 25 x 15mm. *East Yorkshire*. Jim Halliday/035. Drawing © Anne Hodgson.

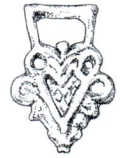

450. Copper alloy; cast; one-piece; moulded-relief and openwork. Comparable with no. 451 except a fleur-de-lis within a linear heart with a beaded border creating engrailed edges; a small rounded knop projects into the loop; a projecting ridged and ribbed collar at juncture of the plate and hook; 31.96 x 16.6mm. *South Lincolnshire*. Drawing © Nick Griffiths.

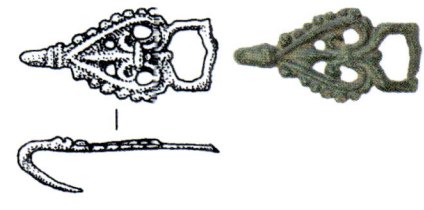

451. Copper alloy; cast; one-piece; moulded-relief and openwork. Comparable with no. 450 except without the beaded border, a grooved angular knop either side and a projecting ridged double-pellet collar at the juncture of the plate and hook; 28.75 x 15.12mm. *River Thames foreshore, London*. Drawing © Nick Griffiths.

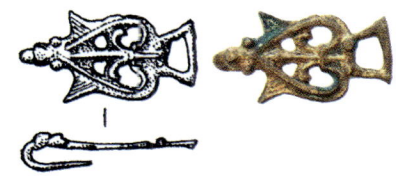

452. Copper alloy; cast; one-piece; moulded-relief and openwork. A linear heart the bifurcate end of which has a trefoil pointing inwards; a swag extends almost to the loop; a small rounded knop projects into the loop; an openwork small disc in one side, while the other side has a pit which on similar hooks is open, therefore is probably unfettled; 33 x 19mm. *North Dorset*. Drawing © Patrick Read.

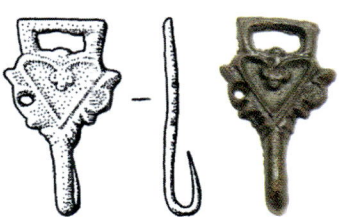

HOOKED-CLASPS & EYES

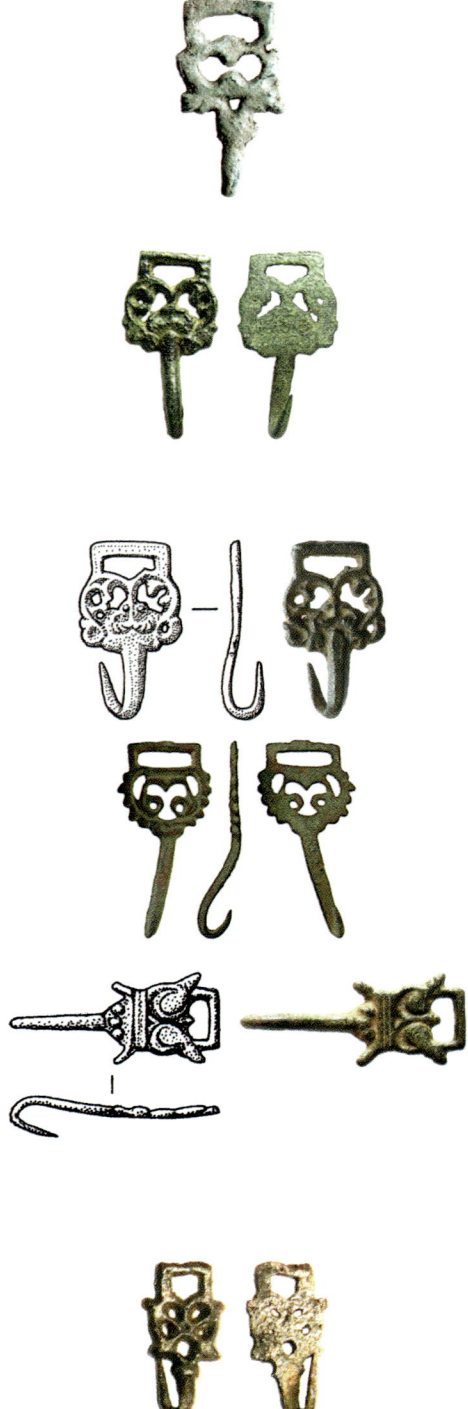

453. Copper alloy; cast; one-piece; moulded-relief and openwork. A swag, and a shallow ridged collar at the juncture of the plate and hook; 33.5 x 17.1mm. *Buckinghamshire*. Portable Antiquities Scheme BUC-580C51. Photograph © Buckinghamshire County Council.

454. Copper alloy; cast; one-piece; moulded-relief and openwork. Comparable with no. 455 except a heart with small flowers, one either side at the bifurcate end and a conjoined pair above the hook; a swag at the juncture of the plate and hook; partially unfettled; 31.35 x 15.97. *South-West Yorkshire*. Portable Antiquities Scheme SWYOR-062EB3. Photographs © West Yorkshire Archaeology Service.

455. Copper alloy; cast; one-piece; moulded-relief and openwork. Comparable with no. 454 except a partially openwork swag and lacking the small flowers; 29.35 x 16mm. *Nottinghamshire*. United Kingdom Detecting Finds' Database 11478. Drawing © Patrick Read.

456. Copper alloy; cast; one-piece; moulded-relief and openwork. Confronted spirals within a linear heart and an engrailed edge; a small swag at the juncture of the plate and hook; 32.9 x 15.7mm. *Isle of White*. Portable Antiquities Scheme IOW-DC8014. Photographs © Isle of White Council.

457. Copper alloy; cast; one-piece; moulded-relief. Two transverse grooves surmounted by confronted spirals, their conjoined running-ends terminating in a tiny knop that projects into the loop, two oblique elongated knops either side form a saltire; a band of three pellets at the juncture of the plate and hook; 34.12 x 14.36mm. *South-East Dorset*. Drawing © Nick Griffiths.

458. Copper alloy; cast; one-piece; moulded-relief and openwork. A five-spoked wheel, four spokes of which protrude and form small rounded knops, two either side; a protruding ridged and rounded collar at the juncture of the plate and hook; 25 x 14mm. *Isle of White*. Photographs © Mary Winch.

HOOKED-CLASPS & EYES

Early post-medieval Class E, Type 8

Figurative

459. Copper alloy; cast; one-piece; convex; moulded-relief. A hollow-domed boss bearing a human facing-mask; a projecting ridged collar at the juncture of the plate and hook; 35 x 14.2mm. *Suffolk*. Drawing © Patrick Read.

460. Copper alloy; cast; one-piece; moulded-relief and openwork. A possible stylised moustachioed human facing-mask; the chin is formed from a solid-domed boss and the eyes, two openwork small discs; the hair is represented by linked spirals with a central tiny knop projecting into the loop; a shallow ridged collar at the juncture of the plate and hook; 25 x 11mm. *Northamptonshire*. Peter Woods CH14. Drawing © Roy Turland, photograph © Peter Woods.

461. Copper alloy; cast; one-piece; moulded-relief and openwork. Two birds perched on foliate; a trefoil of pellets and a projecting ridged and obliquely-ribbed collar at the juncture of the plate and hook; 37.2 x 18.1mm. *Northamptonshire*. Peter Woods CH58. Drawing © Roy Turland, photograph © Peter Woods.

462. Copper alloy; cast; one-piece; convex; moulded-relief. A multi-petalled flower, the centre a hollow-domed boss with a saltire, a central pellet and a pellet in each quadrant; bordered by shallow recessed ovals. Incomplete, hook-point broken off; 30 x 16mm. *North Yorkshire*. Jim Halliday/001. Drawing © Anne Hodgson.

463. Copper alloy; cast; one-piece; moulded-relief. Comparable with no. 464 except a six-petalled double rose; 32 x 14mm. *River Thames foreshore, London*. Drawing © Patrick Read.

464. Copper alloy; cast; one-piece; moulded-relief. Comparable with no. 463 except the centre of the rose is cross-hatched. Incomplete, hook-point broken off; 34 x 18mm. *East Devon*. Drawing © Patrick Read.

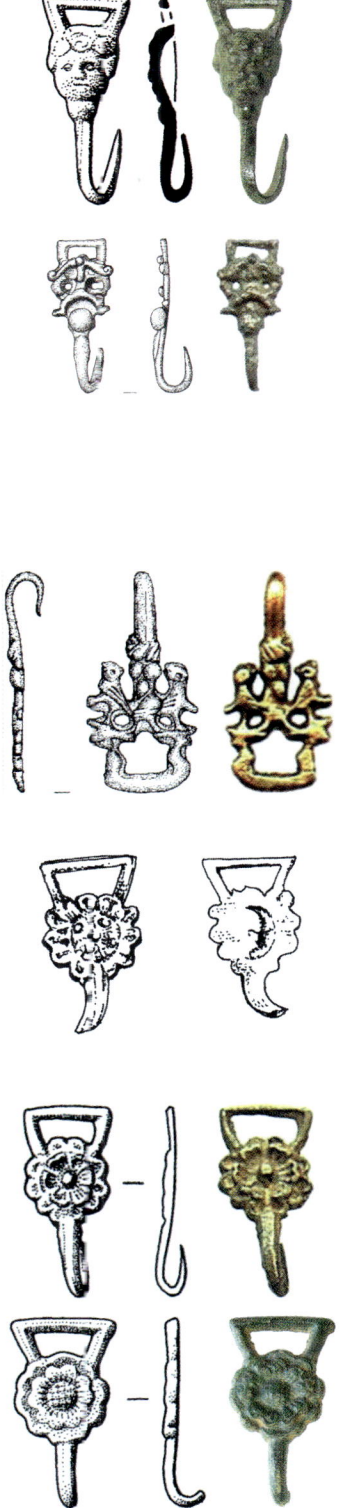

HOOKED-CLASPS & EYES

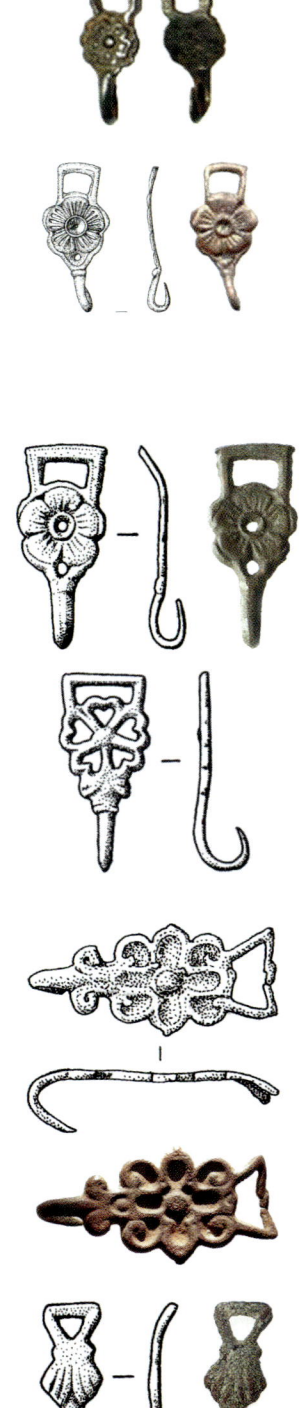

465. Copper alloy; cast; one-piece; moulded-relief. A five-petalled double rose; 29 x 12.6mm. *East Yorkshire*. United Kingdom Detecting Finds' Database 10049. Photographs © Richard Last.

466. Copper alloy; cast; one-piece; moulded-relief and openwork. Comparable with no. 467 except a five-petalled rose; a narrow ridged collar at the juncture of the plate and hook; a central small drilled-hole and another near the collar were probably not for seperate decorative features; 25 x 11mm. *Northamptonshire*. Peter Woods CH9. Drawing © Roy Turland, photograph © Peter Woods.

467. Copper alloy; cast; one-piece; moulded-relief. Comparable with no. 466 except larger; 34.43 x 10.5. *North Oxfordshire*. Drawing © Patrick Read.

468. Copper alloy; cast; one-piece; moulded-relief and openwork. A five-petalled rose, each petal heart-shaped; a debased swag and a projecting ribbed collar at the juncture of the plate and hook; 35.5 x 15mm. *North Yorkshire*. Jim Halliday. Drawing © Anne Hodgson.

469. Copper alloy; cast; one-piece; moulded-relief. A four-petalled flower with sepals; a projecting collar formed from addorsed spirals at the juncture of the plate and hook; 38.91 x 20.09mm. *The Netherlands*. Drawing © Nick Griffiths.

470. Copper alloy; cast; one-piece; moulded-relief. A scallop shell, comparable with nos 471-473 except; a projecting angular collar at the juncture of the plate and loop; 25.47 x 10.07mm. *South Somerset*. Drawing © Patrick Read.

HOOKED-CLASPS & EYES

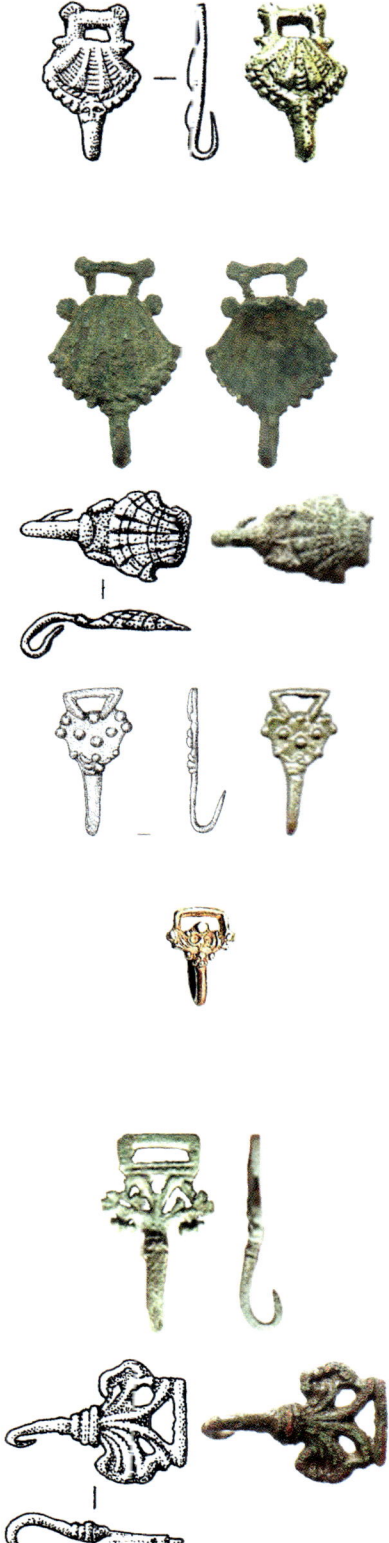

471. Copper alloy; cast; one-piece; moulded-relief. Comparable with nos 470, 472-473 except the curved edge is beaded and engrailed; a ridged collar at the juncture of the plate and hook; and a rounded knop on either corner of the loop; 27 x 10.07mm. *River Thames foreshore, London*. Drawing © Patrick Read.

472. Copper alloy; cast; one-piece; moulded-relief. Comparable with nos 470-471, 473 except a small scallop-shell knop either side near the loop. Loop fractured where it joins the plate on one side, corroded; 34 x 21mm. *Somerset*. United Kingdom Detecting Finds' Database 9973. Photographs © Nick Martin.

473. Copper alloy; cast; one-piece; moulded-relief. Comparable with nos 470-472 except a ridged collar with three-pellets at the juncture of the plate and hook. Incomplete, loop broken off; 26 x 15.21mm. *East Devon*. Drawing © Nick Griffiths.

474. Copper alloy; cast; one-piece; moulded-relief. Possibly representing a berry; multiple pellets, some of which form rounded knops around the edge, a ridged ribbed collar at juncture of the plate and hook; 25.47 x 10.07mm. *Northamptonshire*. Peter Woods CH5R. Drawing © Roy Turland, photograph © Peter Woods.

475. Silver-gilt; cast; one-piece; moulded-relief. A swag edged by small rounded knops on the hook side and a large pellet forming a knop within the loop; 16.5 x 11.3mm. *Wiltshire*. Portable Antiquities Scheme B4CF38. Treasure case M&ME 441. Photograph © Salisbury and South Wiltshire Museum.

476. Copper alloy; cast; one-piece; moulded-relief and openwork. Two fronds emerging from a swag that has three small pellets either side on the edge nearest the hook; a transverse groove between the swag and the loop; a ribbed collar at the juncture of the plate and hook; 33.5 x 18.5mm. *Buckinghamshire*. Portable Antiquities Scheme BUC-242f76. Photographs © Buckinghamshire County Council.

477. Copper alloy; cast; one-piece; moulded-relief and openwork. A swag; a projecting ridged and ribbed collar at the juncture of the plate and hook; 29.38 x 20.15mm. *Buckinghamshire*. Drawing © Nick Griffiths.

HOOKED-CLASPS & EYES

478. Copper alloy; cast; one-piece; moulded-relief. A tri-lobed leaf (?) a strawberry. Incomplete, hook broken off and loop fractured; 19 x 19mm. *River Thames foreshore, London*. Drawing © Nick Griffiths.

479. Copper alloy; cast; one-piece; moulded-relief and openwork. Intertwined vine tendrils, emerging from what is considered an urn; two small loops, perhaps additional attachment-holes, and a small rounded knop either side; a projecting ridged and two-knobbed collar at the juncture of the plate and hook. Incomplete, hook-point broken off; 38 x 29mm. *North Yorkshire*. Drawing © Anne Hodgson.

480. Copper alloy; cast; one-piece; moulded-relief and openwork. A lyre enclosing two confronted spirals surmounted by a cross-hatched sub-lozenge, possibly a pinecone; a projecting collar with trefoil terminals at the juncture of the plate and loop; a stylised swag and a shallow ridged collar at the juncture of the plate and hook; 33 x 15mm. *River Thames foreshore, London*. Drawing © Patrick Read.

481. Copper alloy; cast; one-piece; openwork. Interpreted as the letter A with serifs; a shallow ridged collar at the juncture of the plate and hook; 26 x 14.5mm. *Lincolnshire*. United Kingdom Detecting Finds' Database 9137. Photograph © Andy Germaney.

Early post-medieval Class E, Type 9

Asymmetrical

482. Copper alloy; cast; one-piece; moulded-relief and openwork. A transverse rectangular panel formed from small circles and a meridian ridge; a small rounded knop protrudes into the loop; hook distorted, now straight; 38 x 16mm. *East Yorkshire*. Photographs © Stan Raymond.

483. Copper alloy; cast; one-piece; moulded-relief and openwork. Comparable with no. 484 except two addorsed spirals, each enclosing a pellet, surmounted by a quatrefoil of four small and one large pellet; a rounded eye either side; 47 x 18mm. *Norfolk*. Portable Antiquities Scheme NMS-7E8085. Photograph © Norfolk Museums and Archaeology Service.

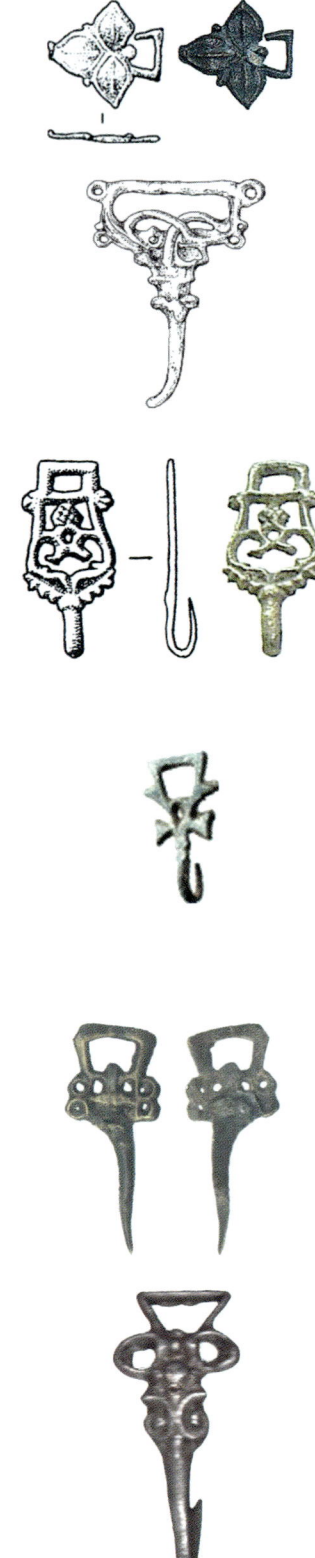

HOOKED-CLASPS & EYES

484. Copper alloy; cast; each section is one-piece; moulded-relief and openwork. Two almost identical sharp-hooked clasps, both comparable with no. 483 except only one eye, one attached either end of a copper-alloy circular-section single-link chain by a copper-alloy split-ring. Incomplete, the eye on both clasps is broken. Each hook is 37.24 x 15.7mm, chain L192mm, overall L266.48mm. *The Netherlands.* Drawings © Nick Griffiths.

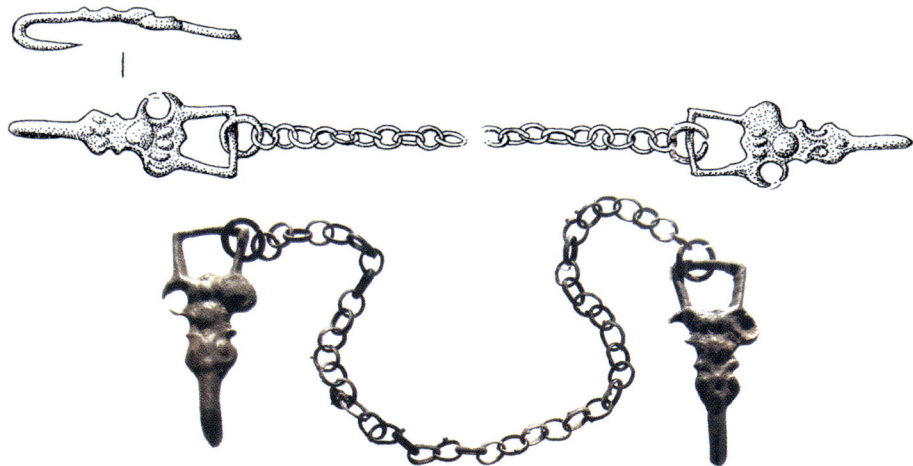

Early post-medieval Class F single sharp-hooked clasps

Class F, Type 1 cast copper-alloy single sharp-hooked clasps have rectangular attachment-loops with two circular attachment-holes, a feature noted as apparently unusual. All other observations for Class E single sharp-hooked clasps apply equally. Decoration is moulded-relief; *c.*16th century.

Early post-medieval Class F, Type 1

Rectangular

Two circular attachment-holes

485. Copper alloy; cast; one-piece; moulded-relief. Comparable with no. 486 except a transverse broad groove with a ridge on the loop side; a pointed knop (one distorted) each side of the plate near the hook; a ridged collar at the juncture of the plate and hook; 29 x 15mm. *South Somerset.* Drawing © Patrick Read.

486. Copper alloy; cast; one-piece; moulded-relief. Comparable with no. 485 except a transverse cabled ridge either side of the groove and a ridged ribbed collar with a tiny pellet above; 27 x 14mm. *Hertfordshire.* Drawing © Patrick Read.

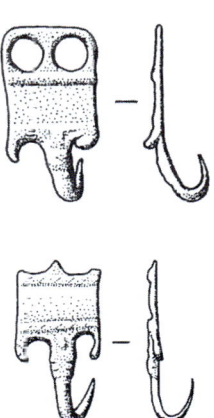

Early post-medieval Class G single sharp-hooked clasp

This Class G, Type 1 cast copper-alloy single sharp-hooked clasp has a sub-rectangular attachment-loop with four attachment-holes, again a feature noted as apparently unusual. All other observations for Class E single sharp-hooked clasps apply equally. Decoration is moulded-relief; *c.*16th century.

Early post-medieval Class G, Type 1

Figurative

Four sub-circular/sub-rectangular attachment-holes

487. Copper alloy; cast; one-piece; convex; moulded-relief and possibly openwork. A scallop shell; 26 x 15.4mm. Incomplete, hook broken off and two stubs of a possible openwork collar. *Northamptonshire.* United Kingdom Detecting Finds' Database 12952. Photographs © Russell Fergie.

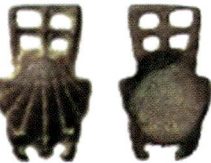

Early post-medieval Class H single sharp-hooked clasps

Rounded attachment-loops distinguish Class H single sharp-hooked clasps from Class E. Designated as Type 1 circular/sub-circular, Type 2 oval, Type 3 shield-shaped and Type 5 figurative. All are cast copper-alloy and appear one-piece, though no. 495 may have had a separate decorative feature therefore perhaps is composite; no. 496 has a glass appliqué, similar to Roman period glass, and possibly represents reuse of classical material, while no. 497 would have had an inset gem. Other observations for early post-medieval Class E single sharp-hooked clasps apply equally. All are *c.*16th century.

Early post-medieval Class H, Type 1

Circular/Sub-circular

488. Copper alloy; cast; one-piece; convex; moulded-relief. A hollow-domed boss bearing a possible six-petalled rose or leonine mask; much abraded; 30 x 16mm. *South Devon.* After Read 1988, fig. 19, no 4 and pp 94, no. 5; and 1995, no. 762.

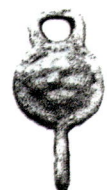

489. Copper alloy; cast; one-piece; convex; moulded-relief. A hollow-domed boss bearing a clockwise eight-armed impeller within a beaded border. Incomplete, hook broken off; 18 x 12mm. *Worcestershire.* Photographs © Paul Roberts.

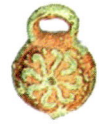 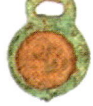

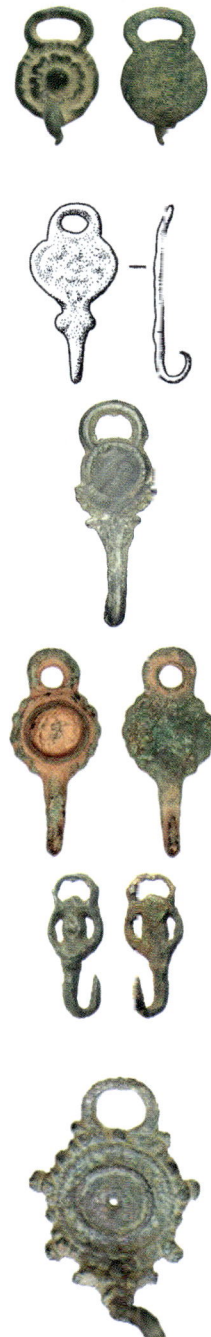

490. Copper alloy, cast; one-piece; moulded-relief. A seven-petalled double rose; hook distorted forwards, 22.2 x 12.8mm. *Hertfordshire*. Portable Antiquities Scheme BH-644F84. Photographs © St Albans Museum.

491. Copper alloy; cast; one-piece; moulded-relief. Possibly a flower, a projecting ridged trefoil collar at the juncture of the plate and hook; much abraded; 32 x 15mm. *East Devon*. Drawing © Patrick Read.

492. Copper alloy; cast; one-piece; moulded-relief. A raised edge; a swag and a projecting ridged collar at the juncture of the plate and hook; 38.5 x 13mm. *Norfolk*. Portable Antiquities Scheme NMS-1D0B93. Photograph © Norfolk Museums and Archaeology Service.

493. Copper alloy; cast; one-piece; moulded-relief. A linear circle bordered by a beaded and engrailed edge; 35.6 x 15.1mm. *Somerset*. Portable Antiquities Scheme SOMDOR-963C34. Photographs © Somerset County Council.

494. Copper alloy; cast; one-piece; moulded-relief and openwork. A median septum-bar with a circular indeterminate motif; 24.2 x 9.6mm. *East Yorkshire*. United Kingdom Detecting Finds' Database 10064. Photographs © Richard Last.

495. Copper alloy; cast; one-piece; moulded-relief and openwork. A central small drilled-hole within two concentric linear circles; a beaded border creating an engrailed edge with two rounded knops either side; a swag and a ridged collar at the juncture of the plate and hook. The central hole may have held a seperate decorative feature; hook distorted; *c*.50 x *c*.28mm. *Norfolk*. Portable Antiquities Scheme NMS-39C154. Photograph © Norfolk Museums and Archaeology Service.

HOOKED-CLASPS & EYES

496. Copper alloy; cast; one-piece; moulded-relief and openwork. A linear circle with a central circular drilled-hole within a beaded and engrailed edge; a swag and a ridged collar at the juncture of the plate and hook; in the circle is a pale-green glass roundel appliqué with a milled-effect edge, inlaid into the appliqué is a separate dark-blue glass roundel into which seven pellets are inlaid, white in the centre, surrounded by two light-blue, two dark-blue and two (?) white - the whole resembles a six-petalled flower. When found, soil held the roundel in place. Precisely how the roundel was affixed to the main plate is uncertain; although there is now no sign, possibly it had an integral shaft, thereby making it a stud, which was secured in the hole in the plate by glue. This glass appliqué is reminiscent of Roman work and is plausibly such, and perhaps represents reuse of a Roman-period object; 54.4 x 22.63. *South-West Dorset*. Drawing © Nick Griffiths.

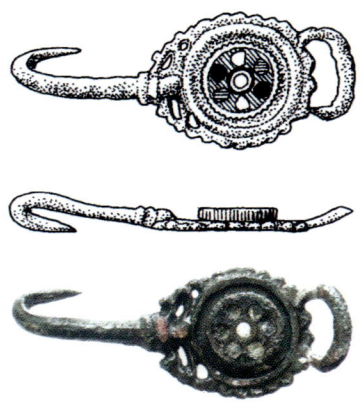

497. Copper alloy; cast; one-piece; moulded-relief. A recessed circle with four claws, presumably a setting for a now missing gem; a slightly projecting ridged collar at the juncture of the plate and loop; a multi-ribbed collar at the juncture of the plate and hook; 33.28 x 8.33mm. *South-West Dorset*. Drawing © Nick Griffiths.

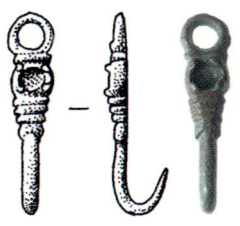

Early post-medieval Class H, Type 2

Oval

498. Copper alloy; cast; one-piece; moulded-relief. Pellets, ovals and curlicues; a large trefoil collar with an annulet, spirals and pellets at the juncture of the plate and hook; 38.83 x 11.43mm. *The Netherlands*. Drawing © Nick Griffiths.

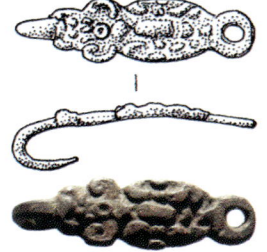

Early post-medieval Class H, Type 3

Shield-shaped

499. Copper alloy; cast; one-piece; moulded-relief and openwork. Comparable with nos 317-318; 37 x 15mm. *North Yorkshire*. Jim Halliday/54. Drawing © Anne Hodgson.

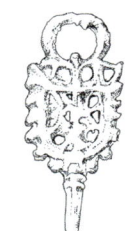

HOOKED-CLASPS & EYES

Early post-medieval Class H, Type 4

Figurative

500. Copper alloy; cast; one-piece; moulded-relief and openwork. Possibly a tri-lobed leaf (?) a strawberry; two openwork small discs are perhaps additional attachment-holes. Incomplete, hook broken off; 27 x 18mm. *South-East Dorset*. Drawing © Patrick Read.

501. Copper alloy; cast; one-piece; moulded-relief and openwork. A swag and a projecting ridged collar at the junction of the plate and hook; 32 x 17mm. *Northamptonshire*. Portable Antiquities Scheme NARC-A230A6. Photographs © Northamptonshire County Council.

502. Copper alloy; cast; one-piece; moulded-relief and openwork. A six-petalled rose, each petal a trefoil; 35.80 x 18mm. *Suffolk*. Portable Antiquities Scheme SF-F95233. Photographs © Suffolk County Council Archaeological Service.

503. Copper alloy; cast; one-piece; moulded-relief. A multi-petalled flower within a foliate border; a human facing-mask collar at the juncture of the plate and hook; 44 x 14.8mm. *River Thames foreshore, London*.

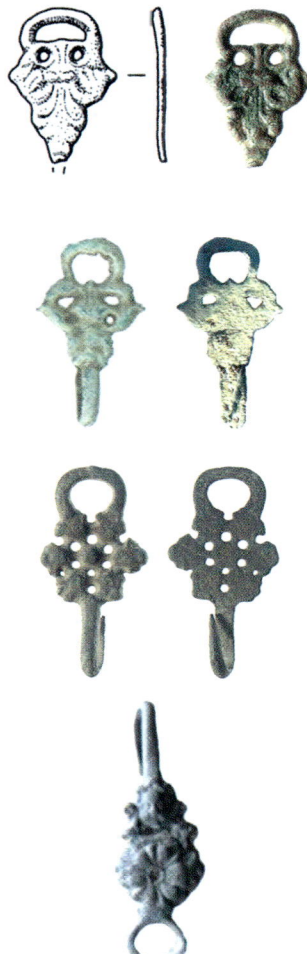

Early post-medieval Class I single sharp-hooked clasps

Single sharp-hooked clasps designated as Class I, Types 1-4 are compositely constructed of copper-alloy or silver; either cast, sheeting or part cast, part sheeting and part wire, with rounded attachment-loops. Other characteristics are similar to those of Class E single sharp-hooked clasps. No. 509 is possibly a tooth-pick. All are c.16th century; though no. 508 is perhaps early 16th. No. 507 is curious and it may be a completely different type of object.

Early post-medieval Class I, Type 1

Circular

504. Copper alloy; cast; three-piece; convex; moulded-relief and openwork. Comparable with nos 505-506. A flat plate with an engrailed edge, a swag and a ribbed collar at the juncture of the plate and hook. A separate domed-head rivet pierces a separate hollow-domed eight-spoked wheel and the main plate before securing; 52.02 x 22.63mm. *Nottinghamshire.* Portable Antiquities Scheme DENO-147FB4. Photographs © Derby City Council.

505. Copper alloy; cast; three-piece; convex; moulded-relief and openwork. Comparable with nos 504, 506 except the hollow-dome is a five-petalled rose with heart-shaped petals, 44 x 21mm. *North Lincolnshire.* Photographs © Stan Raymond.

506. Copper alloy; cast; three-piece; convex; moulded-relief and openwork. Comparable with nos 504-505 except less openwork in the swag, Incomplete, hook broken off and separate copper-alloy rivet missing; 35.84 x 21.66mm. *Derbyshire.* Drawing © Nick Griffiths.

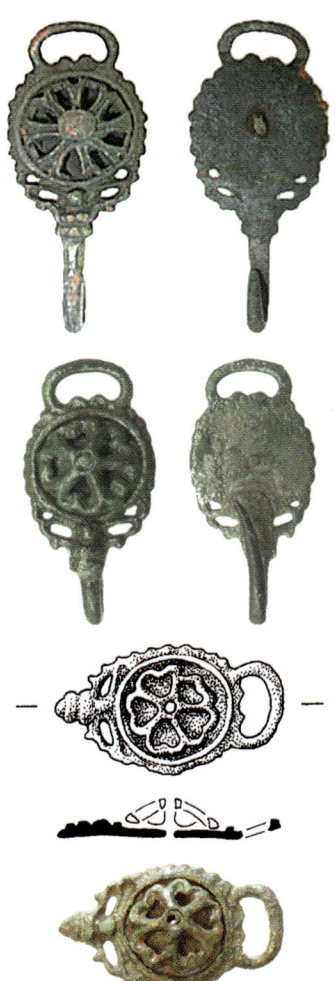

Early post-medieval Class I, Type 2

Sub-ovate

507. Copper alloy; sheeting; convex; three-piece; sporadic white-metal coating on the front and both sides of the hook, probably tin. A distorted hollow-dome. A separate tapered sheet with a hook at one end and a rounded eye at the other is secured to the back with a separate copper-alloy rivet; 23.4 x 13.3mm. *Hertfordshire.* Portable Antiquities Scheme BH-4AAC70. Photographs © St Albans Museum.

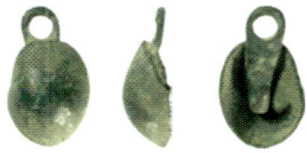

Early post-medieval Class I, Type 3

Lozenge-shaped

508. Copper alloy; sheeting and wire; three-piece, engraved. An equal-armed cross, each arm of which has feathered terminals, with a central saltire; all within a linear border. A separate soldered wire loop and wire hook; 25.02 x 17.28mm. *East Anglia.* Drawing © Patrick Read.

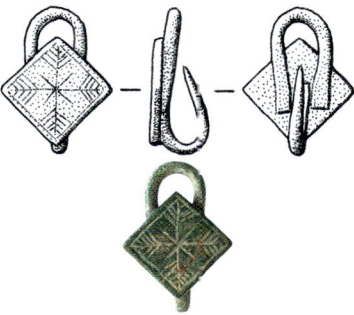

Early post-medieval Class I, Type 4

Cylindrical

509. Silver; possibly part cast part sheeting and perhaps wire; possibly three-piece; engraved. A hollow (?) sheeting cylindrical body with cross-hatching within two transverse lines. A (?) separate soldered rectangular-section (?) wire rounded loop and circular cap. A separate soldered tapered rectangular-section (?) wire/cast hook and circular cap. The body is distorted and torn; 24 x 5.5mm. *Hampshire.* Treasure case 2002 T98. Photographs © the Trustees of The British Museum.

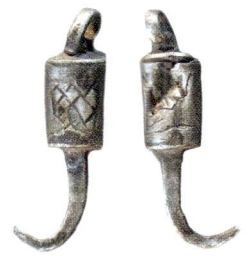

Early post-medieval Class J single sharp-hooked clasp

A seemingly unusual category of cast copper-alloy single sharp-hooked clasp designated as Class J, Type 1 is one-piece sub-rectangular with two rounded attachment-loops. All other observations made for Class E single sharp-hooked clasps apply equally; *c.*16th century.

HOOKED-CLASPS & EYES

Early post-medieval Class J, Type 1

Sub-rectangular

Two attachment-loops

510. Copper alloy; cast; one-piece; moulded-relief. Comparable with nos 485-486. Incomplete, hook broken off; 33.43 x 15.75mm. *Leicestershire*. Drawing © Nick Griffiths.

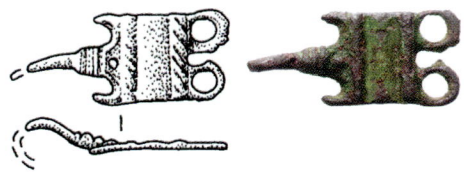

Early post-medieval Class K single sharp-hooked clasps

Class K single sharp-hooked clasps are either cast or part cast and part sheeting, in silver or lead/tin, and have angular attachment-loops. They differ from Classes A-J single sharp-hooked clasps by having separate embedded or soldered wire hooks, therefore are compositely constructed. Decoration is moulded-relief or engraved and some are gilded. Designated as Type 1 circular, Type 2 rectangular/sub-rectangular, Type 3 trefoil, Type 4 heart-shaped and Type 5 figurative. No. 516 has a drilled-hole, possibly for a separate decorative feature. The evidence from the River Thames, London provides a pretty secure date range of *c*.1450 - 1500.

Early post-medieval Class K, Type 1

Rectangular/Sub-rectangular

511. Silver-gilt; cast and wire; two-piece; engraved and moulded-relief. Two four-petalled flowers; a ridged zoomorphic collar at the juncture of the plate and hook; a separate soldered silver wire hook; 31 x 13.25mm. *South-East Dorset*. Treasure case 2002 T114. Acc. No. DORCM 2006.23 in the collections at Dorset County Museum and published with the permission of The Dorset Natural History and Archaeological Society at the Dorset County Museum. Photographs © Val MacRae.

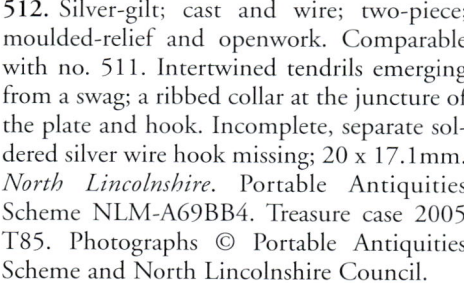

512. Silver-gilt; cast and wire; two-piece; moulded-relief and openwork. Comparable with no. 511. Intertwined tendrils emerging from a swag; a ribbed collar at the juncture of the plate and hook. Incomplete, separate soldered silver wire hook missing; 20 x 17.1mm. *North Lincolnshire*. Portable Antiquities Scheme NLM-A69BB4. Treasure case 2005 T85. Photographs © Portable Antiquities Scheme and North Lincolnshire Council.

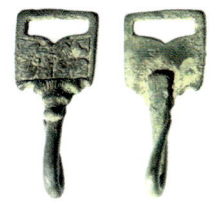

513. Silver-gilt; cast and wire; two-piece; moulded-relief. Comparable with no. 512 except the swag and collar are slightly different; 26 x 17mm. *South-East Dorset*. Photographs © Ken Wheatley.

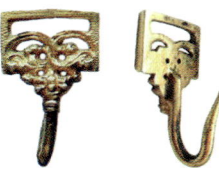

HOOKED-CLASPS & EYES

Early post-medieval Class K, Type 2

Circular

514. Lead/tin and iron; cast and wire; two-piece; moulded-relief. A circular panel bearing a six-petalled double rose (the outer petals resemble crowns) within a linear border. Incomplete, a remnant of separate embedded iron wire hook, rust staining on reverse; 21.1 x 14.8mm. *Isle of White*. Portable Antiquities Scheme IOW-0D7002. Photographs © Isle of White Council.

515. Lead/tin and iron; cast and wire; two-piece; moulded-relief; engraved. A circular panel bearing the sacred monogram IHS in Lombardic script. Incomplete, a remnant of separate embedded iron wire hook; 20.6 x 15.12mm. *Bedfordshire*. Drawing © Patrick Read.

516. Lead/tin and copper alloy; cast and wire; two-piece; moulded-relief and openwork. A beaded border. Incomplete, a remnant of separate embedded wire hook; a central drilled-hole may have held a separate decorative feature; 22 x 15mm. *River Thames foreshore, London*. Drawing © Nick Griffiths.

517. Lead/tin and probably copper alloy or iron; cast and probably wire; two-piece; moulded-relief. Very crude. A recessed circle with a central pellet surrounded by (?) four pellets. Incomplete, edge of the plate broken off, and probable separate embedded copper-alloy or iron wire hook missing; 28.7 x 21mm. *North Yorkshire*. Portable Antiquities Scheme LVPL-0DF707. Photographs © Portable Antiquities Scheme and the Trustees of National Museums Liverpool.

518. Silver-gilt; cast and probably wire; two-piece; moulded-relief. A heart within a floral garland. Incomplete, separate soldered probable wire hook missing; 16 x 12.3. *Lincolnshire*. Treasure case 2003 T26. Photographs © the Trustees of The British Museum.

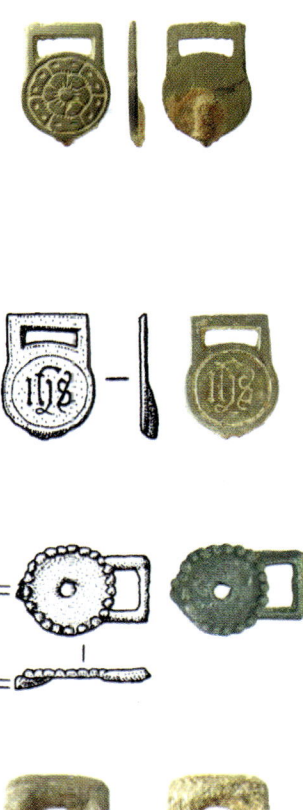

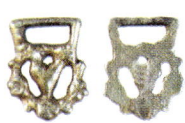

Early post-medieval Class K, Type 3

Trefoil

519. Lead/tin and copper alloy; cast and wire; two-piece; shallow convex; moulded-relief. A stylised three-petalled rose with sepals. A separate embedded wire hook; 25 x 12mm. *River Thames foreshore, London*. Drawing © Patrick Read.

520. Lead/tin and copper alloy; cast and wire; two-piece; moulded-relief. Comparable with no. 519. Incomplete, a small piece of plate broken off and a remnant of separate embedded wire hook; 24.5 x 15mm. *South-West Wiltshire*. Drawing © Patrick Read.

521. Lead/tin and probably copper alloy; cast and wire; two-piece; moulded-relief. Tiny pellets arranged as a trefoil of small stylised flowers within a raised border. Incomplete, separate embedded wire hook missing; 28.5 x 18.5mm. *River Thames foreshore, London*. Drawing © Nick Griffiths.

522. Lead/tin and probably copper alloy; two-piece; convex; moulded-relief. A trefoil of hollow-domed bosses, each boss has five voided radiating lines with pellets in the interstices; a beaded border. Incomplete, separate embedded wire hook missing and a small hole in one boss; 27.2 x 21.5mm. *River Thames foreshore, London*. Drawing © Patrick Read.

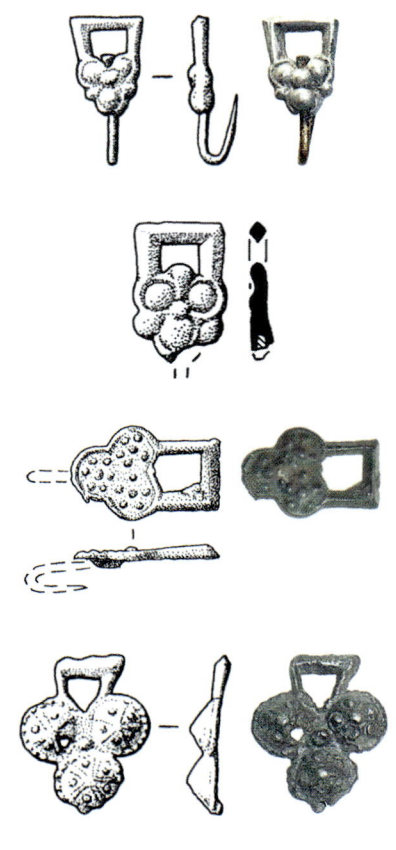

Early post-medieval Class K, Type 4

Heart-shaped

523. Lead/tin and iron; cast; two-piece; moulded-relief. Comparable with no. 457 except a small fleur-de-lis projects into the loop, two transverse grooves and curvilinear at the juncture of the plate and hook. Incomplete, a remnant of separate embedded iron wire hook; 22.72 x 15.5mm. *Essex*. Portable Antiquities Scheme ESS-5AFC81. Photographs © Colchester Museums.

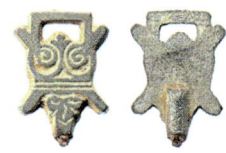

Early post-medieval Class K, Type 5

Figurative

524. Silver-gilt; cast and wire; two-piece; convex; moulded-relief. A solid acorn; a separate soldered distorted wire hook; 19.06 x 0.99mm. *East Devon.* Drawing © Patrick Read.

525. Silver-gilt; cast and wire; two-piece; moulded-relief. A five-petalled double rose; a separate soldered distorted wire hook; 22.4 x 0.98mm. *Derbyshire.* Portable Antiquities Scheme E4550. Photographs © Derby City Council.

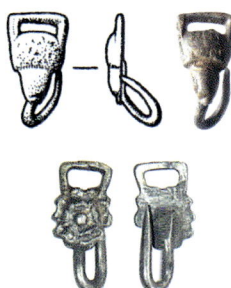

Early post-medieval Class L single sharp-hooked clasps

Class L cast copper-alloy single sharp-hooked clasps are designated as Type 1 circular and Type 2 triangular. Otherwise comparable with Classes A-K except lacking distinct partitioned attachment-loops - instead the main plates are annular, thereby serving as attachment-loops. No. 527 perhaps originally had a solid centre and a rectangular attachment-loop (pers. comm. Jim Halliday): the latter is not evident from the drawing, although a small projection inside the loop could possibly be a remnant of the infill of the plate; the angle of the hook on no. 526 is anomalous; *c.* 16th century.

Early post-medieval Class L, Type 1

Circular

526. Copper alloy; cast, one-piece; moulded-relief. A ridged ribbed collar at the juncture of the loop and hook; hook-point distorted; 31.1 x 13.8mm. *North Lincolnshire.* Portable Antiquities Scheme SWYOR-E9FC82. Photograph © and courtesy of the West Yorkshire Archaeology Service.

527. Copper alloy; cast, one-piece; moulded-relief. A swag and a ridged ribbed collar at the juncture of the loop and hook; a small bifurcate projection located at the top inside of the loop; 27 x 14mm. *East Yorkshire.* JH/069. Drawing © Anne Hodgson.

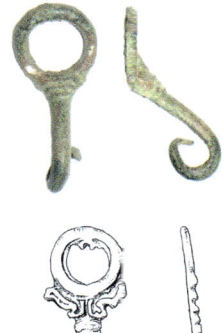

Early Post-Medieval Class L, Type 2

Triangular

528. Copper alloy; cast; one-piece; moulded-relief. A cinquefoil on each apex of the attachment-end and another forms a projecting ridged collar at the juncture of the plate and distorted hook; 30.61 x 15.31mm. *Surrey.* Portable Antiquities Scheme SUR-873D44. Photo © Surrey County Council.

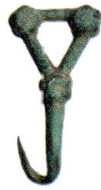

Early post-medieval Class M single sharp-hooked clasps

Distinctive by a lack of attachment-loops, Class M single sharp-hooked clasps were attached by stitching through openwork or attachment-holes in the plate. Type 1 is shield-shaped and Type 2 figurative. Cast in either copper-alloy or silver, they are otherwise comparable with Classes A-J; *c*.16th century.

Early post-medieval Class M, Type 1

Shield-shaped

529. Copper alloy; cast; one-piece; moulded-relief and openwork. Three debased fleurs-de-lis within a linear shield; a debased fleur-de-lis knop on the attachment-end; engrailed edges; a shallow ridged collar at the juncture of the plate and hook; openwork utilised for attachment; 29 x 15mm. *South-West Wiltshire*. Drawing © Patrick Read.

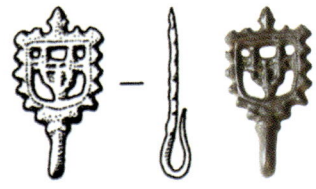

Early post-medieval Class M, Type 2

Figurative

530. Silver; cast; one-piece; moulded-relief. A possible acorn at the juncture of the plate and hook and three trefoils; three attachment-holes; 19 x 12.7mm. *Suffolk*. Treasure case 2004 T274. Photographs © the Trustees of The British Museum.

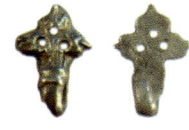

Early post-medieval Class N single sharp-hooked clasp

This cast compositely constructed silver-gilt loopless sharp-hooked clasp is designated as Class N, Type 1 and is sub-lozenge shaped with an unusual single forward-facing sharp-hook. Rounded attachment-knops used for stitching. Under the **Treasure Act 1996** declared not Treasure as less than 300 years old; notwithstanding, it is stylistically probably *c*.16th century.

Early Post-Medieval Class N, Type 1

Figurative

531. Silver-gilt; cast; two-piece; moulded-relief and openwork. A spray emerging from a three-lobed leaf (?) a strawberry, each lobe of which is a trefoil; the spray supports a large ring; three rounded attachment-knops, one each side immediately above the end of each frond and another attached to the middle trefoil of the leaf. A separate flat-section sharp-hook with two longitudinal grooves is soldered to the reverse of the ring and between the spray. Striations on the reverse of the plate are perhaps deliberate; 24 x 14mm. *South Somerset*. Treasure case 2003 T109. Drawing © Patrick Read.

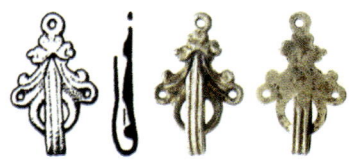

Early post-medieval Class O single sharp-hooked clasp

Designated Class O, Type 1 this alarmingly flimsy single recurving sharp-hooked clasp is compositely constructed from copper-alloy sheeting and circular-section wire, decorated with ground-supported filigree. Unusually, and similar to many early medieval sharp-hooked clasps, the plate has pierced attachment-holes. Possibly late 15th early 16th century.

Early post-medieval Class O, Type 1

Circular

532. Copper alloy, sheeting, wire and ground-supported twisted wire filigree: two-piece; sporadic gilding overall. An extremely thin-gauge sheeting plate with a trefoil collar at the juncture of the hook and what is perhaps a knop at the other end, now distorted towards the obverse; two oval attachment-holes; a wire border; one end of the separate wire hook is flattened and soldered to the reverse of the collar and plate. Corroded, which has fractured the wire border and plate at one of the attachment-holes; 31.48 x 16.78mm. *Buckinghamshire*. Drawing © Nick Griffiths.

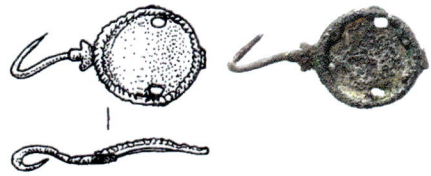

Early post-medieval Class P single sharp-hooked clasp

That riveting is the attachment method differentiates this single recurving sharp-hooked clasp from Classes E-O and Q. Designated as Class P, Type 1 sub-circular, it is constructed from copper-alloy sheeting and tentatively assigned as late 15th - *c.*17th century.

Early post-medieval Class P, Type 1

Sub-circular

533. Copper alloy; sheeting; one-piece; convex; die-stamped; sporadic gilding on the obverse. A hollow-domed boss with a laterally-projecting rim with a V-shaped notch either side; a further similar notch each side of the shank at its juncture with the plate forms an angular collar; a central rivet-hole retains a separate copper-alloy rivet; 34 x 17mm. *South-East Dorset*. Drawing © Patrick Read.

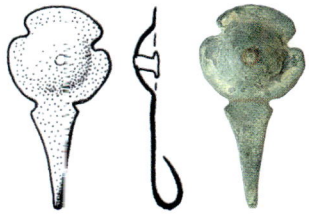

Early post-medieval Class Q single sharp-hooked clasps

Compositely constructed single sharp-hooked clasps designated as Class Q, Type 1 comprise a cast lead/tin plate into which is embedded a separate copper-alloy circular-section wire hook and combined rounded attachment loop: Type 2 is compositely constructed from sheeting and circular-section wire copper-alloy, also with a rounded loop. All are probably *c*.16th century.

Early post-medieval Class Q, Type 1

Ovoid

534. Lead/tin and copper-alloy; cast and wire; two-piece; shallow convex; moulded-relief. A central pellet and a trefoil of solid-domed bosses, each boss within a beaded annulet; evidence of abraded decoration on each boss, perhaps annulets and beads. An embedded separate copper-alloy combined wire hook and loop. Incomplete, edge much abraded; 22.99 x 13.05mm. *South-East Dorset*. Drawing © Patrick Read.

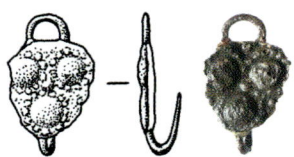

535. Lead/tin and copper-alloy; cast and wire; two-piece. Incomplete, much corroded. Outline of the combined hook and eye are clearly visible; 26 x 12mm. *North Gloucestershire*. Photographs © John Bromley.

536. Copper alloy; sheeting and wire; four-piece; die-stamped or repoussé. A foliate and floral panel outlined with cabling all within a beaded border. A separate soldered sheeting reverse-plate, wire loop and wire hook; 30 x 19mm. Incomplete, edge broken away in two places and hook broken off. *Norfolk*. Portable Antiquities Scheme NMS-1E13B2. Photograph © Norfolk Museums and Archaeology Service.

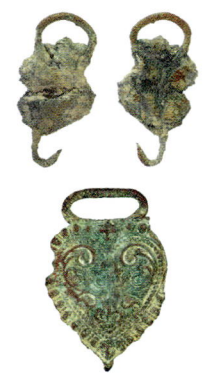

Early post-medieval unclassified single sharp-hooked clasps

Four compositely constructed single sharp-hooked clasps which are missing their attachment-loops, however, all are probably Class K. Three are circular while the fourth is an indeterminate shape.

537. Silver-gilt; cast and wire; two-piece; moulded-relief. A fleur-de-lis within a four-petalled rose; a separate soldered hook. Incomplete, probable angular loop broken off; 21.04 x 13.35mm. *Suffolk*. Portable Antiquities Scheme SF-9CCB15, Treasure case 2007 T256. Photographs © Suffolk County Council Archaeological Service.

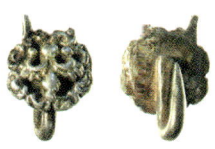

538. Silver; cast, sheeting and wire; four-piece; moulded-relief. Comparable with no. 539. Resembles a stylised flower, the cast plate has three equidistant globular knops either side. A separate domed-head rivet pierces a pair of sheeting multi-slotted roves placed one above the other, the upper one smaller, and then the plate before securing. Incomplete, indeterminate-shape loop and point of separate soldered silver wire hook broken off; 22.5 x 18.98mm. *Suffolk*. Portable Antiquities Scheme SF-96ED71. Photographs © Suffolk County Council Archaeological Service.

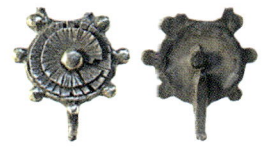

539. Silver-gilt; cast, sheeting and wire; four-piece; moulded-relief. Comparable with no. 538 except a multi-petalled rove, the petals of which have multiple longitudinal striations, and a large domed-head rivet; 21.5 x 15mm. Incomplete, indeterminate-shape loop broken off. *Suffolk*. Portable Antiquities Scheme SF-E85546. Photographs © Portable Antiquities Scheme.

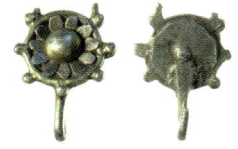

540. Lead/tin and copper alloy; cast and wire; two-piece; moulded-relief. A central pellet and annulets on a raised roundel surmounted by a large pellet flanked either side by a small pellet; a possible large rounded knop at the juncture of the plate and hook. A separate embedded distorted copper-alloy wire hook. Incomplete, loop broken off and edge corroded away; 36.06 x 14.48mm. *Warwickshire*. Drawing © Patrick Read.

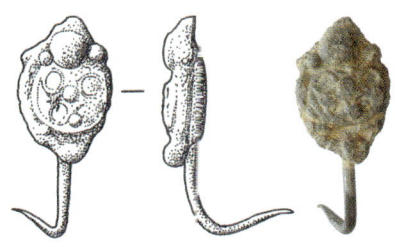

Early post-medieval Class R double sharp-hooked clasps

Either cast or sheeting, Class R copper-alloy clasps comprise a central decorated plate with a recurving tapering sharp-hook either end. Like early medieval Class L double recurving sharp-hooked clasps, invariably called 'cloak clasps' or 'cloak fasteners', but again the same caveats apply. The contour of the hooks could mean that some are havettes, though this hypothesis is conjectural (see below). Two forms are noted: Type 1 has a rectangular/sub-rectangular plate, and Type 2 circular/sub-circular. Decoration is either moulded-relief or punched; c.15th - c. early 16th century. Clasps of this form are not evident in contemporary iconographic or documentary sources.

A comparable but smaller and more delicate form of Type 1 clasp made from a thin strip of sheeting copper-alloy was found in a c.1538 archaeological context in York (Ottaway and Rogers 2002, fig 1491, no. 15222).

Early post-medieval Class R, Type 1

Rectangular/Sub-rectangular

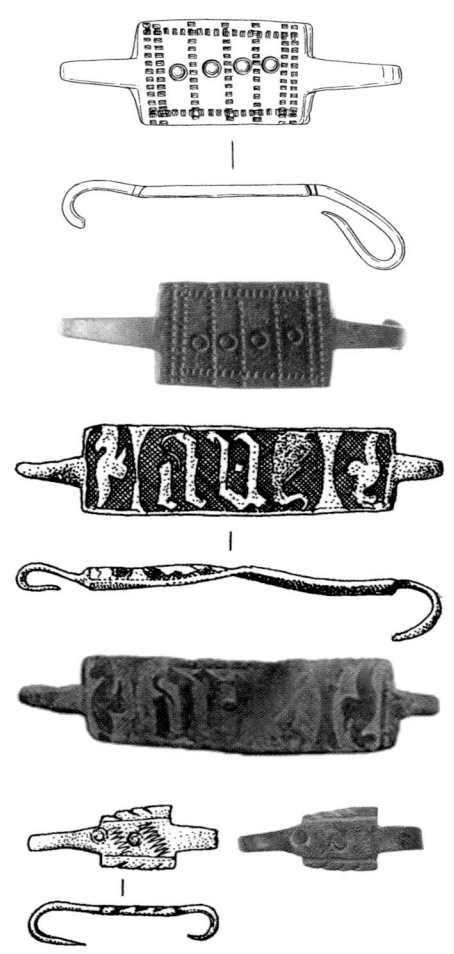

541. Copper alloy; cast; one-piece; punched and engraved or compass-inscribed. Seven transverse bands of annulets, the two bands at either end being voided; and a longitudinal band of ovals bordering either side; thereby forming four rectangular panels each containing an annulet on or close to the median; a hook either end. Incomplete, one hook broken off; 55 x 17mm. *Suffolk*. Portable Antiquities Scheme SF-E78FC7. Drawing © Donna Wreathall, photograph © Suffolk County Council Archaeological Service.

542. Copper alloy; cast; one-piece; moulded-relief. A rectangular panel bearing AVE - probably abbreviated Ave Maria - in black-letter script, flanked either side with a bird-like motif on a cross-hatched field; a hook either end; 67.5 x 15.5mm. *Hampshire*. Portable Antiquities Scheme HAMP1396. Photograph © Winchester Museum Service. Drawing © Nick Griffiths.

543. Copper alloy; sheeting; one-piece; engraved and punched. Two median annulets and two oblique bands of zigzags with a linear and hatched border either side; a hook either end, one large and one small; 26.68 x 23.39mm. *River Thames foreshore, London*. Drawing © Nick Griffiths.

HOOKED-CLASPS & EYES

Early post-medieval Class R, Type 2

Sub-circular

544. Copper alloy; sheeting; engraved. Ten unequally-spaced radiating bands of zigzgs; a hook either end; 36.7 x 24mm. Incomplete, one hook broken off. *Norfolk*. After Margeson 1993, fig. 9, no. 80. Drawing © and reproduced courtesy of Norfolk Museums and Archaeology Service.

Early post-medieval Class R, Type 3

Cordate

545. Copper alloy; cast; one-piece; punched or drilled. A central heart, the obverse has a median band and border of pits, the reverse shows where the punch or drill has almost penetrated the metal; projecting from either side of the bifurcate end is an integral exceedingly long strip bent at the end into a hook; 78.3 x 15.9 x 8.6mm. *North Yorkshire*. Portable Antiquities Scheme SWYOR-128363. Photographs © West Yorkshire Archaeology Service.

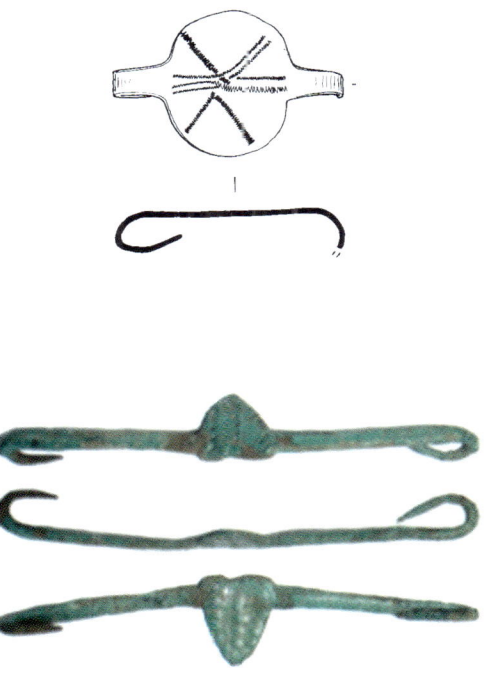

Early post-medieval Class S double sharp-hooked clasps

Class S clasps are compositely constructed from sheeting copper-alloy and are differentiated from Class R by a separate strip with a recurving sharp-hook either end. Each section has a central rivet-hole and secured together by a separate copper-alloy rivet.

Like Class R, these are frequently called cloak-clasps but again supposition. The 45° angle of the hooks on no. 546 is comparable with hooks on havettes (see below) though for this particular clasp such a use is most unlikely. The plate of no. 549 is oriented in the rectangular; this is possibly unintentional as most other similar clasps in the known record are oriented as a lozenge, another exception being one from Meols and recorded in Egan *et al* 2007, Pl. 45, no. 3038. One form is recognised, designated as Type 1, and assigned as *c.*15th - *c.*16th century.

Early post-medieval Class S, Type 1

Lozenge-shaped

546. Copper alloy; sheeting; three-piece; engraved. Comparable with nos 547-549. Eight bands of zigzags radiating from a central rivet-hole, bordered by zigzags. A separate double-hook is secured to the back by a separate copper-alloy rivet; 44 x 30mm. *South Devon*. After Read 1988, fig 19, no. 7; and 1995, no. 766. Drawing © Patrick Read.

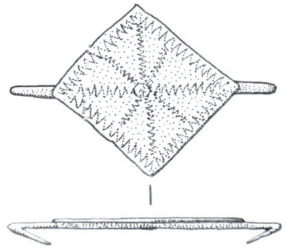

547. Copper alloy; sheeting; engraved; three-piece. Comparable with no. 546, 548-549 except one median band of zigzags and the double-hook strip, both ends of which taper from the middle, is wider. Incomplete, plate broken in two places and partially missing; L48mm. *Norfolk*. After Margeson 1993, fig. 9, no. 81. Drawing © and reproduced courtesy of Norfolk Museums and Archaeology Service.

548. Copper alloy; sheeting; three-piece; engraved. Comparable with nos 546-547, 549 except the plate is elongated and has three transverse bands of zigzags bordered by zigzags. Incomplete, two points of the plate and both hook-points broken off; 37 x 20mm. *East Devon*. After Read 2001, no. 822, described as a brooch. Drawing © Patrick Read.

549. Copper alloy; sheeting; three-piece; engraved. Linear and oblique bands of zigzags within a zigzag border otherwise comparable with nos 546-548. Incomplete, one hook-point broken off; plate 25 x 23mm, hook L41mm. *Norfolk*. Portable Antiquities Scheme NMS-7DC651. Photographs © Norfolk Museums and Archaeology Service.

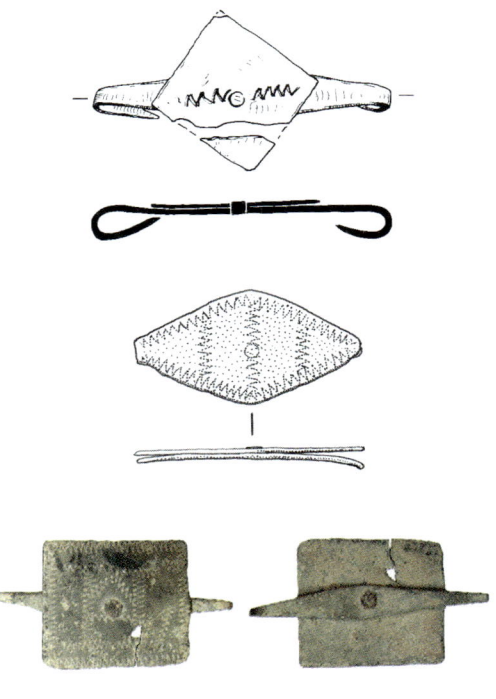

Early post-medieval Class T double sharp-hooked clasp

Designated as Class T, Type 1, this substantial compositely constructed clasp has a cast lead/tin plate into which is embedded a separate iron circular-section tapering wire recurving double sharp-hook. Decoration is moulded-relief. Recovered from a c.16th - c.17th-century deposit.

Early post-medieval Class T, Type 1

Sub-Rectangular

550. Lead/tin and iron; cast and wire; two piece; moulded-relief and openwork. Two lappets each side of the plate, each pair linked by a bar with a central globular knop on the outside edge, thereby forming narrow openwork; the plate and lappets are cross-hatched; each end of the plate has a trefoil formed from one large and three small domed-bosses, each large boss within an annulet; both ends of the plate terminate with a trefoil formed from one large and two small globular knops. The back of the plate has a median ridge into which is embedded a separate iron wire bent at each end into a hook. Both sides of the plate are coated with a now black substance, possibly bitumen. Incomplete, a small piece of plate and a globular knop broken off; 81 x 25mm. *River Thames foreshore, London*. Drawing © Patrick Read.

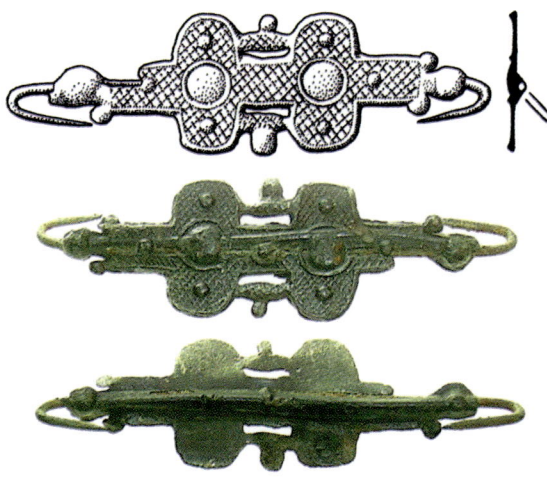

Early post-medieval Class U triple sharp-hooked clasp

Undoubtedly a high-status item, a substantial silver-gilt clasp, perhaps a hat ornament, designated as Class U, Type 1. Soldered to the reverse of the ornately cast plate are three circular-section tapering wire recurving sharp-hooks.

This remarkable piece is thought to have a possible parallel, securing the cloak worn by St Margaret of Antioch, depicted in a c.1518-27 stained-glass window in the Chapel of the Vyne, Sherborne St John, Hampshire. Disappointingly, close study of St Margaret's gold-coloured probable trefoil-shaped jewel is unconvincing, for it does not appear to have three hooks: it is perhaps an agrafe, a large brooch used for fastening a robe or cloak, fashionable between the mid-13th and 15th centuries (Fig. 16.1-2).

The chapel also has an early 16th-century stained-glass window that shows Catherine of Aragon with a linked pair of elaborate gold-coloured trefoil-jewels securing her cloak to the bodice. These jewels are also thought to have three hooks but again inspection suggests otherwise: yes, a protrusion is visible between each leaf, but it is impossible to say whether they are hook-shanks. A more likely description is matching brooches, or bosses provided with rings on the reverse, through which a chain or cord was threaded; the chain or cord could be drawn, thereby allowing the cloak to be adjusted at the throat (Fig. 17).

Interestingly, a contemporary drawing of Queen Elizabeth I in the margin of the 1599 Town Charter of Axbridge, Somerset, shows her cloak fastened at the throat by a circular jewel with four projections that are possibly loops or hooks: nonetheless, caution is advised, for it could be a cruciform brooch the projections of which are gems (Fig. 18.1-2).

Important evidence is provided in a 1577 portrait of Sir Edward Hoby; attached near the crown of his hard high hat is what appears to be a trefoil-boss jewel with three projections (Fig. 19.1-2). Close inspection, however, reveals this is perhaps three separate domed circular clasps arranged as a trefoil, each with a slightly curved projection. The curved projections are likely to be sharp-hooks piercing the fabric. If indeed individual clasps, each would have needed an attachment-loop or aperture for holding stitches, thereby keeping them in place. Early post-medieval single sharp-hooked clasps Classes C and D would fit the bill but as the backs are not visible, impossible to confirm. Sir Edward's hat-jewel may well be a Class U triple sharp-hooked clasp with granular decoration similar to that on hat-hook no. 714 (see below). Consideration should be given to one or more hat-hooks, however, as no part of the S-shaped sharp-hook found on most hat-hooks, or a recurving hook, would be visible, this hypothesis can be discounted (see below).

Early post-medieval Class U, Type 1

Circular

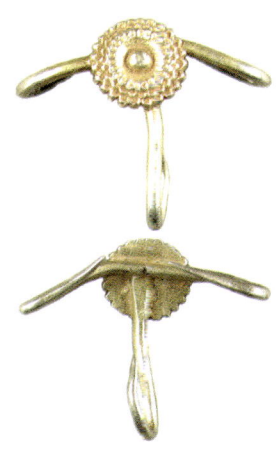

551. Silver-gilt; cast and wire; four-piece; moulded-relief. The plate is in the form of a multi-petalled chrysanthemum-like flower. Soldered to the back is a separate transverse wire with a hook at each end; a second separate wire extends laterally from the centre of the plate, one end of which is soldered and the other end terminates in a hook; 36 x 41mm. *Lincolnshire*. Treasure case 2006 T55. Photographs © the Trustees of The British Museum.

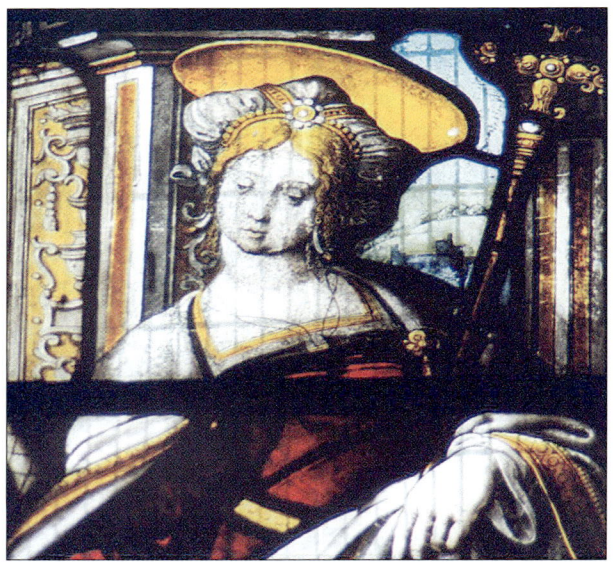

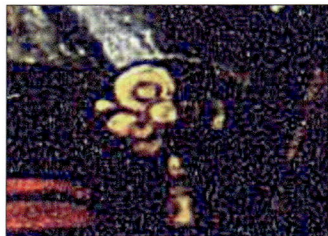

Fig. 16.1. St Margaret of Antioch, depicted in a c.1518-27 stained-glass window in the Chapel of the Vyne, Sherborne St John, Hampshire. Note (?) clasp on her left breast. Photograph reproduced courtesy of The National Trust.

Fig. 16.2. Detail of St Margaret's (?) clasp. Photograph reproduced courtesy of The National Trust.

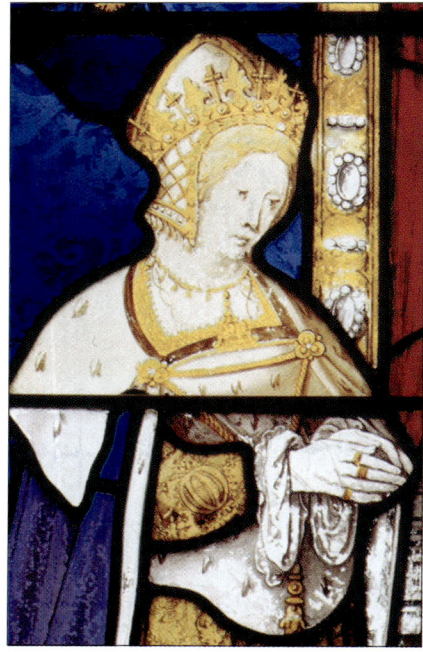

Fig. 17. Catherine of Aragon depicted in a 16th- century stained-glass window in the Chapel of the Vyne, Sherborne St John, Hampshire. Note the linked pair of gold-coloured trefoil-jewels securing her cloak to the bodice. Photograph reproduced courtesy of The National Trust, © NTPL/ Derrick E Whitty.

HOOKED-CLASPS & EYES

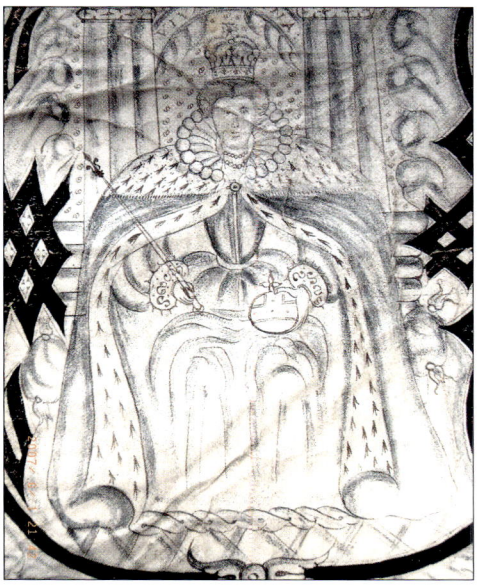

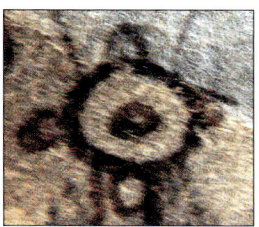

Fig. 18.2. Detail of Queen Elizabeth's throat jewel. Photograph © Val MacRae.

Fig. 18.1. A 1599 drawing of Queen Elizabeth 1 in the Town Charter of Axebridge, Somerset. Note her cloak fastened at the throat by a circular jewel with four projections. Photograph © Val MacRae.

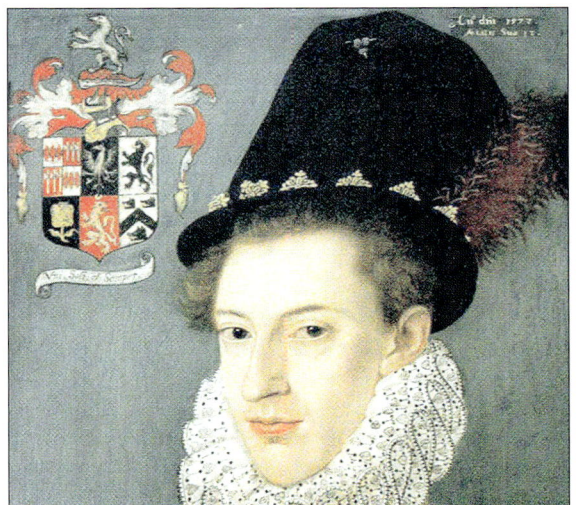

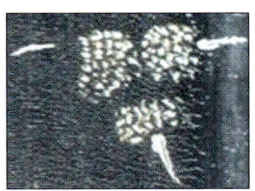

Fig. 19.2. Detail of Sir Edward Hoby's hat clasp/s. Note the three curved projections. Photograph © Val MacRae.

Fig. 19.1. Sir Edward Hoby 1577, anonymous artist. Note clasp/s secured near the crown of his high hat. Private collection. Photograph © Val MacRae.

Early post-medieval Class V quadruple sharp- and blunt-hooked clasps

Designated as Class V, Type 1, each of the clasps described here is compositely constructed from sheeting and circular-section tapering wire with four recurving sharp or blunt hooks. The lozenge-shaped plates makes them comparable with a quadruple sharp-hooked clasp in Egan and Forsyth 1997, fig. 15.10, but the hooks are arranged differently, where it is suggested that theirs perhaps had an association with probable 16th-century women's head-dress.

Early post-medieval Class V, Type 1

Lozenge-shaped

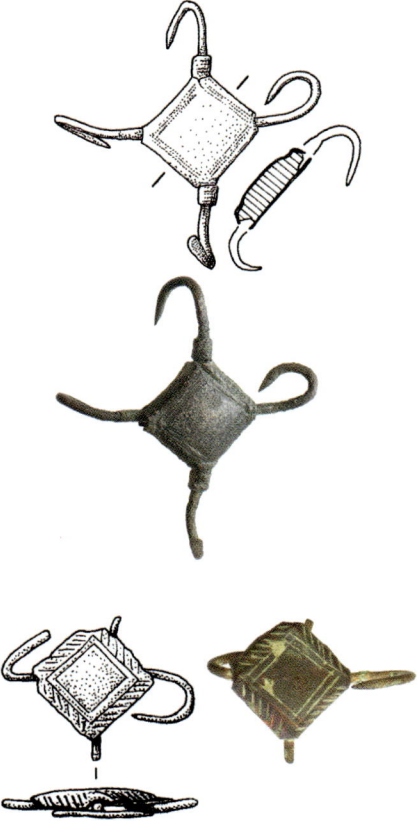

552. Copper alloy and lead/tin; sheeting and wire; probably eight or more pieces; shallow convex; engraved. Comparable with no. 553. A hollow-domed front-plate with a voided lozenge bordered by hatching, a small section removed from each apex, thereby forming an opening. The back-plate is flat and attached to the front-plate by lead which fills the space between the two plates. A separate wire with a sharp-hook at one end and a blunt-hook at the other, is sandwiched between the plates and protrudes through two of the openings - around the wire where it exits the plates either side is crimped or soldered a separate sheeting sleeve, presumably as stops. Another separate wire with a sharp-hook either end crosses the first wire and protrudes through the other two openings - marks on the wire either side of the plate suggest missing sleeves; plate 18.18 x 18.11mm, overall 45.96 x 41.14mm. *Norfolk*. Drawing © Patrick Read.

553. Copper alloy; sheeting and wire; probably eight or more pieces; shallow convex; engraved. Comparable with no. 552 except incomplete. Lead/tin residue on the inside of both plates. A separate wire, with a sharp-hook at one end and a 45° bend the other, forming a blunt-hook, is sandwiched between the plates and protrudes from two of the openings and now swivels freely; however, a mark on the wire suggests the lead/tin secured it with the hook facing to the front and the 45° bend rearwards. Another separate wire crosses the first wire and protrudes through the other two openings: although both ends appear clean cut and unbroken, feasibly it may have had a hook either end, 31.62 x 23.7mm. *North-East Kent*. Drawing © Nick Griffiths.

5: EARLY POST-MEDIEVAL WIRE CLASPS

Although many of the preceding sharp- or blunt-hooked clasps have separate wire hooks and/or attachment-loops, it is expedient to differentiate clasps made predominantly from wire. In the main, wire is circular-section, though square- or flattened-section are recorded here. Decoration is confined to engraving (seemingly uniquely), twisting a single wire or two wires together to form a barley-twist, soldered appliqués or plates, fine-gauge wire spiral binding or beads.

Early post-medieval Class A wire single sharp-hooked clasps

Two forms of Class A circular-section copper-alloy wire single sharp-hooked clasps are catalogued here, designated as Types 1-2, both of which are from safe archaeological contexts. No. 554 is simply made and assigned as 1500-25, while no. 555 is more complicated and dated as 1690-1730/60. If the separate attachment on Type 2 originally did hold another hook, it should be reclassified.

Early post-medieval Class A, Type 1

554. Copper alloy; wire; one-piece. One end is bent into a figure-of-eight forming two transverse attachment-spirals; the shank is barley-twisted and bent into a hook but whether recurving or forward-facing is unclear; 25 x 15.5mm. *Ridderstraat, Amsterdam*. Amsterdam Historical Museum/Bureau of Monuments and Archaeology, Department of Archaeology, Amsterdam, inventory no. ML12-198. Photograph © Wiard Krook, Bureau of Monuments and Archaeology, Department of Archaeology, Amsterdam.

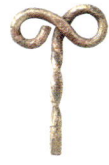

Early post-medieval Class A, Type 2

555. Copper alloy; wire. Hooked-section: one-piece; a wire tapered at both ends then bent and barley-twisted together to form an attachment-loop at one end and a hook at the other, either recurving or forward-facing. Separate link: two-piece; a wire spiralled at each end, one of which is attached to the hook's attachment-loop; a separate thinner-gauge wire spiralled around the shank is in turn decorated with a spiral of very fine-gauge wire. The link is perhaps from a chain or alternatively may have held a second hook; overall L58mm. *Norfolk*. After Margeson 1993, fig. 9, no. 87. Drawing © and reproduced courtesy of Norfolk Museums and Archaeology Service.

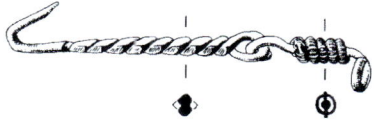

Early post-medieval Class B wire single sharp-hooked clasp

An unusual clasp designated as Class B, Type 1. Compositely constructed from copper-alloy square-section wire, with a single recurving sharp-hook and a small front-plate or appliqué. Comparable with Class K, Type 2 and probably *c*.16th - *c*.17th century.

Early post-medieval Class B, Type 1

556. Copper alloy; wire and sheeting; two-piece; die-stamped. A square-section wire bent into a triangular loop the end of which butts against the shank; while the other end is bent into a hook. A separate sheeting lozenge-shaped front-plate or appliqué with a four-petalled flower is soldered over the butt seam; 29.18 x 13.3. *The Netherlands*. Drawing © Nick Griffiths.

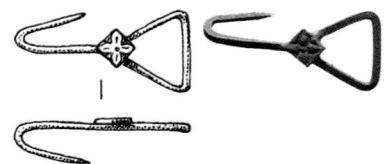

Early post-medieval Class C wire single sharp-hooked clasps

Five Types of Class C compositely constructed single sharp-hooked clasp made of circular-section copper-alloy or silver wire are recognised. Most are plain though no. 558 has simple engraving and is perhaps gilded. This decoration is presumably on the front which means Type 1 hooks are recurving, but whether this is the case with Types 2-4 is uncertain.

Type 1 comprises two pieces of wire bent together as a reef knot, with one end forming a hook; there is opine that the other end originally also had a hook; however, each specimen in the known record is single-hooked. If originally they were double-hooked, it is reasonable to believe one would have revealed itself by now.

Recoveries of Type 1 clasps from archaeological contexts at Fastolf Place, London (Egan 2005, fig. 25, no. 157) and Austin Friars, Leicester (Mellor and Pearce 1081, fig. 49, no. 40) provide a date range of possibly 15th - 16th century. Sixteenth- - 17th-century deposits in the River Thames foreshore in London have produced many clasps in this category for members of The Society of Thames Mudlarks. Paradoxically, they appear uncommon finds for metal-detectorists, although one is recorded from Surrey (Portable Antiquities Scheme SUR-04F848). An apparent indeterminate form of probable early post-medieval wire clasp is reused as a suspension-mount for an early 13th-century harness-pendant recorded by Nick Griffiths (Fig. 20).

Type 2 is possibly *c*.15th - *c*.17th century; Type 3 *c*.1500 - *c*.1550 and stylistically is comparable with fig. 53, no. 284 in Egan 2005 (a chatelaine). A substantial portion of a late 16th - early 17th-century compositely constructed copper-alloy wire probable head-dress from the River Thames foreshore, London, included a single sharp-hooked clasp comparable with Type 4, no. 561 (Murdoch 1991, no. 212); and Type 4, no. 562 is possibly also an ornament from women's head-dress assigned the same date and is comparable with another example from London (Egan and Forsyth 1997, fig. 15.10). Two clasps similar to Type 4 are erroneously recorded as Anglo-Saxon wrist-clasps in West Stow The Anglo-Saxon Village, vol 1, *East Anglian Archaeological Report No. 24*, 1985. Wire clasps of any category are apparently common finds in the Netherlands for metal-detectorists.

HOOKED-CLASPS & EYES

Early post-medieval Class C, Type 1

557. Copper alloy; wire; two-piece. Comparable with no. 558. Two wires bent as a reef knot thereby forming an oval attachment-loop; the end of one wire projects and forms a hook; 27 x 16mm. *River Thames foreshore, London.* Drawing © Nick Griffiths.

558. Silver; wire; two-piece; engraved; sporadic gilding. Comparable with no. 557 except the front is decorated with five groups of oblique lines; 25.53 x 14.27mm. *River Thames foreshore, London.* Drawing © Nick Griffiths.

Early post-medieval Class C, Type 2

559. Copper alloy; wire; two-piece. An oval loop with one end bent laterally at 90º forming a long-shanked hook; similarly at 90º, the running-end is bent into a lateral short stub which is then seized to the hook-shank by a separate thinner-gauge wire; 28 x 20mm. *River Thames foreshore, London.* Drawing © Nick Griffiths.

Early post-medieval Class C, Type 3

560. Copper alloy; wire; four-piece. A wire with a hook at one end while the other is spiralled into a loop; either side of the shank is a separate wire with an outward-facing spiral at each end, these wires are seized to the shank with a thinner-gauge wire. In places the main wires are flattened; 29.2 x 14.65mm. *River Thames foreshore, London.* Drawing © Nick Griffiths.

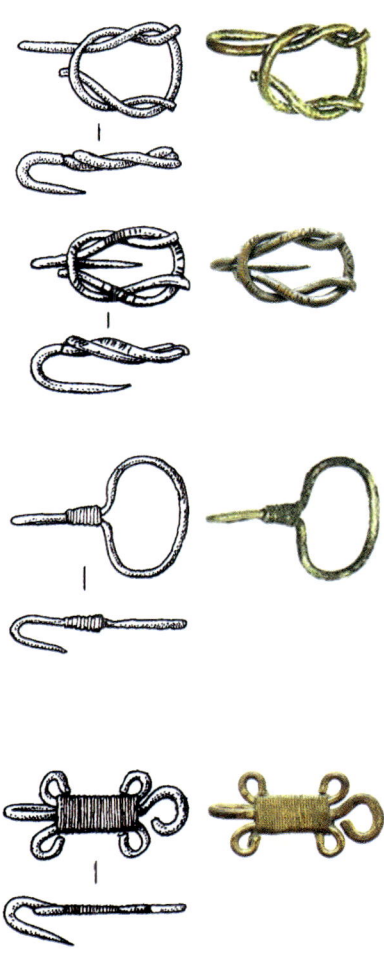

Early post-medieval Class C, Type 4

561. Copper alloy; wire; three-piece. Comparable with no. 560. A heavy-gauge wire bent into a sub-triangular loop, each running-end of which is spiralled back to butt against the side of the frame; a separate wire of the same gauge, one end of which is coiled around the middle of the loop while the other end is formed into a hook, is secured to the main frame by a thinner-gauge wire twisted around and between the two spirals; 32 x 23mm. *Norfolk.* Portable Antiquities Scheme NMS-8030D3. Photograph © of Norfolk Museums and Archaeology Service.

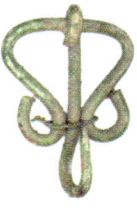

562. Copper alloy; wire; probably four-piece. Comparable with no. 561 except the hook-shank is seized to the main frame by a thinner-gauge wire, and the whole length of hook-shank and each side of the frame are bound with thinner-gauge wire; 31 x 14.5mm. *River Thames foreshore, London.* Drawing © Patrick Read.

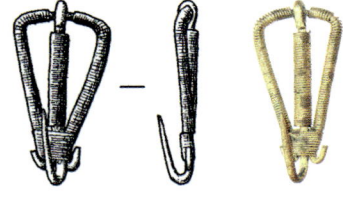

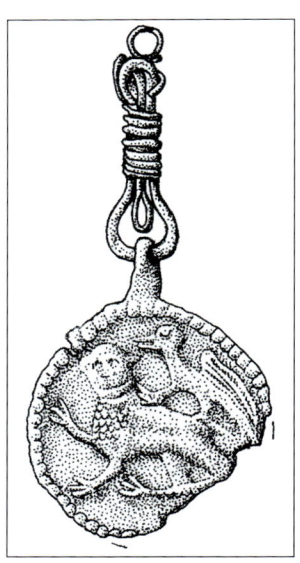

Fig. 20. An indeterminate form of probable early post-medieval wire clasp reused as a suspension-mount for an early 13th-century sheeting copper-alloy circular repoussé harness-pendant. Drawing © Nick Griffiths.

Early post-medieval Class D wire double sharp-hooked clasps

Double sharp-hooked clasps made from silver or copper-alloy circular-section tapering wire are designated as Class D, Types 1-2. Type 1 is plain, while Type 2 has a barley-twist shank. Comparable clasps are known in the Netherlands, recovered in considerable numbers from archaeologically stratified contexts and secure 16th-century deposits by metal-detectorists.

Early post-medieval Class D, Type 1

563. Copper alloy; wire; one-piece. A plain shank; L47mm. *Norfolk.* After Margeson 1993, fig. 9, no. 82. Drawing © and reproduced courtesy of Norfolk Museums and Archaeology Service.

Early post-medieval, Class D, Type 2

564. Copper alloy; wire; one-piece. A flattened barley-twist shank; 50 x 5mm. *South-East Dorset.* United Kingdom Detecting Finds' Database 2918. Photograph © Rod Blunt.

565. Silver; wire; one-piece. A barley-twist shank; one hook-point distorted outwards; 34.38 x 11.26mm. *South-West Dorset.* Drawing © Nick Griffiths.

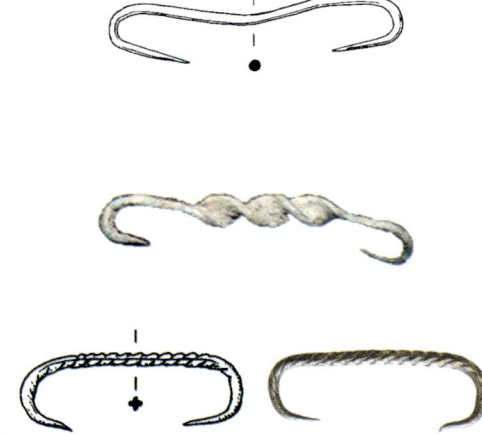

Early post-medieval Class E wire double sharp-hooked clasps

Copper-alloy circular-section wire clasps with a recurving sharp-hook at either end of a shank are designated as Class E, Types 1 and 2, both of which are compositely constructed. Again these are perhaps ornaments from women's head-dress and comparable with examples in Egan and Forsyth 1997. In Murdoch 1991, no. 213, one virtually identical as Type 2 is described as a 'chain clasp' assigned to the first half of the 17th century; while the same piece published in Egan and Forsyth 1997, fig. 15.10, is assigned as probably the second half of the 16th century or early 17th. These clasps are known from 16th- - 17th-century contexts in the Netherlands.

Early post-medieval Class E, Type 1

Double-hooked

566. Copper alloy; wire; probably three-piece. Comparable with no. 567. A bowed wire with a sharp hook either end; a second wire with a small projecting spiral either end is seized to the main shank by thinner-gauge wire; L32mm. *River Thames foreshore, London.* Drawing © Nick Griffiths.

567. Copper alloy; wire; four-piece. Comparable with no. 566 except two pieces of addorsed wire, the ends of which are bent into a spiral, are seized one either side of the shank; L37mm. *River Thames foreshore, London.* Drawing © Nick Griffiths.

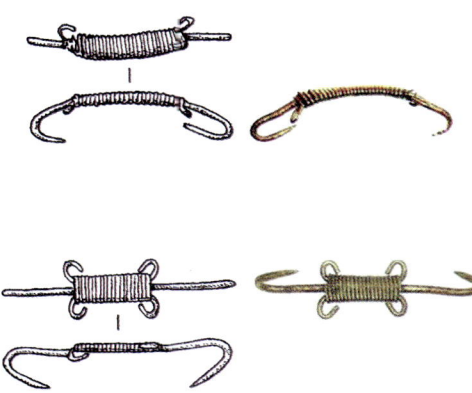

Early post-medieval Class E, Type 2

568. Copper alloy; wire; possibly eight-piece. A central wire with a sharp-hook either end, flanked both sides with a bowed wire the ends of which are bent into flattened spirals; the three wires are seized together near their ends with a thinner-gauge wire; the central and two side wires retain fragments of spirals of very fine-gauge wire which originally covered all three main wires; the central wire has three now black bone beads, one in the centre and one near each hook. Incomplete, much of the decorative spiralled wire is missing; 62.6 x 21mm. *River Thames foreshore, London.* Drawing © Nick Griffiths.

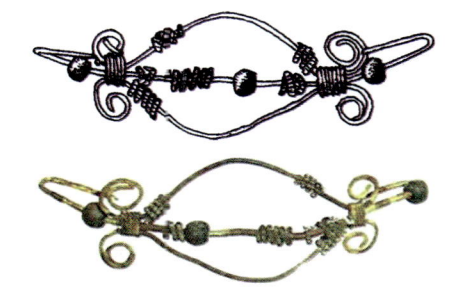

Early post-medieval Class F wire triple sharp-hooked clasps

Although the preceding triple sharp-hooked clasp no. 541 is perhaps a male item, Class F triple recurving sharp-hooked clasps are considered as possible components of women's head-dress ornament. Two forms are noted, both compositely constructed from copper-alloy circular-section wire, and designated as Types 1 and 2. Type 1 comprises two wires with decorative wire spirals around both sections, and Type 2 four wires, of which no. 570 has decorative beads, and wires on no. 571 are partially flattened. Likely to be assigned as second half of the 16th century into the early 17th. No. 570 is from a 1600-1700 archaeological context. Similar examples of both types are known in the Netherlands.

Early post-medieval Class F, Type 1

569. Copper alloy; wire; two-piece. A wire bent into a hook at either end; a separate wire is coiled at one end around the first wire and has a hook at the other; remnants of separate thinner-gauge twisted wire, three on the horizontal wire and two on the vertical; 50 x 20.5mm. *South-East Dorset*. Drawing © Nick Griffiths.

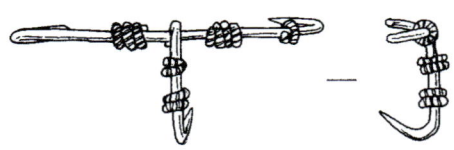

Early post-medieval Class F, Type 2

570. Copper alloy; wire; four-piece. Comparable with no. 571. A wire bent into a sharp-hook at one end and a spiral at the other, the hook and spiral face alternate directions; either side of the shank is a separate wire, one of which is bent at 90° with a hook at one end and an outward-facing spiral the other, the second wire is broken and just the spiral remains; these wires are seized to the shank with a thinner-gauge wire and a remnant of finer-gauge twisted wire is located around the shank near the hook; a now light-green bone bead decorates both the main and lateral shank (originally the beads were white, stained by copper-alloy corrosion products); W31.8mm. *Norfolk*. After Margeson 1993, fig. 9, no. 89. Drawing © and reproduced courtesy of Norfolk Museums and Archaeology Service.

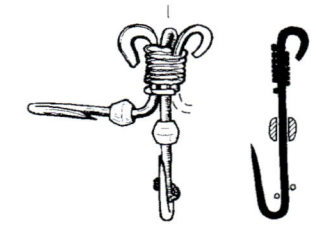

571. Copper alloy; wire; four-piece; engraved. Comparable with no. 570 except the lateral arms are splayed and all three shanks are flattened and have two longitudinal grooves (see enlargement), and without beads; 27.56 x 36.93mm. *County Durham*. Drawing © Patrick Read.

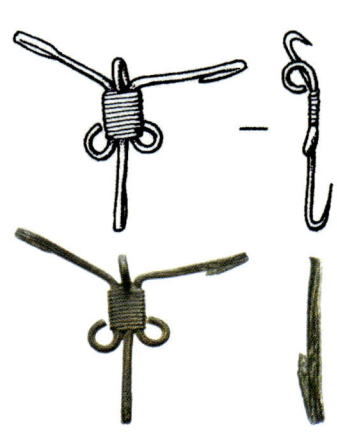

Early post-medieval Class G wire quadruple sharp-hooked clasps

Class G, Type 1 compositely constructed copper-alloy circular-section wire clasps have four recurving sharp-hooks, and are comparable with Class E, Type 1. Perhaps also associated with women's head-dress assigned to the second half of the 16th century into the early 17th.

Early post-medieval Class G, Type 1

572. Copper alloy; wire; three-piece. Comparable with no. 573. Two wires, both ends of each bent into a hook offset inwards; the shanks are seized together by thinner-gauge wire; L33mm. *River Thames foreshore, London.* Drawing © Nick Griffiths.

573. Copper alloy; wire; three-piece. Comparable with no. 572 except the hooks are in the same plane as the body; L38mm. *River Thames foreshore, London.* Drawing © Nick Griffiths.

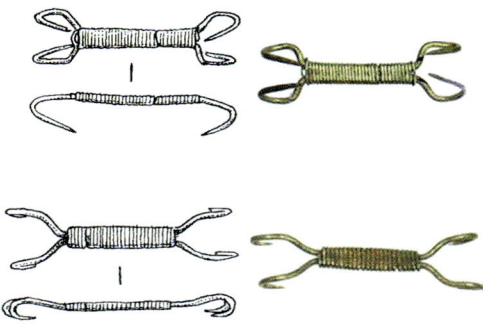

Early post-medieval Class H wire single blunt-hooked clasp

A compositely constructed copper-alloy circular-section barley-twist wire blunt-hook designated as Class H, Type 1. The blunt-hook suggests it may have functioned in tandem with a wire eye. From a secure archaeological 1600-1700 context.

Early post-medieval Class H, Type 1

574. Copper alloy; wire; two-piece. Two wires bent in the centre and then twisted together to form a circular attachment-loop and a barley-twist shank and hook; L30mm. *Keizersstraat, Amsterdam.* Historical Museum/Bureau of Monuments and Archaeology, Department of Archaeology, Amsterdam, inventory no. MZ23-341. Photograph © Wiard Krook, Bureau of Monuments and Archaeology, Department of Archaeology, Amsterdam.

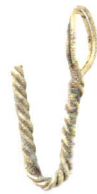

Early post-medieval Class I wire chatelaine blunt-hooks

Designated as Class A, Types 1-2 these compositely constructed circular-section copper-alloy wire blunt-hooks frequently have partially or wholly flattened sections. Damaged clasps often show multiple transverse grooves in the main wires occasioned when hammering separate thinner-gauge wire seizing (No. 578 and fig. 21). Archaeological excavations at Pontefract Castle, Yorkshire, between 1982-86, produced two chatelaine blunt-hooks, one from a 17th-century context and the other post-1649. No. 573 is comparable with two *c.*1500-50 presumed chatelaine-hooks, one in Egan and Forsyth 1997 and the other in Egan 2005, fig. 53, no. 284. Nos 576, 578 are from *c.*16th - *c.*17th-century deposits, and nos 575, 577 may be assigned to the same period.

Early post-medieval Class A, Type 1

575. Copper alloy; wire; three-piece. A wire bent into a slightly open bight, the two halves forming the hook and shank, and each running-end formed into an attachment-loop and then back in the same plane before spiralling outwards. A second wire is set inside the open bight of the shank and hook and terminates at the base of the two attachment-loops; the whole is seized together by thinner-gauge wire; 52 x 29mm. Incomplete, part of one spiral broken off and separate suspension-chains missing. *North Yorkshire.* United Kingdom Detecting Finds' Database 9411. Photographs © Lance Todd.

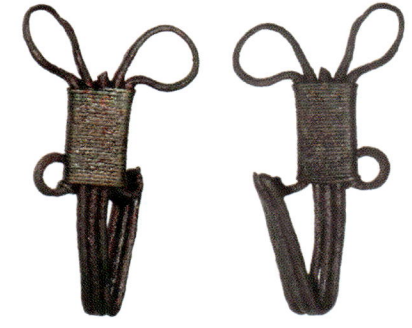

Early post-medieval Class A, Type 2

576. Copper alloy; wire; five-piece. Comparable with nos 577-578. A wire bent into a slightly open bight, the two halves forming part of the shank, and each running-end tightly spiralled inwards; a second wire bent into a tight bight and hooked at the bottom is set inside the open bight; two wires, each tightly spiralled inwards at both ends, lie one each side of the shank and the whole is seized together by thinner-gauge wire; after securing, the seizing, shank and spirals have been flattened. Two sides of the shank are broken and the hook is so distorted it is now lying flat; 54.5 x 26mm. *River Thames foreshore, London.* Drawing © Nick Griffiths.

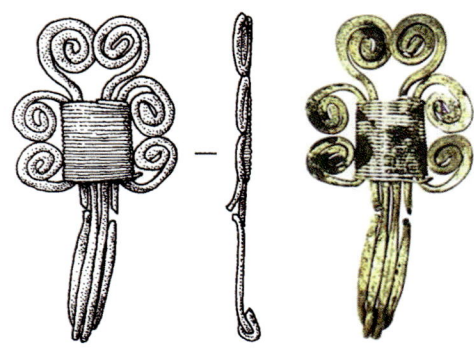

577. Copper alloy; wire; probably six-piece. Comparable with nos 576, 578 except a trefoil of spirals at one end, and the orientation of one spiral is anomalous; 52.5 x 28mm. *Wiltshire.* Drawing © Ian Bell and reproduced courtesy of Wiltshire Heritage Museum.

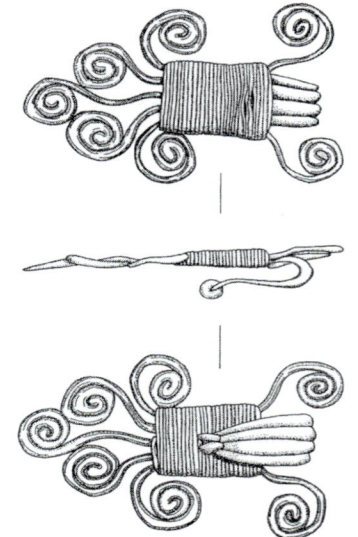

578. Copper alloy; wire; five-piece. Comparable with nos 576-577 except virtually the entire length of every wire, including the thin-gauge wire seizing, is flattened. Incomplete, part of the thin-gauge wire is broken off, revealing transverse grooves; one of the small spirals retains a tiny fragment of extremely thin-gauge wire, perhaps from a larger decorative element; 44.6 x 23.3. *River Thames foreshore, London.*

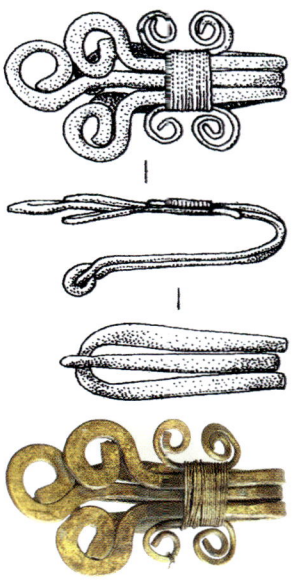

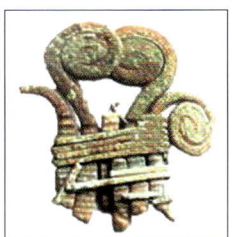

Fig. 21. An incomplete Class A copper-alloy chatelaine blunt-hook. Note transversely grooved main wires. *Provenance unknown.* Photograph © Phil Edwards.

Early post-medieval unclassified wire possible clasps

The incompleteness of no. 579, a complex piece, precludes saying whether it is a clasp or had some other function, such as a component of women's head-dress or even a brooch. Compositely constructed from copper-alloy circular-section wire with bead decoration, on stylistic grounds it is tentatively assigned to the second half of the 16th century into the early 17th. No. 580 is now known to be a late medieval brooch that may have operated in pairs (pers. comm. Geoff Egan) (information arrived too late to reclassify this object). The nearest parallel in the known record is from an archaeological *c.*1400-50 context in London (Egan and Pritchard 1991, 164, no. 1338).

Early post-medieval unclassified

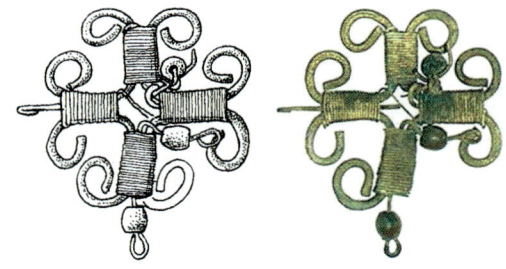

579. Copper alloy; wire; at least ten parts. Four addorsed arcs of wire, each of which has spiralled ends, form an equal-armed cross, each arm is seized together by thinner-gauge wire; a thinner-gauge wire is threaded through one seizing and each end has a now black bone bead and a spiral; the seizing of a second arm also traps a similar thin wire, the projecting end of which forms a small possible sharp-hook or loop; fragments of finer-gauge wire are threaded and/or twisted through the remaining seizings, one has a now black bone bead attached; damage precludes determining their original fixing. Incomplete, an indeterminate number of wires and beads missing, one arc of wire broken and other wires distorted; 42 x 37mm. *River Thames foreshore, London.* Drawing © Nick Griffiths.

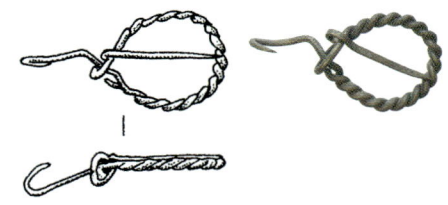

580. Copper alloy; wire; two-piece. A length of circular-section wire bent and barley twisted together to form a small eye at one end and a presumably forward-facing sharp-hook at the other, the twisted section is bent into a bight and the hook threaded through the eye, thereby forming a ring. One end of a separate flattened wire pin is coiled just below the small eye; 31.06 x 16.32. *River Thames foreshore, London.* Drawing © Nick Griffiths.

6: LATE MEDIEVAL TO LATE POST-MEDIEVAL WIRE BLUNT-HOOKED AND EYE CLASPS AND WIRE RINGS

Late medieval to late post-medieval Class A wire single blunt-hooked and eye clasps

Comprising two separate sections, a blunt-hook and an eye, circular-section wire clasps are designated as Class A. Each section may be one-piece or composite construction. One section is formed into a blunt-hook with a spiral either side for stitching to a garment and the other section an eye with similar attachment-spirals. Spirals are either close-butted to or ajar from the shank or eye, though on several the ends of the spirals are soldered to the shank of the hook or eye, and the two wires forming the shank of another are also soldered together.

One Class and five sub-types are recognised: Type 1 is a single strand of bent wire, usually with no decorative element other than white-metal coating (either silver or tin), though examples with transverse ribs are known from the Netherlands (Nos 586-588) and on a $c.$1605-10 doublet in the Germanisches Nationalmuseum, Nuremburg (Arnold 1985, nos 146, 151, 152). An exceptional Type 1 hook, with die-stamped decoration, is also recorded from the Netherlands (No. 590). On Type 1a the two sections of wire forming the hook-shank or eye are twisted once (and sometimes flattened, presumably to prevent untwisting) before being bent into attachment-spirals; Type 1b comprises one wire twisted, or two strands of wire twisted together (both described as barley twist), before being formed into a hook or eye; Type 1c is a combination of Types 1a and 1b; Type 1d is a single strand of wire hammered flat to form the hook and then tapering towards the opposite end where it is again flattened and then drilled with two attachment-holes (a comparable but decorated $c.$1615-20 example is in the Germanisches National Museum, Nuremburg; see Arnold 1985, pp 87); and Type 1e is unusual as one running-end turns inwards and forms an attachment-eye and then continues down the inside of the shank and back up between the two sides of the hook (Fig. 27).

Recorded metals for Class A are: Type 1 - copper alloy, steel or silver; Types 1a and 1d - copper alloy; Types 1b and 1c - copper-alloy or silver, and Type e - silver. Type 1 ribbed or die-stamped decorated examples and Types 1b and 1d appear unrecorded from Britain, and those published here are from either Amsterdam or a wrecked Dutch East Indiaman. The Type e wire blunt-hooked and eye clasps shown in Fig. 27 are also apparently absent from the known record outside of Bath Museum of Costume. Silver or steel wire blunt-hooked and eye clasps are rare from both archaeological and metal-detecting contexts though extant on surviving 19th-century dress. The reason why metal-detectorists will rarely find steel clasps of this form is due to their poor survival in ploughsoil, elimination by discrimination, or, if solid rust, the lack of conductivity. Manufactory proof for wire blunt-hooked and eye clasps from Britain is absent, a situation apparently similar in Amsterdam, though it is suspected (pers. comm. Wiard Krook). If not the Netherlands, Germany is the likeliest source for these clasps (pers. comm. Wiard Krook). The dating for the Amsterdam clasps in this category and catalogued here is secure: no. 593 - 1500-50; nos 590, 592, 594 - 1575-1600; and no. 588 - 1650-1700.

In the 19th and 20th centuries on copper-alloy examples a blackening agent was occasionally applied, although the nature of this substance remains unidentified. As with some Nuremberg-made 16th-century brass thimbles, heating and dipping in linseed oil would possibly achieve this effect (Holmes 1985). It appears different from the now black coating, (?) bitumen, frequently seen on some late medieval and early post-medieval small metalwork.

The blunt-hook and eye wire clasp has its roots in the Scandinavian Roman Iron Age, then being adapted as wrist-clasps (Hines 1984, Class A) by the Scandinavians who brought them to Britain in the late 5th century. Notwithstanding, in Hungary the loop and spiral arrangement can be traced back even further, to a $c.$11th - 9th century B.C. suite of gold wire jewellery (Tait 2006), and, interestingly, each of the two Romano-British silver penannular brooches in the

Wheathampstead Hoard (Treasure case 2002 T83) has terminals in this form. A few Class A wrist-clasps with beaded or ribbed spirals are in the known record (Hines 1984). The distribution of wrist-clasps is mainly confined to north, east and south-east England with copper-alloy wire examples being less common than silver. However, the odd outrider is recorded from the west of England, with one from Wiltshire and another from Devon (Read 1995, no. 173). Wrist-clasps are beyond the remit of this present work.

The Kunsthistorisches Museum, Vienna, has possibly the earliest portrait to clearly show Type 1 wire blunt-hooked and eye clasps - the *Ferraran court jester, Gonella*, painted *c*.1445 by Jean Fouqet: the open neck of Gonella's doublet has two hooks on one side while on the other is an eye (Fig. 22).

From *c*.1405 cote-hardies may have fastened at the back with Type 1 wire blunt-hooked and eye clasps, and between the 1620s and 1680s attached men's breeches to doublets. Waugh 1964 mentions several interesting snippets, two of which in 'the *Academy of Armoury* 1688, read "The EYES, OR HOLDERS; are small Wiers made round through which Breeches hooks are put, to keep them from falling"; and "In the BREECHES, there are several parts: The WAIST-BAND, The HOOKS"; and in a '1638 BILL FROM THE VERNEY PAPERS "16 Mar. 1638 For Collr and belypeeces and hookes and eyes to a buffe coate 00: 02 : 06...".

Class A, Type 1, and sub-Types 1a and 1d wire blunt-hooked and eye clasps were found in the wreck of the Dutch East India Company jachct *Vergulde Draeck* lost off Western Australia in 1656 (Nos 589, 593 and fig. 31). The shanks of Types 1, and sub-types 1a and 1d hooks vary in length, with the longest at around 100mm being fitted at the back of the breeches where they were the most likely to come undone (nos 581, 591, 595 and fig. 23). Interestingly, the *Vergulde Draeck* wire clasps nos GT3116, GT3131 and GT3162 are thought to be military-style and probably from a bandolier, however, there is no evidence to support such a use. More likely they are from breeches and doublets.

The limited surviving contemporary dress retaining one or both sections of Type 1 wire blunt-hooked and eye clasps in the Victoria and Albert Museum, London, reveals the following:

1620s doublet - six *eyes* along the back waist-seam.
Late 1630s doublet - two *eyes* along the front waist-seam and eight the back.
1630s doublet and breeches - nine *eyes* along the waist-seam arranged around front
    and back of doublet, with nine *hooks* around front and back waist-band of the breeches.
1640s breeches (2 pairs) - each has one *hook* at the front waist-band and two at the back.
1650s doublet - two *eyes* along the front waist-seam and two at the back.

Apart from securing doublets to breeches, cuffs of men's doublets were sometimes fastened with Type 1 wire blunt-hooked and eye clasps; and from at least the 16th century they were used to fasten the fronts of women's jackets. Six pairs were used to attach detachable sleeves to women's *c*.1580-1600 doublets. A girl's loose gown of *c*.1600-10 is secured at the front with six pairs; and the front of a women's bodice of the same date has 18 pairs. Class A, Type 1 and its sub-types may have also performed as cloak-clasps (see below). The Littlecote Collection, kept at the Royal Armouries, has a 17th-century buff-coat with a wire blunt-hook stitched on the inside of the front (Royal Armouries III 1942); tufts of thread and rust-marks on this garment, and on other buff-coats in the collection, suggests this was the method of fastening for all.

Evidence that Type 1 wire eyes were not used solely in tandem with wire hooks comes from the Dutch East India Company fluit *Lasdrager* lost off Yell, Shetland in 1653: a recovered cast copper-alloy one-piece domed button has a Type 1 wire eye attached through its loop (Green 1977) (Fig. 29).

Surviving contemporary dress shows that the popularity of wire blunt-hooked and eye clasps continued into and beyond the 19th century, for example the false front of a *c*.1745-55 pet-en-l'air is attached to the bodice with 20 pairs and an eye stitched to each shoulder of the same garment may have secured a handkerchief worn at the neck; twelve pairs fasten the front of a *c*.1775-85 women's caraco jacket; the bodice of a *c*.1775-85 women's gown is fastened at the front with 9 pairs; a *c*.1795-1803 women's silk robe bodice is fastened at the front with two pairs, as is the bodice of *c*.1795-1803 women's robe; *c*.1824-7 and *c*.1827-29 evening dresses are each fastened at the back with four pairs; a *c*.1826-28 women's cloak fastened at the throat with one pair; a *c*.1829-31 wedding dress has several pairs on the waist-band and at the bodice side opening; the waist-band of a *c*.1837-41 morning dress has one pair; the bodice of a *c*.1839-45 silk day dress uses 9 pairs to fasten the back; 15 pairs fasten the back of a 1849-50 bodice; a *c*.1864-67 crinoline fitted with two pairs on the waist-band; one pair fastened the throat of a *c*.1875-76 dress; one pair attached a *c*.1880-82 bustle frill to the bodice, and the skirt of an evening dress attached to the bodice with two pairs; an 1894 skirt waist-band secured by two pairs; a *c*.1901-2 reception gown has two pairs at the waist-band and ten securing the bodice front; and a *c*.1911-12 day dress uses numerous pairs to fasten the skirt opening, bodice front and waist to bodice (Figs 24-27). Similar usage, albeit on a lesser scale, continued throughout the 20th century and they are found on women's underwear today (the latter clasps often have a white synthetic coating).

During the 19th century a small metal bar, either sheeting or wire, with an attachment-eye either end, was occasionally substituted for an eye (Fig. 28). Perhaps a cruder form of the latter was found in a 1690-1730/60 context in Norwich (No. 596); however, this is possibly a distorted example of the perceived conventional Class A, Type 1 eye.

From the early 19th century Type 1 copper-alloy wire blunt-hooked and eye clasps were worn by army personnel - two or three pairs fastened the necks of tunics, and mess and stable jackets had many pairs down the front. Moreover, from the late 19th century until at least the mid-1970s two pairs fastened the necks of operational fire-tunics used by fire brigades in this country: police tunics were similarly fastened into the 1950s. Apart from with occupational and civilian dress, they remain current as curtain hooks and fasteners on tents and marquees.

Irrespective of date, Types 1-3 wire eyes are either circular or sub-circular, and it was custom sometimes to hammer flat the hooks and/or shanks of both hooks and eyes, as evident on several catalogued here. Other than those hooked sections with very long shanks, which suggests they are from breeches, wire blunt-hooked and eye clasps, either hooks or eyes, found detached are impossible to determine where they were used.

As Type 1 are still used today, precise assignment is difficult unless found in a datable context, and they are easily confused with certain early medieval Class A wrist-clasps. No. 588 is identical to hooks that secured breeches to doublets and is probably 17th century, while those found on the River Thames foreshore in London are *c*.16th - *c*.17th century.

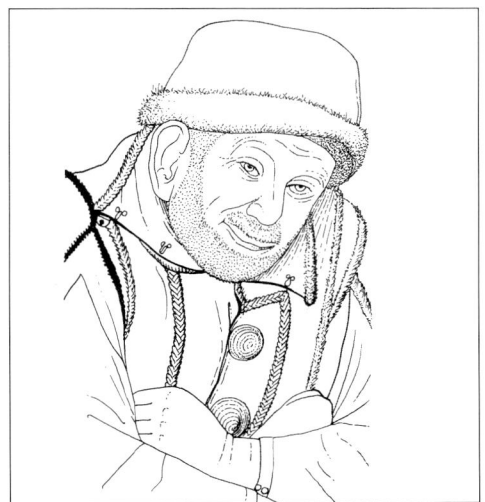

Fig. 22. The *Ferraran court jester, Gonella*, *c*.1445. Redrawn from the portrait by Jean Fouqet in the Kunsthistorisches Museum, Vienna. Note the Class A, Type 1 wire blunt-hooked and eye clasps on the open neck of the doublet.

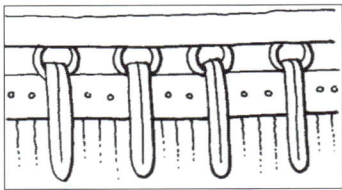
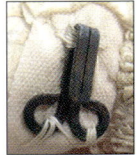
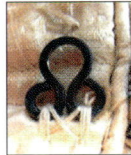

Fig. 23. Reconstruction of how Class A, Type 1 wire blunt-hooked and eye clasps were attached to men's breeches and doublets. Note the length of the hooks. Redrawn from Cunningtons 1963.

Fig. 24. Class A, Type 1 wire blunt-hooked and eye clasp on the back of a 1742-44 woman's robe. Note the blackened square-section wire. BATMC 1.09.658 and BATMC 1.09.1003. Photographs © Val MacRae and reproduced courtesy of Bath Museum of Costume.

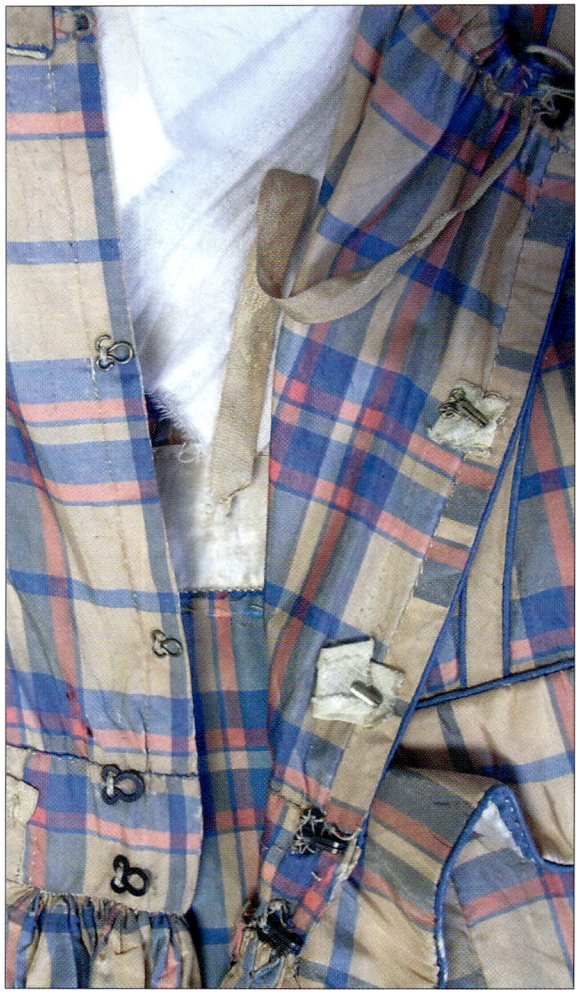

Fig. 25. Class A, Type 1 wire blunt-hooked and eye clasps on the back of an 1821-25 woman's dress. Note the variations in size, both blackened or uncoated, which suggests that some are probably later replacements, but which are contemporary is uncertain. BATMC 1.09.966. Photograph © Val MacRae and reproduced courtesy of Bath Museum of Costume.

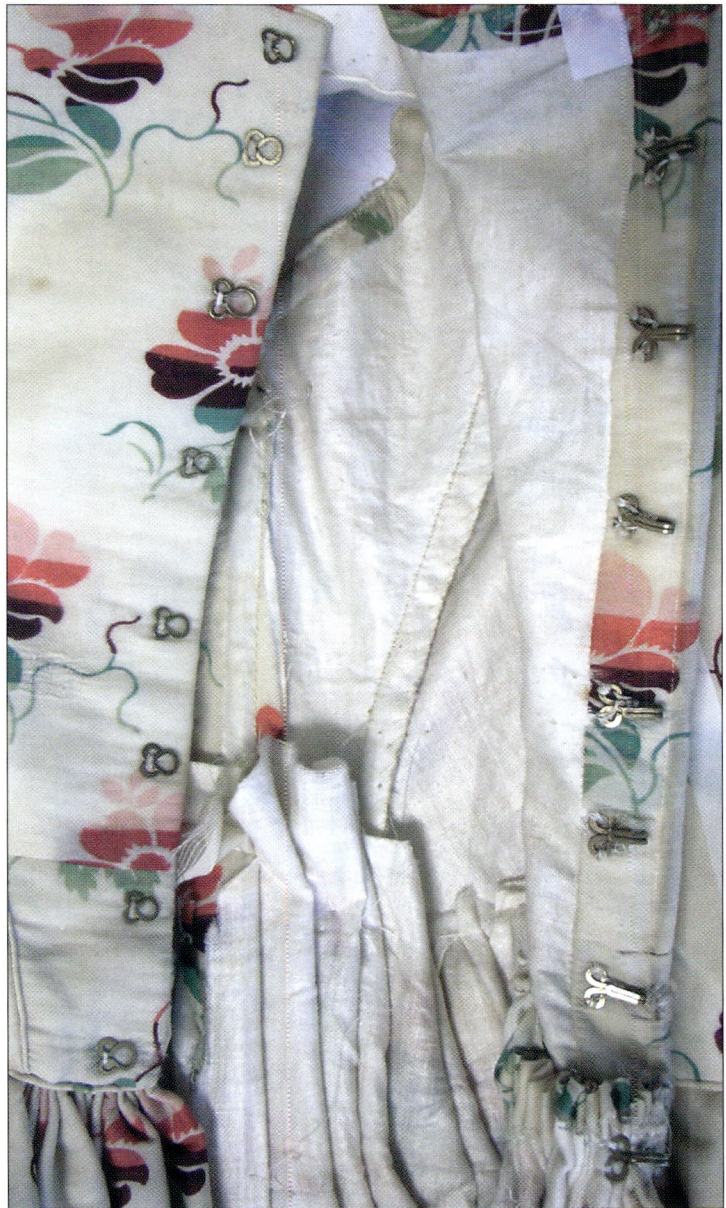

Fig. 26. Class A, Type 1 wire blunt-hooked and eye clasps on the back of a woman's dress, date unknown but probably 18th or 19th century. Note the difference in size and colour which suggests some are replacements; several appear to be silver. BATMC 1.09.1003. Photograph © Val MacRae and reproduced courtesy of Bath Museum of Costume.

HOOKED-CLASPS & EYES

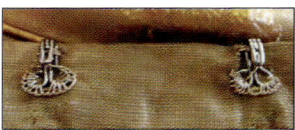

Fig. 27. Class A, Type 1e probable silver wire blunt-hooks on the back of an 1824-26 woman's dress. BATMC 1.09 1270. Photograph © Val MacRae and reproduced courtesy Bath Museum of Costume.

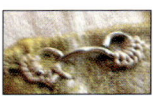

Fig. 28. A Class A, Type 1 probable silver wire bar-type eye on the back of an 1824-26 women's dress. BATMC 1.09 1270. Photograph © Val MacRae and reproduced courtesy Bath Museum of Costume.

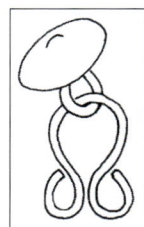

Fig. 29. Sketch of the button and a Class A, Type 1 wire eye recovered from the Dutch East India Company fluit *Lasdrager* lost off Yell, Shetland in 1653. Drawing © Patrick Read.

Early post-medieval Class A, Type 1

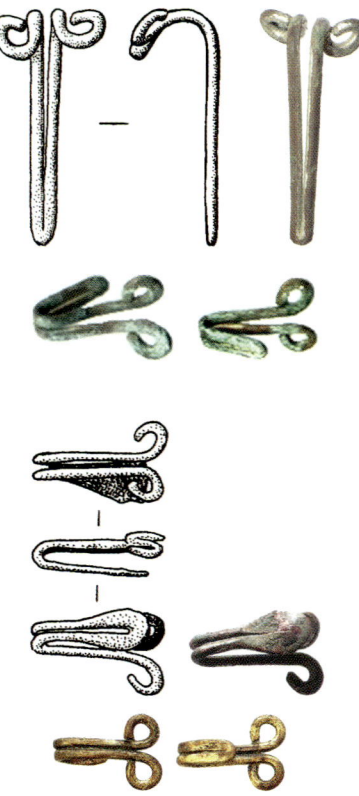

581. Copper alloy; wire; one-piece; sporadic white-metal coating, probably tin. Hooked-section: bent in the centre to form a long tapering hook, each running-end is bent in the same plane as the shank and then into a laterally projecting close-butted attachment-spiral; 40 x 18.5mm. *West Dorset*. Drawing © Patrick Read.

582. Copper alloy; wire; one-piece. Hooked-section: the shank is bent back on itself midway to form a hook; 22 x 10mm. *Cambridgeshire*. United Kingdom Detecting Finds' Database 3017. Photographs © Cheryl Hodgson.

583. Copper alloy; wire; one-piece; sporadic white-metal coating, probably tin. Hooked-section: the hook is flattened and the attachment-spirals are ajar; 22 x 13mm. *South-West Wiltshire*. Drawing © Nick Griffiths.

584. Copper alloy; wire; one-piece. Hooked-section: comparable with nos 582-583 except the hook is less flattened and the attachment-spirals are close-butted; 16.02 x 11.55mm. *River Thames foreshore, London*.

585. Copper alloy; wire; one-piece. Eye-section: bent in the centre to form an eye, each running-end is bent in the same plane as the eye and then into a laterally projecting close-butted attachment-spiral; the spirals and most of the eye are slightly flattened; 16.29 x 12.24mm. *River Thames foreshore, London.*

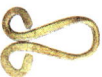

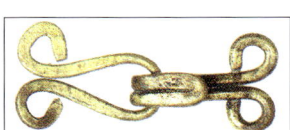

Fig. 30. Nos 582-583 shown linked together. Drawing © Nick Griffiths.

586. Copper alloy; wire; one-piece. Hooked-section: slightly flattened and shallow ribbed; 18 x 13.08mm. *The Netherlands.* Drawing © Nick Griffiths.

587. Copper alloy; wire; one-piece. Eye-section: comparable with no. 585 except the eye is more rounded; 15.15 x 10.03mm. *The Netherlands.* Drawing © Nick Griffiths.

588. Copper alloy; wire; one-piece; engraved. Eye-section: comparable with no. 587 except ribbed; 14 x 14.8mm. *Prins Hendrikkade, Amsterdam.* Historical Museum/Bureau of Monuments and Archaeology, Department of Archaeology, Amsterdam, inventory no. PH1-119. Photograph © Wiard Krook, Bureau of Monuments and Archaeology, Department of Archaeology, Amsterdam.

589. Copper alloy; wire; one-piece. Hooked-section: heavier-gauge wire and slightly ajar spirals; 33.12 x 25.33mm. *South Somerset.*

590. Copper alloy; wire; one-piece; die-stamped. Hooked-section: the shank and attachment-spirals are square-section and the hook is flattened; the front of the spirals and shank are cross-hatched with quatrefoils in the lozenges, and the hook has vine and foliate; 33 x 18.2mm. *Weesperstaat, Amsterdam.* Historical Museum/Bureau of Monuments and Archaeology, Department of Archaeology, Amsterdam, inventory no. MX-215. Photograph © Wiard Krook, Bureau of Monuments and Archaeology, Department of Archaeology, Amsterdam.

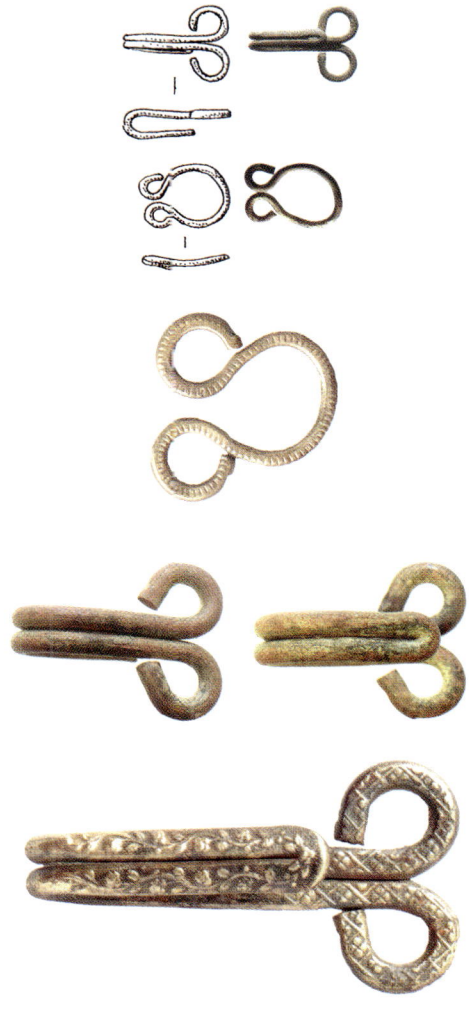

Early post-medieval Class A, Type 1a

591. Copper alloy, wire; one-piece. Hooked-section: bent in the centre to form a long hook, each running-end is twisted once and bent in the same plane as the shank and then into laterally projecting ajar attachment-spirals, the hook is flattened and the remainder of the wire, slightly so; 41.1 x 15mm. *Western Australia*. Dutch East India Company Jacht *Vergulde Draeck*. Western Australian Maritime Museum acc. no. GT3116. Photograph © Western Australian Maritime Museum.

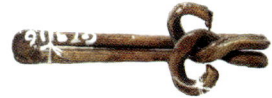

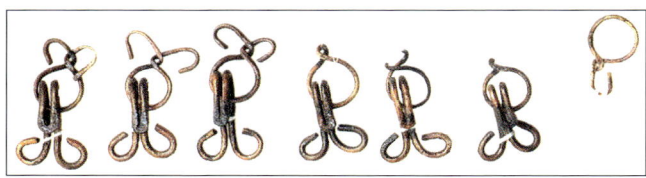

Fig. 31. Class A, Type 1 hooks and Type 1a eyes, all are one-piece copper-alloy wire; the latter twisted before forming attachment-spirals. Average dimensions - hooks 14.5 x 11.3mm, eyes 11.3 x 7.7mm. Some eyes possibly incomplete, attachment-spirals perhaps broken off. Found grouped together on the Dutch East India Company Jachct *Vergulde Draeck* lost off *Western Australia* in 1656. Western Australian Maritime Museum acc. no. GT3121. Photograph © Western Australian Maritime Museum.

Early post-medieval Class A, Type 1b

592. Silver; wire; one-piece. Hooked-section: barley-twist; 9 x 0.59mm. *Weesperstraat, Amsterdam*. Historical Museum/Bureau of Monuments and Archaeology, Department of Archaeology, Amsterdam, inventory no. MWEX-102. Photograph © Wiard Krook, Bureau of Monuments and Archaeology, Department of Archaeology, Amsterdam.

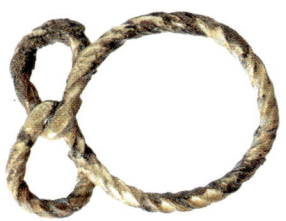

Early post-medieval Class A, Type 1c

593. Copper alloy; wire; one-piece. Eye-section: barley-twist; 22 x 17.2mm. *Keizersstraat, Amsterdam*. Historical Museum/Bureau of Monuments and Archaeology, Department of Archaeology, Amsterdam, inventory no. MZ3-842. Photograph © Wiard Krook, Bureau of Monuments and Archaeology, Department of Archaeology, Amsterdam.

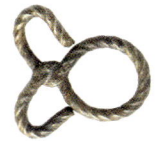

594. Silver; wire; one-piece. Eye-section: barley-twist; 5 x 0.51mm. *Weesperstraat, Amsterdam.* Historical Museum/Bureau of Monuments and Archaeology, Department of Archaeology, Amsterdam, inventory no. MWEX-100. Photograph © Wiard Krook, Bureau of Monuments and Archaeology, Department of Archaeology, Amsterdam.

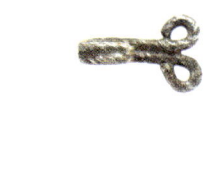

Early post-medieval Class A, Type 1d

595. Copper alloy; wire; one-piece. Hooked-section: flattened and bent to form a long-shanked hook at one end and two drilled attachment-holes the other; 47.7 x 0.9mm Eye-section: Type 1a; 20.09 x 14mm; attached to the hook. *Western Australia.* Dutch East India Company Jacht *Vergulde Draeck*. Western Australian Maritime Museum acc. no. GT3131 and GT3162. Photograph © Western Australian Maritime Museum.

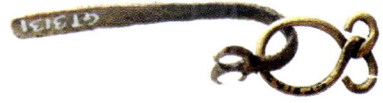

596. Copper alloy; wire; one-piece. Eye-section: shallowly bent, each running-end is bent in the same plane as the shank and then into a close-butted attachment-spiral. Possibly a bar form (see fig. 28), but perhaps distorted; L27.6mm. *Norfolk.* After Margeson 1993, fig. 10, no. 93. Drawing © and reproduced courtesy of Norfolk Museums and Archaeology Service.

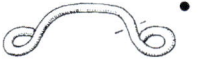

Late medieval to late post-medieval Class B wire single blunt-hooked and eye clasps

Designated as Class B, Types 2-3, these wire blunt-hooked and eye clasps are identical to the preceding Class A, Type 1 but have separate cast or sheeting decorative plates - either circular, triangular, or trefoil - soldered to the front. Silver and copper-alloy are the recorded metals. The completeness of no. 598 means it stands alone in the present assemblage. The decorative nature of the plates suggest they were designed to be on view, therefore particularly suitable for fastening cloaks at the neck (see below), though this remains conjectural. Those applied with ground-supported filigree decoration are stylistically *c.*16th century, and the others are possibly the same attribution or even *c.*17th.

HOOKED-CLASPS & EYES

Early post-medieval Class B, Type 2

Circular

597. Silver-gilt; cast and wire; two-piece; shallow convex; moulded-relief and open-work. Eye-section: a plate bearing a heart wreathed by equidistant small flowers. A separate wire bent in the centre to form an eye, each running-end bent in the same plane as the eye and then into a laterally projecting slightly ajar close-butted attachment-spiral, is soldered to the back; 20.8 x 13.33mm. *Suffolk*. Portable Antiquities Scheme SF-80A9F7. Photographs © Suffolk County Council Archaeological Service.

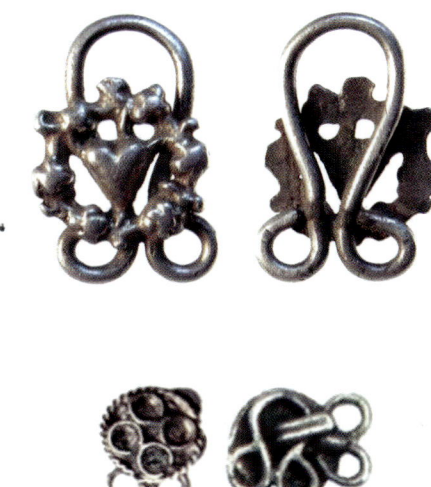

598. Silver; sheeting and wire; ground-supported straight and twisted wire filigree. Hooked-section: two-piece; a plate applied with a quatrefoil of touching small straight wire annulets within a twisted wire border (one annulet possibly retains a remnant of a twisted wire S); remnants of green glass stones set within three of the annulets. A separate wire bent in the centre to form a hook, each running-end is bent in the same plane as the shank and then into a laterally projecting close-butted attachment-spiral, is soldered to the front. Eye-section: one-piece (attached to the hooked section); a wire bent in the centre to form an eye, each running-end bent in the same plane as the shank and then into a laterally projecting close-butted attachment-spiral. The ends of all four attachment-spirals, and between each set of spirals, are soldered to the respective shank or eye; plate D6-7mm, hook 8 x 6mm. *Nottinghamshire*. Treasure case T379. United Kingdom Detecting Finds' Database 9472. Photographs © Alan Ridgeway.

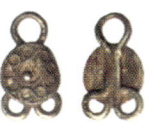

599. Silver; sheeting and wire; two-piece; ground-supported twisted wire filigree and a granule. Eye-section: a plate applied with an off-centre granule imitating a cabochon gem within a wire annulet surrounded by nine smaller wire annulets, a wire border. A separate wire bent in the centre to form a long-shanked eye, each running-end bent in line with the shank and then into a laterally projecting close-butted attachment-spiral, is soldered to the back; the wires of the shank and the ends of the attachment-spirals are soldered. The off-centre granule suggest sloppy work during the fusion process, or inferior soldering; 18.4 x 10.7mm. *Bedfordshire*. Portable Antiquities Scheme BH-0174E0. Treasure case 2006 T584. Photograph © St Albans Museum.

600. Silver-gilt; sheeting and wire; three-piece; die-stamped and ground-supported straight and twisted wire filigree. Hooked-section: a plate applied with two concentric twisted wire circles infilled with alternate twisted and straight wire quatrefoils, ovals and stylised tulips. A central separate soldered sheeting appliqué - a hatted human facing-bust. Incomplete; a large section of the plate and filigree broken off, a remnant of separate soldered wire hook; D15mm. *Suffolk*. United Kingdom Detecting Finds' Database 10557. Photograph © Neil Blatherwick.

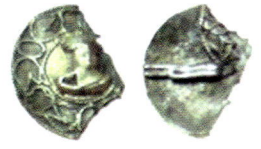

Early post-medieval Class B, Type 3

Triangular

601. Silver-gilt; sheeting and wire; two-piece, convex and flat; die-stamped and ground-supported twisted wire filigree. Eye-section: a plate applied with a trefoil of hollow-domed bosses, each bordered by a wire annulet; the three sides are edged with similar wire. A separate wire bent in the centre to form an eye, each running-end bent in the same plane as the shank and then into a laterally projecting close-butted or slightly ajar attachment-spiral, is soldered to the back. Incomplete, one apex of the plate and section of wire border broken off; 23.5 x 19.5mm. *North Yorkshire*. Drawing © Nick Griffiths.

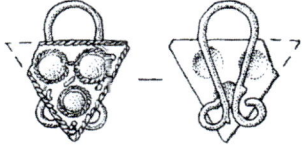

602. Silver-gilt; sheeting and wire; five-piece, convex and flat; die-stamped and ground-supported twisted wire filigree and a granule. Eye-section: the three bosses are separate entities, each soldered to the main-plate, and a granule imitating a cabochon gem in the centre of the trefoil and the close-butted seam of the spirals and shank are soldered; 1.78 x 1.27mm. *East Yorkshire*. Portable Antiquities Scheme LAN-CUM-DF7DD1. Treasure case 2008 T8. Photographs © of the Portable Antiquities Scheme.

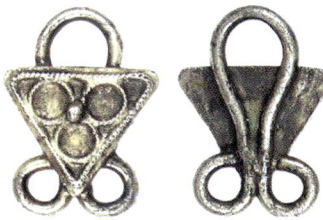

603. Silver-gilt; sheeting and wire; possibly five-piece, convex and flat; possibly die-stamped and ground-supported twisted wire filigree and granules. Eye-section: the three bosses are perhaps separate entities, each soldered to the main-plate, and four granules around the border and another in one of the annulets, imitating cabochon gems, and the close-butted seam of the spirals are soldered. Incomplete, a central granule from two of the annulets and a further two granules in the border are missing; additionally, the granule remaining in an annulet, and the central granule, have slipped. These flaws suggest sloppy work during the fusion process, or inferior soldering; 1.54 x 1.34mm. *East Yorkshire*. Portable Antiquities Scheme LANCUM-DF9A36. Treasure case 2007 T565. Photographs © the Portable Antiquities Scheme.

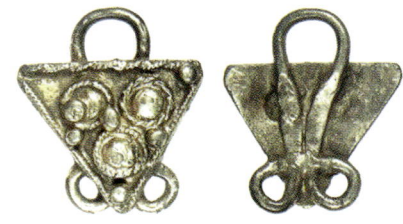

604. Silver-gilt; cast and wire; two-piece. Eye-section: a plate with imitative ground-supported straight and twisted wire filigree and granules - a central large granule within six smaller granules and a raised border; a trefoil with a central granule, each lobe raised, at each apex. The granules imitating cabochon gems. A separate wire bent in the centre to form an eye, each running-end bent in the same plane as the eye and then into a laterally projecting close-butted attachment-spiral, is soldered to the back; 14.5 x 12.9mm. *Suffolk*. Treasure case 2002 T124. Photographs © the Trustees of The British Museum.

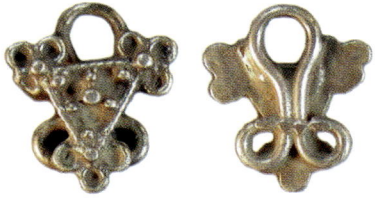

Early post-medieval Class B, Type 4

Trefoil

605. Silver-gilt; cast and ground-supported twisted wire filigree and a granule; two-piece. Eye-section: a plate applied with a central granule imitating a gem, each lobe has a twisted wire annulet. A separate wire bent in the centre to form an eye, each running-end bent in the same plane as the shank and then into a laterally projecting close-butted attachment-spiral, is soldered to the back; 17 x 11.7mm. *East Yorkshire*. Treasure case 2004 T450. Photographs © The Portable Antiquities Scheme.

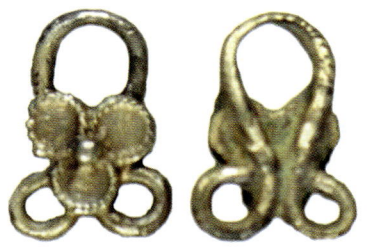

Late medieval to late post-medieval Class C wire single blunt-hooked and eye clasp

Formed from a single strand of circular-section wire bent similarly as the eyes of the preceding Classes A and B wire blunt-hooked and eye clasps, Class C, Type 1 is attached to a separate pivoting copper-alloy folded sheeting plate. Whether it functioned in conjunction with a hook is conjectural but it is reasonable to believe it did. Possibly *c*.15th - *c*.17th century.

Early post-medieval Class C, Type 1

Rectangular

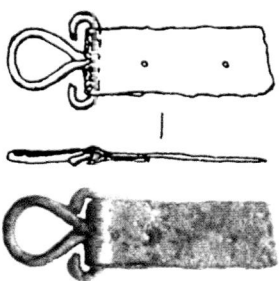

606. Copper alloy, sheeting and wire; two-piece; undecorated. The plate, which has two median rivet-holes, is folded back on itself at one end thereby providing an axis point; the centre of the fold is slotted. A separate wire bent in the centre to form an eye, each running-end is bent in the same plane as the shank and then into a laterally projecting close-butted or slightly ajar attachment-spiral; the eye projects through the slot in the fold of the plate and is free to pivot; 45 x 17mm. *South Devon*. After Read 1988, no. 8; and 1995, no. 773. Drawing © Patrick Read.

Early post-medieval wire rings

Small one-piece rings, simply formed by coiling copper-alloy circular-section wire and twisting together once the running-ends, sometimes slightly flattened. Two forms are apparent, both similar to Class A Types 1a and 1b wire blunt-hooked and eye clasps. Although recorded from many archaeological contexts in Britain and the Netherlands, they are apparently uncommon finds for metal-detectorists, a dearth perhaps due to a failure of recognition? Examples interpreted as fasteners (but for what is unclear) were found positioned on the line of the arms of skeletons in burials at St Margaret's Church, Magdalen Street, Norwich, (Margeson 1963) (Nos 607-609); excavations at 61-64 High Street, Southampton have been interpretted as multiple reinforcing of purses against cut-purse thieves; others lying near the throat of a silk bag or purse in St Cuthbert's tomb in Durham Cathedral are thought to date from the 1542 reinterment of the body (Egan 2005); and textile fragments have been occasionally found around them. Their fragility makes them unlikely candidates for the aforementioned Cunningtons 'strong metal rings' stitched to 1630s doublets from which breeches were suspended. They are not apparent on any surviving contemporary dress, and such a use seems unsuitable as the twisted sharp ends would surely soon damage the fabric. British archaeological contexts provide a date range from *c*.1450 - *c*.1900; while those from Amsterdam archaeological contexts are dated at 1500-1550.

Apart from lacking the defining attachment-spirals, these rings are identical to the eyes on several of the early post-medieval Class A, Type 1a wire blunt-hooked and eye clasps recovered from the aforementioned vessels *Vergulde Draeck* and *Lasdrager*; and Type 1b as those from Amsterdam. Indeed, some of the eyes from the preceding wrecks have only one attachment-spiral or none at all, but nos 607 - 611 are interpreted as intentional rings.

Early post-medieval Class A, Type 1a

607. Copper alloy; wire; one-piece. Ring possibly distorted; 18 x 6mm. *Norfolk*. After Margeson 1993, fig. 10, no. 99. Drawing © and reproduced courtesy of Norfolk Museums and Archaeology Service.

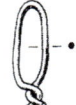

608. Copper alloy; wire; one-piece. 15.2 x 10.5mm. *Norfolk*. After Margeson 1993, fig. 10, no. 100. Drawing © and reproduced courtesy of Norfolk Museums and Archaeology Service.

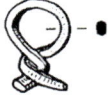

609. Copper alloy; wire; one-piece. 17 x 12mm. *Norfolk*. After Margeson 1993, fig. 10, no. 101. Drawing © and reproduced courtesy of Norfolk Museums and Archaeology Service.

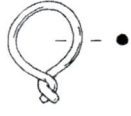

Early post-medieval Class A, Type 1b

610. Copper alloy; wire; two-piece. Barley-twist; 17 x 12.2mm. *Rotterdammersloot, Amsterdam*. Historical Museum/Bureau of Monuments and Archaeology, Department of Archaeology, Amsterdam, inventory no. MZ5-846 (1). Photograph © Wiard Krook, Bureau of Monuments and Archaeology, Department of Archaeology, Amsterdam.

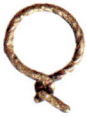

611. Copper alloy; wire; two-piece. Comparable with no. 610 except flattened where the wires are twisted together; 22 x 17.2mm. *Lange Keizersdwarsstraat, Amsterdam*. Historical Museum/Bureau of Monuments and Archaeology, Department of Archaeology, Amsterdam, inventory no. MZ2-370. Photograph © Wiard Krook, Bureau of Monuments and Archaeology, Department of Archaeology, Amsterdam.

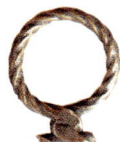

7: EARLY POST-MEDIEVAL BLUNT-HOOKED AND EYE CLASPS

Early post-medieval Class A single blunt-hooked and eye clasps

Blunt-hooked and eye clasps designated as Class A are substantially cast from copper-alloy or silver and are prolific finds for metal-detectorists, evidence which suggests widespread use by the civilian populace. The Commonwealth arms, or part of them, decorating the front of some perhaps implies official or semi-official use on buff-coats or jerkins worn by the military and/or civilians (Robinson 1999); and the lion (?) holding a crown borne on no. 624 may be a Royalist version (pers. comm. Geoff Egan). Frustratingly, these clasps are not evident in contemporary depictions of such apparel, nor is there any specific mention in primary or secondary documentation. None in the known record retain evidence of rivets in the attachment-holes, therefore presumably they were stitched on, like those on a woollen felt-coat in the Museum of London (discussed below, fig. 31.1-2, nos 698-699).

It is convenient to designate these clasps into 16 Types, all of which comprise two presumably matching parts. One, the male, has a single blunt-hook with either a rounded or angular terminal, and the other, the female, an angular or rounded eye. These hooked sections differ from most of the aforementioned recurving sharp-hooked clasps, for the hooks, so far as is known, always curve forward. The hook passes through the eye and the two sections are secured together by tension.

The following design features are common to both sections of all: Type 1 circular with three attachment-knops; Type 2 oval with three attachment-knops, some have a collar, frequently projecting and/or ridged, at the juncture of the plate and hook; Type 3 oval/ovoid with four attachment-knops; Type 4 oval/ovoid with five attachment-knops; Type 5 shield-shaped with three attachment-knops; Type 6 sub-lozenge shaped with three attachment-knops; Type 7 figurative with three attachment-knops; Type 8 oval with three attachment-knops and two ornamental knops - the end knop is frequently collared; Type 9 oval/ovoid with four attachment-knops and an ornamental knop; Type 10 sub-lozenge shaped with three attachment-knops and ornamental knops; Type 11 sub-circular with one attachment-knop which has one or two holes, two attachment-holes in the plate, and a collar at one or more ends; Type 12 sub-pentagonal with one attachment-knop which has one or two holes, two attachment-holes in the plate, and a collar at one or more ends; Type 13 figurative with one attachment-knop and two attachment-holes in the plate; Type 14 oval with two attachment-holes in the plate, and an ornamental knop; Type 15 ovoid with openwork utilised for attachment; and Type 16 oval/ovoid with openwork utilised for attachment, and an ornamental knop; some have a collar at one end. Attachment- and ornamental-knops are either rounded, angular or debased trefoil.

The predominant metal is copper-alloy while lead/tin appears to be much less common and only two of silver are catalogued here. In this present assemblage all are flat unless otherwise stated. Although some are plain, the majority have either moulded-relief, engraved, punched or openwork decoration; several are champlevé enamelled and some are white-metal coated, probably tin. Characteristically, many are crude and unfettled; however a minority are well finished.

Apart from possible use with coats, other applications should be considered, for example on leather or textile satchels, saddle-bags or straps. Interestingly, a Class A, Type 6 hooked-section (with enamel residue) found in Amsterdam has been described as a book-clasp (Baart *et al* 1977), although this identification is doubtful (pers. comm. Wiard Krook). It is noteworthy that the Amsterdam blunt-hooked clasp is the only example recovered from an archaeological context in that city. Despite popular belief, there is not any evidence for these clasps being worn for fastening cloaks, mantles or capes.

It is difficult to understand precisely what fastened the necks of cloaks, mantles or capes throughout history. It is thought that during the Iron Age laces or toggle fasteners were used to fasten dress, the latter perhaps being the frequently found copper-alloy toggles with simple attachment-loops (Read 2005). This same form of fastener continued into the Roman period where it seems to have possibly been used alongside copper-alloy button-and-loop fasteners or button-like objects as shown by the evidence of the Camomile Street soldier (Bishop, M C, London and Middlesex Archaeological Society, 34, 1983, and Read 2005, fig. 1).

Rogers 2007 provides the most up-to-date published evidence on the wearing of cloaks, capes and mantles by early Anglo-Saxon women, and the metal fasteners used, namely: large cruciform or square-headed brooches, florid cruciform and great square-headed brooches, annular brooches, reused Romano-British disc brooches, penannular brooches, small-long brooches and buckles. All of these fasteners are technically clasps. It seems that during the Anglo-Saxon period fasteners other than ones made of metal were current, for example the Cunningtons 1973 state that '...in the 11th century men's cloaks were fastened with a *brooch* or *tie* at the shoulder or beneath the chin; but the nobility used a *cord* threaded through attached *metal rings* stitched to opposite edges...'; and on 12th-century men's cloaks '...the upper *corner of the neck edge on one side* was pulled through [an] *S ring* stitched to the opposite corner, and then *knotted* to keep it in position. Otherwise ornamental *clasp* or *brooch* used'. Others than the Cunningtons state that Tudor period cloaks were usually just draped across the shoulders, for the surviving examples have no incisions or marks to suggest that cord or leather ties or metal fasteners were used, and metal fasteners are absent in contemporary iconography. Notwithstanding, other than being left unfastened, the several styles of cloak (men's or women's) current in the 16th and 17th centuries did use cords, sashes or points (that is aglets, metal lace-tags) for neck fastenings; or were buttoned into worked (sewn) cord eyes at the neck or down the front; or secured with wire blunt-hooked and eye clasps; or wire blunt-hooks and worked cord eyes. These wire blunt-hooked and eye clasps were probably the preceding early post-medieval Classes A and B, therefore the hypothesis that Tudor period cloaks probably were not secured by metal clasps is refuted. Although unproven, there is good reason to believe that a type of clasp made from a pair of relatively large one-piece metal buttons linked by a copper-alloy or iron wire did indeed perform such a function in the mid/late 17th century (Read 2005, no. 132.). No. 826 is a good example of an early 19th-century cloak-clasp used by the military.

The aforementioned Class A, Type 6 hooked-section found in Amsterdam is from a secure archaeological 1550-1650 context, a broad date range which indicates they were perhaps used in Britain as early as the mid-16th century, though this must remain conjectural. Either the whole or part of the Commonwealth arms borne by some provides a secure 1649-60 attribution for these pieces. It is reasonable to assume they continued in use throughout the 17th century.

The examples catalogued here are individual finds and en suite pairs definitely found together are absent from the known record. Two comparable with nos 639-644 were discovered close together in Lincolnshire, but three years apart; and it is impossible to prove they are a pair (Portable Antiquities Scheme LIN-BEBCD2). A further two, similar to nos 690-691, came from the same field in Kent (Portable Antiquities Scheme KENT-9578D3) and considered as a pair, however, this is impossible to prove. Stylistically similar blunt-hooked and eye-sections are shown together.

Early post-medieval Class A, Type 1

Three attachment-knops

Circular

612. Copper alloy; cast; one-piece; moulded-relief and openwork. Hooked-section: seven pellets forming a stylised six-petalled flower within two concentric linear circles with alternate pellets between, and transverse bands; two rounded and one debased trefoil attachment-knops; a casting sprue near the end attachment-knop; 38 x 25mm. *South Dorset*. Drawing © Patrick Read.

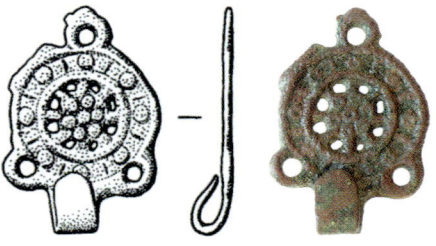

HOOKED-CLASPS & EYES

613. Copper alloy; cast; one-piece; moulded-relief. Eye-section: pellets forming a stylised multi-petalled flower within two concentric linear circles; two attachment-knops are rounded and one trefoil; 34.7 x 19mm. *South Wiltshire*. Drawing © Nick Griffiths.

614. Copper alloy; cast; one-piece; moulded-relief. Eye-section: a stylised sunburst or multi-petalled flower formed from three concentric segmented circles; two rounded and one debased trefoil attachment-knops; one side of the eye is much abraded; 35.5 x 27mm. *South-West Wiltshire*. Drawing © Patrick Read.

615. Copper alloy; cast; one-piece; moulded-relief and openwork. Hooked-section: a six-petalled flower bordered by palmettes; two rounded and one debased trefoil attachment-knops; partially unfettled openwork; 41.83 x 32.49mm. *South Somerset*. Drawing © Patrick Read.

616. Copper alloy; cast; one-piece; moulded-relief and openwork. Eye-section: comparable with no. 615; partially unfettled openwork; 40.5 x 33mm. *East Devon*. Drawing © Patrick Read.

617. Copper alloy; cast; one-piece; moulded-relief and openwork. Hooked-section: a human facing-mask within a curved-arm cross; rounded attachment-knops; a projecting rounded collar, one side abraded, at the juncture of the plate and hook; abraded beading around the edge; a casting sprue near the end attachment-knop; 42.5 x 34.5. *South Somerset*. Drawing © Patrick Read.

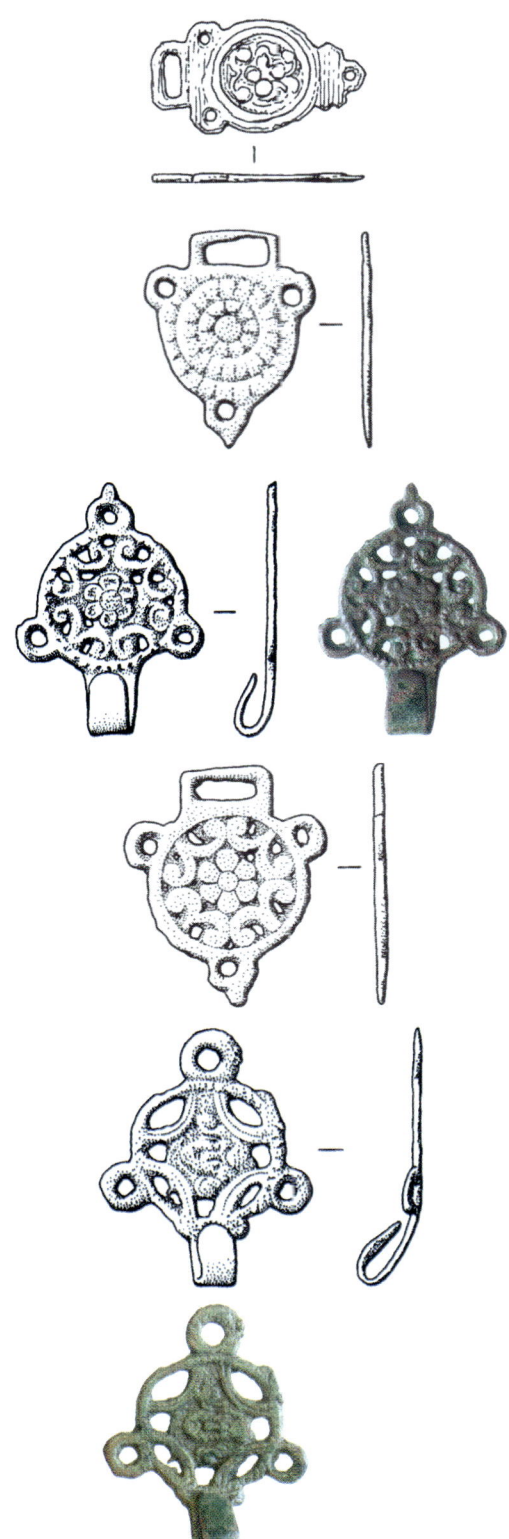

HOOKED-CLASPS & EYES

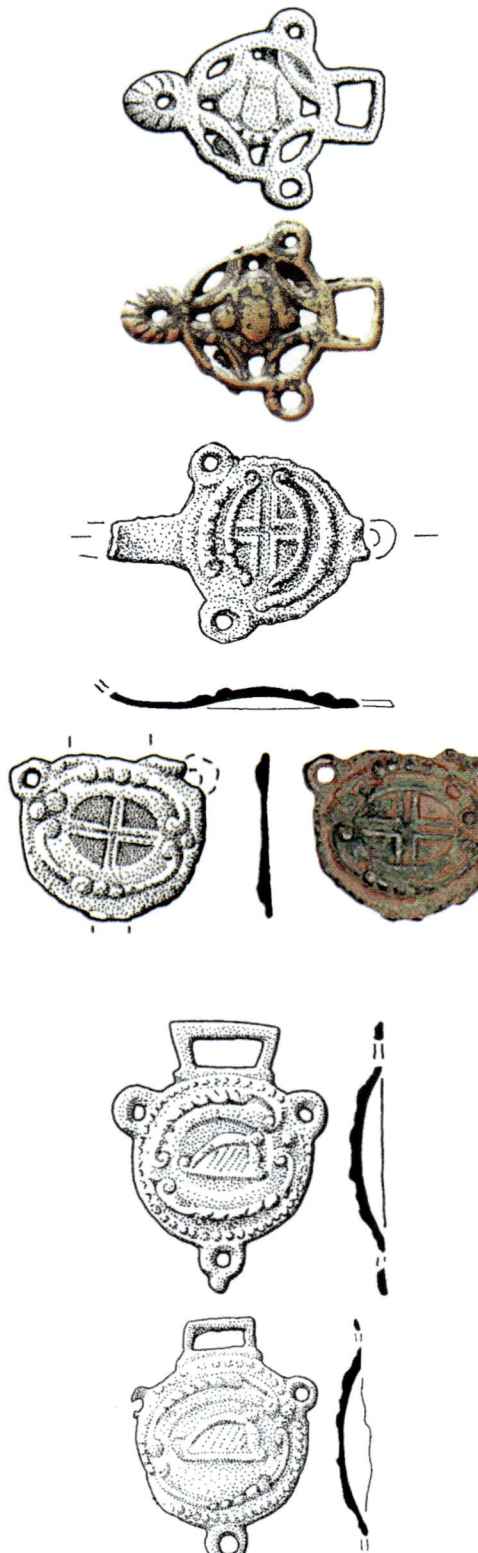

618. Copper alloy; cast; one-piece; moulded-relief and openwork. Eye-section: comparable with no. 617 except the end attachment-knop is larger and multi-grooved; abraded and partially unfettled; 42.5 x 33.5mm. *River Thames foreshore, London*. Drawing © Patrick Read.

619. Copper alloy; cast; one-piece; convex; moulded-relief. Hooked-section: a hollow-dome bearing a wreathed Cross of St George; two rounded attachment-knops. Incomplete, hook and one indeterminate-shaped attachment-knop broken off; 42 x 33mm. *East Devon*. Drawing © Nick Griffiths.

620. Copper alloy; cast; one-piece; moulded-relief. Eye-section: comparable with no. 619; a slightly angular attachment-knop. Incomplete, eye and two indeterminate-shaped attachment-knops broken off; 27.5 x 32.5mm. Found near an English Civil War battle site. *South-East Lincolnshire*. Portable Antiquities Scheme SOMDOR-32754. Drawing © Patrick Read, photograph © Somerset Museums Service.

621. Copper alloy; cast; one-piece; convex; moulded-relief. Eye-section: a hollow-dome bearing a wreathed Irish harp within a beaded border; two rounded and one debased trefoil attachment-knops; a slightly projecting angular collar at the juncture of the plate and eye; 45 x 35mm. *South Somerset*. Drawing © Patrick Read.

622. Copper alloy; cast; one-piece; convex; moulded-relief. Eye-section: comparable with nos 621, 623 except the loop is smaller and the collar has rounded ends. Incomplete, one rounded attachment-knop worn through; 43 x 30mm. Found near an English Civil War battle site. *South Somerset*. Drawing © Patrick Read.

HOOKED-CLASPS & EYES

623. Copper alloy; cast; one-piece; convex; moulded-relief. Eye-section: comparable with nos 621-622 except white-metal coated, probably tin, and lacking the collar and beaded border; 43 x 30.5mm. Found near an English Civil War skirmish site. *South Devon.* Drawing © Patrick Read.

624. Copper alloy; cast; one-piece; shallow convex; moulded-relief. Hooked-section: a hollow-dome bearing a rampant lion right (?) holding a crown within a beaded border; two rounded and one debased trefoil attachment-knops. Incomplete, hook broken off; 43 x 32mm. *Bedfordshire.* United Kingdom Detecting Finds' Database 9503. Photograph © Danny Mills.

Early post-medieval Class A, Type 2

Three attachment-knops, some with a collar, projecting and/or ridged

Oval

625. Copper alloy; cast; one-piece; convex; undecorated. Hooked-section: two rounded attachment-knops. Incomplete, one attachment-knop is worn through and one of indeterminate-shape is broken off; 28.5 x 16mm. *South Devon.* Drawing © Patrick Read.

626. Copper alloy; cast; one-piece; convex; undecorated. Hooked-section: comparable with no. 625 except the hook is longer and all the attachment-knops are rounded; 43.19 x 19mm. *South Somerset.* Drawing © Patrick Read.

627. Copper alloy; cast; one-piece; shallow convex; undecorated except coated in a now black substance, possibly bitumen. Hooked-section: the front is flattened and both edges are bevelled; two rounded attachment-knops. Incomplete, hook broken off and one probable rounded attachment-knop worn through; 27.08 x 14.77mm. *East Devon.* Drawing © Patrick Read.

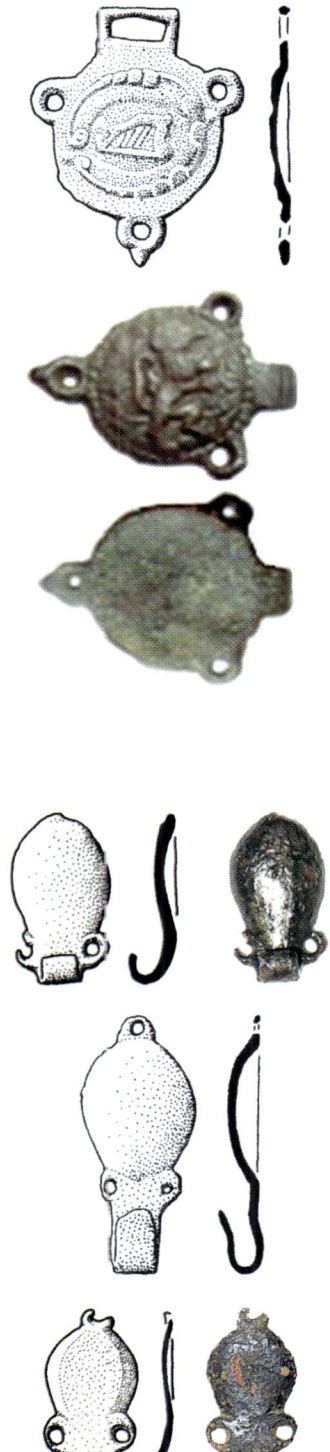

HOOKED-CLASPS & EYES

628. Copper alloy; cast; one-piece. Eye-section: comparable with no. 627 except flat, rounded attachment-knops, and white-metal coated, probably tin; 34 x 18mm. *South Somerset*. Drawing © Patrick Read.

629. Copper alloy; cast; one-piece; convex; moulded-relief. Hooked-section: a hollow-dome bearing longitudinal vine tendrils forming sub-lozenge shaped panels on a stippled field; rounded attachment-knops; 32 x 18mm. *South Somerset*. Drawing © Patrick Read.

630. Copper alloy; cast; one-piece; convex; moulded-relief. Hooked-section: a hollow-dome with a flower and foliate on a stippled field; rounded attachment-knops; white-metal coated, probably tin; 39 x 16mm. *South-East Dorset*. Drawing © Patrick Read.

631. Copper alloy; cast; shallow convex; moulded-relief. Eye-section: comparable with no. 630. Incomplete, part of the eye broken off, abraded; 37 x 16mm. *East Devon*. Drawing © Patrick Read.

632. Copper alloy; cast; one-piece; convex; moulded-relief champlevé enamel. Hooked-section: a hollow-dome with vine tendrils forming sub-lozenge shaped panels infilled with white and dark-blue enamel, each panel also has a quatrefoil of pellets; rounded attachment-knops. Incomplete, hook broken off; 40 x 17mm. *Hampshire*. United Kingdom Detecting Finds' Database 10482. Photographs © Martin Reed.

633. Copper alloy; cast; one-piece; convex; moulded-relief. Eye-section: a hollow-dome with a chequered field; one rounded and one debased trefoil attachment-knops. Incomplete, one probable rounded attachment-knop broken off; 36 x 20mm. *East Devon*. Drawing © Patrick Read.

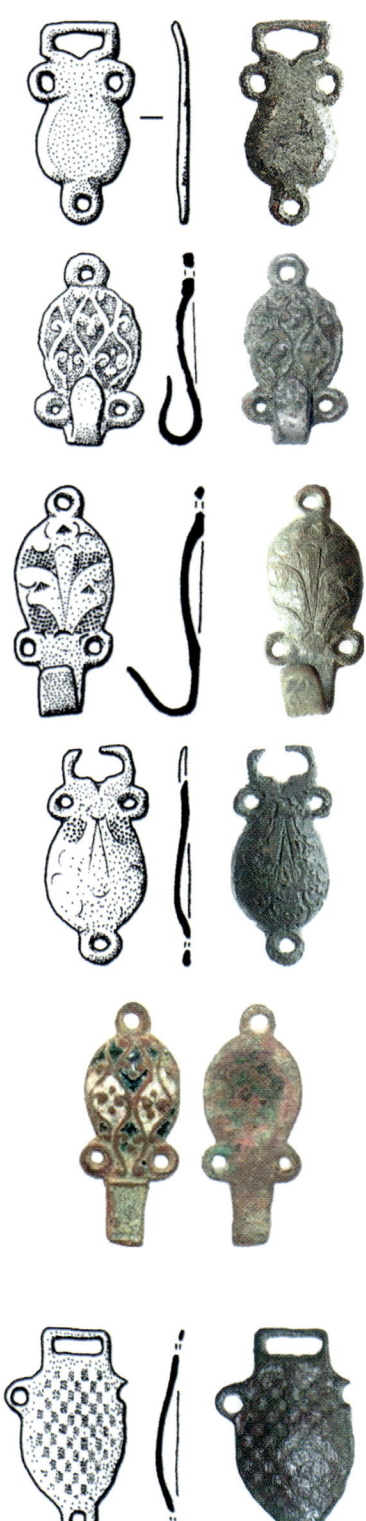

HOOKED-CLASPS & EYES

634. Copper alloy; cast; one-piece; convex; moulded-relief. Eye-section: comparable with no. 633 except the chequered field is higher relief; 40.5 x 24.75mm. *South Wiltshire*. Drawing © Nick Griffiths. Salisbury and South Wiltshire Museum ID 1610.

635. Copper alloy; cast; one-piece; undecorated except white-metal coated, probably tin. Eye-section: debased trefoil attachment-knops; a slightly projecting ridged and rounded collar at the juncture of the plate and eye; 35.5 x 30.5mm. *South Somerset*. Drawing © Patrick Read.

636. Copper alloy; cast; one-piece; undecorated except white-metal coated, probably tin. Hooked-section: comparable with nos 635, 637 except a projecting angular collar at the juncture of the plate and hook; 39.5 x 38mm. *South Somerset*. Drawing © Patrick Read.

637. Copper alloy; one-piece; undecorated. Hooked-section: comparable with nos 635-636 except the hook is much shorter; 35.05 x 27.88mm. *East Devon*. Drawing © Patrick Read.

638. Silver; cast; one-piece; undecorated. Hooked-section: the front is shallow concave; rounded attachment-knops; a projecting bifurcate-ended collar at the juncture of the plate and hook; 39.25 x 27mm. *South-East Dorset*. Drawing © Ken Wheatley.

639. Copper alloy; cast; one-piece; engraved and punched; white-metal coated, probably tin. Hooked-section: a spray of three flowers bordered by ring-and-dot motifs; debased trefoil attachment-knops; a projecting angular collar at the juncture of the plate and hook; 41 x 29.5mm. *South Somerset*. Drawing © Patrick Read.

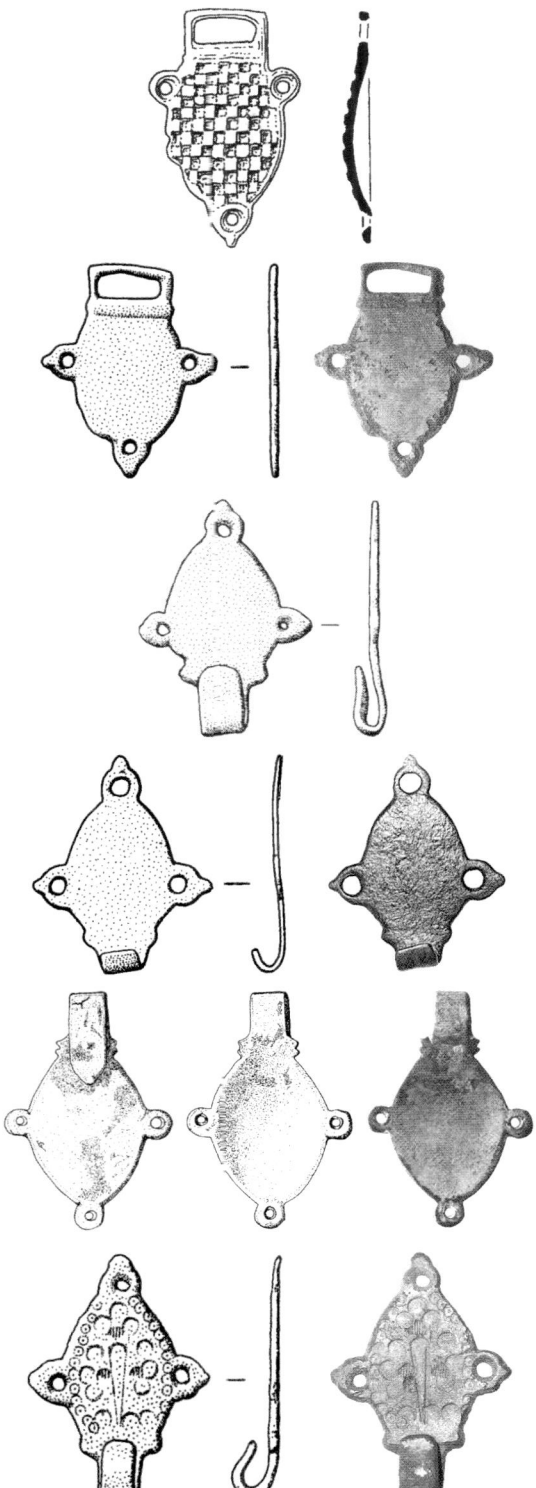

640. Copper alloy; cast; one-piece; engraved and punched. Hooked-section: comparable with nos 639, 641-644 except bordered by small annulets and uncoated. Incomplete, hook broken off; 40 x 37mm. *East Devon*. Drawing © Patrick Read.

641. Copper alloy; cast; one-piece; engraved and punched. Eye-section: comparable with nos 639-640; 642-644; 36 x 28mm. *South-East Dorset*. Drawing © Patrick Read.

642. Copper alloy; cast; one-piece; engraved and punched Eye-section: comparable with nos 639-641, 643-644 except white-metal coated, probably tin; 38 x 37mm. *River Thames foreshore, London*. Drawing © Nick Griffiths.

643. Copper alloy; cast; one-piece; engraved and punched. Eye-section: comparable with nos 639-642, 644 except a ridged collar at the juncture of the plate and eye. Incomplete, eye broken off; 36 x 30mm. *North Dorset*. Drawing © Patrick Read.

644. Copper alloy; cast; one-piece; engraved and punched. Eye-section: comparable with nos 639-643 except the collar is slightly projecting and ribbed; 38 x 29.5mm. *River Thames foreshore, London*. Drawing © Patrick Read.

645. Copper alloy; cast; one-piece; convex; moulded-relief. Hooked-section: a hollow-dome bearing a human facing-mask and foliate; rounded attachment-knops; a projecting rounded collar at the juncture of the plate and end knop. Incomplete, hook broken off; 37 x 12.5mm. *Gloucestershire*. United Kingdom Detecting Finds' Database 10531. Photograph © Jerry Morris.

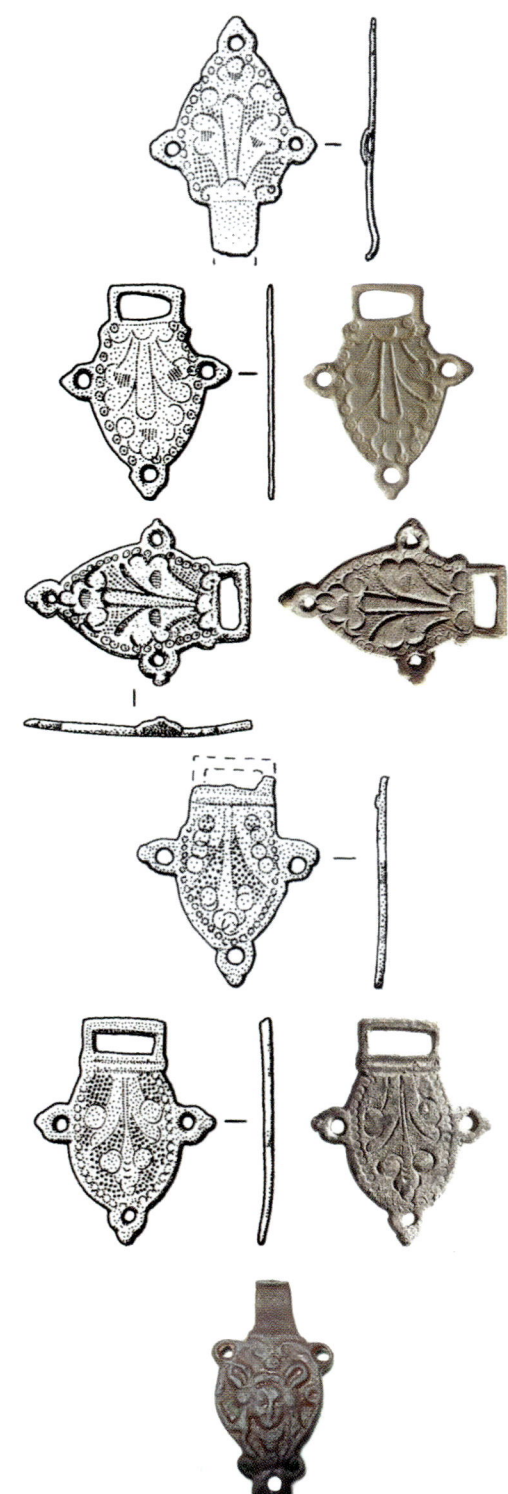

HOOKED-CLASPS & EYES

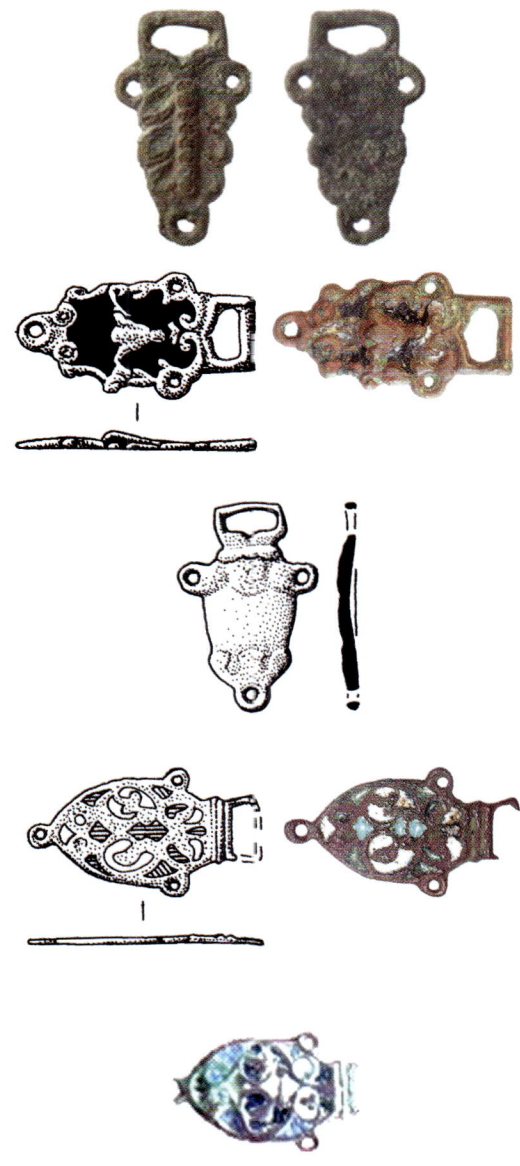

646. Copper alloy; cast; one-piece; moulded-relief. Eye-section: a median segmented band with three oblique ovoids either side; engrailed sides; rounded attachment-knops. Possible champlevé enamel missing; 39 x 22mm. *Wiltshire*. Portable Antiquities Scheme WILT-BA0526. Photographs © Salisbury and South Wiltshire Museum.

647. Copper alloy; cast; one-piece; moulded-relief; champlevé enamel. Eye-section: a bell-shaped flower emerging from a border of tendrils, foliate and two small flowers; dark-blue and white enamel in the field; engrailed sides; rounded attachment-knops; 38.17 x 21.17. *Wiltshire*. Drawing © Nick Griffiths.

648. Copper alloy; cast; one-piece; shallow convex; moulded-relief. Eye-section: a hollow-dome bearing a trilobate band at the eye end; a ridged trilobate collar at the juncture of the plate and eye and a more pronounced version at the end opposite the eye; rounded attachment-knops; 35.5 x 23mm. *East Devon*. Drawing © Patrick Read.

649. Copper alloy; cast; one-piece; moulded-relief champlevé enamel. Eye-section: a white, blue and green enamelled possible winged insect; rounded attachment-knops; a slightly projecting rounded and ribbed collar at the junction of the plate and hook. Incomplete, section of eye broken off; 37.53 x 16.3. *South Somerset*. Drawing © Nick Griffiths.

650. Copper alloy; cast; one-piece; moulded-relief champlevé enamel. Eye-section: intertwined vine tendrils and foliate infilled with white, light- and dark-blue enamel; two rounded attachment-knops; a slightly projecting ridged and rounded collar at the junction of the plate and hook. Incomplete, eye and one indeterminate-shaped attachment-knop broken off; 32 x 22mm. *Essex*. United Kingdom Detecting Finds' Database 4953. Photograph © Chris Chandler.

651. Copper alloy; cast; one-piece; moulded-relief. Hooked-section: transverse orientated plate; a hollow-dome bearing a two addorsed small flowers on stalks and with leaves springing from a median bar and pellet within a hatched border; a rounded knop at the attachment-end and a projecting angular collar at the juncture of the plate and hook. Incomplete, hook and three indeterminate-shaped attachment knops broken off, corroded; 35.09 x 25.09mm. *Staffordshire*. Drawing © Patrick Read.

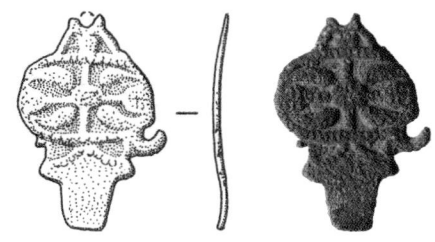

Early post-medieval Class A, Type 3

Four attachment-knops

Oval/ovoid

652. Copper alloy; cast; one-piece; moulded-relief champlevé enamel. Hooked-section: a dark-blue enamelled winged insect. Incomplete, hook and indeterminate-shaped attachment-knops broken off; much abraded; 38 x 21.5mm. *North Somerset*. Drawing © Patrick Read.

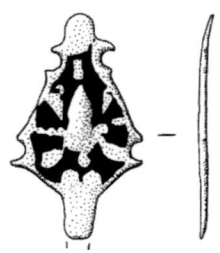

Early post-medieval Class A, Type 4

Five attachment-knops

Oval/ovoid

653. Copper alloy; cast; engraved. Eye-section: comparable with nos 637-642 except two rounded, one debased trefoil, one angular and one probable angular attachment-knops. Incomplete, point of the probable angular attachment-knop broken off; 41 x 21.5. *South Somerset*. Drawing © Patrick Read.

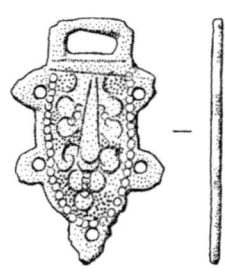

Early post-medieval Class A, Type 5

Three attachment-knops

Shield-shaped

654. Copper alloy; cast; one-piece; convex; moulded-relief. Eye-section: a shallow hollow-dome bearing a crowned fleur-de-lis; rounded attachment-knops. Incomplete, eye broken off; 30 x 20.5mm. *South-West Wiltshire*. Drawing © Patrick Read.

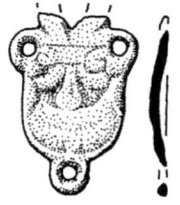

HOOKED-CLASPS & EYES

Early post-medieval Class A, Type 6

Three attachment-knops

Sub-lozenge shaped

655. Copper alloy; cast; one-piece; openwork, otherwise undecorated. Hooked-section: a slightly projecting rounded collar at the juncture of the plate and hook. Incomplete, hook and indeterminate-shaped attachment-knops broken off, much corroded; 40 x 26mm. *South Somerset*. Drawing © Patrick Read.

Early post-medieval Class A, Type 7

Three attachment-knops

Figurative

656. Copper alloy; cast; one-piece; convex; moulded-relief. Hooked-section: a hollow-dome with radiating grooves, a scallop shell; rounded attachment-knops; 35.5 x 18mm. *North Dorset*. Drawing © Patrick Read.

657. Copper alloy; cast; one-piece; convex; moulded-relief. Hooked-section: comparable with nos 656, 658-659 except wider and a much shorter hook; the front is coated in a now black substance, possibly bitumen. Incomplete, indeterminate-shaped attachment-knops broken off; 33 x 22mm. *East Devon*. Drawing © Patrick Read.

658. Silver; cast; one-piece; convex; moulded-relief. Hooked-section: comparable with nos 656-657, 659 except an engrailed edge; hook distorted; 29 x 16.9mm. *Oxfordshire*. Treasure case 2004 T257. Photographs © The Portable Antiquities Scheme.

659. Copper alloy; cast; one-piece; convex; moulded-relief. Eye-section: comparable with nos 656-658 except narrower. Incomplete, part of eye broken off; 36.37 x 16.29mm. *East Devon*. Drawing © Patrick Read.

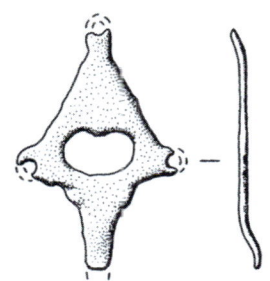

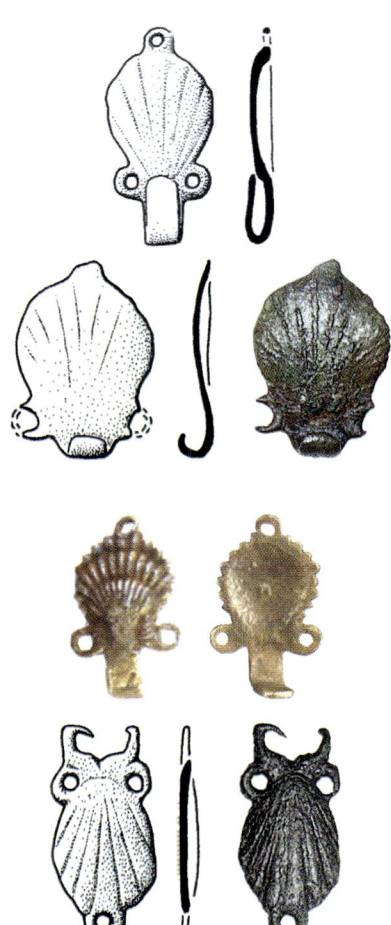

660. Copper alloy; cast; one-piece; shallow convex; engraved and moulded-relief. Hooked-section: a hollow-dome representing an acorn; two rounded and one debased trefoil attachment-knops; 37.81 x 22.14mm. *South-West Wiltshire*. Drawing © Patrick Read.

661. Copper alloy; cast; one-piece; convex; engraved and moulded-relief. Eye-section: comparable with no. 660. Incomplete, eye broken off and one rounded attachment-knop worn through; 36.5 x 21.5mm. *South Devon*. Drawing © Patrick Read.

662. Copper alloy; cast; one-piece; moulded-relief. Hooked-section: Prince of Wales Feathers; two angular and one rounded attachment-knops; a projecting ridged and angular collar at the juncture of the plate and hook. Incomplete, a small piece of the end attachment-knop broken off; 40.2 x 20.2mm. *Buckinghamshire*. Drawing © Patrick Read.

Early post-medieval Class A, Type 8

Three attachment-knops and two ornamental knops; the end attachment-knop is frequently collared

Oval

663. Copper alloy; cast; one-piece; moulded-relief. Hooked-section: an oval panel bearing possible foliate and floriate within a beaded border; rounded attachment-knops, the end one with a projecting rounded collar; a debased bifurcate ornamental knop either side; white-metal coated, probably tin. Incomplete, hook broken off; 43 x 22.5mm. *South-East Dorset*. Drawing © Patrick Read.

664. Copper alloy; cast; one-piece; moulded-relief. Eye-section: comparable with no. 663; 38 x 22.3mm. *East Devon*. Drawing © Patrick Read.

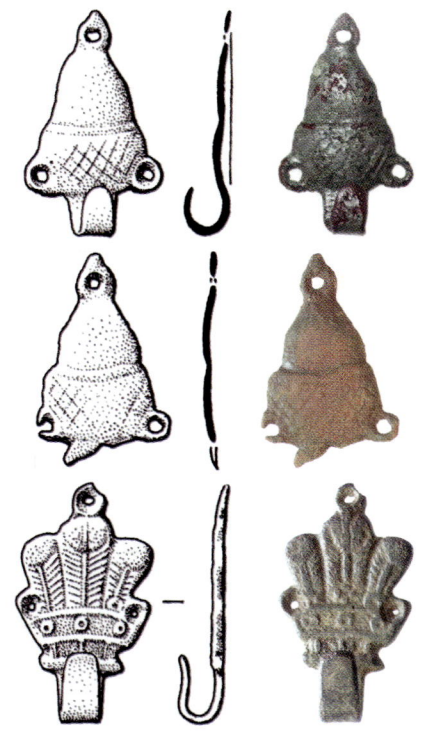

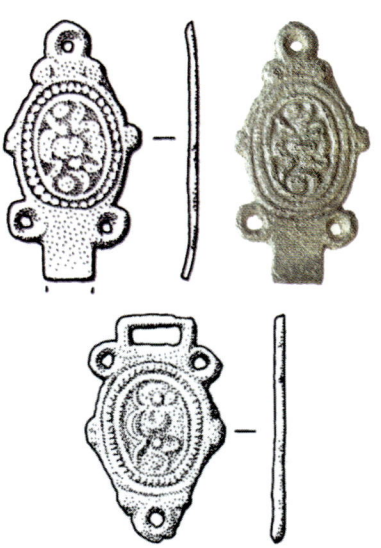

HOOKED-CLASPS & EYES

665. Copper alloy; cast; one-piece; moulded-relief. Eye-section: an oval panel bearing foliate and floriate; a bifurcate ornamental knop either side; 39 x 21mm. *South-West Lincolnshire*. Drawing © Nick Griffiths.

666. Copper alloy; cast; one-piece; moulded-relief. Hooked-section: a possible standing human facing-figure; rounded attachment-knops, the end one with a projecting rounded collar; an ornamental knop either side, one bifurcate and the other debased trefoil. Incomplete, the edge of one attachment-knop worn through and the edge of another broken; 35.5 x 23.5mm. *East Devon*. Drawing © Patrick Read.

667. Copper alloy; cast; one-piece; moulded-relief. Eye-section: comparable with no. 666 except the main decorative element, which is similar, is a fleur-de-lis and oblique bands on a median band; opposite the fleur are four slightly oblique bands with an indeterminate-shape either side. This design perhaps represents a wheat-sheaf, the horizon and sun rays; 37 x 23.5mm. *Mid-Dorset*. Drawing © Patrick Read.

668. Copper alloy; cast; one-piece; moulded-relief. Eye-section: an oval panel bearing a human facing-mask wearing a headdress within a beaded border; rounded attachment-knops, the end one collared; a bifurcate ornamental knop either side; white-metal coated, probably tin. Incomplete, part of eye broken off and distorted; 40 x 23.5mm. *South-East Dorset*. Drawing © Patrick Read.

669. Copper alloy; cast; one-piece; moulded-relief. Hooked-section: a lion passant right; rounded attachment-knops, the end one with a projecting rounded collar; a bifurcate ornamental knop either side. Incomplete, hook broken off; 37.5 x 21.5mm. *South Somerset*. Drawing © Patrick Read.

670. Copper alloy; cast; one-piece; moulded-relief. Eye section: comparable with no. 669 except facing left; 37 x 22mm. *Gloucestershire*. Photograph © Kath Hurcombe.

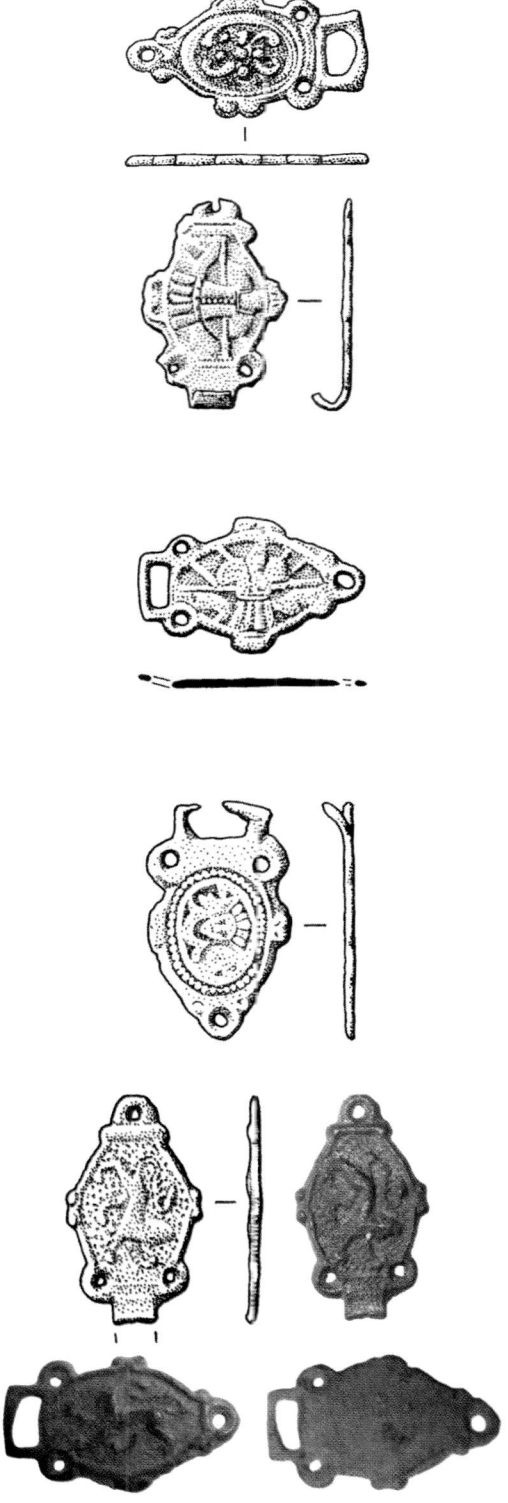

671. Copper alloy; cast; one-piece; moulded-relief. Hooked-section: a horse and rider right, (?) a cavalier, on a cross-hatched field; rounded attachment-knops, the end one with a projecting rounded collar; a bifurcate ornamental knop either side; 42.33 x 21.19mm. *South-East Dorset*. Drawing © Patrick Read.

672. Copper alloy; cast; one-piece; moulded-relief. Eye-section: comparable with no. 671 except riding left. Incomplete, loop broken off, distorted and corroded; 30 x 20mm. *Worcestershire*. United Kingdom Detecting Finds' Database 9938. Photographs © Mark Arrowsmith.

673. Copper alloy; cast; one-piece; moulded-relief. Hooked-section: wreathed Commonwealth Arms; rounded attachment-knops, the end one with a spiral collar; a bifurcate ornamental knop either side; one edge is slightly unfettled; 42.5 x 20mm. *Wiltshire*. Wiltshire Heritage Museum enq. 270. Drawing © Nick Griffiths.

674. Copper alloy; cast; one-piece; moulded-relief. Eye-section: comparable with no. 673 except the arms are reversed, 37 x 21.5mm. *Mid-Somerset*. Drawing © Patrick Read.

675. Copper alloy; cast; one-piece; moulded-relief. Eye-section: Cross of St George within a part wreathed and part schematised border; hatching near the loop; rounded attachment-knops, the end one with a projecting rounded collar; a rounded ornamental knop either side; 44 x 24.5mm. *South-East Dorset*. Drawing © Patrick Read.

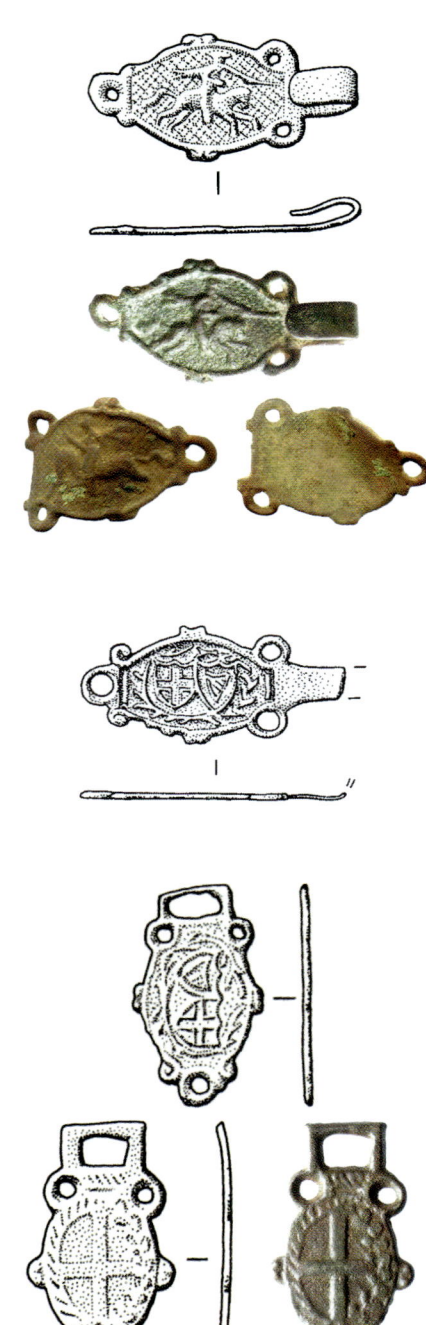

Early post-medieval Class A, Type 9

Four attachment-knops and an ornamental knop

Oval/Ovoid

676. Copper alloy; cast; one-piece; moulded-relief champlevé enamel. Hooked-section: a dark-blue and white enamelled possible dancing human figure; rounded attachment-knops; a rounded ornamental knop on the end. Incomplete, hook broken off and some enamel missing; 31.5 x 20.5mm. *South-East Dorset*. Drawing © Nick Griffiths.

677. Copper alloy; cast; one-piece; moulded-relief. Eye-section: a central four-petalled flower bordered by spirals; rounded attachment-knops; a rounded ornamental knop on the end. The loop is much abraded; 37.1 x 27.81mm. *South Somerset*. Drawing © Patrick Read.

678. Copper alloy; cast; one-piece; moulded-relief. Eye-section: a human facing-bust on a field of pellets and annulets; rounded attachment-knops; a rounded and obliquely grooved ornamental knop on the end resembles a scallop shell; 37 x 25mm. *South Somerset*. Drawing © Patrick Read.

679. Copper alloy; cast; one-piece; moulded-relief. Eye-section: thought to be a stylised fleur-de-lis bordered by spirals but perhaps a winged insect, possibly originally champlevé enamelled; a rounded and obliquely grooved ornamental knop on the end resembles a scallop shell; 38 x 25mm. *Gloucestershire*. United Kingdom Detecting Finds' Database 7081. Photographs © Paul Roberts.

680. Copper alloy; cast; one-piece; moulded-relief champlevé enamel. Eye-section: comparable with no. 679 except with an indeterminate motif in black, green and white enamel. Incomplete, one attachment-knop worn through; 38 x 25mm. *Wiltshire*. Wiltshire Heritage Museum acc. no. ST9966. Drawing © Nick Griffiths.

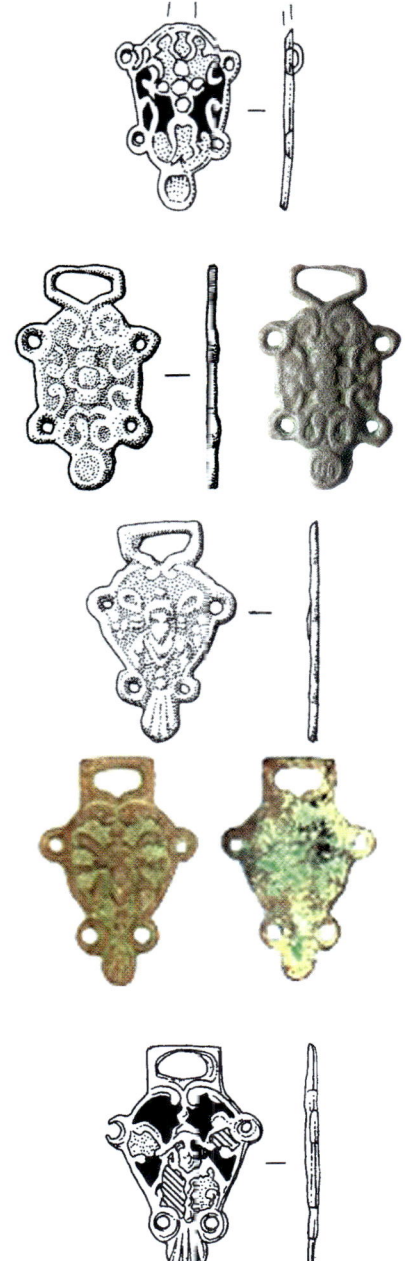

Early post-medieval Class A, Type 10

Three attachment-knops and ornamental knops

Sub-lozenge shaped

681. Copper alloy; cast; one-piece; moulded-relief. Hooked-section: a four-petalled flower with sepals bordered by two addorsed spirals, a transverse segmented band near the hook and two transverse bands at the opposite end; rounded attachment-knops, the end one with a projecting rounded collar; a bifurcate ornamental knop either side; 44 x 25mm. *South-West Wiltshire*. Drawing © Patrick Read.

682. Copper alloy; cast; one-piece; moulded-relief. Hooked-section: comparable with nos 681, 683-685 except the flower is more ornate and two transverse bands at either end. Incomplete, hook broken off; 37.5 x 27mm. *South-East Dorset*. Drawing © Patrick Read.

683. Copper alloy; cast; one-piece; moulded-relief. Eye-section: comparable with nos 681-682, 684-685 except white-metal coated, probably tin; 39.11 x 24.65mm. *North Dorset*.

684. Copper alloy; cast; one-piece; moulded-relief. Eye-section: comparable with nos 681-683, 685 except the flower is less ornate and the gap is wider between the two bands at the end opposite the eye. Incomplete, one attachment-knop worn through; 39 x 25mm. *South Somerset*. Drawing © Patrick Read.

685. Copper alloy; cast; one-piece; moulded-relief. Eye-section: comparable with nos 681-684 except the flower is less ornate, one transverse band at either end; the end attachment knop is a debased trefoil; 38 x 22.5mm. *North Dorset*. Drawing © Patrick Read.

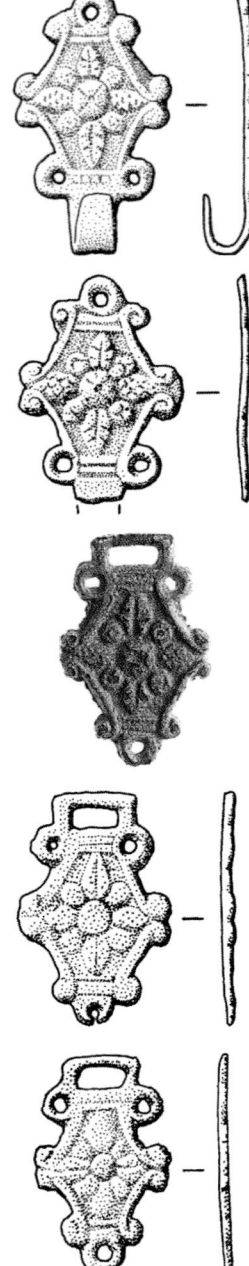

HOOKED-CLASPS & EYES

Early post-medieval Class A, Type 11

One attachment-knop with either one or two holes, two attachment-holes in the plate, and a collar at one or more ends

Sub-circular

686. Copper alloy; cast; one-piece; moulded-relief. Eye-section: a central four-petalled flower on a field of tendrils and foliate, a small three-petalled flower in each quarter; a slightly projecting rounded collar at the juncture of the plate and eye and at the juncture of the plate and debased trefoil attachment-knop, a further attachment-hole either side of the plate; 38 x 21mm. *Cornwall*. Portable Antiquities Scheme CORN-914120. Photograph © Cornwall County Council.

687. Copper alloy; cast; one-piece; moulded-relief champlevé enamel. Hooked-section: a white, light-blue and (?) black (?) dark-blue enamelled butterfly; a slightly projecting rounded collar at the juncture of the plate and trefoil knop which has an attachment-hole either side; a further attachment-hole either side of the plate. Incomplete, hook broken off; 46 x 24mm. *Essex*. United Kingdom Detecting Finds' Database 8673. Photographs © Brian Smyth.

688. Copper alloy; cast; one-piece; openwork. Hooked-section: a lozenge and a heart, a trefoil projects into the latter; a trefoil attachment-knop; an attachment-hole either side of the plate; two slightly angular ornamental knops either side; a projecting angular collar at the juncture of the plate and hook; 46.5 x 23.5mm. *South Devon*. Drawing © Patrick Read.

689. Copper alloy; cast; one-piece; openwork. Eye-section: comparable with no. 688; 42.5 x 24.5. *South-East Lincolnshire*. Drawing © Patrick Read.

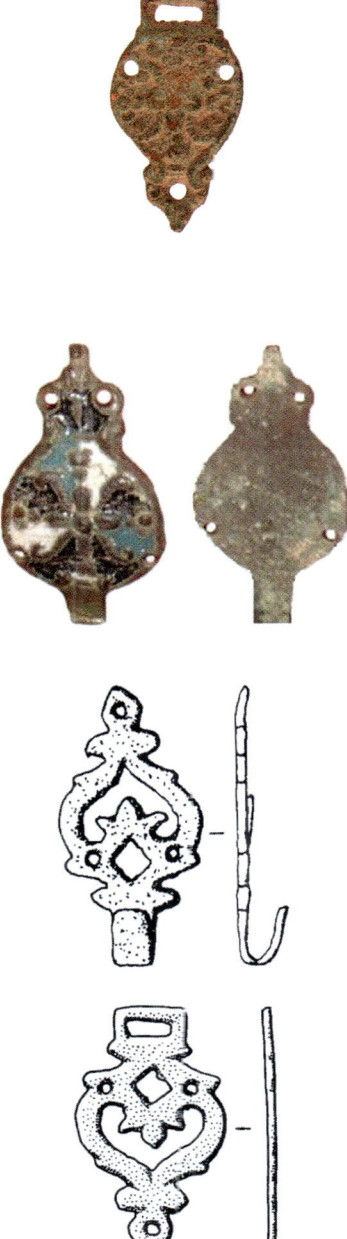

Early post-medieval Class A, Type 12

One attachment-knop with either one or two holes, two attachment-holes in the plate, and a collar at one or more ends

Sub-pentagonal

690. Copper alloy; cast; one-piece; moulded-relief. Hooked-section: a four-petalled flower with sepals and fronds; a rounded attachment-knop with a projecting spiral collar; an attachment-hole either side of the plate; a slightly projecting rounded and ridged angular collar at the juncture of the plate and hook. Incomplete, hook broken off and slightly unfettled; 40 x 20.5mm. *South-West Dorset.* Drawing © Patrick Read.

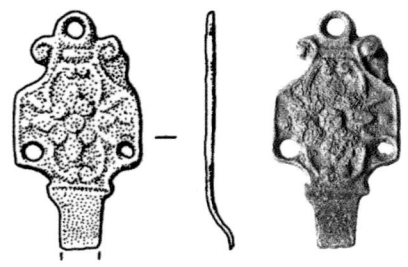

691. Copper alloy; cast; one-piece; moulded-relief. Eye-section: comparable with no. 690, slightly unfettled; 39 x 25mm. *South Somerset.* Drawing © Patrick Read.

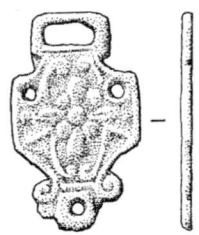

Early post-medieval Class A, Type 13

One attachment-knop, and two attachment-holes in the plate

Oval

692. Copper alloy; cast; one-piece; moulded-relief and openwork. Eye-section: a central large lozenge-shaped flower, tendrils, foliate and small multi-petalled flowers; a rounded attachment knop on the end; a grooved collar at the juncture of the plate and hook. Incomplete, loop broken off; 36 x 19mm. *East Yorkshire.* Photographs © Stan Raymond.

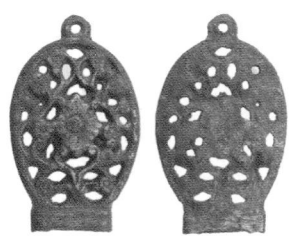

Figurative

693. Copper alloy; cast; one-piece; moulded-relief. Eye-section: a fleur-de-lis with (?) stamens or (?) seeds; a rounded attachment-knop, an oval attachment-hole either side of the plate; a transverse beaded band at the juncture of the plate and eye; 37.3 x 24.1mm. *Northamptonshire.* Peter Woods CH201. Drawing © Roy Turland, photograph © Peter Woods.

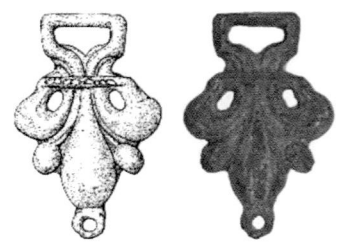

HOOKED-CLASPS & EYES

Early post-medieval Class A, Type 14

Two attachment-holes in the plate, and an ornamental knop

Oval

694. Copper alloy; cast; one-piece; engraved, punched and openwork. Hooked-section: a central four-petalled flower on a field of dots; an obliquely grooved trefoil ornamental knop on the end; 37 x 20.5mm. *East Devon*. Drawing © Patrick Read.

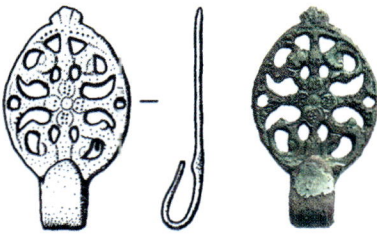

Early post-medieval Class A, Type 15

Openwork utilised for attachment

Ovoid

695. Copper alloy; cast; one-piece; convex; moulded-relief and openwork. Eye-section: a hollow-dome with intertwined vine tendrils, foliate and floriate; the front has a black/brown coating, possibly bitumen. Incomplete, a section of probable rounded eye broken off; 31 x 17mm. *South-West Dorset*. Drawing © Patrick Read.

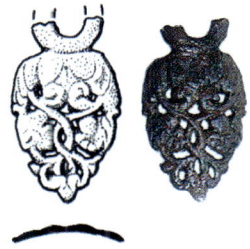

Early post-medieval Class A, Type 16

Openwork utilised for attachment, and an ornamental knop; some with a collar at one end

Oval/Ovoid

696. Copper alloy; cast; one-piece; moulded-relief and openwork. Hooked-section: a quatrefoil with foliate in the angles; an ornamental trefoil knop on the end. Incomplete, hook broken off; 31 x 22mm. *Norfolk*. Portable Antiquities Scheme NMS-84C863. Photograph © Norfolk Museums and Archaeology Service.

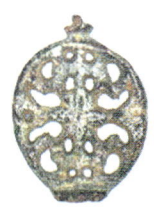

697. Copper alloy; cast; one-piece; convex; moulded-relief and openwork. Eye-section: a hollow-dome with vine tendrils, foliate and floriate emerging from a vase-like object, a projecting collar with bifurcate ends (formed from foliate) at the juncture of the plate and eye; 38 x 29.5mm. *South Somerset*. Drawing © Patrick Read.

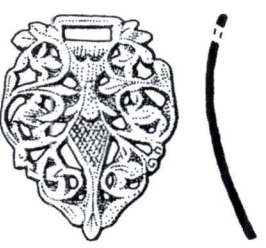

Early post-medieval Class B single blunt-hooked and eye clasps

The only surviving contemporary dress with still attached blunt-hooked and eye clasps similar to the preceding early post-medieval Class A is in the Museum of London, 14 pairs of which (one eye missing and several broken) fasten the front of a woollen felt-coat assigned as 1620-30 (acc. no. A7582) (Fig. 32.1-2). Until recently this coat was thought to be buff-leather and its robustly cast copper-alloy scallop-shaped clasps, which are stitched on, are definitely different to the preceding Class A for the hooks are recurving. The outlines of marks on the coat are similarly-shaped as the clasp-plates themselves, indicating that the clasps have been repositioned or are perhaps replacements. Designated as Class B, outside of the Museum of London, these clasps (their only examples) are unparalleled.

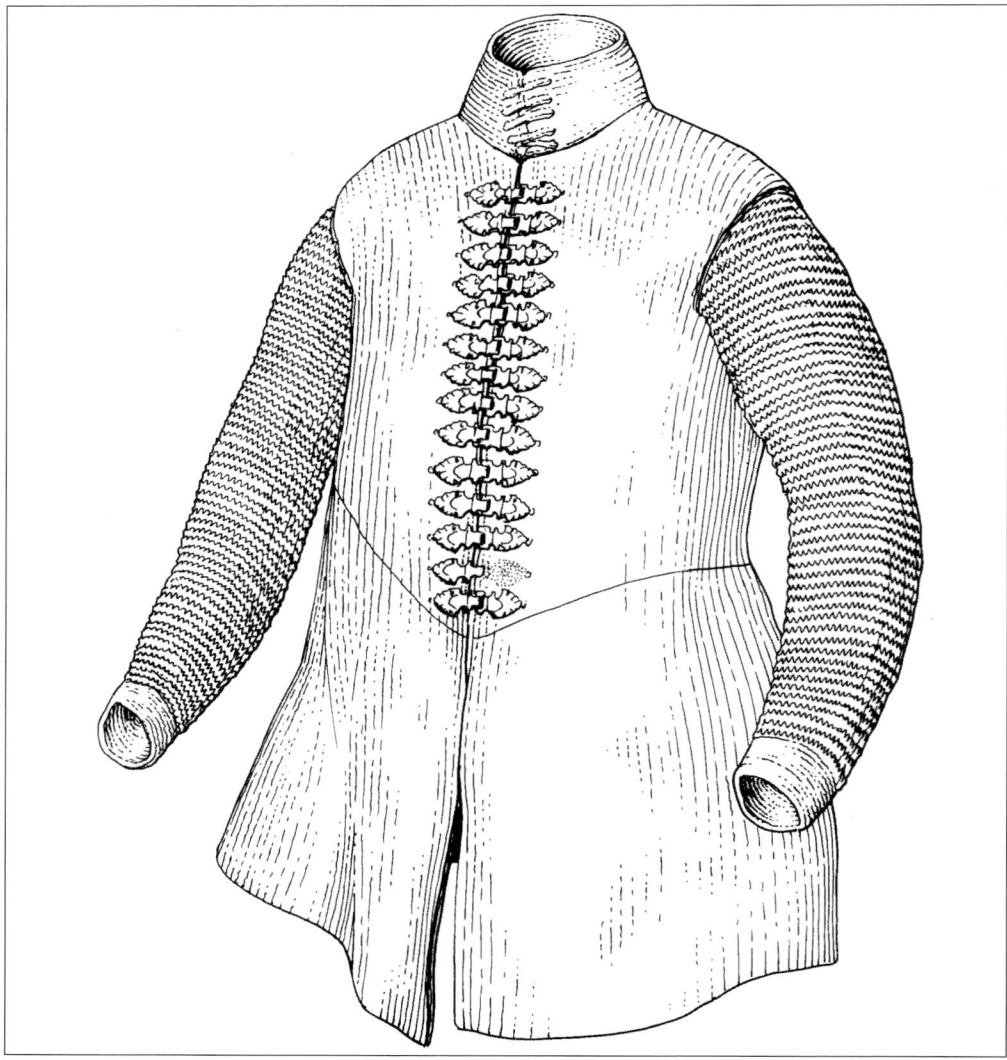

Fig. 32.1. Drawing of a 1620-30 woollen felt-coat in the Museum of London. Note 14 pairs of Class B scallop-shaped blunt-hooked and eye clasps (one eye missing and several broken) securing the front. Museum of London acc. no. A7582. *Formerly part of the Ernest Crofts R.A. collection.* Drawing © Nick Griffiths.

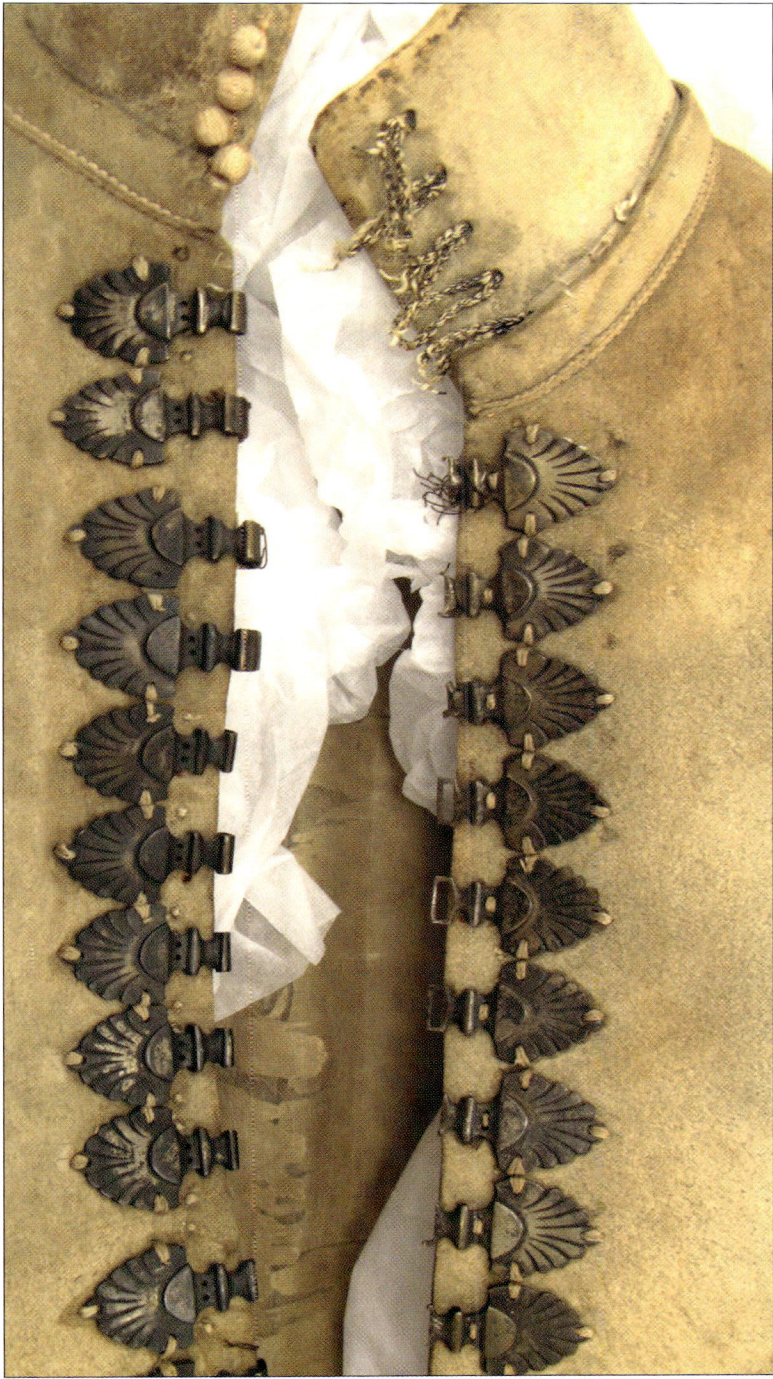

Fig. 32.2. Scallop-shaped cast copper-alloy Class B blunt-hooked and eye clasps on the front of a 1620-30 woollen felt-coat in the Museum of London. One eye missing and several broken. Note stitching through attachment-holes, and marks on the felt. Museum of London acc. no. A7582. *Formerly part of the Ernest Crofts R.A. collection.* Photograph © and reproduced courtesy of the Museum of London.

HOOKED-CLASPS & EYES

Figurative

698. Copper alloy; cast; one-piece; moulded-relief. On coat, hooked-section: a scallop-shaped plate with three drilled attachment-holes and an engrailed edge; a long, cusped shank with a central projecting ridged collar, and a similar collar at the bend of the hook, two transverse drilled-holes near the plate, the hook is broad with a square terminal; 42 x 23. *Provenance unknown other than from the Ernest Crofts R.A. collection.* Museum of London acc. no. A7582. Drawing © Nick Griffiths.

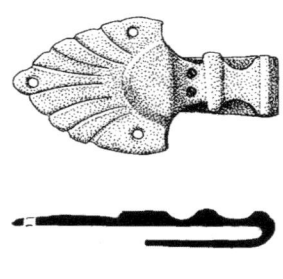

699. Copper alloy; cast; one-piece; moulded-relief. On coat, eye-section: comparable with no. 698; 38 x 23. *Provenance unknown other than from the Ernest Crofts R.A. collection.* Museum of London acc. no. A7582. Drawing © Nick Griffiths.

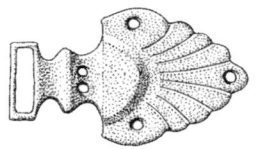

Early post-medieval Class C single blunt-hooked clasp

Although similar but much smaller, this cast lead/tin blunt-hooked clasp does not fit comfortably within either Class A or B, therefore is designated as Class C, Type 1. The plate has seven attachment-holes, presumably for stitching, and as both sides are decorated, it suggests the hook could be recurving or forward-facing. Use in tandem with a matching eye, which are absent from the known record, is plausible, though a worked-eye is a possibility. A late 16th- - *c.*17th-century attribution is likely.

Early post-medieval Class C, Type 1

Circular

700. Lead/tin; cast; one-piece; moulded-relief, recessed and openwork. Hooked-section: unusually, both sides of this clasp are decorated, therefore which is the front and which is the back is uncertain - perhaps it could have been worn with the hook either recurving or forward-facing. Each side mirrors the other - linear, curvilinear, spirals and an ovate; six equidistant small rounded knops; the openwork, seven circular holes, some of which would have served as attachment-holes; 25 x 18mm. *South Devon.* After Read 1988, pp 122, no. 1; and 1995, no. 767. Drawing © Patrick Read.

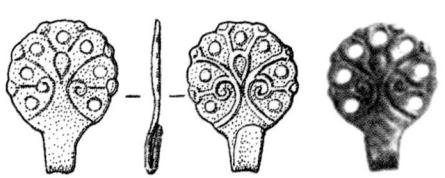

Early post-medieval Class D single blunt-hooked clasp

This Class D cast silver blunt-hooked clasp is the only example in the known record. Whether used with a matching companion eye is unknown though a worked-eye is possible. Each side has a tiny rounded attachment-knop for stitches, and the hook is forward-facing. A 16th- - 17th-century attribution is possible.

Early post-medieval Class D, Type 1

Two knops with attachment-holes and four ornamental knops

Trefoil

701. Silver; cast; one-piece; moulded-relief. Hooked-section: three facing human-masks; rounded attachment-knops; two tiny rounded knops on the end opposite the hook are perhaps stubs from an attachment-loop though they appear ornamental, another rounded ornamental knop either side, one abraded; 18 x 16mm. *North Yorkshire.* Jim Halliday. Drawing © Anne Hodgson.

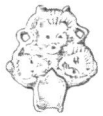

Early post-medieval Class E single blunt-hooked clasp

It is difficult to accept that this tiny cast silver object is anything other than the male section of a blunt-hooked and eye clasp, or, alternatively, engaged with a worked-eye. Its hook has a stand-alone orientation among clasps in the present assemblage. Designated as Class E, Type 1. Said by finder to be from a *c.*16th- - *c.*17th-century context.

Early post-medieval Class E, Type 1

Two attachment-holes

Lozenge-shaped

702. Silver; cast; one-piece; undecorated. Hooked-section: the plate has two median attachment-holes suitable for either stitching or riveting; the hook, which terminates in a globular knop, is in the same plane as the plate; 16.48 x 7.48mm. *River Thames foreshore, London.* Drawing © Nick Griffiths.

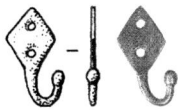

Early post-medieval Class F single blunt-hooked and eye clasps

These copper-alloy clasps comprise two cast one-piece sections - a blunt-hook and an eye, and are designated as Class F, Type 1. Recorded examples are white-metal coated. Common to one end of each section is a T-shaped toggle, presumably for slotting into small slits cut in leather or textile. The nearest comparison is blunt-hooked clasps used as fasteners on 19th-century wooden-soled clogs and shoes; notwithstanding, these items were perhaps used with $c.$16th- - $c.$17th- century sword-belts.

Early post-medieval Class F, Type 1

Asymmetrical

703. Copper alloy; cast; one-piece; moulded-relief and openwork; white-metal coated, probably tin. Hook-section: a heart, both outside edges of which have a slightly rounded knop; either end of the rectangular eye is bifurcate; a projecting, narrow rounded and slightly raised collar at the juncture of the plate and toggle; comparable with no. 704; 27.23 x 16.9. *South Somerset*. Drawing © Nick Griffiths.

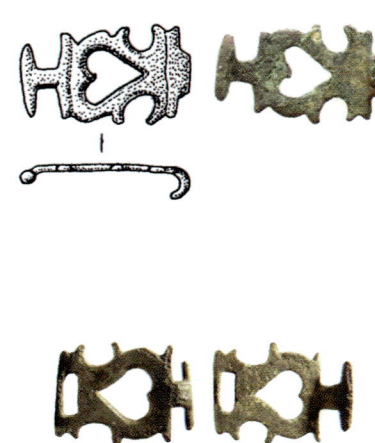

704. Copper alloy; cast; one-piece; moulded-relief and openwork; white-metal coated, probably tin. Eye-section: comparable with no. 703; 22 x 17mm. *Lincolnshire*. Portable Antiquities Scheme LIN-DFAF44. Photograph © the Portable Antiquities Scheme.

Early post-medieval Class G single blunt-hooked clasps

Compositely constructed from copper-alloy sheeting, the provision of such small recurving or forward-facing hooks, which are integral, suggests these are male sections of blunt-hooked and eye clasps. In his invaluable *Material Culture in London in an Age of Transition* 2005, Geoff Egan notes that this category is 'similar in several ways to certain medieval strapends', and nos 592-3 in the same volume are remnants (eyes) of book-clasps. The broad hooks on nos 705-706 indicate they are book-clasps and the narrow hook on no. 707, a strap-end, perhaps for suspending a pendant or suchlike. Attachment was achieved by riveting. Designated as Class G, Types 1 and 2 and assigned as $c.$1550-50 or even earlier. For a comparison see Ottaway and Rogers 2002, fig 1474, no. 14356, which is from a 17th- - 20th-century deposition, therefore perhaps residual.

Early post-medieval Class G, Type 1

Rectangular/Sub-rectangular

705. Copper alloy; sheeting; four-piece; possible openwork, otherwise undecorated. Hooked-section: the attachment-edge of the front-plate has a bifurcate knop on each corner separated by a circular aperture; the hook is an integral extension of the plate and has a slightly angular knop either side; a rivet-hole near each knop and two median drilled-holes may be openwork. The back-plate has straight sides, is similarly pierced and has an integral hook. The plates are secured together, with a space between, with separate copper-alloy rivets; 27 x 21.75mm. *South-West Lincolnshire.* Drawing © Patrick Read.

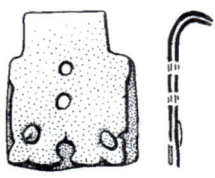

706. Copper alloy; sheeting; four-piece; openwork, otherwise undecorated. Hooked-section: the attachment-edge of the front-plate has a trefoil knop on each corner, the hook is an integral extension of the plate and has a bifurcate knop either side; a median rivet-hole at either end and two transverse drilled-holes. The back-plate has straight sides, is similarly pierced and has an integral hook. A separate copper-alloy rivet secures the two plates with a tapering slight gap between; 34.84 x 26.01mm. *South-East Dorset.* Drawing © Nick Griffiths.

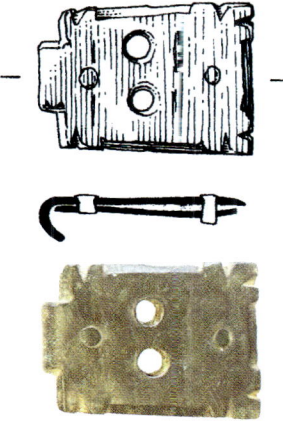

Early post-medieval Class G, Type 2

Rectangular/Sub-rectangular

707. Copper alloy; sheeting; five-piece; undecorated. Hooked-section: the front-plate has four median rivet-holes, two of which are close together at the hook-end, one in the centre, and another at the attachment-end. A smaller sub-rectangular back-plate is similarly pierced. A separate forward-facing hook is secured between the plates by two separate copper-alloy rivets, a third separate copper-alloy rivet secures the other end, the central rivet-hole retains rust residue of an iron rivet; the latter two rivets may have been purely for securing the strap; the space between the plates is tapered, 30.83 x 21.14mm. *South-West Wiltshire.* Drawing © Patrick Read.

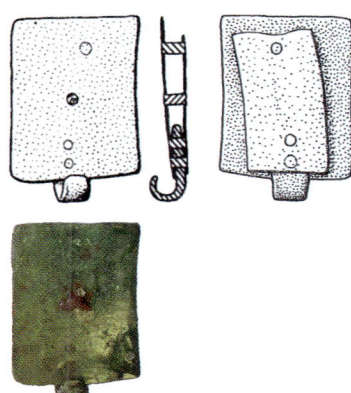

8: MISCELLANEOUS OBJECTS WITH HOOKS, EYES OR LOOPS

Early post-medieval hat-hooks

Increasingly apparent is a fascinating category of precious- or base-metal object with circular-section tapering wire sharp-hooks on the back. Known as hat-hooks (or cap-hooks), they are said to have embellished Tudor men's hats (Gaimster *et al* 2002). The Cunningtons 1970 state that the Milan bonnet, fashionable *c.*1500-30, had a medium to large slashed brim, the tabs of which could be *buttoned* or *looped up* to the crown. No mention is made of hooks whatsoever and what they meant by *looped up* is unclear. Is their word *buttoned* inaccurate, and should they have used the term *hooked*? From the discussion in the introduction to late medieval and early post-medieval single sharp-hooked clasps, we can infer that 'button', 'buttoned' and 'hook', 'hooked' may have had the same meaning. A description in Laver 1963, 'a so-called Milan beret ... [was] fastened with a metal tag', fails to further explain the fastener, either by depiction or textually, whether it therefore means a sharp-hooked clasp is unclear. A posthumous *c.*1520 portrait of Arthur, Prince of Wales shows him wearing a bonnet with two rose jewels attached but whether these have hooks is unknown (Fig 34). As stated earlier, it is the author's opinion that expressions such as 'hooked-tag' or 'dress-hook' (among many others) are best avoided, for such inconsistency is misleading.

No museum in this country or on the Continental mainland has in its collection surviving Tudor men's or women's hats with in situ hat-hooks of the form discussed here. Moreover, among the wealth of Renaissance men's and women's hat-jewels evident in contemporary portraits, uncertainty surrounds whether any were attached by hooks (a possible exception being the afore-mentioned Sir Edward Hoby's hat), although it is known that larger badges or *enseigns* were stitched through small eyes, usually four, placed equidistant around the back (Hackenbroch 1996). Where therefore is the evidence for these hooked-objects being worn on hats? To avoid confusion, however, until disproved, herein the term 'hat-hook' is used.

Of the 21 hat-hooks catalogued here, 16 have S-shaped hooks, on one possible hat-hook it is recurving, and hooks are missing on four: two of the latter are in Gaimster *et al* 2002 where the drawings show them with recurving hooks (Nos 710, 711). Experiments have proved that S-shaped hooks (especially when hook-shanks are squashed towards the backs of the plates) are expedient for piercing and holding together at the desired angle two tabs of textile bonnets; however, recurving hooks by themselves will not keep a hat-hook in place, therefore an additional method of attachment was necessary, for example, stitching. To stitch, an essential requirement is either attachment-loops, -knops, -holes or openwork and only one of Gaimster's examples (No. 711) has such a feature, openwork-filigree. This evidence suggests that two in Gaimster *et al* 2002 (Nos 710-711) are perhaps drawn assuming they had recurving hooks rather than S-shaped. The one with a recurving hook catalogued herein as no. 729 may well be an early post-medieval Class I sharp-hooked clasp. The practice of fashioning sharp-hooks into an S-shape perhaps reaches as far back as at least the 7th - 9th centuries as suggested by a possible Hines Type D Double Spiral-Headed dress- or hair-pin found on the River Thames foreshore, London (Fig. 33): being sheet metal rather than cast and bent into an S-shape makes it unusual for an Anglo-Saxon pin (pers. comm. Geoff Egan). Whether it represents early post-medieval reuse of an Anglo-Saxon pin as a clasp that functioned similarly to the hat-hooks discussed here seems unlikely. On known early post-medieval Double Spiral-Headed pins, the spirals face outwards. A continental - Merovingian / early Carolingian, or Irish origin is possible (pers. comm. Barry Ager).

Only one gold hat-hook, set with a sapphire, is in the surviving repertoire; called the 'Farnham Pin', it is thought to have originally been partially enamelled (No. 708) (after Cherry 1997), and similarly unique is No. 711, which apart from being openwork filigree, is inset with a glass cameo (after Gaimster *et al* 2002). In the same paper it states that there are only two contemporary records of hat-hooks, both in '... the same inventory: that of Richard Goddard, an extremely wealthy Southampton merchant ... "iiii amelde [enamelled] cap hokes", valued at 1s 4d, and "viii cap hokes of brasse", valued at 2s'. No enamelled hat-hook is known to have survived, however, apart from the Farnham Pin, no. 717 was perhaps partially enamelled.

Several of the hat-hooks catalogued here are possibly emblematic, for example those representing a rose or a Lombardic letter S. The third son of Edward III, John of Gaunt (1340-99), Duke of Lancaster, instigated the livery collar of SS, and respective dukes of Lancaster and Lancastrian kings continued to use the SS device on their livery collars. Kings, princes and great lords presented livery collars, which bore their SS or other device, to their followers who wore them to show their allegiance. It is thought that people with the rank of knight or above were rewarded with gold collars of SS, while lesser mortals made do with silver and base-metal collars. Apart from on livery collars, diverse items bearing the S device (or other devices) would undoubtedly be worn by retainers and sympathisers, for example as hat-badges. Precisely what the letter S signifies is uncertain, but '*soverayne*', a word painted many times on a *c.*1420s board over Henry IVs monument in Canterbury Cathedral, or '*souvenez*', meaning 'remember', are possibilities.

The War of the Roses, for more than 30 years a bitter dispute between two sections of the same family, the House of York and the House of Lancaster, which in 1485 resulted in the defeat of King Richard III by Henry Tudor. The emblem of York was a white rose and that of Lancaster, a red rose. Henry Tudor took the crown of England as King Henry VII and married Elizabeth of York, thereby uniting the two families. Henry adopted the Tudor Rose emblem and superimposed the white rose on the red rose, making a double rose. It is probable that hat-hooks in the form of a double rose, and possibly a single rose too, proved the wearer's allegiance to the king.

Hat-hooks with S-shaped hooks are designated Class A, Types 1-4 and that with a recurving hook, Class B, Type 1. All are compositely constructed, either sheeting or part sheeting and part cast, with wire hooks. Separate front- and back-plates, and hooks, are soldered. Shapes and decoration, especially those applied with ground-supported filigree and granules, mirror early post-medieval Class D sharp-hooked clasps, some of which surely would have been en suite items? If correct, it implies that men may have worn sharp-hooked clasps, or, conversely, women also wore hat-hooks.

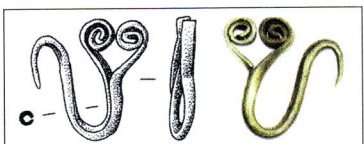

Fig. 33. A possible Hines Type D early medieval Double Spiral-Headed dress- or hair-pin made from copper-alloy sheeting: a tapering circular-section unsoldered butt-seamed shaft formed into an S-shape; 26.5 x 14.5mm (see above discussion). *River Thames foreshore, London*. Drawing © Patrick Read.

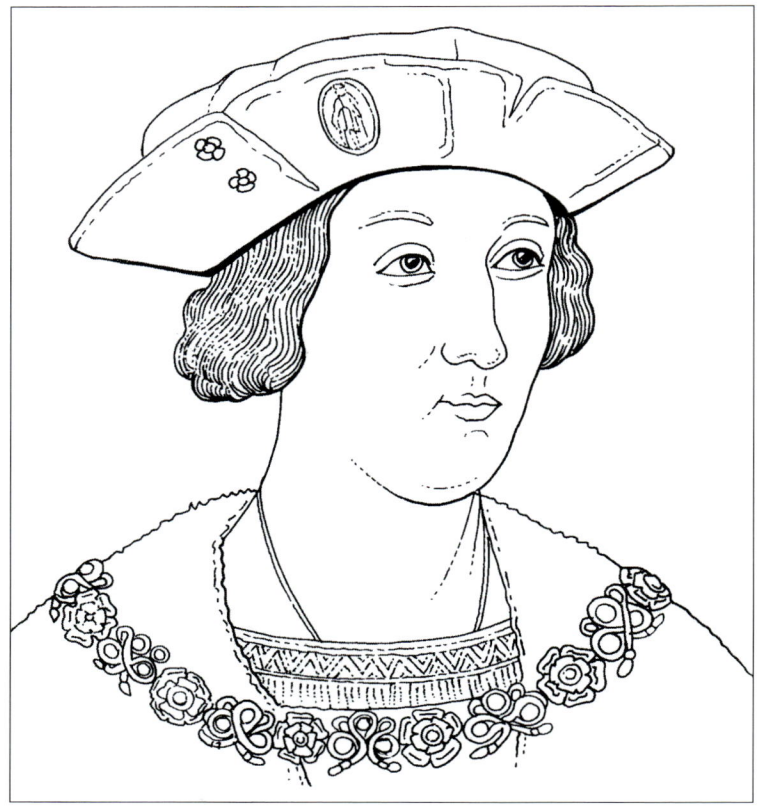

Fig. 34. Arthur, Prince of Wales (1486-1502). Redrawn from a posthumous portrait of *c*.1520. Note two rose jewels, without any sign of hooks, positioned near the slashed brim of his bonnet, and the larger *enseign* badge.

Early post-medieval Class A, Type 1

Circular

708. Gold; sheeting and possibly cast, and wire; seven-piece; engraved and possibly moulded-relief. A possible cast plate with a raised edge into which is soldered a sheeting double five-petalled rose bordered by a coiled wire ring; a cast six-clawed collet rivet pierces the roses and the plate and is then secured; a hexagonal sapphire with a square table-cut face is set in the collet. The front of the plate has cross-hatched striations and the front of each petal, transverse and radiating, possibly as a key for enamel, now missing. A separate soldered S-shaped wire hook; D22.6mm. *Surrey*. After Cherry 1997. Drawing © David Williams; photograph © David Graham.

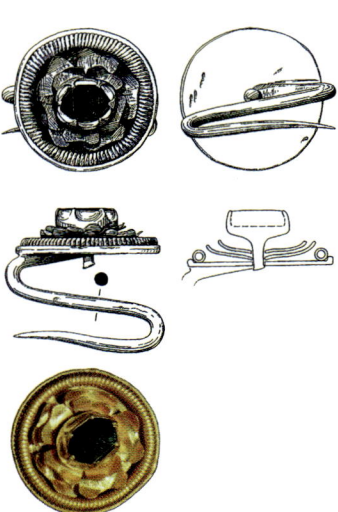

709. Silver; cast and wire; two-piece; engraved. A heart surmounted by a quatrefoil, with T left and A right, (?) Thomas (?) Amor), in black-letter script, within a beaded border. A separate soldered S-shaped wire hook. Incomplete, hook broken; 35 x 20mm. *Gloucestershire*. Portable Antiquities Scheme GLO-721AD7. Photographs © Bristol City Council.

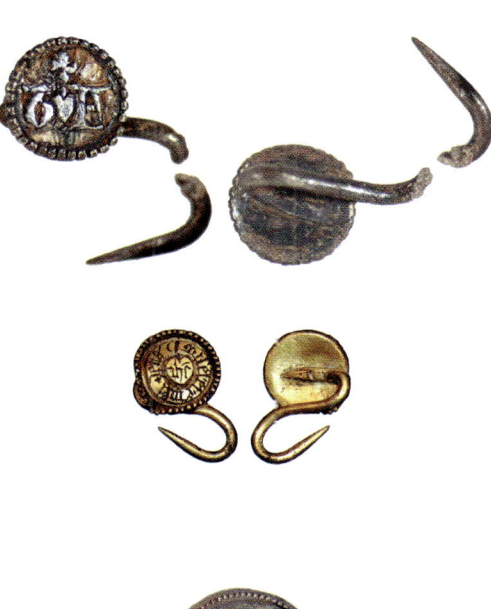

710. Silver-gilt; sheeting and wire; three-piece; engraved. The sacred monogram IHS within a Latin black-letter legend DI MISERERE MEI DEUS [Have mercy on me o God]. A separate soldered slightly damaged beaded wire border and distorted wire hook; 21.59 x 13.09mm. *Lincolnshire*. Photograph © TimeLine Originals.

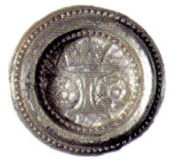

711. Silver-gilt; cast and wire; two-piece; engraved and moulded-relief. An incuse roundel with an I (Jesus) between two seven-petalled roses surmounted by a crown on a cross-hatched field, within two concentric circles, the inner beaded and the outer linear; and a laterally projecting cabled border. Incomplete, the back retains the flattened shank of a separate soldered indeterminate-shape hook: D25mm. *Suffolk*. Treasure case MME 2001 152. Photograph © the Trustees of The British Museum.

712. Silver-gilt; sheeting, wire, and straight and twisted wire openwork filigree and granules; convex; three-piece. A hollow-domed front-plate formed from two concentric large annulets, the inner one of which is oval, the interstice infilled with a contiguous band of two concentric small annulets, each inner annulet has a granule; further tiny annulets, all with a granule, form a border between the internal large oval and the smaller annulets. A central oval glass cameo profile left human-bust in a wire frame, is thought to be post-classical. The sheeting back-plate has an engrailed edge bordered with equidistant granules. Incomplete, several granules missing and the back retains the flattened shank of a separate soldered indeterminate-shape hook; D17mm. *Lincolnshire*. Treasure case MME 2001 174. Photograph © the Trustees of The British Museum.

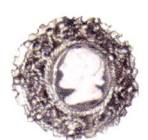

713. Silver-gilt; sheeting and wire; three-piece; convex; die-stamped; ground-supported twisted wire filigree and granules. A hollow-domed front-plate applied with a trefoil, each arm formed from two large concentric annulets, within each is a trefoil of smaller annulets; small annulets, each encircling a granule, in the interstices; a central granule. The back-plate has an engrailed edge. A separate soldered S-shaped wire hook. Incomplete, one granule missing; 21.93 x 15.38mm. *South Somerset*. Treasure case 2005 238. Photographs © Win Weller.

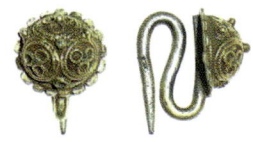

714. Silver-gilt; sheeting and wire; three-piece; convex; die-stamped; ground-supported twisted wire filigree and granules. A hollow-domed front-plate with a central boss within a circle of five bosses; each boss is within an annulet and the whole is within a wire border; granules in the interstices. The back-plate has an engrailed edge. Incomplete, separate soldered indeterminate-shape hook missing; D16mm. *North Yorkshire*. United Kingdom Detecting Finds' Database 14045. Photographs © Garry Jones.

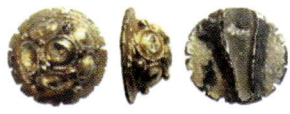

715. Silver-gilt; sheeting and wire; three-piece; convex; ground-supported twisted wire filigree and granules. A hollow-domed front-plate applied with three concentric annulets, the interstices infilled with contiguous small annulets, each with a granule imitating a gem. The back-plate has an engrailed edge. A separate soldered S-shaped wire hook. D16.5mm. *Nottinghamshire*. United Kingdom Detecting Finds' Database 7815. Photographs © John Radford.

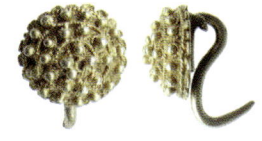

Early post-medieval Class A, Type 2

Trefoil

716. Silver-gilt; sheeting and wire; seven-piece; die-stamped; convex; ground-supported twisted wire filigree and granules. A trefoil of hollow-domed bosses, each with a trefoil of large annulets and a central granule, each annulet encircles a trefoil of small annulets and a central granule. The back-plate has an engrailed edge. A separate domed-head split-pin pierces a six-petalled rove and the back-plate before splaying: each petal of the rove has multiple striations, possibly as a key for enamel of which no evidence remains. A separate soldered S-shaped wire hook; 23.75 x 23.5mm. (see Cherry pp 393, no. 5, 1997). *South-East Dorset*. Drawing © Nick Griffiths.

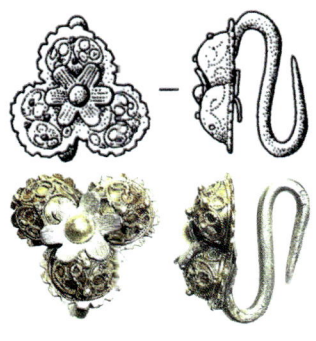

Early post-medieval Class A, Type 3

Lozenge-shaped

717. Silver-gilt; probably cast, and wire; possibly seven-piece. Multiple striations radiating from a circular collet in which is set a pinkish unidentified cabochon gem; each apex has a large granule, imitating cabochon gems. Incomplete, two marks on the back are consistent with a missing separate spot-soldered indeterminate-shape hook, therefore this piece appears to be a hat-hook ; two apexes of the plate are distorted upwards; 21.5 x 11.91mm. *North Dorset*. Photographs © Roy Mcleod.

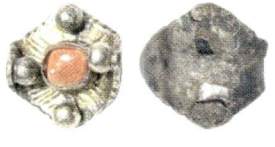

Early post-medieval Class A, Type 4

Figurative

718. Silver-gilt; cast and wire; two-piece; moulded-relief. A four-petalled flower with sepals. A separate soldered S-shaped wire hook; 15 x 14mm. *Isle of White*. Treasure case 2004 T359. Photographs © Isle of White Council.

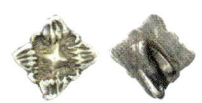

HOOKED-CLASPS & EYES

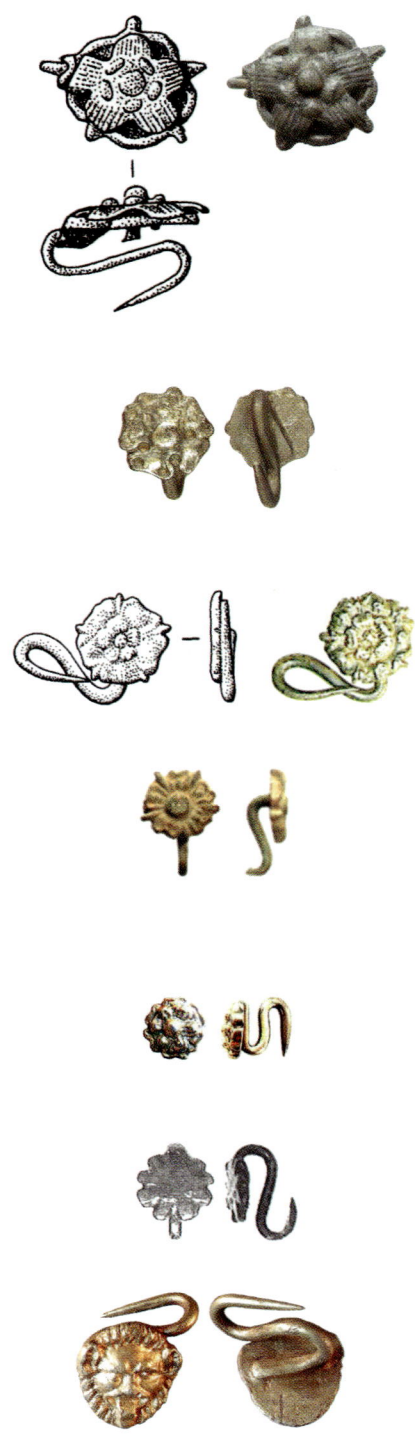

719. Lead/tin and copper alloy; cast and wire; four-piece; moulded-relief. The back-plate has five-petals with sepals between, and a central rivet-hole. A separate front-plate with five longitudinally grooved petals (not for enamel here, as base-metal), also with a central rivet-hole, is secured to the back-plate with a separate lead/tin rivet. Resembles a five-petalled double rose. A separate embedded S-shaped copper-alloy wire hook; 26.68 x 23.39mm. *River Thames foreshore, London*. Drawing © Nick Griffiths.

720. Silver-gilt; cast; two-piece; moulded-relief. A five-petalled rose with sepals. A separate soldered S-shaped wire hook; D13mm. *North Yorkshire*. Treasure case 2004 T191. Photographs © the Trustees of The British Museum.

721. Silver-gilt; cast and wire; two-piece; moulded-relief. A double five-petalled rose with sepals. A separate soldered distorted S-shaped wire hook; D15mm. *South Somerset*. Drawing © Patrick Read.

722. Copper alloy; cast and wire; two-piece; moulded-relief. A five-petalled rose with sepals. A separate soldered S-shaped wire hook. Incomplete, hook-point broken off; 18.1 x 13.1mm. *Hertfordshire*. Portable Antiquities Scheme BH-0769D0. Photographs © St Albans Museum.

723. Silver-gilt; cast and wire; convex; two-piece; moulded-relief. A six-petalled double rose. A separate soldered S-shaped wire hook; D11.9mm. *Hampshire*.

724. Copper alloy; cast and wire; two-piece; moulded-relief. A stylised nine-petalled flower. A separate soldered S-shaped wire hook; D12.5mm. *North Yorkshire*.

725. Silver-gilt; cast and wire; shallow convex; two-piece; moulded-relief. A facing-mask of a lion with protruding tongue. A separate soldered S-shaped wire hook; 15.7 x 15.3mm. *North Somerset*. Treasure case 2005 T184. Photographs © the Trustees of The British Museum.

726. Silver-gilt; cast and wire; two-piece; moulded-relief and openwork. Christ crucified, with Mary standing on the left and John the Baptist on the right. A separate soldered S-shaped wire hook; 13.31 x 10mm. *Suffolk*. Portable Antiquities Scheme SF-B4F136. Photographs © Suffolk County Council Archaeological Service.

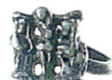

727. Silver-gilt; cast and wire; two-piece; moulded-relief and openwork. A Lombardic S, possibly meaning 'Salvator', an invocation to Christ, the Saviour, or associated with the Lancastrian collar of SS. A separate soldered S-shaped wire hook; 12.8 x 9.48mm. *South Yorkshire*. Drawing © Patrick Read.

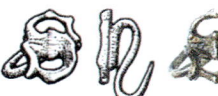

728. Silver-gilt; cast and wire; two-piece; moulded-relief. A three-lobed leaf (front view unavailable). A separate soldered S-shaped wire hook; 10.7 x 8.5mm. *Suffolk*. Portable Antiquities Scheme SF-970504. Photographs © Suffolk County Council Archaeological Service.

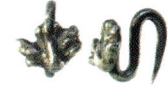

Early post-medieval Class B, Type 1

Rectangular

729. Silver; cast and wire; two-piece; moulded-relief and openwork. The plate has a septum bar, thereby forming two square apertures, a sub-rectangular projection on one side with two quatrefoils on the front; the frame, septum bar and the plate are grooved. A separate soldered recurving wire hook; 15.3 x 13.9mm. *Suffolk*. Portable Antiquities Scheme SF-CDFS2. Treasure report 2004 T417. Photographs © Suffolk County Council Archaeological Service.

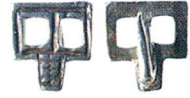

Early post-medieval single sharp-hooked collar-clasp

Livery neck-collars worn by supporters or retainers of royalty or lords are well-documented, for example Murdoch 1991 and Cherry 1994 (see hat-hooks). Contemporary with livery-collars were non-emblematic decorative neck-collars, both precious- or base-metal, often set with gems, that also comprise a chain of separate links. The central link of both forms of collar has a single recurving sharp-hooked clasp on the back for piercing the dress at the nape, thereby preventing the collar from slipping (Egan 2005). The one catalogued here is presumably from a collar and possibly c.16th century or a little earlier. Designated as Class A, Type 1 its attachment-loops are oriented transverse to the plate, whereas a silver collar of SS in the Museum of London has a collar-clasp with links in the same plane as the plate (MoL 84.80). This latter feature is noted on the gold SS link shown below (Fig. 35) and other collars in contemporary iconography.

Early post-medieval Class A, Type 1

Rectangular

730. Gold; cast, sheeting and wire; six-piece; moulded-relief. A rectangular collet set with a cracked grey and white jasper stone; a border of imitative granules; engrailed edges. A separate circular-section wire attachment-loop is soldered transversely to each apex of the plate. A separate soldered recurving hook, which is either sheeting or flattened wire; 16.83 x 15.86. *Lancashire*. Drawing © Patrick Read. Reproduced courtesy of TimeLine Originals.

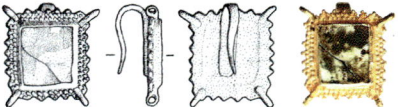

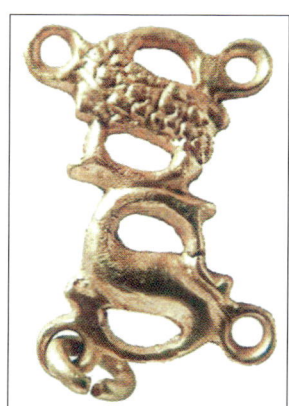

Fig. 35. A link from a late 14th- - 15th-century gold collar of SS found by the author and now in Wiltshire Heritage Museum, Devizes. Note the in the same plane orientation of the four attachment-loops and separate wire link attached to one. This is the only surviving link from a gold collar of SS of this date; it is the only recorded conjoined SS link; and only the second surviving piece of Gothic gold jewellery bearing the letter S - the other is the Middleham finger-ring in York Museum. *Wiltshire*. Treasure case 2005 T442.

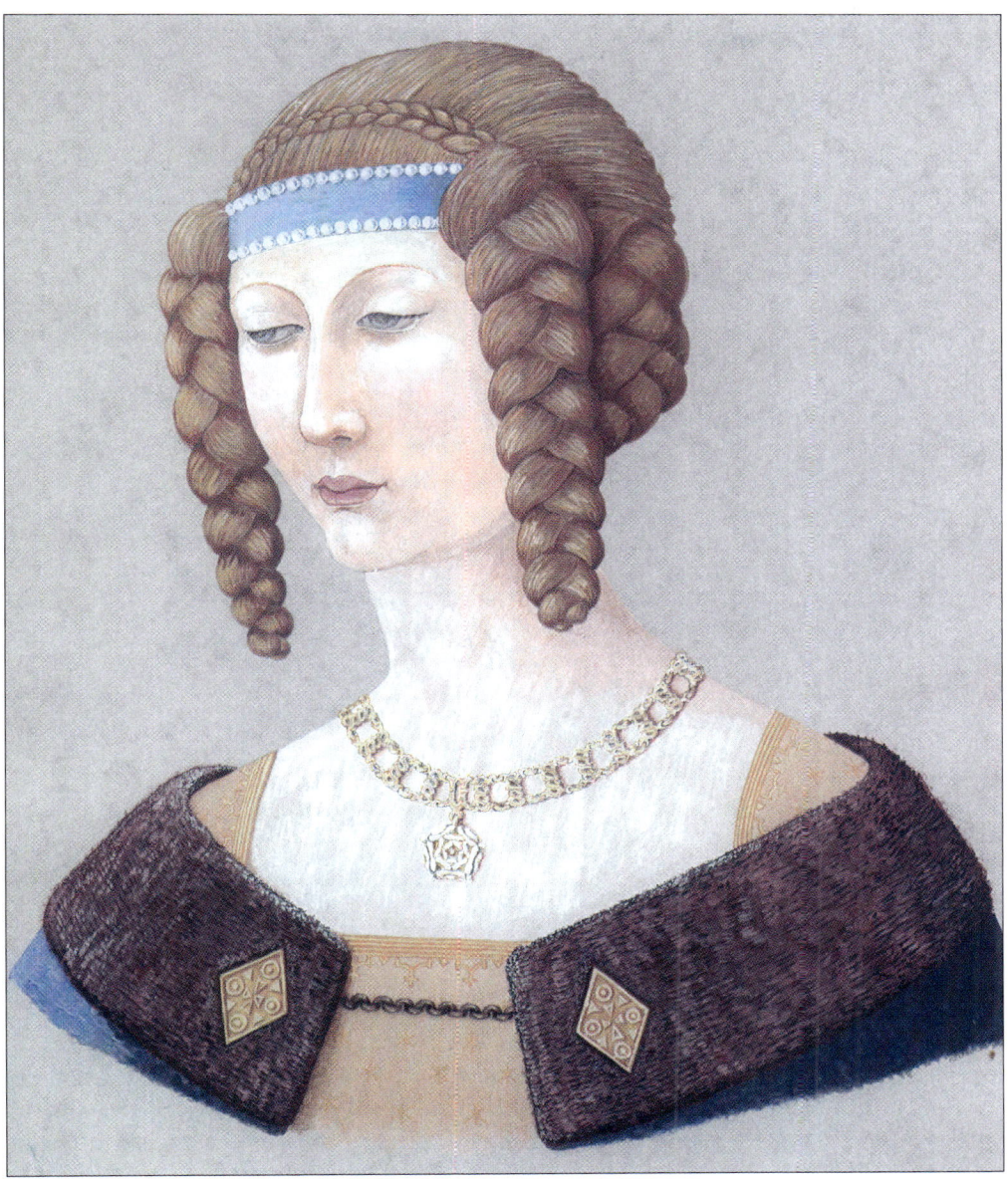

Fig. 36. A reconstruction portrait of a *c.*1350 - *c.*1500 woman, by Helen Stanford, shows her wearing a gold livery collar of SS based upon the SS link in fig. 35. Women's livery collars are generally smaller and lighter than men's, however, they could still move around, therefore a sharp-hooked collar-clasp would probably have been affixed at the nape of the neck. The cloak is shown fastened at the neck by two lozenge-shaped jewels both of which would have a loop on the back - the chain has a hook at both ends which were secured to the loops. Displayed in Wiltshire Heritage Museum, Devizes. Portrait © Helen Stanford 2008. Photograph © and reproduced courtesy of Wiltshire Heritage Museum.

Early and late medieval nummular brooches

A specific category of composite brooch-, badge- or fastener-like object called nummular brooches is especially made from sheeting or cast copper-alloy or cast lead/tin, often coin-like, designated as Class A, or adapted from a silver hammered coin or a copper-alloy jetton, designated as Class B. The non-specifically numismatic examples have either engraved, compass-inscribed, punched or moulded-relief decoration, or a combination. Nummular brooches seem to have appeared sometime in the 9th century and remained sporadically popular possibly into the 17th century.

Three types of attachment-mechanism, and one sub-type, are apparent. Type 1 is a separate narrow tapering strip of sheeting with a recurving sharp-hook at one end while the other has a 90º or 45º bend drilled to form an attachment-loop. This strip is secured to the obverse with a separate rivet through a central rivet-hole in the plate and strip. Type 1a is similar, though both riveting or soldering to the obverse are known, except the attachment-loop is formed by rolling the metal into a cylinder that may spiral either inwards towards the hook or outwards towards the plate. On Type 2 the hook and attachment-eye are separate entities, each made from slightly flattened circular-section wire, both of which are soldered to the obverse. Type 3 is an apparently more ubiquitous method, a hinge-pin and catch-plate (similar mechanisms are found on Anglo-Saxon Disc-brooches), commented on by Robinson 1990, and sub-divided by Williams 2001 into arrangements a, b and c.

An interesting nummular brooch variant found at Winchester, Hampshire (Dolly and Mays 1990, no. 2006) is noteworthy for it comprises two *c.*865-75 base-silver pennies seemingly riveted together, obverse to (?) reverse; its attachment-mechanism is Type 3, Williams arrangement b.

With the exception of no. 737, which is double-reversed, all nummular coin- or jetton-brooches in the known record have the reverse, which on the issues selected, is a form of cross, facing to the front, perhaps denoting a religious significance. The majority of coin-brooches in the known record have their reverses gilded though gilding on both sides is known.

A Class A circular nummular brooch with a runic inscription, suggesting an Anglo-Saxon milieu, is known from South-East Lincolnshire, and Henry II coins identically adapted imply a date of 1180-89; though of course such reuse could have occurred long after, therefore caution is advised when assigning dates.

Interestingly, although generally called 'brooches', it seems that this identification is tentative. If those with Type 3 attachment-mechanism are indeed brooches, which is plausible, they surely would have been purely decorative or used only with fine textiles for the design and flimsiness of pins and catch-plates would not facilitate fixture to thick textiles. Both Robinson and Williams suggest that [nummular] coin- or jetton brooches perhaps may have been symbolic, therefore are more likely to have been badges worn on personal dress. Notwithstanding, it is very obvious that Types 1, 1a and 2 attachment-mechanisms contrast with Type 3 in that their design is inconsistent with using pins. The badges theory is plausible, for the attachment-loops are suitable for stitching to dress or textile straps and the hooks possibly linked into small metal- or worked-eyes or directly into textile; however, perhaps they functioned as lightweight clasps worn with delicate fabrics. This disparity means that nummular brooches with Type 3 attachment-mechanism are outside the remit of this present work. No. 731 is *c.*11th - *c.*12th century; no. 732 *c.* mid-14th century; while dates of the remainder are mentioned in the respective descriptions.

Early and late medieval Class A, Type 1

Circular

731. Copper alloy; sheeting; three-piece; engraved, punched and compass-inscribed. Six bands of zigzags radiating from a central rivet-hole within a linear circle and ring-and-dot motifs and a border of tiny zigzags. A Type 1 combined hook and 90° attachment-loop is secured to the undecorated back by a separate copper-alloy rivet, the head of which has a central dot; D24mm. *South-East Lincolnshire*. After Read 2001, no. 775, described as a 'disc-brooch or possible dress-fastener'. Drawing © Patrick Read.

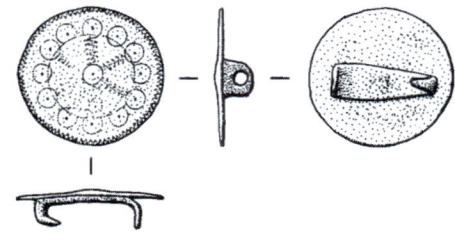

Early or late medieval Class A, Type 1a

Elaborate quatrefoil

732. Copper alloy; cast and sheeting; three-piece; moulded-relief; champlevé enamel and sporadic gilding. Resembles a four-petalled rose with sepals. A lion passant guardant left within a square with a central rivet-hole; a lozenge at each apex of the square; a fleur-de-lis in each interstice; a raised border; blue enamel in two lozenges and in part of the field of the square. A Type 1a (spiralled outwards) combined hook and attachment-loop is secured to the back by a separate copper-alloy rivet; 33 x 35mm. This clasp is adapted from a pseudo heraldic stud, the stump of which is visible on the back. *Billingsgate, London*. After Clark *et al* 1995, fig. 53, no. 81. Drawing © Nick Griffiths.

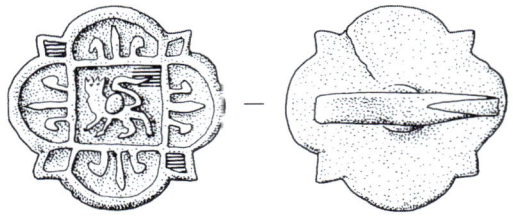

Early and late medieval Class B, Type 1

733. Silver, gilded reverse; two-piece. Adapted from an Edward I new coinage penny, Tower Mint (uncertain class), 1279-1307. Obv: EDW REX ANGL DNS HYB. Rev: civitas London. A Type 1a (spiralled inwards) combined hook and attachment-loop is soldered to the obverse. Incomplete, hook distorted and point broken off. D18.5mm. *South Wiltshire*. Portable Antiquities Scheme DOR-403D81. Photographs © Somerset County Council.

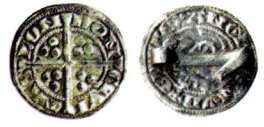

734. Copper alloy; three-piece. Adapted from an Edward 1 jetton variant, 1293-96 - Fox Class 4; Berry Type 1; Mitchener, no. 90. Obv: bust Class 7 within two concentric beaded circles, the inner broken by the crown, a border of alternate roses and strokes; a central rivet-hole. Rev: a cross fleury with expanded ends, with a star or crescent in the quadrants, and two concentric circles (possibly beaded), a border of alternate roses and strokes, some of which are curved. A Type 1a combined hook and attachment-loop (spiralled outwards) is secured to the obverse by a separate copper-alloy rivet. Incomplete, hook point broken off; D12.5mm. *Norfolk*. After Margesson 1993, no. 66. Drawing © and reproduced courtesy of Norfolk Museums and Archaeology Service.

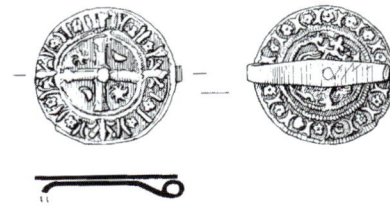

735. Copper alloy; three-piece. Adapted from an Edward II double-back jetton variant, 1310-14 - Berry Type 14; Mitchener, no. 150. Obv: a short cross moline within a beaded circle bordered by pellets and a beaded circle; a central rivet hole. Rev: identical. The Type 1a combined hook and attachment-loop (spiralled inwards) is secured by a separate copper-alloy rivet; D21.2mm. *Wiltshire*. WHM acc. no. 1987.112.1. After Robinson 1990. Drawing © Nick Griffiths and reproduced by permission of Wiltshire Archaeological and Natural History Society.

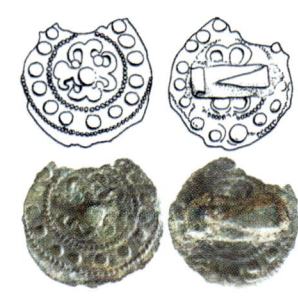

736. Copper alloy; three-piece. Adapted from a jetton variant. Obv: three chevrons with above left a crescent within a shield, a five-petalled rose left and right and a possible pellet above; a beaded circle and a border of alternate saltires and five-petalled roses; a central rivet-hole. Rev: a triple-stranded cross fleury with a star or crescent in each quadrant; two concentric circles, the outer beaded and the inner wire, and a saltire in each segment of the border. A Type 1 combined hook and 45° attachment-loop is secured to the reverse by a separate copper-alloy rivet. The cross fleury with Plantagenet 'star and crescent' emblems provides a date of between *c.*1280-1343 (see Mitchiner 1988, nos 172 and 173a for similar reverses); the shield and chevron design is known from Burgundian, the Netherlands, in the 15th century, thereby providing a reasonably safe attribution. D26mm. *South-East Lincolnshire*. After Read 2001, no. 821, described as a brooch. Drawing © Patrick Read.

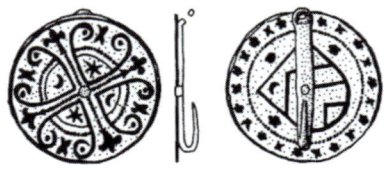

Early and late medieval Class B, Type 2

737. Silver; gilded reverse; three-piece. Adapted from a Louis IV of France gros-tournois, c.1266-70. A Type 2 separate hook and attachment-loop are soldered to the obverse; D unrecorded. *Hampshire*. Treasure case 2001 T23. Photographs © the Trustees of The British Museum.

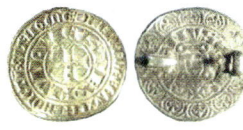

Late medieval and early post-medieval havettes

An uncommon form of double sharp-hooked clasp is the havette (or habick, harbick or shearman's hook) used in the production of woollen cloth to enable the fuller (shearman) to shear the nap. One hook of a havette pierced the selvedge of the newly-woven cloth at each corner and then held it taut by securing the opposite hook into a padded cropping-board.

Essentially, confirmed havettes are either cast or sheeting copper-alloy or wrought-iron with a distinctive 45° angle recurving hook either end of a straight or slightly bowed arm and some form of grip, normally in the centre, to assist in attaching or removing. On known havettes grips are either a rectangular block (Class A) or barley twist (Class B). Rectangular grips have moulded-relief or engraved decoration. An iron havette found by a Mudlark on the River Thames foreshore in London has saltires inscribed on its grip and shaft (No. 738); this same mark is depicted in the Arms of the Clothworkers' Company of London (Fig. 37) granted in 1530 (Egan 1979). Each of three havettes depicted in the Arms of the Shearman of London (incorporated with the Fullers as the Company of Clothworkers in 1527-8) has three equidistant knob-like grips all of which appear to be marked with a saltire (Fig. 38) (Egan 1979). A version of the Clothworkers' Arms published in 1677, and a probably unreliable variation of the same Arms published in the 19th century, shows grips formed from looped shafts (Figs 39-40) (Egan 1979): the hooks on these havettes are anomalous with the 45° hooks on Class A, Type 1 havettes and if they existed, were probably wire. With its looped grip on the underside, the havette in the unattributed Arms seems impractical and Egan comments that the illustrator possibly was unfamiliar with a havette's function.

Interestingly, saltires are noted on the grips of four other havettes catalogued here - two from archaeological contexts in Winchester (Nos 739, 742), and two found by metal-detectorists, Nottinghamshire (No. 740) and Buckinghamshire (No. 741) respectively. Yet another marked with a saltire was recovered from an archaeological deposit in Exeter, Devon, (Goodal *et al* 1984, fig. 193, no. 177). An important sheeting copper-alloy havette is recorded here as no. 745, whose hooks lie at the characteristic 45° and the arm is bowed but where it differs, apart from being heavy-gauge sheeting, is a drilled-hole instead of a grip. This hole does serve very well as a grip, or it may be for attaching to a cord or thong or simply hanging on a nail or peg when not in use. If the author's identification (supported by Nick Griffiths) is correct, it is unparalleled, and included here as Class C, Type 1.

Although in the north of England havettes continued in use into the 19th century, they appear to be uncommon finds: the known record shows that few have been recovered from archaeological excavations, and the four here are the only confirmed examples recorded from Britain by metal-detectorists. All are assigned as late medieval early post-medieval.

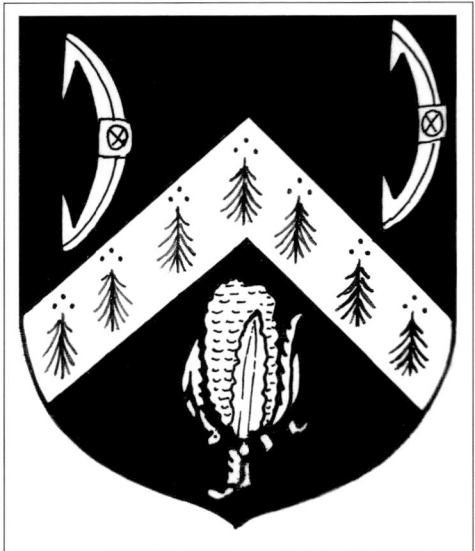
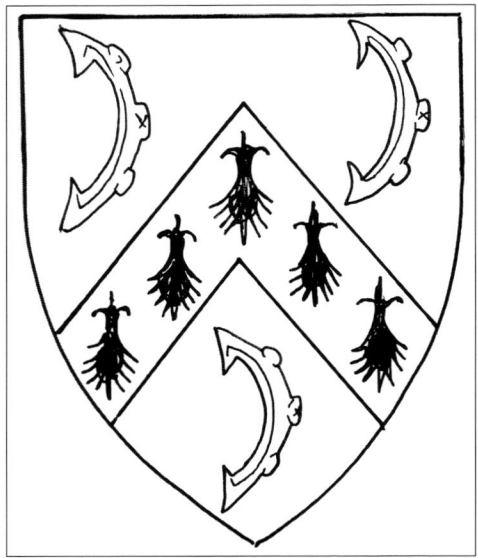

Fig. 37. Arms of the Clothworkers' Company of London from the grant of 1530. Note havette grips bearing saltires. Redrawn from the *Transactions of London and Middlesex Archaeological Society vol. 30*. 1979, courtesy of Geoff Egan.

Fig. 38. Arms of the Shearman of London, incorporated in 1527/8 with the Fullers as the Company of Clothworkers'. Note havette triple grips apparently bearing saltires. Redrawn from the *Transactions of London and Middlesex Archaeological Society vol. 30*. 1979, courtesy of Geoff Egan.

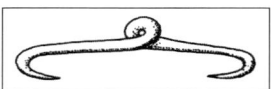

Fig. 39. A havette on a 1677 version of the Clothworkers' Arms. Note the looped grip on the shaft. Redrawn from the *Transactions of London and Middlesex Archaeological Society vol. 30*. 1979, courtesy of Geoff Egan.

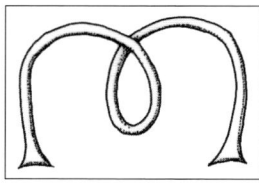

Fig. 40. A havette on a 19th-century unattributed version of the Clothworkers' Arms. Note the loop on the underside of the havette; the illustrator possibly was unfamiliar with a havette's function (pers. comm. Geoff Egan). Redrawn from the *Transactions of London and Middlesex Archaeological Society vol. 30*. 1979, courtesy of Geoff Egan.

HOOKED-CLASPS & EYES

Late medieval early post-medieval, Class A, Type 1

738. Iron; wrought; engraved; one-piece. A rectangular-section grip with a saltire on the front and either side; the slightly bowed arms, both of which has on the front two circular knobs with a saltire, terminate with a sharp-hook; L89.5. *River Thames foreshore, London.* Redrawn from the *Transactions of London and Middlesex Archaeological Society* 30. 1979, courtesy of Geoff Egan. Museum of London collection.

739. Iron; wrought; engraved; one-piece. A (?) rectangular-section grip with on the front a saltire; a separate length of (?) iron wire is wound around the grip, thereby forming a grooved effect; each straight arm terminates with a sharp-hook; L64mm. *Winchester.* Redrawn courtesy of Clarendon Press, Oxford, from *Winchester Studies, 7.ii*: Object and Economy in Medieval Winchester, pp. 240, no. 308.

740. Copper alloy; cast; one-piece; moulded-relief or engraved. A rectangular-section grip with on the front a saltire within two transverse lines that continue down the sides, each side has a further three lines; a straight arm terminating with a sharp-hook. Incomplete, one arm and hook broken off; 36.39 x 9.6mm. *Nottinghamshire.* Drawing © Patrick Read.

741. Copper alloy; cast; one-piece; moulded-relief or engraved. A rectangular-section grip with on the front a saltire and two lines either end that continue down each side; each straight arm terminates with a sharp-hook. Incomplete, one hook-point broken off; L63.3mm. *Buckinghamshire.* Portable Antiquities Scheme BUC-08A034. Photograph © Buckinghamshire County Council.

742. Copper alloy; cast; one-piece; moulded-relief or engraved. A rectangular-section grip with on the front a saltire within two transverse lines; each slightly bowed arm terminates with a sharp-hook; L67mm. *Winchester.* Redrawn courtesy of Clarendon Press, Oxford, from *Winchester Studies, 7.ii*: Object and Economy in Medieval Winchester, pp. 240, no. 310.

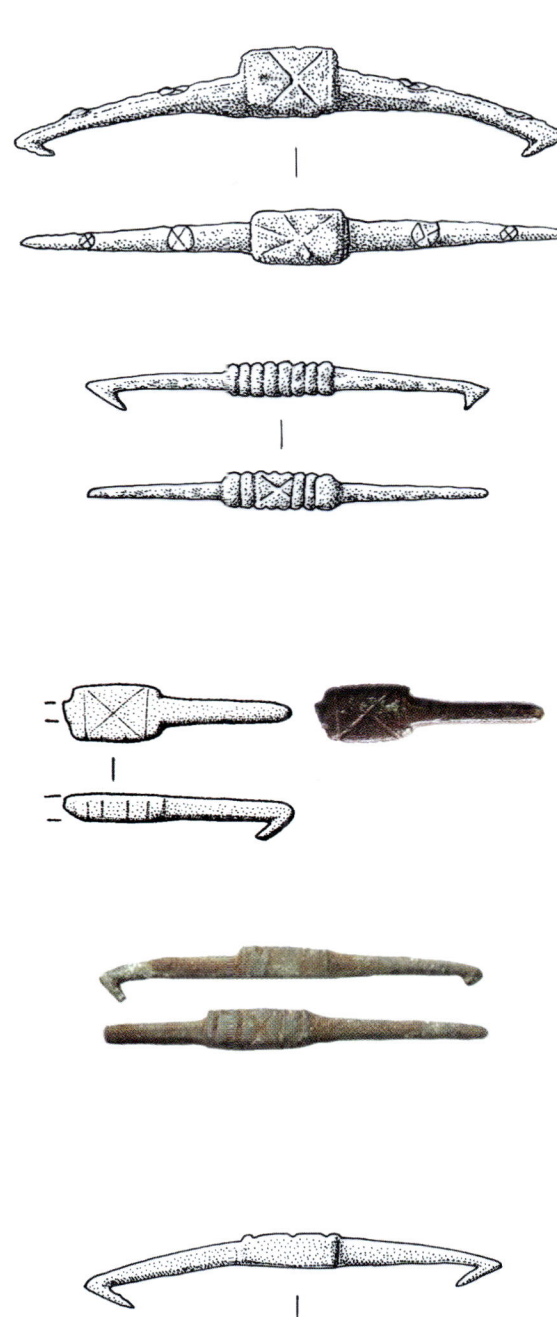

743. Copper alloy; cast; one-piece; moulded-relief or engraved. A rectangular grip with oblique nicks on each edge; each slightly bowed arm terminates with a sharp-hook; L71mm. *Winchester*. Redrawn courtesy of Clarendon Press, Oxford, from *Winchester Studies, 7.ii*: Object and Economy in Medieval Winchester, pp. 240, no. 307.

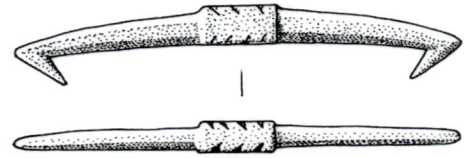

Late medieval early post-medieval, Class B, Type 1

744. Iron; wrought; one-piece. A barley-twist grip; each straight arm terminates with a sharp-hook; L102mm. *Winchester*. Redrawn courtesy of Clarendon Press, Oxford, from *Winchester Studies, 7.ii*: Object and Economy in Medieval Winchester, pp. 240, no. 309.

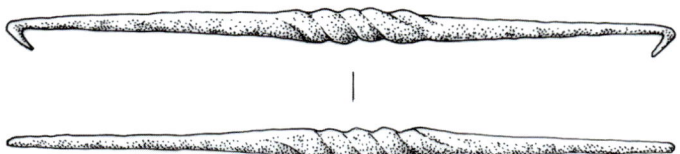

Late medieval early post-medieval, Class C, Type 1

745. Copper alloy; sheeting; one-piece; undecorated. The lower edge is straight and the upper bowed, a drilled-hole in the apex, each arm terminates with a sharp-hook; filing striations both sides; 73.93 x 15.47 x 4.31mm, hole D1.89mm. *North Dorset*. Drawing © Nick Griffiths.

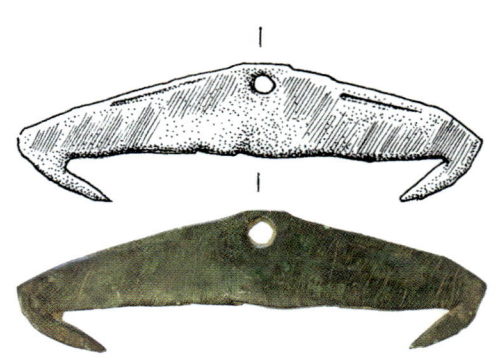

Early and late post-medieval possible single blunt-hooked clasps

Three stylistically similar objects compositely constructed from copper-alloy sheeting and wire are perhaps male sections of blunt-hooked and eye clasps, however, their forward-facing hooks may have suspended secondary items. Attachment would presumably have been by inserting the wire eye or eyes through slits in the dress and securing with a pin, similar to modern military badges. The incompleteness of no. 746 means the hook is indeterminate, notwithstanding, blunt is probable. Designated as Class A, Types 1-2, the latter have decorative appliqués. No. 746 is tentatively assigned as *c.*16th - *c.*17th-century but could be *c.*19th century as are nos 747-748.

Early post-medieval Class A, Type 1

Figurative

746. Copper alloy; sheeting and wire; three-piece; concave; die-stamped and engraved; gilded overall. A scallop-shell; a linear border terminating in a spiral either side of a cross-hatched panel at the juncture of the plate and hook. On the back a separate soldered sheeting or flattened wire blunt-hook and wire loop. Incomplete, hook-point broken off; 21.27 x 20.26mm. *South-West Lincolnshire*. After Read 2001, no. 354, described as a mount or possible pilgrim's badge (the latter unlikely). Drawing © Patrick Read.

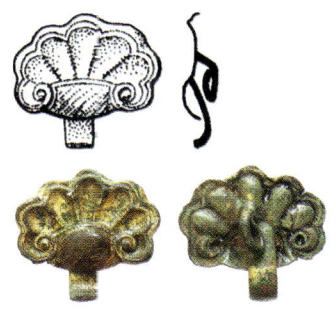

Early post-medieval Class A, Type 2

Sub-octagonal

747. Copper alloy; cast, sheeting and wire; five-piece; die-stamped. An octagon with a raised edge bordered by foliate; secured in the octagon by a separate cast copper-alloy rivet is a bevelled-edged white mother-of-pearl appliqué, the rivet-head is shaped as an AD 1600-50 long-fingered glove with a pointed-tab gauntlet. On the back a separate soldered sheeting or flattened wire hook and two wire eyes. One corner of the plate and both eyes are distorted; 36.9 x 27.3mm. *West Dorset*. Drawing © Patrick Read.

Figurative

748. Copper alloy; sheeting and wire; four-piece. A stylised multi-petalled flower with a white mother-of-pearl multi-petalled appliqué secured to the front by a separate domed-head rivet. On the back a separate soldered sheeting or flattened wire hook and wire eye. Incomplete, a section of the appliqué broken off and the plate is distorted; 26.41 x 21.25mm. *North Dorset*. Drawing © Nick Griffiths.

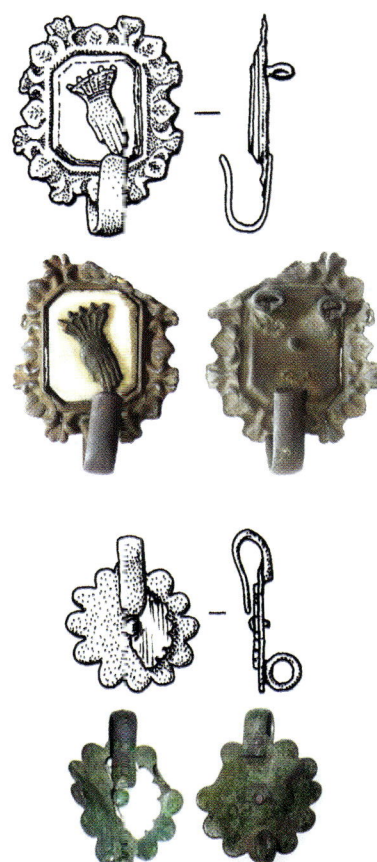

Early post-medieval unclassified eyes

Whether these eye-like objects functioned in tandem with possibly matching hooks, either sharp or blunt, is conjectural. Alternatively, all are suitable for attaching to a strap or garment and used for suspending secondary objects about the person. No attempt at a classification is made here. The heart-shaped maker's mark on no. 751 is not Swedish, therefore is probably English. No. 749 is tentatively assigned as *c.*15th - *c.*17th century; no 750 is *c.*16th - *c.*17th century; no. 751 is *c.* late 16th century, while no. 752 is stylistically 16th-century but equally could be a 19th-century.

Oval

749. Copper alloy; sheeting; one-piece; undecorated. Two transverse attachment-holes, presumably for separate rivets, and a rounded eye; 25 x 24mm. *South Devon.* After Read 1998, no. 9; and 1995, no. 770. Drawing © Patrick Read.

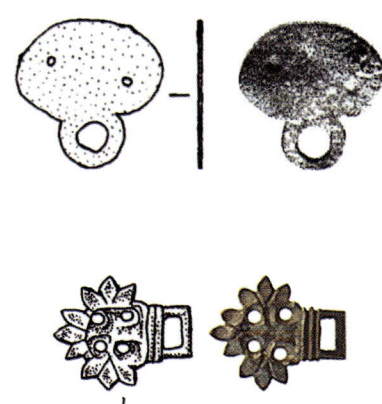

Trefoil

750. Silver; cast; one-piece; moulded-relief. A recessed cross-paty with an attachment-hole in each quadrant; three trefoil knops, the lobes of which are dished; a ridged and ribbed collar at the juncture of the plate and eye; 22.1 x 19.4mm. *Wiltshire.* Drawing © Nick Griffiths, photograph © and reproduced courtesy of Salisbury and South Wiltshire Museum.

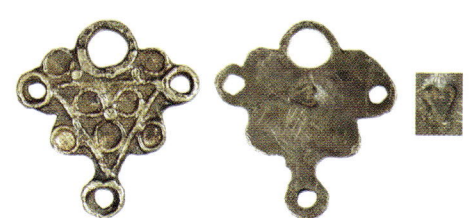

Triangular

751. Silver-gilt. The 2004 Treasure Annual Report provides an inadequate description. Either sheeting or cast; one-piece. If cast, the decoration is probably imitative ground-supported filigree and granules; if sheeting, probably ground-supported straight and twisted wire filigree and granules. A central granule within a trefoil of annulets and a raised linear border; four annulets, one either side of a circular attachment-eye and one in a rounded knop either side; two granules in the interstices near the eye, evidence of a further two granules near the apex-end annulets; a circular attachment-loop on each apex; a punched heart on the back is probably a maker's mark (see enlargement); dimensions unrecorded. *Buckinghamshire.* Treasure case 2004 T183. Photographs © The Portable Antiquities Scheme.

HOOKED-CLASPS & EYES

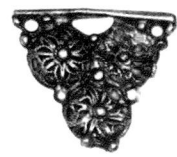

752. Silver; sheeting and wire; four-piece; convex; straight and twisted wire openwork-filigree and granules. A trefoil of hollow-domed bosses, each boss a stylistic eight-petalled flower with a central granule, smaller and larger granules in the field; the granules imitate cabochon gems. The sheeting back-plate has a semi-circular aperture forming an eye the outside edge of which is rolled into a cylinder, presumably for strength; at each end of and alongside the eye is an attachment-hole, an attachment-knop either side between the bosses. One boss and rolled edge distorted; 24 x 20mm. *Leicestershire*. Portable Antiquities Scheme LEIC-E62221. Photograph © Leicestershire County Council/Portable Antiquities Scheme.

Early post-medieval unclassified toggle-clasps

These two-section clasps, one with an eye and the other a toggle-bar or -disc, are thought to be from sword-belts and hangers: by inserting the toggle through the eye and twisting, the two halves are locked together. Nos 768-769 are easily confused with Roman bow brooches. Toggle-bars and -discs are usually raised and the former are always transverse. With one exception, no. 766, which is cast and sheeting composite construction, every section catalogued here is one-piece. All are copper-alloy, predominantly cast, though no. 767 is sheeting. All were riveted to a presumably leather or textile strap. At this time insufficient information precludes attempting a classification; however, they are tentatively designated as Types 1-11. Their vine and foliate decoration makes nos 758-762 comparable with other *c.*16th-century sword-belt fittings catalogued below, and it is likely that most of the remainder are *c.*16th - *c.*17th century. Each of the two sections of nos 753 and 765 respectively, were found together.

Early post-medieval, Type 1

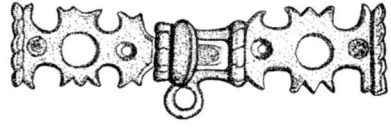

753. Copper alloy; cast; both sections are one-piece; moulded-relief, engraved and openwork. Toggle-section: the plate has a central circular hole and a rivet-hole either end, the one at the attachment-end retains residue of an iron rivet; both sides have two deep cusps and trefoil and bifurcate knops; the outside edge of the raised toggle-bar is curved; the edge of the attachment-end is cabled. Eye-section: the plate is identical except for a cabled collar at the juncture of the body and eye, and circumferential ribs around the end-bar of the eye; a circular suspension-loop on one side of the eye. The attachment-end rivet-hole retains residue of an iron rivet; toggle-section 37.5 x 15.5mm, eye-section 41 x 16.5mm. *South East Dorset*. Drawing © Ken Wheatley.

HOOKED-CLASPS & EYES

754. Copper alloy; cast; one-piece; moulded-relief, engraved and openwork. Toggle-section: comparable with no. 753 but which shows the raised toggle-bar; 44.5 x 17mm. *South Wiltshire*. Drawing © Nick Griffiths.

755. Copper alloy; cast; one-piece; moulded-relief, engraved and openwork. Eye-section: comparable with nos 753-754 but which shows the curved end-bar; the middle rivet-hole retains residue of an iron rivet; 45 x 19.5mm. *South Wiltshire*. Drawing © Nick Griffiths.

Early post-medieval, Type 2

756. Copper alloy; cast; one-piece; moulded-relief, engraved and openwork. Eye-section: the plate has a central circular hole and a rivet-hole either end, both of which retain residue of iron rivets; engrailed side edges; the edge of the attachment-end is cabled and a cabled collar at the juncture of the plate and eye; the curved end-bar of the eye, which is fractured, is cabled; a circular suspension-loop on one side of the eye and another near the collar, both distorted; 49.5 x 20mm. *South-East Dorset*. Drawing © Nick Griffiths.

Early post-medieval, Type 3

757. Copper alloy; cast; one-piece; moulded-relief, engraved and openwork. Toggle-section: comparable with nos 753-756 except much smaller, the attachment-edge has two small grooves; a rivet-hole at the attachment-end retains residue of an iron rivet; a sub-rectangular transverse toggle-bar and a rounded knop; 28.5 x 13mm. *South Somerset*. Drawing © Patrick Read.

Early post-medieval, Type 4

758. Copper alloy; cast; engraved and moulded-relief. Eye-section: a trefoil plate with vine tendrils and foliate; a rivet-hole in the middle lobe retains residue of an iron rivet and another rivet-hole near a transverse ridged and hatched collar at the juncture of the plate and eye; the eye has a hatched rounded end-bar and a circular suspension-loop; 46 x 20mm. *Buckinghamshire*. Drawing © Nick Griffiths.

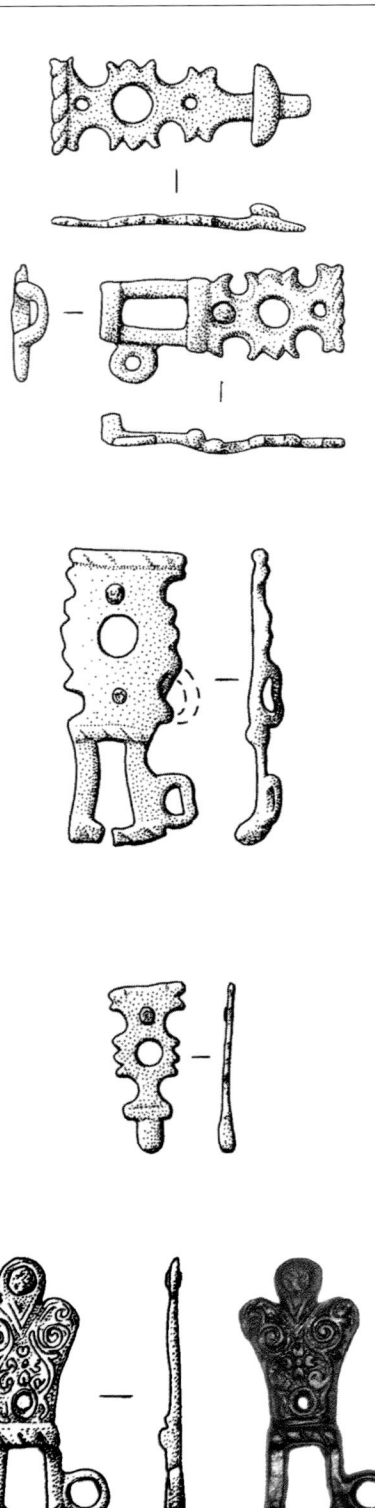

HOOKED-CLASPS & EYES

Early post-medieval, Type 5

759. Copper alloy; cast; one-piece; moulded-relief. Eye-section: the plate resembles a seven-lobed leaf with foliate and floriate; rivet-holes either end retain residue of iron rivets; a circular eye with a cross-shaped aperture and a circular suspension-loop; 43 x 23.5mm. *South-West Wiltshire*. Drawing © Nick Griffiths.

760. Copper alloy; cast; one-piece; moulded-relief. Eye-section: comparable with no. 759 except six-lobed and a sub-rectangular aperture in the eye. Both rivet-holes retain residue of iron rivets; 41 x 22mm. *East Devon*. After Read 2001, fig 26, no. 372. Drawing © Patrick Read.

761. Copper alloy; cast; one-piece; engraved and moulded-relief. Toggle-section: comparable with nos 759-760 except different decoration; a raised disc-toggle with an anticlockwise nine-armed impeller; 39.2 x 18.5mm. *North Dorset*. Drawing © Patrick Read.

Early post-medieval, Type 6

762. Copper alloy; cast; one-piece; moulded-relief. Eye-section: an asymmetrical plate with foliate and floriate, a rivet-hole either end, a ridged foliate collar at the juncture of the plate and rectangular eye, which has a rounded end with foliate, and a circular suspension-loop; 44 x 21mm. *Cheshire*. Drawing © Nick Griffiths.

Early post-medieval, Type 7

763. Copper alloy; cast; one-piece; convex; moulded-relief. Toggle-section: the oval plate has a debased trefoil knop with a transverse ridged collar; a transverse ridged and grooved collar at the juncture of the plate and disc-toggle; rivet-holes in the trefoil knop and near the collar retain residue of iron rivets; 49.5 x 12mm. *South Somerset*. Drawing © Patrick Read.

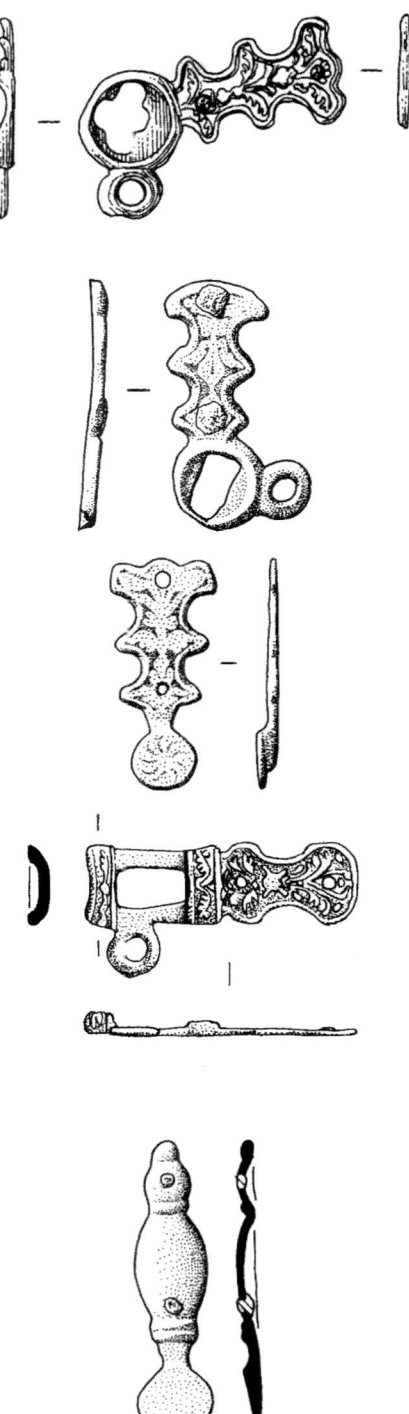

HOOKED-CLASPS & EYES

764. Copper alloy; cast; one-piece; convex; moulded-relief. Eye-section: comparable with no. 763 except more pronounced collars; a circular eye with a sub-rectangular aperture and circular suspension-loop; the rivet-hole near the eye retains residue of an iron rivet; 50.6 x 24.71mm. *South Dorset*. Drawing © Patrick Read.

765. Copper alloy; cast; one-piece; convex; moulded-relief. Comparable with no. 763-764 except both the eye- and toggle-sections have a series of transverse ridges. The rivet-holes retain separate copper-alloy rivets; toggle-section L43.5mm, eye-section L48.3mm. *Suffolk*. Photographs © TimeLine Originals.

Early post-medieval, Type 8

766. Copper alloy; cast and sheeting; two-piece; engraved. Toggle-section: a cast sub-rectangular plate having a rectangular attachment-loop at one end and a debased trefoil with a transverse cylindrical toggle; at the other; foliate and floriate within curvilinear and hatched borders; 34 x 16mm. A sheeting plate bent in the centre and folded around the axis-bar of the toggle-section, a deep cusp either side creates a debased trefoil at the folded end; the attachment-end has a rivet-hole (which pierces both folds) and two cusps in the edge; foliate within a linear and dotted border; 45.5 x 9.5mm. *Buckinghamshire*. Drawing © Nick Griffiths.

Early post-medieval, Type 9

767. Copper alloy; sheeting; one-piece; undecorated. Toggle-section: a rectangular plate narrowing to shank and a semi-circular toggle at one end and a shallow rounded knop at the attachment-end; two transverse rivet-holes either end and another in the centre, three of which retain separate copper-alloy rivets; 45.72 x 11.63. *South Somerset*. Drawing © Patrick Read.

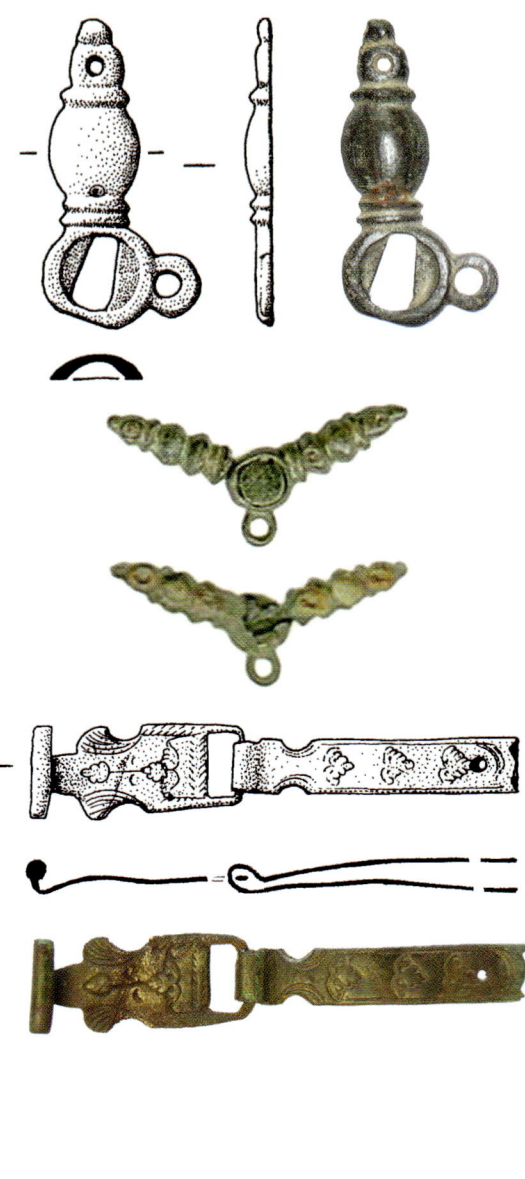

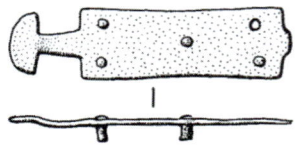

Early post-medieval, Type 10

768. Copper alloy; cast; one-piece; moulded-relief. Toggle-section: a sub-triangular plate with a projecting, ridged and ribbed collar at the juncture of the plate and curved toggle-shank, a sub-cylindrical toggle; the attachment-end is cusped; four longitudinal grooves run from the attachment-end, which has two transverse rivet-holes, to near the collar; a drilled pit close to one rivet-hole probably represents a manufacturing error. The back has a raised boss near the juncture of the plate and shank; 37 x 18mm. *East Devon*. Drawing © Patrick Read.

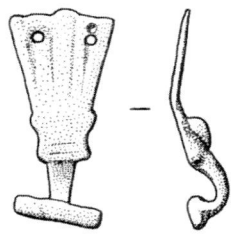

769. Copper alloy; cast; one-piece; moulded-relief. Comparable with no. 768 except three rivet-holes, a tiny drilled-hole, and more grooves. Incomplete, toggle and shank broken off, or perhaps a broken eye-section and rust residue around the boss on the back; 31 x 19. *South Somerset*. Drawing © Patrick Read.

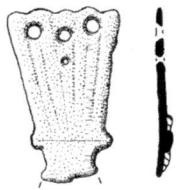

Early medieval and early post-medieval unclassified hooks, eyes or loops

Other metal-fittings with some form of hook, eye or loop are recognised. We have a good understanding of how many of these often substantial objects functioned, for example, with sword-belts or baldricks and as neck-clasps on military cloaks, but the purpose of others remains conjectural. Where known, respective descriptions include function and attribution. No attempt is made at a classification or typology. Copper alloy, primarily cast, and occasionally sheeting, is the predominant metal of the surviving material, while cast silver or lead/tin is less evident. Although rarely recovered in a recognisable or stable condition, wrought iron is also seen. Most are one-piece though several are compositely constructed. Some are plain, while others are moulded-relief, engraved, white-metal coated or inlaid with silver. Hooks are either forward-facing or recurving and may be sharp or blunt; however, S-shaped clasps have in the same plane hooks, frequently zoomorphic. Riveting, either integral or separate, is the commonest method of attachment to leather or textile straps. The possible earliest piece in this present assemblage (No. 803) possesses Roman characteristics (pers. comm. Nick Griffiths), however, dating is left open; no. 770 is believed to be *c.*11th-century Anglo-Saxon or Anglo-Scandinavian while all others are individually dated. Caution is advised with assigning S-shaped clasps for they have been fashionable from at least the 16th century and are still used today; notwithstanding decorative features provide useful dating aids.

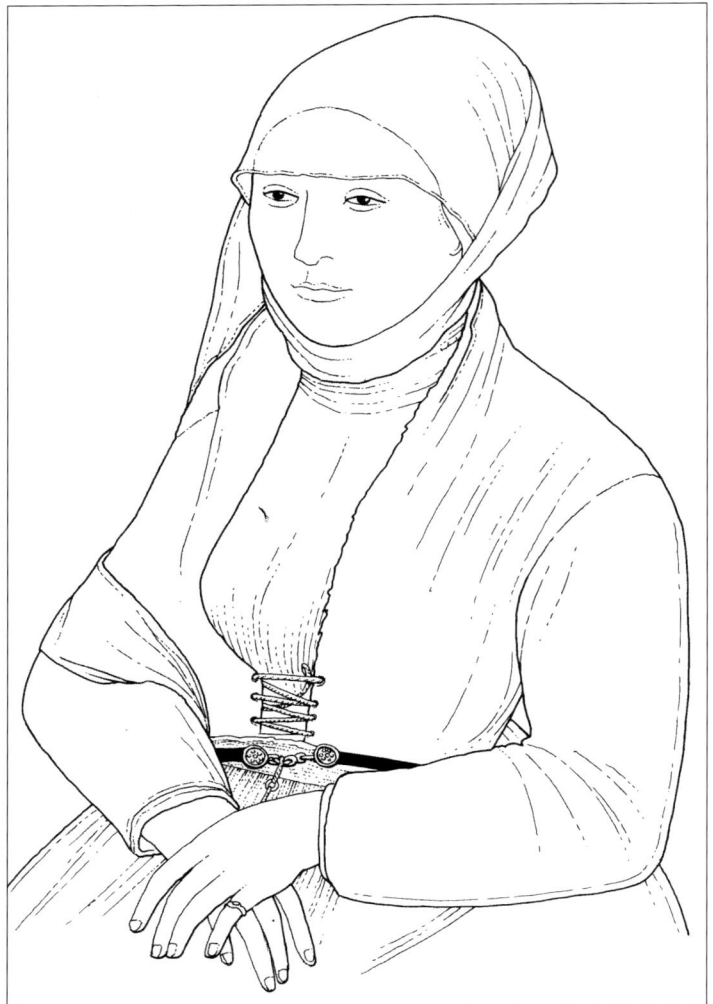

Fig. 41.1. Redrawing of '*A young woman*', by Hans Holbein the Younger (probably his wife), 1523-24. Note her girdle fastened with a metal-clasp from which hangs a chain or lanyard and ring.

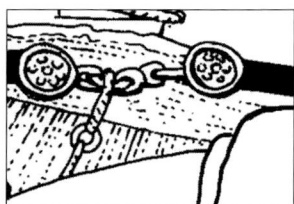

Fig. 41.2. Detail of the young woman's clasp; it is impossible to say to which Class it belongs.

HOOKED-CLASPS & EYES

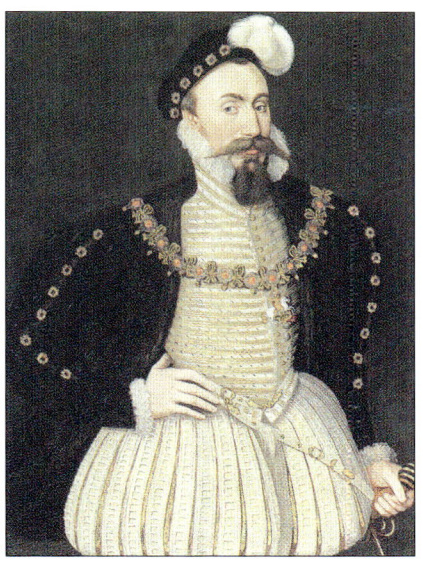

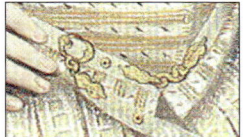

Fig. 42.1. Robert Dudley, Earl of Leicester (1532? - 88), unknown artist, c.1575, the National Portrait Gallery collection, Montacute House, Somerset. Note the S-shaped clasp and other metal-fittings on his sword-belt and hanger.

Fig. 42.2. Detail of the S-shaped clasp and other metal-fittings on the Earl of Leicester's sword-belt and hanger.

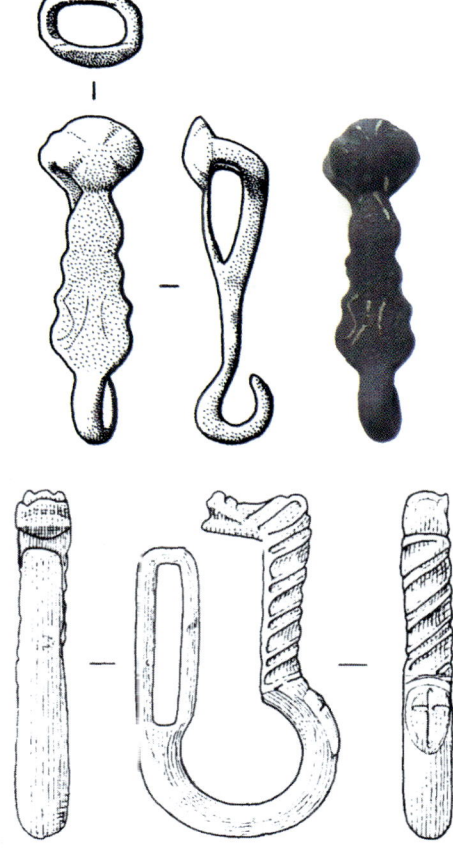

770. Copper alloy; cast; one-piece; engraved and moulded-relief. A sub-lozenge shaped plate with engrailed edges and Ringerike-style sporadic degraded white inlay; the narrow end of the plate has a sub-circular convex head bearing a saltire formed from triangular grooves; on the back an arm extends at an angle to just below the head where it becomes bifurcate, one arm linking with either side of the head, thus forming an aperture; the opposite end of the plate tapers into a circular-section recurving sharp hook; 54 x 17mm. Possibly a link from a strap-distributor; *c.* early 11th century. *South-West Wiltshire*. After Read 2001, fig. 4, no. 39. Drawing © Patrick Read.

771. Copper alloy; cast; one-piece; moulded-relief. A circular-section rod bent into a forward-facing hook, the attachment-end is flattened and pierced laterally with a long slot; the hook-end projects beyond the slot and has a retrograde three-dimensional zoomorphic terminal, the outside of this section has multiple oblique grooves and a Norman-style shield bearing a Latin Cross; 57.5 x 32.3mm. A strap was presumably threaded through the slot and a secondary object, (?) a purse, suspended from the hook; possibly *c.*13th - *c.*15th century. *Wiltshire*. Drawing © Nick Griffiths. Reproduced courtesy of Wiltshire Heritage Museum.

HOOKED-CLASPS & EYES

772. Copper alloy; cast; one-piece; moulded-relief. Comparable with nos 771, 773 except having a pointed mousing-bar inside the loop, lacking the oblique grooves and a plain shield; 54.21 x 26.34mm. Possibly *c*.13th -*c*.15th century. *Hertfordshire.* Portable Antiquities Scheme BH-4A9D88. Photographs © St Albans Museum.

773. Copper alloy; cast; one-piece; undecorated. Comparable with nos 771-772 except a plain terminal, without the mousing-bar and perhaps a poorly formed plain shield; 58.3 x 25.4mm. Possibly *c*.13th - *c*.15th century. *Dorset.*

774. Copper alloy; cast; one-piece; undecorated. A circular-section tapering rod with a biconvex terminal at one end, while the other end is bent into a blunt-hook which could be recurving or forward-facing; the inside bend of the hook is abraded; 34.06 x 16.19mm. The design suggests this was held vertically and a secondary object suspended from the hook, possibly an equine object; possibly *c*.13th - *c*.15th century. *South-East Dorset.* Drawing © Patrick Read.

775. Copper alloy; cast; one-piece; moulded-relief. Comparable with no. 774 except a part circular- and part semi-circular section rod with a tapering square-section three-dimensional zoomorphic terminal at one end, while the other end is bent into a blunt-hook which could be recurving or forward-facing; L54mm. Possibly *c*.13th - *c*.15th century. After Read 1995, no. 363. *South Devon.* Drawing © Patrick Read.

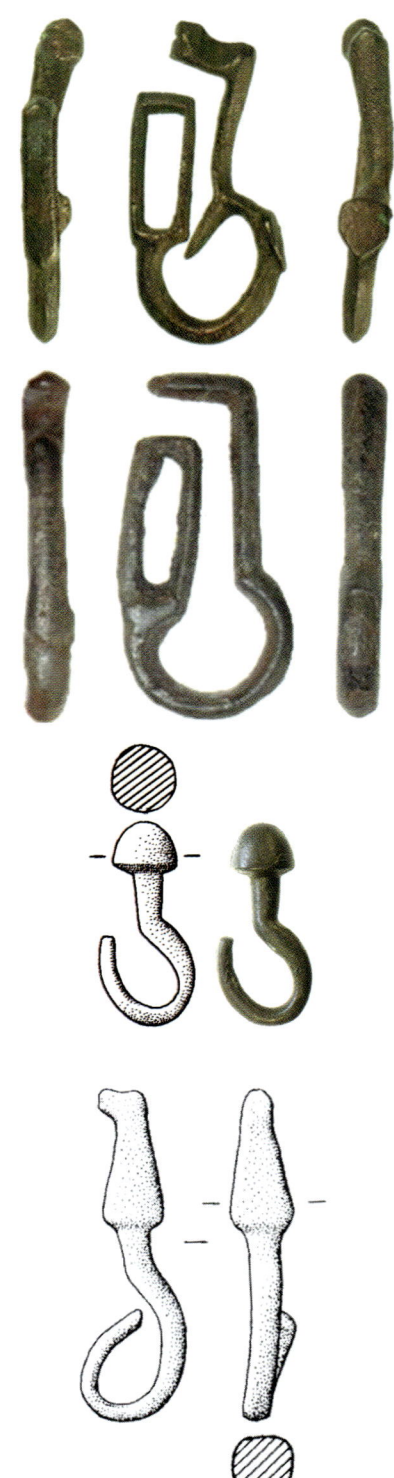

HOOKED-CLASPS & EYES

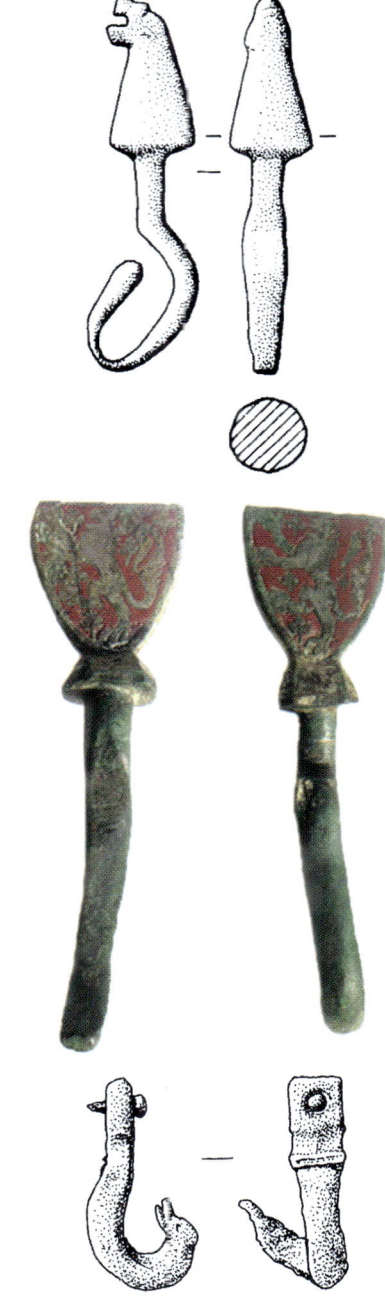

776. Copper alloy; cast; one-piece; moulded-relief. Comparable with no. 774-775 except totally circular-section; the inside bend of the hook is much abraded; L63mm. Possibly c.13th - c.15th century. *South Devon*. After Read 1995, no. 362. Drawing © Patrick Read.

777. Copper alloy; cast; one-piece; moulded-relief; champlevé enamel and gilding. A shield-shaped plate bearing on each side a gilded rampant lion on a red enamelled field; a part circular- and part D-shaped section hook, now distorted; a projecting conical collar at the juncture of the plate and hook; 90 x 24.5mm. An equine object, c.14th century. *Cumbria*. Portable Antiquities Scheme LAN-CUM-9F42C2. Photographs © the Portable Antiquities Scheme.

778. Copper alloy; cast; one-piece; moulded-relief. A sub-circular section rod bent into a hook flattened at one end and drilled with a rivet-hole retaining a separate copper-alloy globular-head rivet; on the probable back and below the rivet-hole are two contiguous sub-rectangles and a projecting grooved collar; the orientation of the rivet and the decoration suggests the distorted hook, which is zoomorphic, is forward-facing; L35mm. Presumably for riveting to a strap and suspending a secondary object from the hook; possibly c.13th - c.15th century. *South-West Dorset*. Drawing © Nick Griffiths.

779. Copper alloy; cast; one-piece; moulded-relief. A triangular-section rod with a debased trefoil attachment-knop at one end and an expansion with a rivet-hole at the other; the rod is then flattened and bent into a recurving blunt-hook; 49.5 x 0.63mm. Presumably for riveting to a strap and suspending a secondary object from the hook; possibly *c.*13th - *c.*15th century. *Suffolk.* Portable Antiquities Scheme SF-D0F262. Photograph © Suffolk County Council Archaeological Service.

780. Copper alloy; sheeting; one-piece; undecorated. A sub-rectangular plate with two median drilled rivet-holes; a forward-facing blunt-hook; 30 x 15mm. Possibly from a sword-belt used in tandem with a separate eye-section or riveted direct to a strap, tentatively assigned as *c.*16th - *c.*17th century. *Norfolk.* Photographs © Robert Green.

781. Copper alloy; cast; one-piece; engraved and moulded-relief. The plate design is comparable with toggle-clasps nos 753-755, 757 which suggests they are en suite items assigned to the same date. At one end is a recurving central (?) blunt-hook, while at the other end a similar but longer recurving (?) blunt-hook extends from one corner. Whether these protuberances are hooks for attaching to, or suspending a secondary object from, is uncertain. The corner (?) hook could have slotted through a slit in, for example, a strap, though it does seem illogical to have only one and on a corner. Another possibility is a strap-slide, the central (?) hook of which is distorted; 34 x 15mm; *c.*16th century. *Buckinghamshire.* Portable Antiquities Scheme BUC-91F075. Photographs © Buckinghamshire County Council.

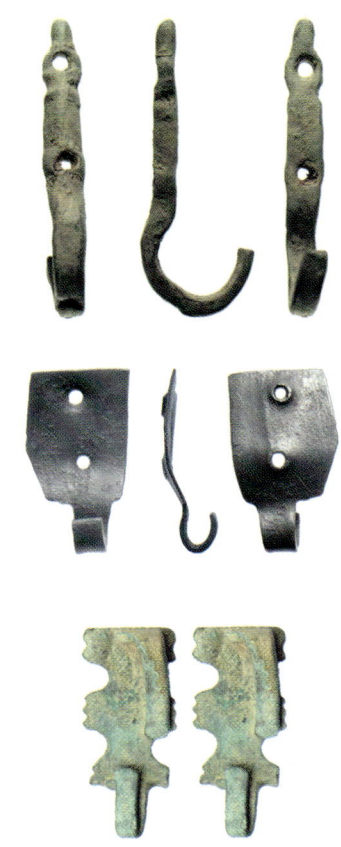

782. Copper alloy; cast; one-piece; moulded-relief. The front median of the sub-rectangular plate is slightly expanded and grooved from the attachment-end to where it narrows into a cusped collar and a forward-facing sharp-hook; the edge of the attachment-end is cusped; rivet-holes either end of the median groove retain residue of iron rivets; 49.36 x 17.49mm. Possibly from a sword-belt, used in tandem with a separate eye-section of similar design, *c.*16th century. *East Devon.* Drawing © Patrick Read.

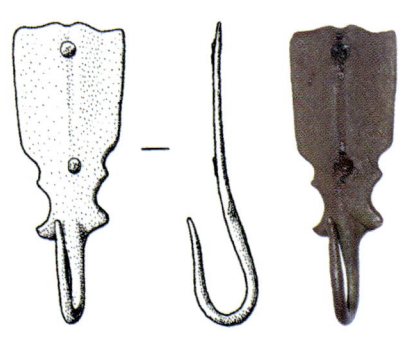

783. Copper alloy; cast; one-piece; moulded-relief. A forward-facing close-butted blunt-hook, eye or loop; comparable with no. 782: 46 x 21mm. A copper-alloy similar object with an S-shaped chain-link attached to its loop - described as a strapend (with caveats) came from a *c*.1530 - *c*.1570 context in London (Egan 2005, fig. 23, no. 148). *East Devon.* Drawing and photograph © Patrick Read.

784. Copper alloy; cast and sheeting; four-piece; moulded-relief and openwork. A cast asymmetrical front-plate with comma and circular apertures, turned-over edges and a central large rivet-hole and a rivet-hole either side on the attachment-edge. A sheeting back-plate similarly pierced with rivet-holes retaining residue of iron rivets. A separate sheeting forward-facing hook with a debased zoomorphic terminal is riveted between the plates through the basal rivet-hole. Incomplete, the side edges of the back-plate are ragged; marks between the rivet-holes on the front-plate are perhaps traces of moulded decoration or corrosion; 38.09 x 20.5mm. Possibly from a sword-belt; *c*.16th - *c*.17th century. *East Anglia.* Drawing © Patrick Read.

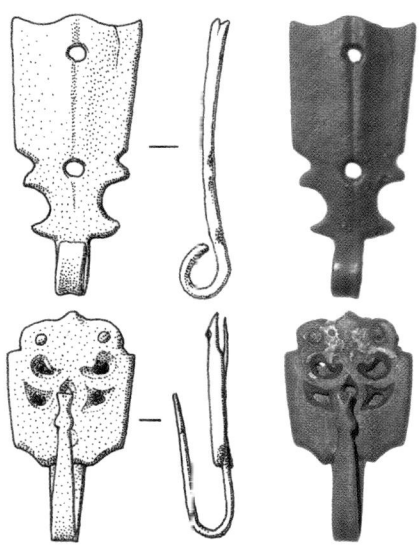

785. Copper alloy; sheeting; one-piece; possibly undecorated. A sub-rectangular plate cut and forged at one end into a circular-section tapering recurving globular-ended hook; the attachment-end of the plate is slightly bifurcate. The front appears undecorated but obscure marks may be vestiges of a design; conversely, possibly corrosion. A rivet-hole nearer the hook-end retains a remnant of separate copper-alloy narrow tube that possibly served as a rivet; 39 x 16mm. Possibly from a sword-belt; *c*.16th - *c*.17th century. *East Devon.* Drawing © Patrick Read.

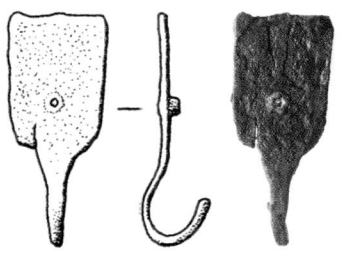

786. Copper alloy; cast; one-piece; moulded-relief. A rectangular plate with at one end a debased trefoil attachment-knop retaining residue of an iron rivet; a transverse grooved collar at the juncture of the plate and tapering circular-section possible hook or suspension-loop. An integral circular-section rivet projects from the back of collar; a small drilled pit in the back of the plate. Incomplete, the point of the hook or suspension-loop is broken off; 47 x 18mm. Possibly from a sword-belt; *c*.16th - *c*.17th century. After Read 2001, fig. 25, no. 355. *East Devon.* Drawing © Patrick Read.

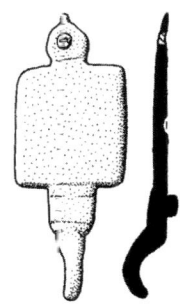

787. Copper alloy; probably sheeting; undecorated. An ovoid plate with a rounded knop on the attachment-end; a projecting angular collar at the juncture of the plate and forward-facing hook; which is circular-section and with a debased zoomorphic terminal; two median rivet-holes, one of which retains residue of iron rivet; 41 x 20mm. Possibly from a sword-belt; *c.*16th - *c.*17th century. *South-East Dorset*. Drawing © Patrick Read.

788. Copper alloy; cast; one-piece; moulded-relief. An ovoid plate with a rounded attachment-knop and vine tendrils, pellets and an annulet; a projecting rounded collar at the juncture of the plate and hook; one rivet-hole retains residue of an iron rivet. Incomplete, hook distorted and point broken off; 54 x 23mm. Possibly from a sword-belt; *c.*16th - *c.*17th century. After Read 2001, fig. 25, no. 358. *South Somerset*. Drawing © Patrick Read.

789. Copper alloy; cast; one-piece; convex; moulded-relief. An ovoid plate bearing a possible abraded floriate design, at one end a rounded attachment-knop with a projecting, ridged and rounded collar, a rivet hole in the plate retains residue of an iron rivet, at the other end a forward-facing circular-section hook with a zoomorphic terminal, representing a swan's neck and head; a rounded knop either side at the juncture of the plate and hook; 50 x 17mm. Possibly from a sword-belt; *c.*16th - *c.*17th century. *South-West Wiltshire*. After Read 2001, fig. 25, no. 360. Drawing © Patrick Read.

790. Copper alloy; cast; one-piece; moulded-relief. An M-shaped plate bearing foliate; two rivet-holes at the hook-end and one at the attachment-end retain separate domed-head copper-alloy rivets and sheeting circular roves; a circular-section forward-facing blunt-hook; 47 x 32mm. From a sword-belt hanger; *c.*16th - *c.*17th century. *River Thames foreshore, London*. Drawing © Nick Griffiths.

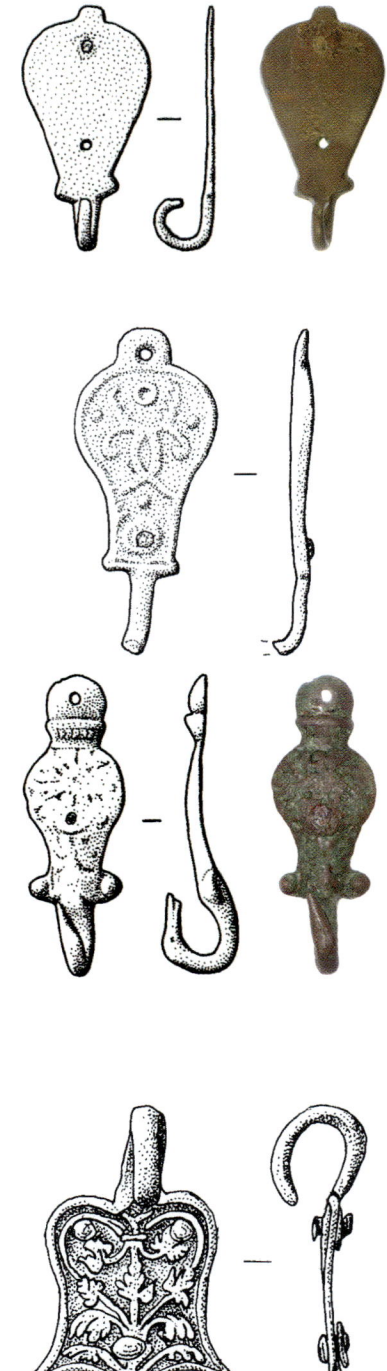

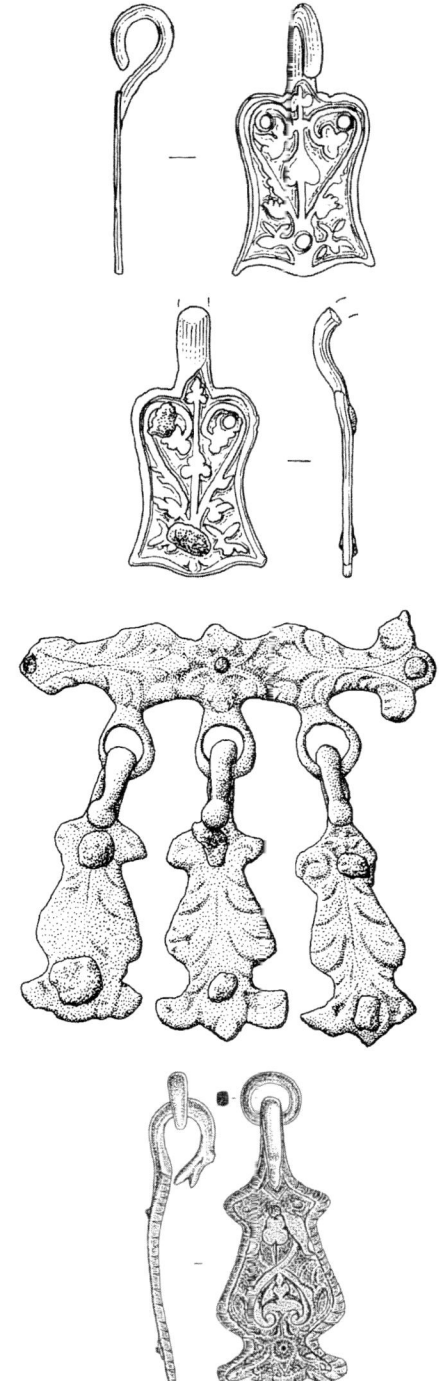

791. Copper alloy; cast; one-piece; moulded-relief. Comparable with nos 790, 792 except narrower and retaining residue of two iron rivets; 45 x 22.5mm. Incomplete, hook broken off. From a sword-belt hanger; *c.*16th - *c.*17th century. *South-East Dorset.* Drawing © Nick Griffiths.

792. Copper alloy; cast; one-piece; moulded-relief. Comparable with nos 790-791 except the decoration is slightly different; 45 x 23mm. From a sword-belt hanger; *c.*16th - *c.*17th century. *South-East Dorset.* Drawing © Nick Griffiths.

793. Copper alloy; cast; each section is one-piece; moulded-relief. An asymmetrical plate bearing foliate and floriate; three rivet-holes, each retaining residue of iron rivets, and three circular suspension-eyes. Suspended from each eye is an asymmetrical similarly decorated plate with a forward-facing close-butted globular-ended hook, rivet-holes either end retain residue of iron rivets. Incomplete, one end of the plate is broken off; plate 67 x 26mm, hooks 49 x 21mm. A sword-belt, hanger; *c.*16th century. *West Somerset.* After Read 2001, fig. 26, no. 373. Drawing © Patrick Read.

794. Copper alloy; cast; one-piece; possibly engraved. Comparable with hook-sections of nos 793, 795 except vine, foliate and floral within a linear and hatched border; residue of iron rivets in the rivet-holes; a forward-facing close-butted blunt-hook with a zoomorphic terminal. A separate copper-alloy ring is suspended in the hook; hooked-section 48 x 21mm, ring D9.5mm. From a sword-belt; *c.*16th century. *Isle of White.* Isle of White Archaeological Unit, A.2001.9.10. Drawing © Frank Basford.

795. Copper alloy; cast; each section is one-piece; possibly engraved. Comparable with the hooked sections of nos 793-794 except different decoration; one rivet-hole retains residue of an iron rivet; hooked-section 44 x 19.5mm, eye-section D13mm. Incomplete, the attachment-eye is broken off a probable asymmetrical plate. From a sword-belt hanger; *c*.16th century. *Wiltshire*. Drawing © Nick Griffiths.

796. Copper alloy; cast; one-piece; shallow convex; undecorated. An ovoid plate with a rounded knop on the attachment-end; two rivet-holes nearer the attachment-end, one retaining residue of iron rivet; a recurving forward-facing close-butted blunt-hook. A separate copper-alloy hexagonal-section pendent ring is suspended in the hook; hook 41 x 13mm, ring D13mm. Possibly from a sword-belt or baldrick; *c*.16th - *c*.17th century. *East Devon*. After Read 2001, fig. 25, no. 363. Drawing © Patrick Read.

797. Copper alloy; cast; one-piece; engraved and moulded-relief. An oval plate bearing a voided curved-armed cross and a central stylised flower formed from seven annulets within an oval, crescents in three of the interstices; a rounded attachment-knop on one end; a slightly projecting ridged collar at the juncture of the plate and hook; a rivet-hole near the collar retains a separate copper-alloy rivet and sheeting circular rove; a forward-facing close-butted blunt-hook. A separate copper-alloy pendent ring suspended in the hook; hook 61 x 27mm, ring D13mm. From a sword-belt; 17th century. *East Devon*. Drawing © Patrick Read.

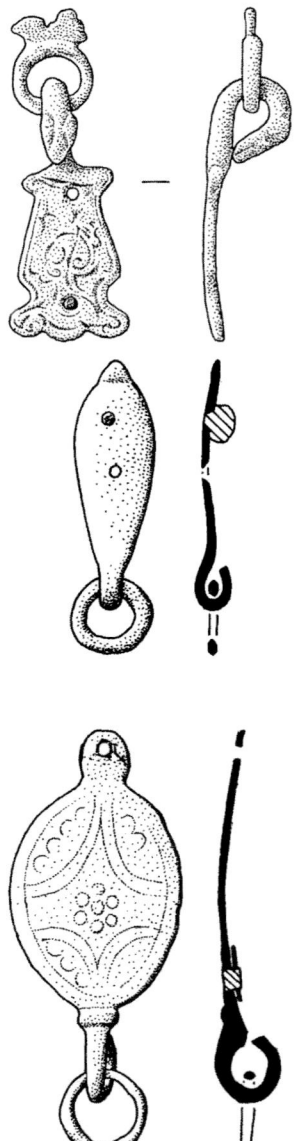

HOOKED-CLASPS & EYES

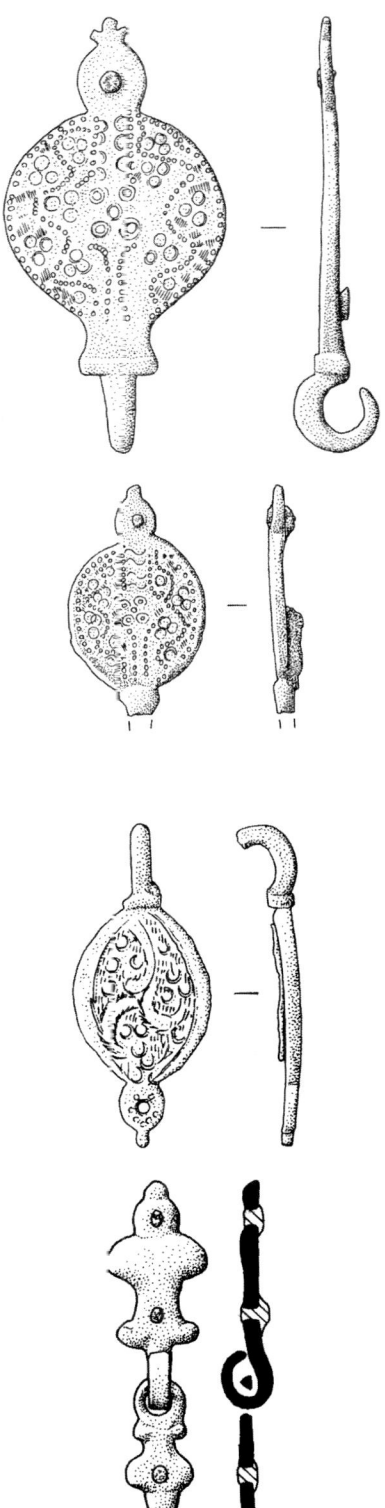

798. Copper alloy; cast; punched. A circular plate bearing curlicues of tiny annulets, larger annulets and ring-and-dot motifs in the interstices, all within a border of tiny annulets; a rounded attachment-knop, retaining residue of an iron rivet, surmounted by a small trefoil-knop on the attachment-end, and at the other a recurving sharp-hook with a projecting ridged collar at the juncture of the plate and hook; an integral rivet on the back near the collar; 72 x 35.5mm. From a sword-belt; 17th century. *Lincolnshire*. Drawing © Nick Griffiths.

799. Copper alloy; cast; punched. An oval plate bearing decoration comparable with no. 798, a debased trefoil attachment-knop, retaining residue of an iron rivet on the attachment-end and a slightly projecting and ridged collar at the juncture of the hook; rust adhering to the back is probably obscuring an integral copper-alloy rivet. Incomplete, hook broken off; 38 x 22mm. From a sword-belt; 17th century. *Lincolnshire*. Drawing © Nick Griffiths.

800. Copper alloy; cast; engraved and possibly punched. An ovoid plate bearing vine and foliate, a debased trefoil attachment-knop at the attachment-end and a slightly projecting and ridged collar at the juncture of the plate and hook. Incomplete, forward-facing hook broken off; 53 x 22mm. From a sword-belt; 17th century. *Wiltshire*. Drawing © Nick Griffiths.

801. Copper alloy; cast; each section is one-piece; moulded-relief. Hooked-section: a trefoil-shaped plate with a rounded knop on the attachment-end, the other end has a forward-facing close-butted blunt-hook with a rounded knop either side; rivet-holes at either end retain residue of iron rivets, 38 x 16mm. Eye-section: comparable with the hooked-section except one rivet-hole retaining residue of an iron rivet, 25 x 11mm. Possibly from a sword-belt or baldrick; *c.*16th - *c.*17th century. *South-East Lincolnshire*. After Read 2001, fig. 25, no. 361. Drawing © Patrick Read.

802. Copper alloy; cast; each section is one-piece; openwork; white-metal coated, probably tin. Hooked-section: a trefoil-shaped plate with a heart aperture and a rounded attachment-knop on the end and a forward-facing close-butted blunt-hook at the other end, a rounded knop either side with a rivet-hole between; both rivet-holes retain residue of iron rivets; 55 x 21mm. Eye-section: incomplete, the surviving part of the plate is comparable with the hooked-section except with a laterally projecting circular eye in which the hooked-section is suspended, a rounded attachment-knop retains residue of an iron rivet, the opposite end has four stubs where it is broken; a second rivet-hole at this end retains a separate copper-alloy rivet, 34 x 32.5mm. Possibly from a sword-belt, baldrick or horse harness; c.16th - c.17th century. *South-West Wiltshire*. Drawing © Nick Griffiths.

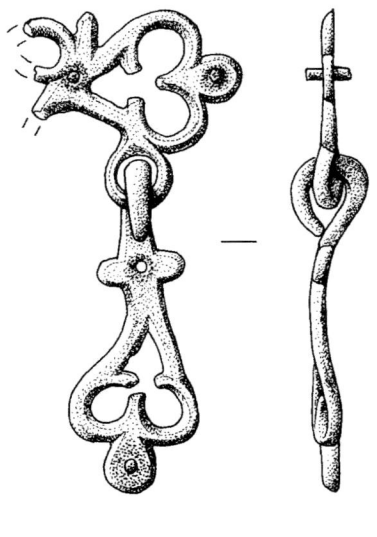

803. Copper alloy; cast and sheeting; each section is one-piece; engraved and moulded-relief. Both sections are virtually identical, notwithstanding, they are sufficiently different, suggesting they are from different moulds or affected by hand-finishing. Each plate is asymmetrical and has chamfered edges and recurving blunt-hooks - one of which is close-butted; trefoil attachment-knops on the ends opposite the hooks are considered zoomorphic, perhaps the heads of birds with outspread wings, the eyes represented by rivet-holes, another rivet-hole at the opposite ends; a projecting, grooved collar at the juncture of the plates and hooks; two oblique grooves either end; the rivet-holes retain separate copper-alloy rivets and sheeting circular roves; beneath two of the roves is a fragment of leather, presumably from a strap; hooks 60.5 x 21mm, eye 60.5 x 20mm, ring D14mm. Possibly from a sword-belt, perhaps Roman period (pers. comm. Nick Griffiths) though could be early post-medieval. *River Thames foreshore, London*. Drawing © Nick Griffiths.

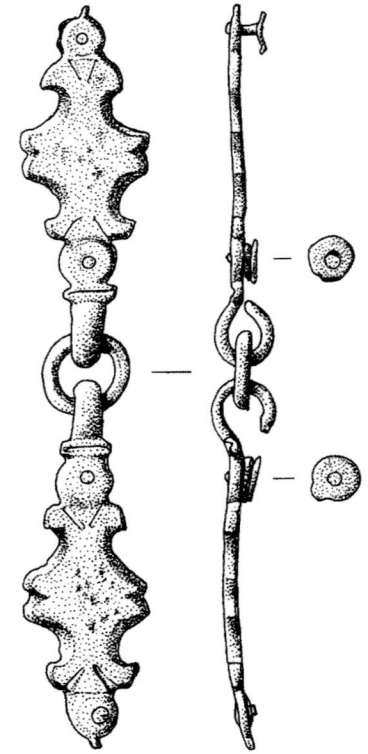

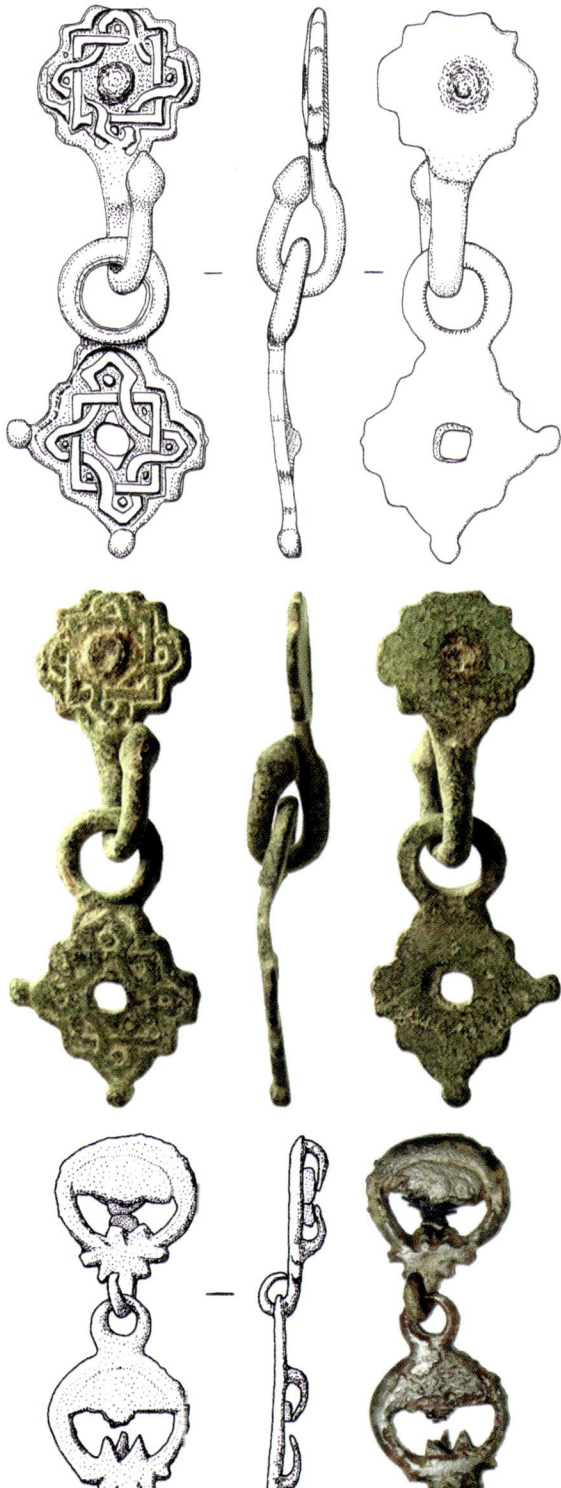

804. Copper alloy; cast; each section is one-piece; moulded-relief or engraved. Hooked-section: a lozenge-shaped plate with a forward-facing circular-section close-butted hook terminating with a pointed globule; engrailed sides; an intertwined square and quatrefoil; a central rivet-hole retains residue of an iron rivet. Incomplete, three apexes and probable globular knops broken off; 34 x 18.2. Eye-section: attached to the hooked-section with which it is comparable but having a circular loop on one apex; and globular knops on two others. Incomplete, one apex and globular knop broken off; plate 36.5 x 22.8, eye external D12.2mm. Possibly from a *c.*16th- - *c.*17th-century sword-belt or baldrick. *Isle-of-White*. Portable Antiquities Scheme IOW-77DB28. Drawing and photographs © Isle of White Council.

805. Copper alloy; cast; each section is one-piece; moulded-relief and openwork. Hooked-section: a circular plate with an asymmetrical aperture, four angular/rounded knops form a collar at the juncture of the plate and forward-facing close-butted sharp-hook; a grooved arc on the front continues the outline of the aperture; two integral sharp-pointed lugs on the back retain a remnant of leather; 27 x 21.5mm. Eye-section: similar except a circular eye at one end and a trefoil of rounded knops on the attachment-end, one lug retains a remnant of leather; 33 x 21.5mm. Each plate is a man in the moon motif plus a star, though this example is poorly cast. Possibly from a sword-belt or baldrick; c.16th - c.17th century. *South Devon*. Drawing © Patrick Read. Photograph © John Parnell.

806. Copper alloy; possibly sheeting; each section is one-piece; white-metal coated, probably tin. Hooked section: a plate with six angular or slightly rounded knops, a forward-facing hook with a slightly expanded terminal; stubs of two integral rivets or lugs on the back, 34 x 21mm. Eye-section: similar, a rounded eye; 28 x 20mm. Possibly from a sword-belt or baldrick; c.16th - c.17th century. After Read 2001, fig. 25, no. 364. *South-West Dorset*. Drawing © Patrick Read.

807. Copper alloy; cast; each section is one-piece; partially convex; undecorated. Hooked-section: a sub-rectangular triangular-section plate with a circular-section forward-facing virtually close-butted blunt-hook with a flattened sub-oval terminal; two integral circular-section rivets on the back; 33.54 x 0.83mm. Eye-section: similar, a rectangular eye which is attached to the hook; 31.6 x 10mm. Possibly from a sword-belt; c.16th - c.17th century. *Isle of White*. Portable Antiquities Scheme IOW-7184A4. Drawing and photographs © Isle of White Council.

808. Copper alloy; cast and sheeting; one-piece; moulded-relief. Comparable with the hooked-section of no. 807 except a rectangular sub-triangular section plate chamfered at one end and a ridged collar at the hook-end; a recurving blunt-hook with a sub-triangular terminal with a groove either side. Two integral circular-section rivets one of which retains a separate sheeting copper-alloy circular rove; 32.74 x 9.08mm. Possibly from a sword-belt; c.16th - c.17th century. *Derbyshire*. Drawing © Nick Griffiths.

809. Copper alloy; cast; each section is one-piece; partially convex; moulded-relief. An asymmetrical plate with oblique grooves and three rivet-holes, the end ones retain residue of iron rivets, a central semi-circular loop projects from one side. Two solid-domed bosses with recurving close-butted blunt-hooks resembling scallop shells have rivet-holes retaining residue of iron rivets, hang from the plate loop; W43mm. Possibly from a sword-belt; c.16th - c.17th century. *River Thames foreshore, London*.

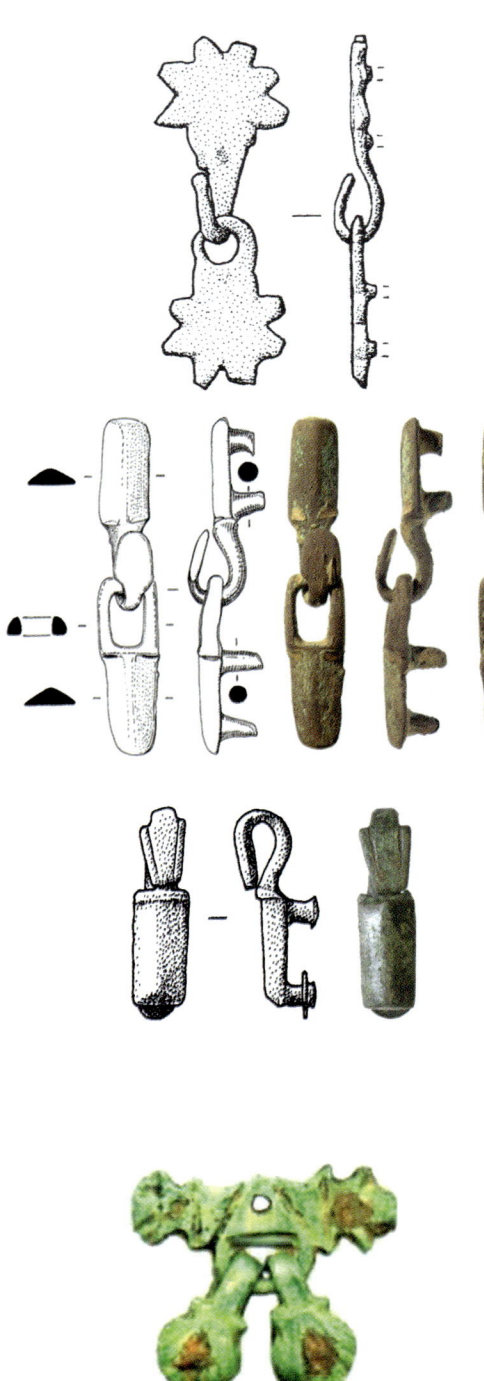

HOOKED-CLASPS & EYES

810. Copper alloy; cast; moulded-relief; one-piece; undecorated except for sporadic white-metal coating, probably tin, on the front. The plate is a stylised six-petalled flower pierced centrally for a separate rivet, probably iron as suggested by rust adhering to the front and back; a forward-facing sharp hook, 26.1 x 15.3mm. Possibly from a sword-belt; *c.*16th - *c.*17th century. *Nottinghamshire.* Portable Antiquities Scheme E4488. Photographs © Derby City Council.

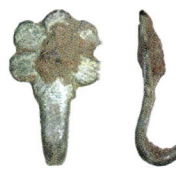

811. Copper alloy; cast; convex; one-piece; moulded-relief and possibly openwork. An ovoid hollow-domed plate with a rounded knop on the attachment-end and a ridged and grooved collar at the juncture of the plate and circular suspension-loop; a rivet-hole near the knop, and three transverse holes in the centre, one or more of which may be rivet-holes; three pits run parallel with these holes; a tapered groove runs towards the knop-end from each of the central holes; 35 x 12.5mm. From a sword-belt; *c.*17th century. *Nottinghamshire.* Drawing © Nick Griffiths.

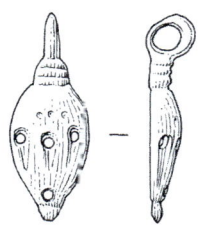

812. Copper alloy; cast and sheeting; eye-section two-piece, clasp one-piece; convex; moulded-relief. Eye-section: an ovoid hollow-domed plate with at the attachment-end a rounded knop and at the other a penannular loop oriented transverse to the plate; a ribbed collar at the juncture of the plate and hook; a rivet hole near the knop retains residue of an iron rivet. Incomplete, a separate sheeting plate formerly soldered to the back is missing; 34 x 14mm. Clasp-section: S-shaped with zoomorphic terminals and a central circular hole is suspended from the loop; 19 x 10mm. From a sword-belt or baldrick; *c.*17th century. *South Devon.* After Read 2001, fig. 25, no. 365. Drawing © Patrick Read.

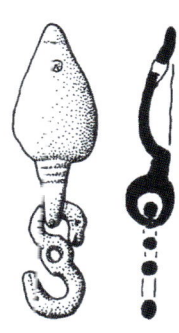

813. Copper alloy; cast and sheeting; two-piece; convex; moulded-relief. A sub-circular hollow-domed plate with three longitudinal facets; at one end is a ridged collared debased trefoil attachment-knop, and the other narrows to a transverse ridge and a recurving close-butted blunt hook. The back has an integral rivet near the hook, to which a now missing separate sheeting plate was secured; 52 x 20mm. From a sword-belt or baldrick; *c.*17th century. *North Dorset.* Drawing © Patrick Read.

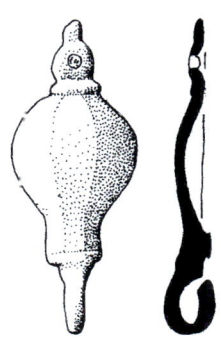

814. Copper alloy; cast; one-piece; convex; moulded-relief. Comparable with no. 813 except four longitudinal pitted bands, a rounded attachment-knop and a sharp-pointed hook; 46 x 19mm. From a sword-belt or baldrick; *c.*17th century. *Isle of White.* Isle of White Archaeological Unit, A.2001.9.23. Drawing © Frank Basford.

815. Copper alloy; cast and sheeting; convex; each section is one-piece, moulded-relief and openwork. Hook-section: an oval hollow-domed plate with at one end a collared trefoil attachment-knop with two pits, at the other end is a recurving close-butted blunt hook; a projecting and ribbed and longitudinal grooved collar at the juncture of the plate and hook. Incomplete, a separate sheeting plate formerly soldered to the back is missing; 44 x 12mm. Attachment-link: an openwork trefoil suspended in the hook; 19 x 13mm. *South Devon.* From a sword-belt or baldrick; *c.*17th century. After Read 2001, fig. 25, no. 362. Drawing © Patrick Read.

816. Copper alloy; cast and sheeting; each section is one-piece; convex; moulded-relief and openwork. Hook-section: a circular hollow-domed plate with at one end a projecting collared debased trefoil attachment-knop retaining residue of an iron rivet, at the other end is a close-butted blunt hook; a rounded collar with transverse V-shaped grooves and a rivet-hole retaining a separate copper-alloy rivet, at the juncture of the plate and hook; 50.5 x 22.5mm. Attachment-link: an openwork trefoil is suspended in the hook; 19 x 11.5mm. *Hampshire.* From a sword-belt or baldrick; *c.*17th century. Drawing © Nick Griffiths.

817. Copper alloy; cast; one-piece; convex; moulded-relief. An ovoid hollow-domed plate with longitudinal ribs; at one end is a collared debased trefoil attachment-knop retaining residue of an iron rivet; a ribbed collar at the juncture of the plate and broken possible loop; the back has an integral plate with an angular end; 35.4 x 15mm. From a sword-belt or baldrick; *c.*17th century. *South Somerset.* Drawing © Patrick Read.

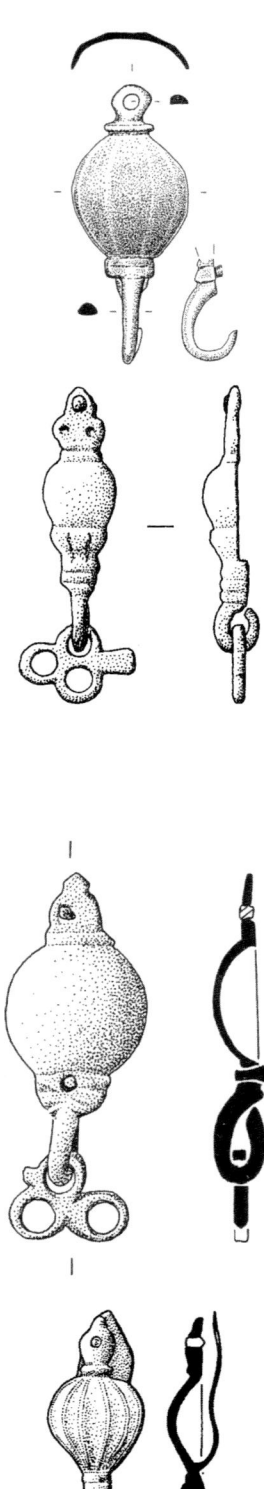

818. Copper alloy; cast; two-piece; convex; moulded-relief and possibly openwork. An ovoid hollow-domed plate with an obliquely grooved trefoil attachment-knop pierced by two transverse holes and a rivet-hole retaining a separate copper-alloy rivet; a ridged collar at the juncture of the plate and distorted recurving sharp-hook; either side of the plate projects laterally and is hatched, an integral rivet on the back near the hook. A separate incomplete copper-alloy sheeting plate is riveted and soldered to the back; 39 x 16mm. Possibly from a sword-belt or baldrick; *c.*17th century. *North Dorset*. Drawing © Patrick Read.

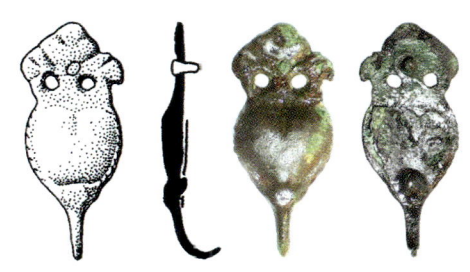

819. Copper alloy; cast; one-piece; moulded-relief. A shield-shaped plate with an oblique broad groove bordered either side by a narrow groove, both ends of the broad groove either side of the plate are recessed; two median rivet-holes; 49 x 20.5mm. Incomplete, suspension-loop broken or worn through. Possibly from a sword-belt; *c.*16th - *c.*17th century. Invariably mistaken for a harness pendant. *Somerset*. Drawing © Nick Griffiths.

820. Copper alloy; cast; one-piece; moulded-relief; sporadic white-metal coating overall (?) silver (?) tin. A heart-shaped split-plate with a median groove; a shepherd's-crook sharp-hook protrudes laterally in the same plane as the plate, a projecting ridged collar at the juncture of the plate and hook; two rivet-holes in the attachment-end retain separate copper-alloy rivets; plate 45.47 x 41.66mm, hook L63.94mm. From a sword-belt hanger; *c.* mid-17th century (Fig. 42). *Provenance unknown, private collection*. Drawing and photograph © Patrick Read, reproduced courtesy of Geoff Hobson.

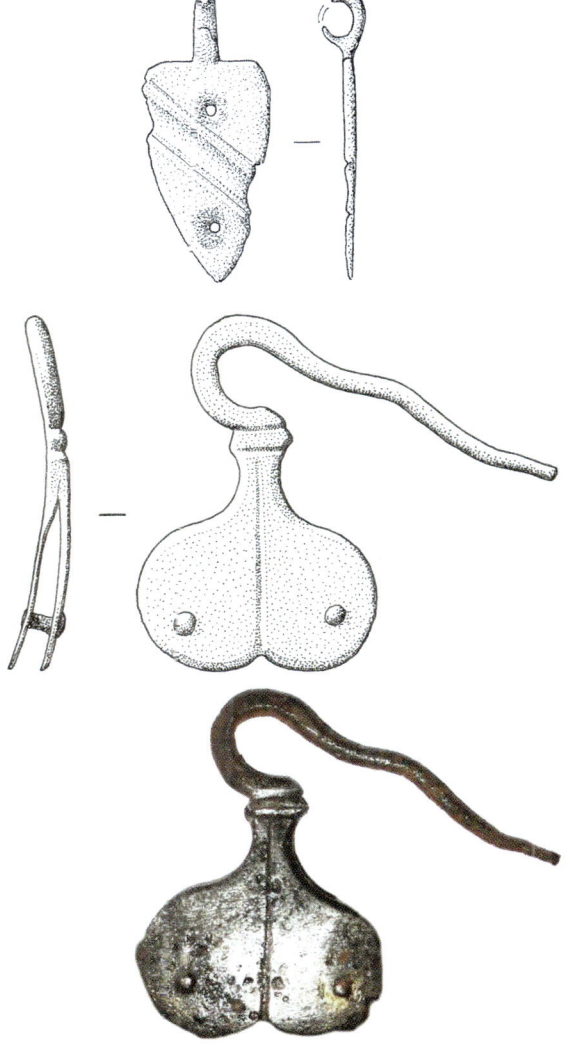

821. Copper alloy; cast; convex; one-piece; moulded-relief; sporadic gilding overall. An ovoid hollow-domed split plate with three longitudinal facets; a recurving sharp-hook with a projecting ridged collar; an integral rivet on the back of the front-plate at the attachment-end; the integral back-plate is pierced by a rivet-hole at the attachment-end; 41.55 x 14.02mm. From a sword-belt hanger; *c.* mid-17th century (Fig. 42). *Provenance unknown, private collection.* Photographs © Patrick Read, reproduced courtesy of Geoff Hobson.

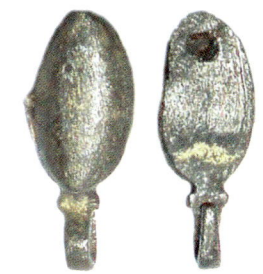

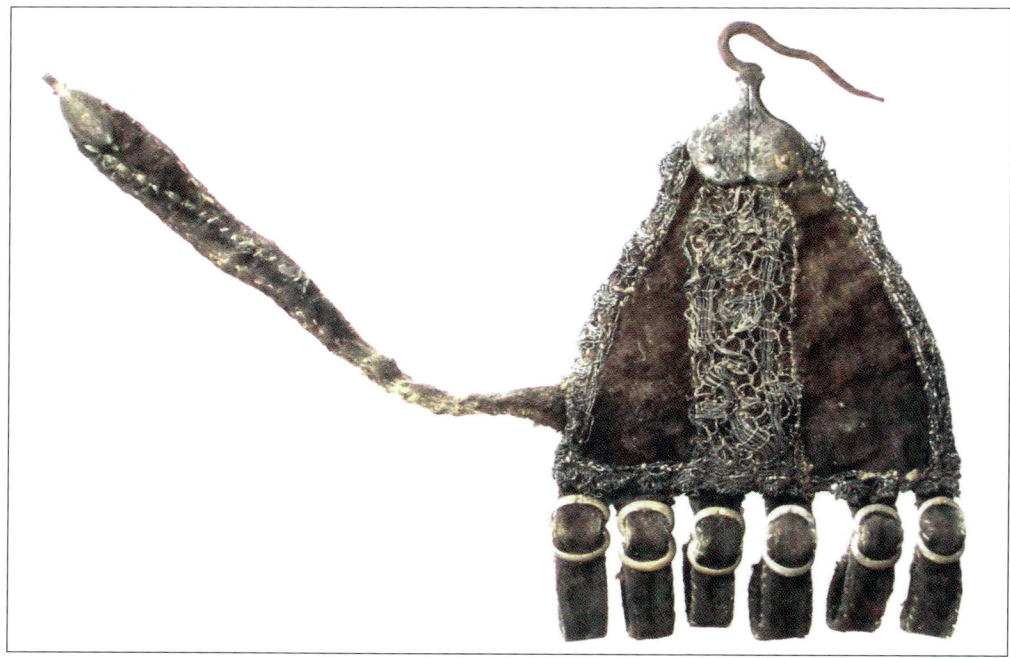

Fig. 43. A buff-leather sword-belt hanger lined on the front with possible shag-pile textile overlaid with a median panel and border of very coarse bobbin lace in metal threads which are possibly silver and silver-gilt. The back is lined with a fine-weave textile which could be either silk or linen. A sharp-hooked clasp is stitched to the apex-end (no. 820). Stitched to the opposite end are six buff-leather straps formed into loops, each lined either side with identical textiles, the opposite ends of which are stitched to the axis-bars of cast copper-alloy double-looped oval slides. A buff-leather strap, also lined either side with the same textiles, is stitched to the wide end of the hanger; the opposite end of the strap terminates with a sharp-hooked clasp (no. 821); *c.* mid-17th century. *Provenance unknown, private collection.* Photograph © Patrick Read, reproduced courtesy of Geoff Hobson.

HOOKED-CLASPS & EYES

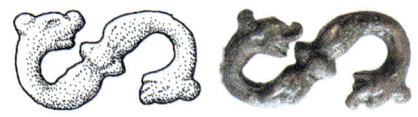

822. Copper alloy; cast; one-piece; flattened three-dimensional moulded-relief; sporadic white-metal coating. Hook-section: S-shaped, the blunt-hooks of which have dragon-headed terminals; a central rounded and grooved knop either side. The close-butted hook would have been affixed as nos 825-826; 30 x 15mm. Possibly from a sword-belt; perhaps *c.* mid-16th - *c.* early 17th century. *South-East Lincolnshire*. Drawing © Patrick Read.

823. Copper alloy; cast; one-piece; flattened three-dimensional moulded-relief. Hook-section: comparable with nos 822, 824-826, the blunt-hooks have (?) bird-headed terminals; a beaded border either side and two central circumferential transverse ridges. The close-butted hook would have been affixed as no. 825-826; 44.5 x 20mm. Possibly from a sword-belt; perhaps *c.* mid-16th - *c.* early 17th century though could be modern. *River Thames foreshore, London*. Drawing © Nick Griffiths.

824. Copper alloy; cast; one-piece; flattened three-dimensional moulded-relief. Hook-section: comparable with nos 822-823, 825-826, snake form; the underside at the head end is much abraded; 42.59 x 20.63. Possibly from a 19th-century military or police belt but perhaps from a more modern belt. *South Somerset*.

825. Copper alloy; cast and wire; hooked-section is one-piece, strap-link two-piece; flattened three-dimensional moulded-relief; sporadic black coating, possibly bitumen. Hook-section: comparable with nos 822-824, 826, (?) swan-headed terminals; a central circumferential hatched band with a ridge and four leaves either side; L37.02mm. Strap-link: circular-section wire with a separate soldered transverse eye by which it is attached to one of the hooks; distorted. From a *c.* mid-16th-century sword-belt. *River Thames foreshore, London*.

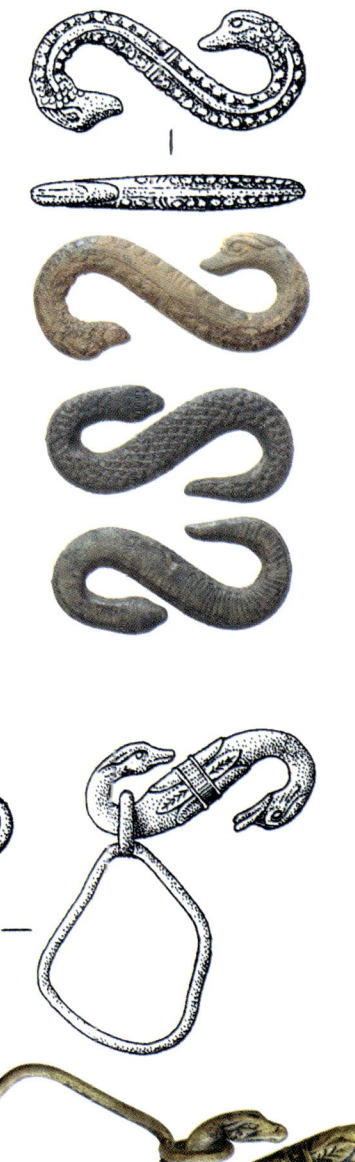

826. Copper alloy; cast; part convex; each section is one-piece; three-dimensional moulded-relief; gilded. Hook-section: comparable with nos 822-825 except (?) bird-headed terminals and a plain circumferential band with a leaf either side; L27.09mm. Eye-section: an oval hollow-domed boss bearing a lion's facing mask and with a laterally projecting border of hatching and asymmetrical-shapes, and a rectangular attachment-loop at one end while the other has a loop transverse to the plate to which the S-clasp is attached by the close-butted hook. Incomplete, loop broken off, now repaired, and a matching eye-section missing; 38.73 x 26.08mm. An early 19th-century military cloak-clasp. *East Devon.* Drawing © Patrick Read.

827. Copper alloy; cast, sheeting and wire; convex hooked-sections are one-piece and moulded-relief. Cast hooked-sections are similar: both have hollow-domed bosses with rounded split attachment-ends pierced by rivet-holes retaining separate copper-alloy rivets, projecting ridged collars either side of the boss and recurving close-butted blunt-hooks - one has an additional ridged collar on the attachment-end. A braided-wire strap with sheeting strapends is secured by the rivets to each hooked-section. Whether the strapends are folded or single sheets is indeterminate. Each hooked-section has attached a separate cast asymmetrical connector with a large kidney-shaped aperture and two smaller holes in a debased trefoil knop. Hooked-sections 32.44 x 12.29mm and 29.48 x 12.67mm; connectors 21.99 x 19.08mm and 22.64 x 18.72mm; strapends 13.17 x 7.61mm and 12.18 x 8.43mm; strap 247 x 7.50mm; overall length of strap and hooked-sections 292mm. Comparable with two connectors in Egan 2005, nos 173-4; and others are recorded from the Netherlands, Germany and Belgium. Possibly for suspending knife scabbards and other accessories; assigned between the 15th and 17th centuries. *Amsterdam.* Drawings © Nick Griffiths.

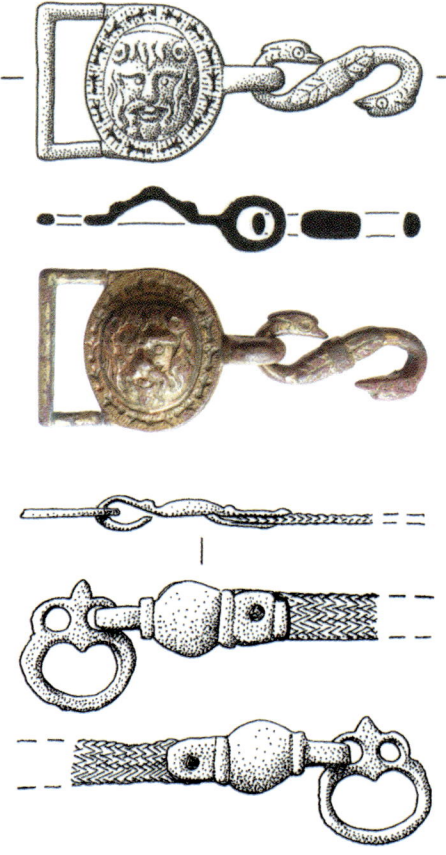

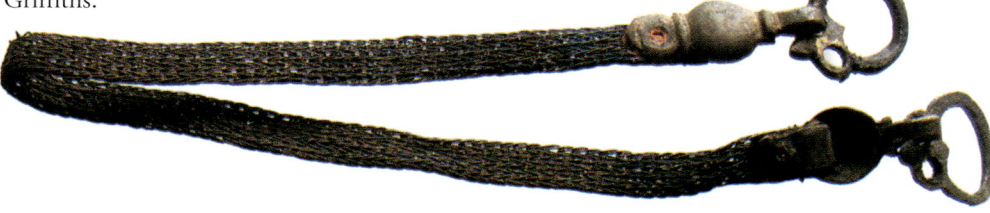

828. Copper alloy; cast; one-piece; open-work. A trefoil plate with circular and lozenge-shaped apertures and a projecting bifurcate collar at the juncture of the plate and recurving close-butted blunt-hook; rivet-holes either end retain separate copper-alloy rivets. A separate copper-alloy pendent ring is suspended in the hook; hook 48.8 x 11mm, ring D12.5mm. A strap-mount for suspending a secondary object; *c.*17th century. *Isle of White.* Portable Antiquities Scheme IOW-0A0576. Drawing © Isle of White Council.

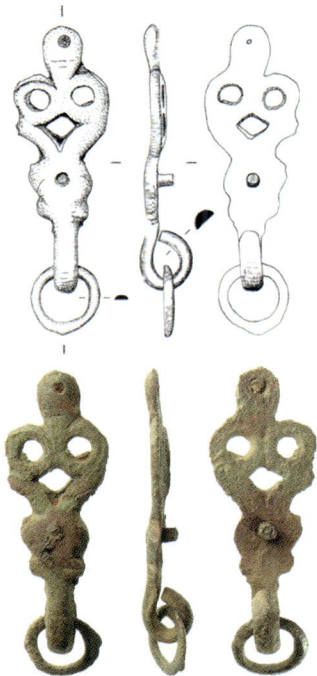

Early post-medieval strap-hooks with integral loops

These cast copper-alloy objects are comparable with Class F, Type 3 single recurving sharp-hooked clasps, and differentiated only by their extremely long blunt- or sharp-hooks. The decorated fronts of three imply they were meant to be seen, and although seemingly suitable for such a use, there is no evidence on surviving dress that they attached breeches to doublets. Perhaps the hooks clipped over leather or textile straps, thereby ensuring the correct orientation when viewed from the front, and a secondary object such as a key, purse, knife or chatelaine suspended from the integral loop. Interestingly, no evidence of abrasion is noted on the loops of those catalogued here. A comparable example was recovered from a 17th-century context at Flowerdew Hundred, Virginia, in the United States of America.

Oval

829. Copper alloy; cast; one-piece; moulded-relief. A plate with a circular loop at one end and a long blunt-hook at the other; a projecting rounded and transversely single grooved collar between the loop and plate; a similar collar but with two grooves at the juncture of the plate and hook; 59 x 16mm. *South Devon.* Photographs © John Parnell.

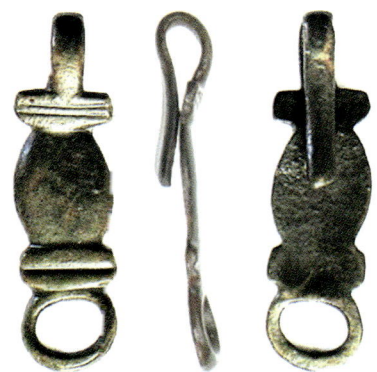

Figurative

830. Copper alloy; cast; one-piece; moulded-relief and openwork. Interpreted as the torso of a human female facing-figure, possibly wearing a pigtail hairstyle and with a girdle around the hips; a circular attachment-loop and a blunt-hook; corroded; 56.8 x 24.4mm. *Herefordshire*. Portable Antiquities Scheme HESH-9F8A61. Photograph © Birmingham City Council.

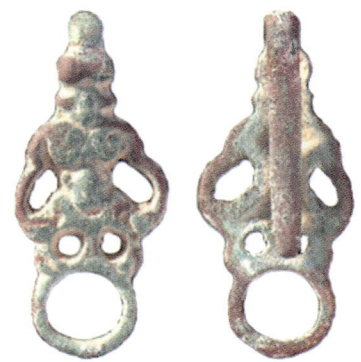

831. Copper alloy; cast; one-piece; moulded-relief and openwork. Comparable with no. 830 except the figure appears to be a long-haired and bearded man wearing a girdle around the hips. Incomplete, hook broken off (by how much is uncertain); 54 x 24mm. *Lincolnshire*. Portable Antiquities Scheme LIN-79D1C5. Photograph © the Portable Antiquities Scheme.

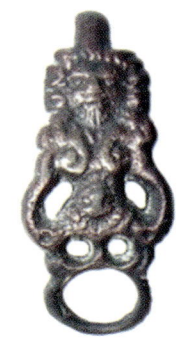

Bibliography

Allan, J P. Medieval and Post-Medieval Finds from Exeter, 1971-1980. *Exeter Archaeological Report 3*. 1984.

Andrews, D and Milne, G. (eds). Wharram: A Study of Settlement on the Yorkshire Wolds, vol 1, Copper-alloy objects by Goodall, A R. *The Society of Medieval Archæology Monograph 8*. 1981.

Arbman, H. Birka I: *Die Gräber, Stockholm / Uppsala*. 1943.

Arnold, J. *Perukes and Periwigs*. 1970.

---- *Handbook of Costume*. 1973.

---- *Patterns of Fashion 1: Englishwomen's dresses, cut and construction of women's clothing c.1660-1860*. 1964.

----*Patterns of Fashion 2: Englishwomen's dresses and their construction c.1860-1940*. 1966.

----*Lost from Her Majesty's Back*. 1980.

----*Patterns of Fashion 3: the cut and construction of clothes for men and women 1560-1620*. 1985.

----*Queen Elizabeth's Wardrobe Unlocked*. 1988.

Ashelford, J. *A Visual History of Costume The Sixteenth Century*. 1983.

----*The Art of Dress: Clothes and Society 1500-1914*. 1996.

Axbridge Town Charter 1599, Somerset Record Office D/B/Ax Box 52.

Baart, J (*et al*). Opgravingen in Amsterdam, *Fibula-Van Dishoeck, Haarlem, Amsterdam*. 1977.

Baclawski, K. *The Guide to Historic Costume*. 1995.

Bailey, G. *Detector Finds*. 1992.

----*Buttons and Fasteners 500BC - AD1840*. 2004.

Bagley, P. *The Encyclopaedia of Jewellery Techniques*. 1986.

Baumgarten, L and Watson, J with Carr F. *Costume Close-up: Clothing Construction and Pattern 1750-1790*. 1999.

Berry, G. *Medieval English Jettons*. 1974.

Biddle, M. *Object and Economy in Medieval Winchester, vols 1 and 2*. 1990.

Bishop, M C. The Camomile Street Soldier Reconsidered, in *London and Middlesex Archaeological Society Transactions 34*. 1983.

----*Lorica Segmentata, vol. 1, A Handbook of Articulated Roman Plate Armour*. 2002.

Blackburn, M A S and Bonser M J. Single Finds of Anglo-Saxon and Norman Coins, in *British Numismatic Journal 55*. 1985.

Blackley, F D and Hermansen, G (eds). *The Household Book of Queen Isabella of England for the Fifth Regnal Year of Edward II 8th July 1311 to 7th July 1312*. 1971. BM MS. Cotton Nero C VIII, fols. 121-152.

Blackmore, D. *Arms and Armour of the English Civil Wars*. 1990.

Blunt, C E. The Coinage of Athelstan 924-939. *British Numismatic Journal, vol 42*. 1974.

Boucher, F. *A History of Costume in the West*. 1967.

Bradfield, N. *Costume in Detail - Women's dress 1730-1930*. 1981.

Burnston, S. *Fitting and Proper: 18th Century Clothing from the Collection of the Chester County Historical Society*. 1998.

Byrde, P. *The Male Image*. 1979.

Capelle, T. Die frühgeschichtliche Metallfunde von Domburg auf Walcheren, *Nederlandse Oudheden, vol. 5, pp. 19, Taf. 11, 177*. 1976.

Cherry, J. The Farnham Pin, in *The Antiquaries Journal, vol 77*. 1997.

----*The Middleham Jewel and Ring*. 1994.

Clark, J (ed). Medieval Finds from Excavations in London: 5, *The Medieval Horse and its Equipment c.1150-c.1450*. 1995.

Crowfoot, E, Pritchard F and Staniland, K. Medieval finds from Excavations in London: 4, *Textiles and Clothing, 1150-1450*. 1992.

Crummy, N. The Roman small finds from excavations in Colchester 1971-9; *Colchester Archaeological Report 2.* 1995.

Cummings, V. *A Visual History of Costume The Seventeenth Century.* 1984.

Cunnington, W C and Cunnington, P. *Handbook of English Mediaval Costume.* 1973.

---- *Handbook of English Costume in the 16th Century.* 1970.

---- *Handbook of English Costume in the 17th Century.* 1963.

---- *Handbook of English Costume in the 18th Century.* 1972.

---- *Handbook of English Costume in the 19th Century.* 1966.

Cunnington, P and Lucas, C. *Occupational Costume in England from the 11th Century to 1914.* 1968.

Department of National Heritage. *Treasure Trove Reviewing Committee Annual Report 1995-96.*

Davenport M. *The Book of Costume, vol 1.* 1956.

DCMS. *Treasure Annual Report 2001, 2002, 2003* and *2004.*

DCMS. *Annual Report 2001/02-2002/03, 2004/5* and *2005/6.*

Dolley, M. The Nummular Brooch from Sulgrave, in *England before the Conquest.* 1971.

Dolley, M and Mays, M. Nummular Brooches, in *Southampton Finds Volume Two:* The Gold, Silver and other Non-Ferrous Alloy Objects from Hamwic, and the Non-Ferrous Metalworking Evidence. 1995.

Egan G and Forsyth, H. Wound Wire and Silver Gilt: changing fashions in dress accessories c.1400 - c.1600, in *The Age of Transition, The Archaeology of English Culture 1400-1600.* 1997.

Egan, G. A Shearman's Hook from London, in *Transactions, London and Middlesex Archaeology Society, vol. 30.* 1979.

---- Medieval Finds from Excavations in London: 6, *The Medieval Household Daily Living c.1150-c.1450.* 1998.

---- Material Culture in London in an age of transition, Tudor and Stuart period finds *c*1450-*c*1700 from excavations in Southwark. *MoLAS Monograph 19.* 2005.

Evans, J. *Dress in Medieval France.* 1952.

Ewing, T. *Viking Clothing.* 2006.

Feugère, M. *Weapons of the Romans.* 2002.

Gaimster, D. Two Post-Medieval sword-belt fittings from Pyecombe, West Sussex, in *Sussex Archaeological Collections, vol. 126.* 1988.

Gaimster, D; Hayward, M; Mitchell, D and Parker, K. Tudor Silver-Gilt Dress-Hooks: A New Type of Treasure Find in England, in *The Antiquaries Journal, vol. 82.* 2002.

Gaimster, D and Stamper, P (eds). *The Age of Transition, The Archaeology of English Culture 1400-1600.* 1997.

Geake, H. The Use of Grave-Goods in Conversion-Period England c.600-c.850, *BAR British Series 261.* 1997.

Geake, H and Kenny, J (eds). *Early Deira: Archaeological Studies of the East Riding in the fourth to ninth centuries AD.* 2000.

Green, J. The Loss of the Batavia 1629. *Western Australian Maritime Museum Excavation Report, BAR International Series 489.* 1989.

Green, J N (ed). The loss of the Verenigde Oostindische Compagnie Jacht *Verguide Draeck*, Western Australia 1656. *British Archaeological Report Supplementary Series 36(i) and (ii).* 1977. Appendix to the above, similar loss of the Verenigde Oostindische Compagnie fluit *Lasdrager* off Yell, Shetland 1653.

Green, M. *A Landscape Revealed, 10,000 Years on a Chalkland Farm.* 2000.

Griffiths, D, Philpot R A, and Egan, G. *MEOLS, The Archaeology of the North Wirral Coast.* 2007.

Goodall, A R. Metalwork, Copper-Alloy Objects, chapter VIII in *The Society of Medieval Archaeology Monograph 8.* 1979.

Hackenbroch, Y. *Enseignes: Renaissance Hat Jewels.* 1996.

Halls, Z. *Men's Costume 1580-1750.* HMSO 1970.

Hattat, R. *Brooches of Antiquity*. 1987.
---- *Ancient Brooches and Other Artefacts*. 1989.
Herald, J. *Renaissance Dress in Italy 1400-1500*. 1981.
Hines, J. *Clasps Hektespenner Agraffen: Anglo-Scandinavian Clasps of Classes A-C of the 3rd to 6th centuries A.D. Typology, Diffusion and Function*. 1993.
Hinton, D. *A Catalogue of the Anglo-Saxon Metalwork 700-1100 in the Department of Antiquities, Ashmolean Museum, Oxford*. 1974.
---- *Medieval Jewellery*. 1982.
---- *Gold and Gilt, Pots and Pins, Possessions and People in Medieval Britain*. 2005.
Hinton, D (*et al*). The Gold, Silver and other Non-Ferrous Alloy Objects from Hamwic, and the Non-Ferrous Metalworking Evidence: *Southampton Finds Vol. Two*. 1995.
Holme, R. (ed. R C Alston). *Academy of Armory 1668, English Linguistics 1500-1800*, No. 294. 1972.
Holmes, E F. *A History of Thimbles*. 1985.
Hook, M and Macgregor, A. *Medieval England*. 1997.
Houston, M G. *Medieval Costume in England and France*. 1965.
Hume, I N. *Artifacts of Colonial America*. 1969.
Johns, C. *The Jewellery of Roman Britain: Celtic and Classical-style Traditions*. 1996.
Kelly, F M and Schwabe R. *A Short History of Costume and Armour 1066-1800*. 1972.
Knight, J K. Late Roman and Post-Roman Caerwent, Some Evidence from Metalwork, in *Archaeologia Cambrensis, vol CXLV (1996)*. Cambrian Archaeological Association.1998.
Köhler, C. *A History of Costume*. 1928 and 1963.
Laver, J. *Costume of the Western World, Elizabethan and Jacobean 1558 - 1625*. 1951.
---- *Costume*. 1963.
Leach, P. *Ilchester, vol. 1, Excavations 1974-5*. 1982. Western Archaeological Trust.
Leahy, K. *The Anglo-Saxon Kingdom of Lindsey*. 2007.
Leloir, M. *Histoire Du Costume, De L'antiquité à, vol 12*. 1914.
Lightbrown, R W. *Mediavel European Jewellery*. 1992.
London Museum Catalogues: No.5, *Costume*. 1946.
MacLeod, C. *Tudor and Jacobean Portraits in the National Portrait Gallery collection at Montacute House*. 2002.
Mackrell, A. *An Illustrated History of Fashion, 500 Years of Fashion Illustration*. 1997.
Malcolm-Davies and Mikhaila, J and N. *The Tudor Tailor*. 2006.
Margeson, S. Norwich Households: Medieval and Post-Medieval Finds from Norwich Survey Excavations 1971-1978. *East Anglian Archaeology Report No. 58*. 1993.
Marks, R and Williamson, P (eds). *Gothic - Art for England 1400-1547*. 2003.
Marshall, C. *Buckles Through The Ages*. 1986.
Mellor, J E and Pearce, T. The Austin Friars, Leicester; *CBA Research Report 35*. 1981.
Mikhaila, N and Malcolm-Davies, J. *The Tudor Tailor: Reconstructing sixteenth-century dress*. 2006.
Mitchiner, M. *Medieval Pilgrim and Secular Badges*. 1986.
---- *Jettons, Medalets and Tokens, The Medieval Period and Nuremburg, vol 1*. 1988.
Mollett, J W. *Dictionary of Art and Archaeology*. 1994.
Murdoch, T. *Treasures and Trinkets. Jewellery in London from pre-Roman times to the 1930s*. 1991.
Müller, C and Kemperdick S (*et al*). *Hans Holbein the Younger, The Basel Years 1515-1532*. 1996.
Murawski, G. *Benet's Artefacts of England and the United Kingdom*. 2000 and 2003.
Ottaway, P and Rogers, N. *Craft, Industry and Everyday Life: Finds from Medieval York. The Archaeology of York, vol 17: The Small Finds*. CBA. 2002.
Owen-Crocker, G R. *Dress in Anglo-Saxon England*. 1986.
Parks Canada. *Man's Coat 1730-1750: A Visual Guide to cut and construction*. 1995.
---- *Lady's Gown 1730-1770: A Visual Guide to cut and construction*. 1997.

Philipson, J, (ed). *Archaeologia Aeliana, vol IX*. 1981.
Portable Antiquities Scheme Finds' Database.
Princely Magnificence, Court Jewels of the Renaissance, 1500-1630. Debrett's Peerage Ltd in association with the Victoria and Albert Museum. 15th October 1980 - 1st February 1981.
Proceedings of the Somerset Archaeology and Natural History Society, vol. 129. 1984-5.
Rahtz, P. *The Saxon and Medieval Palaces at Cheddar*. 1979. BAR.
Rangström, L. *Modelejon Manligt Mode: Lions of Fashion: Male fashion of the 16th, 17th and 18th centuries*. 2002.
Read, B. *History Beneath Our Feet*. 1988 and 1995.
---- *Metal Artefacts of Antiquity, vol 1*. 2001.
---- *Metal Buttons c.900 BC - c.AD 1700*. 2005.
Richardson, T. 'The Buff-coats at Littlecote House', in *The Canadian Journal of Arms Collecting, vol, 26*. 1988.
Roberts, I. Pontefract Castle Archaeological Excavations 1982-86, *West Yorkshire Archaeology Service, Yorkshire Archaeology 8*. 2002.
Robinson, P. Two Medieval Coin Brooches from Wiltshire, in *Wiltshire Archaeological and Natural History Magazine 83*. 1990.
---- Some Copper Alloy Objects from the West Country Depicting the Arms of the Commonwealth, in *Post-Medieval Archaeology 33*. 1999.
Rogers, P W. *Cloth and Clothing in Early Anglo-Saxon England AD 450-700*. 2007.
Rogerson, A and Dallas, C. Excavations in Thetford 1948-59 and 1973-80. *East Anglian Archaeology 22*. 1984.
Rudling, D. A Saxon Coin-Brooch from Alfriston, in *Sussex Archaeological Collections 126*. 1988.
Saunders, P and E (eds). *Salisbury & South Wiltshire Museum Medieval Catalogue: Part 1*. 1991.
Savory, H N. *Guide Catalogue of the Iron Age Collections*. National Museum of Wales. 1976.
Scarisbrick, D. *Tudor and Jacobean Jewellery*. 1995.
Scott, M. *History of Dress: Late Gothic Europe, 1400-1500*. 1980.
---- *A Visual History of Costume: The Fourteenth and Fifteenth Centuries*. 1986.
Shakespear, W. *King Henry IV, Part I, Act II, Sc. Iv*.
Smith, R A. *British Museum Guide to Anglo-Saxon Antiquities*. 1923.
----*British Museum Guide to Early Iron Age Antiquities*. 1925.
Starkey, D (ed.). *The Inventory of King Henry VIII*. 1998.
Steedman, K (*et al*). Excavation of a Saxon Site at Riby Cross Roads, Lincolnshire, in *The Archaeological Journal, vol 151*. 1994.
Stenton, F (gen. ed.). *The Bayeux Tapestry*. 1965.
Swann, J M. *A History of Shoe Fashions*. 1975.
---- *Shoes*. 1982.
---- Shoe fashions to 1600, in *Transactions Museum Assistants, Group 12*. 1973.
Tait, H (ed). *7000 Years of Jewellery*. 2006.
Tarrant, N. *The Development of Costume*. 1994.
Thomas, M D. *Lorica Segmentata, vol. II, A Catalogue of Finds*. 2003.
Thomas, S. *Medieval Footwear from Coventry*. 1980.
Treasure Trove Reviewing Committee, *Annual Report 1995-96*.
Tyrrell, R (*et al*). Riding by in Early-Medieval Bucks, in *Portable Antiquities Scheme South-East Regional Newsletter No. 2*. 2005.
United Kingdom Detector Finds' Database.
Vigeon, E. Clogs or Wooden Soled Shoes, in *Costume, 11*. 1977.
Vince, A (ed.). *Aspects of Saxo-Norman London II, Finds and Environmental Evidence*. 1991.
Untracht, O. *Jewellery Concepts and Technology*. 1982.
Wallraf Richartz Museum, Cologne, Catalogue, 'Genie ohne Namen Der Meister des Bartholomeus-Altars'. 2001.

Waugh, N. *Corsets and Crinolines*. 1954.
---- *The Cut of Men's Clothes 1660-1914*. 1964.
---- *The Cut of Men's Clothes 1600-1900*. 1964.
---- *The Cut of Women's Clothes 1600-1930*. 1968.
Wayment, H. The Stained Glass in the Chapel of the Vyne, *National Trust Studies*. 1980.
Webster, L and Backhouse, J. *The Golden Age of Anglo-Saxon Art*. 1994.
---- *The Making of England: Anglo-Saxon art and culture AD600-900*. 1991.
West, S (*et al*). West Stow The Anglo-Saxon Village, vols 1 and 2, *East Anglian Archaeology Report No. 24*. 1985.
Wild, J P. *Button-and-Loop Fasteners in the Roman provinces*. 1970.
Willan, T S. *A Tudor Book of Rates for the year 1582*. 1962.
Williams, G. Coin brooches of Edward the Confessor and William I, in *British Numismatic Journal 71*. 2001.
Wise, T and Embleton G A. *Saxon, Viking and Norman*, Men at Arms series 85.